Microsoft XNA Game Studio 4.0: Learn Programming Now!

Rob Miles

PUBLISHED BY
Microsoft Press
A Division of Microsoft Corporation
One Microsoft Way
Redmond, Washington 98052-6399

Library of Congress Control Number: 2001012345
ISBN: 978-0-7356-5157-9

Printed and bound in the United States of America.

Microsoft Press books are available through booksellers and distributors worldwide. For further information about international editions, contact your local Microsoft Corporation office or contact Microsoft Press International directly at fax (425) 936-7329. Visit our Web site at www.microsoft.com/mspress. Send comments to mspinput@microsoft.com.

Microsoft and the trademarks listed at http://www.microsoft.com/about/legal/en/us/IntellectualProperty/Trademarks/EN-US.aspx are trademarks of the Microsoft group of companies. All other marks are property of their respective owners.

The example companies, organizations, products, domain names, e-mail addresses, logos, people, places, and events depicted herein are fictitious. No association with any real company, organization, product, domain name, e-mail address, logo, person, place, or event is intended or should be inferred.

This book expresses the author's views and opinions. The information contained in this book is provided without any express, statutory, or implied warranties. Neither the authors, Microsoft Corporation, nor its resellers, or distributors will be held liable for any damages caused or alleged to be caused either directly or indirectly by this book.

Acquisitions Editor: Devon Musgrave
Developmental Editor: Devon Musgrave
Project Editor: Valerie Woolley
Editorial and Production: Waypoint Press
Technical Reviewers: Nick Gravelyn, Kurt Meyer; Technical Review services provided by Content Master, a member of CM Group, Ltd.
Cover: Girvin

Body Part No. X17-37448

To Jake, a great dog who is much missed.

Table of Contents

What do you think of this book? We want to hear from you!

Microsoft is interested in hearing your feedback so we can continually improve our books and learning resources for you. To participate in a brief online survey, please visit:

www.microsoft.com/learning/booksurvey/

Part III Writing Proper Games

What do you think of this book? We want to hear from you!

Microsoft is interested in hearing your feedback so we can continually improve our books and learning resources for you. To participate in a brief online survey, please visit:

www.microsoft.com/learning/booksurvey/

Acknowledgments

I'm not sure if you are meant to have fun writing books, but I do. Thanks to Devon Musgrave, Ben Ryan, Valerie Woolley, and Steve Sagman for making everything fit so well together and to Kurt Meyer and Nick Gravely for making sure it all makes sense. I must also mention the XNA team who keep making a great thing better, year on year, and the Windows Phone team who have made something amazing.

Introduction

With Microsoft XNA, Microsoft is doing something really special. It is providing an accessible means for people to create programs for the Windows PC, Xbox 360, and Windows Phone. Now pretty much anyone can take a game idea, run it on a genuine console, and even send it to market in Xbox Live or the Windows Phone Marketplace.

This book shows you how to make game programs and run them on an Xbox 360, a Microsoft Windows PC, or a Windows Phone device. It also gives you an insight into how software is created and what being a programmer is really like.

Who This Book Is For

If you have always fancied writing software but have no idea how to start, then this book is for you. If you have ever played a computer game and thought, "I wonder how they do that?" or, better yet, "I want to make something like that," then this book will get you started with some very silly games that you and all your friends can have a go at playing and modifying. Along the way, you'll also get a decent understanding of C#, which is a massively popular programming language used by many thousands of software developers all over the world. The C# skills that you pick up in this book can also be used as the basis of a career in programming, should you find that you really enjoy writing programs. And because the design of the C# language is very similar to C, C++, and Java, you will find that your skills can be used with them too.

The book is structured into 19 chapters, starting with the simplest possible XNA program and moving on to show you how to use the Xbox gamepad, the keyboard, sounds, graphics, and network in your games. In the course of learning how to use C# and XNA, you create some very silly games, including Color Nerve, Mind Reader, Gamepad Racer, Bread and Cheese, and Button Bash. You can even download the full versions of these games from *http://www.verysillygames.com* and use them at your next party. The final section shows you how to take your programming skills and use them to create games for the Windows Phone device.

With this book, I show you that programming is a fun, creative activity that lets you bring your ideas to life.

System Requirements

You need the following hardware and software to build and run the code samples for this book. Chapter 1, "Computers, C#, XNA, and You," explains how to set up your environment.

- A Windows PC with 3-D graphics acceleration if you want to run your XNA games on your PC.

- Microsoft Windows Vista or Windows 7.

- Microsoft Visual Studio 2010 C# Express Edition for Windows Phone, Visual Studio 2010 Standard Edition, Visual Studio 2010 Professional Edition, or Visual Studio 2010 Team Suite.

- To test your games on a console, you need an Xbox 360 fitted with a hard disk. Your Xbox 360 must be connected to Xbox Live, and you need to join the App Hub. You will find out how to do this in Chapter 1.

- If you have a Windows Phone you can run XNA games on that as well. Any Windows Phone device can be connected to your PC so you can load your XNA games into it.

Code Samples

All the code samples discussed in this book can be downloaded from the book's detail page, located at:

http://oreilly.com/catalog/9780735651579

Display the detail page in your Web browser, and follow the instructions for downloading the files.

There are also code samples and games at *http://www.verysillygames.com*.

Errata and Book Support

We've made every effort to ensure the accuracy of this book and its companion content. If you do find an error, please report it on our Microsoft Press site at Oreilly.com:

1. Go to *http://microsoftpress.oreilly.com*.

2. In the **Search** box, enter the book's ISBN or title.

3. Select your book from the search results.

4. On your book's catalog page, under the cover image, you'll see a list of links.

5. Click **View/Submit Errata**.

You'll find additional information and services for your book on its catalog page. If you need additional support, please e-mail Microsoft Press Book Support at *mspinput@microsoft.com*.

Please note that product support for Microsoft software is not offered through the addresses above.

We Want to Hear from You

At Microsoft Press, your satisfaction is our top priority, and your feedback our most valuable asset. Please tell us what you think of this book at:

http://www.microsoft.com/learning/booksurvey.

The survey is short, and we read *every one* of your comments and ideas. Thanks in advance for your input!

Stay in Touch

Let's keep the conversation going! We're on Twitter: *http://twitter.com/MicrosoftPress.*

Part I
Getting Started

Chapter 1
Computers, C#, XNA, and You

In this chapter, you will

- Discover what makes a good programmer and what makes a great one.
- See what computers are all about.
- Find out why C# is a language you can love and Microsoft XNA is a framework you can adore.
- Get your system set up so that you can write code.
- Run your first XNA program.

Introduction

Welcome to the wonderful world of Rob Miles—a world of bad jokes, puns, and programming. In this book, I'm going to give you an introduction to the C# programming language and show you how to use C# to create XNA games. If you have programmed before, I'd be grateful if you'd still read all the text. It's worth it just for the jokes, and you may actually learn something as you're laughing.

Learning to Program

If you haven't programmed before, don't worry. Programming is not rocket science. It is, well, programming, and there are many more people in the world who have learned programming than rocket science. The bad news about learning to program is that you have lots of different things to learn when you start, and this can be confusing. But the keys to learning programming are simple:

- **Practice** Do a lot of programming and force yourself to think about things from a problem-solving point of view.
- **Study** Look at programs written by other people. You can learn a lot from studying code that others have created. Figuring out how somebody else did the job is a great starting point for your solution. And remember that in many cases, there is no best solution—just solutions that are better in a particular context. (In other words, sometimes you need an approach that is the fastest or the smallest or the easiest to use, and so on.)

■ **Persistence**   Writing programs is hard work. And you have to work hard at it. The main reason most folks don't make it as programmers is that they give up, not because they are stupid. However, don't get too persistent. If you haven't solved a programming problem in 30 minutes, you should call a timeout and seek help or, at least, walk away from the problem and come back to it. Staying up all night trying to sort out a problem is not a good plan. It just makes you irritable in the morning. If you go to bed, have a nice sleep, and then go back to the problem in the morning, you will be amazed how often you can fix it in just a few minutes. (Later in this book, we'll cover what else you can do if a problem is being stubborn.)

Becoming a Great Programmer

You might think that great programmers can type a thousand words a second, have a mega-sized brain, and are fitted with a socket that lets them connect directly to a computer. This is not true. Especially the socket bit. In my experience, the best programmers are the ones who are the most fun to be with. The ones who you enjoy talking to. The ones who don't get upset when you find a mistake in their programs and who sometimes agree that your solution is better than the one that they invented. I'd much rather work with someone like that than someone who can write a hundred lines of code a minute but who refuses to speak to me if I dare to suggest that one of those lines might be wrong.

Great programmers take care to find out that what they are doing is the right thing. If they are working for a customer, they make sure that the customer gets what the customer wants. They do not assume that they know the best way to do it and just do it their way. They make sure that what they produce is tested and comes with helpful documentation. They work in the team, make coffee when it is their turn, and do whatever it takes to make sure that the project has a happy ending. Of course, they might also fill your office with beach balls, superglue your keyboard to the desk, or cover your chair with aluminum foil, but these are all done in a friendly spirit.

I have secured the services of a great programmer who will be adding Programmer's Points to our text. These are truly words of wisdom, so make sure to take note when you see them.

How the Book Works

Great scientists like Sir Isaac Newton and Benjamin Franklin performed experiments to discover how the world works. Then people like Thomas Edison came along and again experimented with what science and engineering could do to make things that everybody wants. You are going to take a similar experimental approach to learning about programming. By playing with XNA and writing tiny games, you are going to investigate how a computer works and how you can invent new kinds of computer games.

As you go through the text, you should never be more than a page or so away from making something happen with a program, so it helps if you have a computer and an Xbox 360 or Windows Phone nearby so that you can try things out. However, you don't have to have ready access to hardware when you read the text because all the programs in the book are laid out and explained in detail.

Don't be afraid to experiment and try things out yourself. At certain points in the text, I suggest ideas you might find fun to explore. Remember that learning by doing is one of the best ways to pick things up, so feel free to try stuff. One of the great things about creating game programs is that even the code that you get a bit wrong can produce cool-looking results. You might even end up creating an entirely new type of game by mistake!

Remember that the great scientists did not always find it easy to understand immediately what was going on inside their experiments, and the same is true about programming. Some of the things that you do when you write programs do not seem to make much sense at first, so be prepared to have to work to understand what is going on inside the program.

 Note Throughout the chapters, words appearing in *italics* are explained more fully in the Glossary at the end of this book.

C# and XNA

Before you go any farther, it is important that you consider exactly what this book is for. You are going to learn about the *programming language* C# and the XNA *Software Development Kit*. Understanding the difference between the two is key. You are familiar with the idea of a computer program. At the moment, I'm using a word processor to create this text. I started the word processing program, and it is telling my computer to take the text that I type and add it to the document I am writing. The program is the set of instructions that tells the computer what to do with the information it receives from the keyboard.

The C# programming language is a way of expressing that set of instructions. When you create your games, you write lines of C# to tell the computer how to make each game work. You can use C# to create programs that do many other tasks; you can even use it to create your own word processor.

A Software Development Kit (SDK) is a set of prebuilt program components that you can use as part of other programs. The XNA SDK provides program code that will draw things on the screen, play sounds, read the Xbox 360 gamepad, and do lots of other useful things. When you create games, the C# code you write uses these prebuilt features of XNA. Part of becoming a successful programmer is learning how to best use the features provided by an SDK. Experience with the XNA SDK makes it much easier for you to understand how to use other SDKs. A particular SDK has an overall architecture that contains all the features that the SDK provides. This is often called a *framework*.

Getting Started

You are going to create programs on the PC and then either run them on the PC or send them into an Xbox 360 or Windows Phone for execution. Either way, you need to install some tools on your PC.

Installing the Development Environment and the XNA Framework

When developers wanted to write a program on the very first computers, they had to take the back off and actually change the wires in the machine. Fortunately, things have moved on, and now you can use an *Integrated Development Environment* (IDE) to create your code. An IDE gets its name because it provides a single place where you can perform the entire creative process of code development. In an IDE, you can write a program by using the built-in text editor, you can run the program and see what it does, and you can also *debug* the program, which means you stop it and try to find out why it is not doing what you want it to. The IDE you will use is Microsoft Visual Studio 2010 Express Edition for Windows Phone, which also includes Xbox 360 support. This is a version of the hugely powerful Visual Studio product, which is used by professional developers all over the world. At this point, I'm assuming that you have already installed Visual Studio and have it running on your machine. You can download Express editions of Microsoft software for free from *http://www.microsoft.com/Express/*. The setup procedure is quite straightforward, and at the end of the process you are asked to register your copy. Registration does not cost you any money and actually gives you access to even more free resources. There are a number of other Express products that you can install. You can use these in addition to Visual Studio, but they are not required to create XNA games.

 Note If you have other versions of Visual Studio on your machine, you can also use these to write XNA games so long as they include the C# development environment. However, you must make sure that your version of Visual Studio has the latest version of the service packs installed. The App Hub Web site, *http://create.msdn.com*, has up-to-date information on service packs and Visual Studio versions.

Once you have installed the software on your system, you will find a shortcut to Microsoft Visual Studio 2010 for Windows Phone on the Start menu.

Setting Up a PC to Run XNA Games

Once you have installed XNA on your PC, you can use this to create and run games. If you just want to write games on the PC and run them on an Xbox 360 or Windows Phone, you don't need a very powerful machine. So long as it supports the minimum requirements for Visual Studio, you can create game software. The games you are going to create in this book do not require particularly advanced hardware but you will need a machine with reasonable graphical ability to run some of the more advanced examples. You can find the detailed hardware and driver requirements for XNA at *http://msdn.microsoft.com/en-us/ library/bb203925.aspx*.

If you want to create Windows Phone games you can run an emulator program on your PC that lets you see how the games would look on a phone. Because the Windows Phone has powerful graphics acceleration built in, your PC will need at least DirectX version 10 to run the emulator.

XNA games can be controlled by the PC keyboard. If you have a wired Xbox gamepad, you can plug it into a Universal Serial Bus (USB) port on your computer and after the New Hardware Wizard runs, it just works. Windows 7 and Windows Vista have the drivers for the gamepad already loaded. You can also obtain a special adapter that lets your PC communicate with wireless Xbox gamepads.

Setting Up an Xbox 360 to Run XNA Games

If you want the full game developer experience, there is no substitute for actually using a genuine console. In this section, you're going find out how to set up an Xbox 360 and make it ready to receive the games that you are going to write.

To deploy games on your Xbox 360, it must be fitted with a hard disk. This is where the XNA Game Studio Connect application and the programs that you create are stored. Your console must also be connected to the Internet and you must be signed up for a Silver Xbox Live subscription or better. You must also be a Registered or Trial-level member of the App Hub.

App Hub

If you want to deploy games to your Xbox 360 you must be a member of the App Hub. There are a number of different membership levels:

- **Visitor**   A visitor to the App Hub site can download Visual Studio 2010 and educational content. If all you want to do is create and run XNA games on your Windows PC you can just visit the App Hub Web site to download software, find resources, and view the forums.

- **Trial**   A trial member of the App Hub can download the development tools and educational content. He can also deploy XNA games to an Xbox 360. Trial members can also develop Windows Phone applications and publish them in the Windows Phone Marketplace. Trial membership is available from a variety of sources including MSDN Academic Alliance (*http://msdn.microsoft.com/academic/default.aspx*), Microsoft Faculty Connection (*http://www.microsoft.com/education/FacultyConnection*), Microsoft DreamSpark (*http://www.dreamspark.com*), and the Dream-Build-Play contest (*http://www.dreambuildplay.com*). If you are a student on a course of study, ask at your institution to see if it has signed up for any of these initiatives.

- **Registered**   A registered member of the App Hub has all of the abilities of a trial member. Registered members can submit their games for distribution on Xbox Live Indie Games and can also review Community Games submitted by other members. Membership presently costs $99. Registered members of the App Hub can register up to three Windows Phone devices for development

App Hub membership is linked to your Windows Live ID and Xbox Live Gamer Tag. You can find membership details at *http://create.msdn.com*.

XNA Game Studio Connect

The XNA Game Studio Connect program provides the link between your Xbox 360 and the XNA Game Studio application that you use to write games on your Windows PC. When you want to send a program from your Windows PC to the Xbox 360 you must run this program on the Xbox 360. You download the program from Xbox Live and it is stored in your games library on your Xbox. You'll need to start it before each game development session in which you want to test your game on the Xbox.

You don't need this program to run XNA programs that have been downloaded onto your Xbox, these are placed in your game library on your Xbox and you can just run them as you would any other locally stored game.

XNA Game Studio Device Center

Before you can send a game from your Windows PC to your Xbox 360 the two systems must be connected together. Connections between XNA Game Studio and Xbox devices are managed by the XNA Game Studio Device Center application. You can find this on your Start menu, as shown in Figure 1-1. It manages all the devices on which you want to run games you have written.

FIGURE 1-1 Starting the XNA Game Studio Device Center application.

I am presently developing programs for my Xbox 360. My XNA Game Studio Device Center is shown in Figure 1-2. You can add an Xbox by clicking Add Device. You will need to add a device so that you can send programs to it.

You need to use the XNA Game Studio Connect application on your Xbox and the XNA Game Studio Device Center on your Windows PC together the first time you create a connection between your Xbox and your Windows PC. You can get detailed help with the procedure for connecting your Xbox to your PC by clicking the small blue question mark on the right side of the XNA Game Studio Device Center application.

Once you have completed the connection procedure, the PC and Xbox 360 retain the settings that you entered—when you attempt to send a program to the Xbox 360, it should just work.

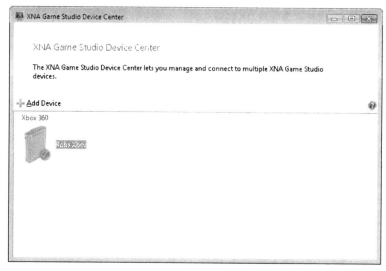

FIGURE 1-2 My XNA Game Studio Device Center.

Setting up a Windows Phone to run XNA games

A Windows Phone device is a very good platform to run XNA games. You can create games for the phone and even sell them from the Windows Phone Marketplace. You can test your games on the Windows Phone emulator which is supplied with Visual Studio 2010. The way that XNA programs work on the phone is exactly the same as how games written for the Windows PC or the Xbox work. However, there are some differences in the way that games are played and used on a mobile device. We will take a detailed look at game development for Windows Phone in the three chapters at the very end of this book.

Note The Zune device is not compatible with Version 4.0 of XNA, which is being used as the basis for the content in this book. If you wish to create games for a Zune you will need to install Visual Studio 2008 and XNA 3.1. These can be used on the same machine alongside Visual Studio 2010 and XNA 4.0. There is no emulator for Zune development and Zune programs cannot be distributed via the Marketplace.

Selling Your Windows Phone Games in the Marketplace

App Hub membership allows you to submit Windows Phone games to the Windows Phone Marketplace. Submissions are carefully checked to make sure that they are suitable for sale. You can create free or paid applications. The Marketplace will collect payments for you.

Connecting a Windows Phone to a Windows PC

Developers can also register their Windows Phone devices so that they can download their own programs into them for testing on a real device. Figure 1-3 shows the registration program in action.

FIGURE 1-3 Registering a Windows Phone for Development.

The Windows Phone device connects to Visual Studio 2010 via the Zune software that is used to transfer media and other content to the device. It does not use the XNA Game Studio Connect program. When you connect the Windows Phone to your PC you should find that the Zune software will run automatically.

When writing a game for a Windows Phone you can use an emulator to show you what it will look like on the device. You can also debug your programs to find out what they are doing, even when they are running inside a phone device.

There are XNA libraries that let you access the music and pictures on your mobile device so that games can use the media content on the device. You can even write custom music players.

Writing Your First Program

You are now going to start from scratch with your first program. It won't actually do much—you won't be writing your own version of Halo just yet—but it does give you an insight into what XNA does and how you can write your own C# bits to produce a cool mood light.

Creating Your First Project

A computer game is not just a program—it is also lots of other bits and pieces that make playing the game fun and interesting. Just about every game has graphics, sounds, 3-D models of game objects, and all sorts of other items that must be created along with the code. This means that when you make a game, you have to manage all these other resources, too. The good news is that the XNA designers have thought of this, and they provide a comprehensive *content management* solution that looks after all these resources. You can just give your game resources to the Content Manager, and it makes sure that they are available to the programs that you write. Later on in the book, I'll show you how to add some content of your own so that you can use a picture of your mom or your dog as a game character.

The content management is part of the *project* mechanism provided by XNA Game Studio. What this means right now is that to create your first game program, you actually have to create an XNA Game Studio project.

To create a project, first start XNA Game Studio if it is not already running. Do this by selecting Microsoft Visual Studio 2010 for Windows Phone from the Start menu.

Note This menu entry is created when XNA Game Studio is installed and contains a link to the version of Visual Studio 2010 installed on your Windows PC. If you are using a different version of Visual Studio 2010 (perhaps you installed XNA Game Studio on top of your installation of Visual Studio 2010 Professional Edition) you might need to look in the Visual Studio 2010 folder in your Program Files.

In XNA Game Studio, select New Project from the File menu, as shown in Figure 1-4. This automatically creates the entire project and the file into which you are going to put your code.

XNA Game Studio can make a whole range of different projects depending on what you actually want to build. The skeletons for each of these types of program are contained in project templates and Starter Kits. You can download and install other Starter Kits from the App Hub Web site. Right now, you are going to use a template to create an empty XNA project.

Figure 1-5 shows all the possible types of projects that can be created. You need to select the project that matches the device on which you want to run the game.

FIGURE 1-4 Opening the New Project dialog box.

 Note Make sure that you create a "Game" and *NOT* a "Game Library"; otherwise, you will not be able to make your program run.

FIGURE 1-5 Creating a new project.

Later in this chapter, I'll show you how you can create a workspace containing multiple projects, one for each target device. For now, you should just choose the one that you want to use; the way that the program works is identical for all. Call the project "MoodLight" because that is what we are building first. You can use the Browse button to select an appropriate destination for the project. You should ensure that the Create Directory For Solution check box is selected so that all the files for this game are held in one place. Once you have done this, click OK to get XNA Game Studio to build the project for you.

When the project has been created, you should see a screen that looks like the one in Figure 1-6. Yours might not look quite the same (it certainly won't have the big arrow pointing at the Start Debugging button), but it should look similar. There are a lot of controls that you can play with. At the moment quite a few are disabled and can't be used, but it still looks confusing the first time that you see it. The key here is not to panic. You are going to use only a few of the buttons to start with, and I'll explain the others as you need them.

Running Your First Program

If you are running your program on a PC, you can just click the Start Debugging button (indicated by the arrow in Figure 1-6), and the program runs. If you are sending your program to an Xbox 360, you must make sure that the XNA Game Studio Connect application is running on your Xbox 360 and that the Xbox has been connected to your Windows PC.

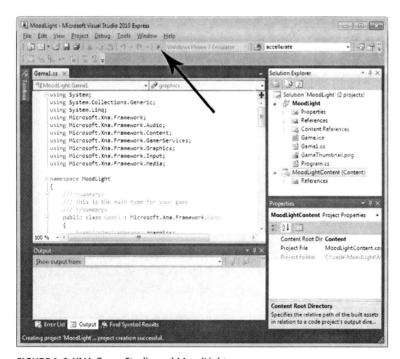

FIGURE 1-6 XNA Game Studio and MoodLight.

When you click the button to run the program, a number of things happen in quick succession:

1. XNA Game Studio *compiles* the *source code* files. The source code of the program is all the lines of C# code that you and XNA Game Studio create that actually describe what you want the computer to do. A compiler is a program that takes source code and creates a set of machine instructions that can be loaded into the computer's processor to control what the computer does. The C# language has a particular specification, and the compiler knows all about the rules in the specification. The compiler rejects any program that it thinks is not correct and tells you about the *compilation errors*. You are going to have to live with the fact that you will see a lot of these errors if you decide to become a computer programmer.

2. Your project might contain a large number of different source files; each of them must be compiled. If all the program source files compile correctly, they are then combined with any resources (for example, images and sounds) that are part of the project.

3. If you are using an external device, either Xbox 360 or Windows Phone, the compiled files are now transferred into it.

4. Finally, XNA Game Studio starts the program running. If you are using a Windows PC, the program runs in a window on the desktop. If you are using an external device, the program takes it over completely. At this point, the window or target device is under the control of your program statements.

When XNA Game Studio produces an empty project, it actually creates a program that will compile and run, so you can just click the Start Debugging button (if you haven't already) and turn the program loose.

When you run the program, the screen turns blue. That's it—nothing else. All that work to turn the screen blue? You could have done that with a can of paint in 30 seconds. The "empty" project from XNA just turns the screen blue, but in Chapter 2, "Programs, Data, and Pretty Colors," you're going to add some code to make it do much cooler things. You're going to make a light that can display millions of possible colors, an ever-changing mood lamp, and finally, the world's first-ever color-changing game.

 Note One slightly irritating thing about Visual Studio is that when the program is running, the organization of the controls in Visual Studio changes. This can confuse a first-time user because menus, toobars, and panes suddenly don't seem to be where they used to be. If you carefully compare Figures 1-6 and 1-7, you notice that a new toolbar has appeared that has buttons that you can use to pause or stop the program.

Stopping a Program

Before you do anything else, you need to stop the program. There are two ways to do this. You can press the Back button on an Xbox 360 gamepad or Windows Phone to instruct the program to finish. If the program is running on a remote device, XNA Game Studio displays a message indicating that the remote connection to the device has been lost. Simply click OK on the message to dismiss it. Alternatively, you can stop the program from within XNA Game Studio by clicking the Stop button indicated by the arrow in Figure 1-7.

If you are using a PC and don't have an Xbox gamepad, you have to stop the program from XNA Game Studio.

Note You should not normally stop your program by using XNA Game Studio. This is like turning off your Xbox 360 rather than quitting a game correctly. It stops the program, but because the program is interrupted, it might not save all the game data properly before it stops. When you make your own game, you should make sure that you provide the player with instructions on how to stop it properly.

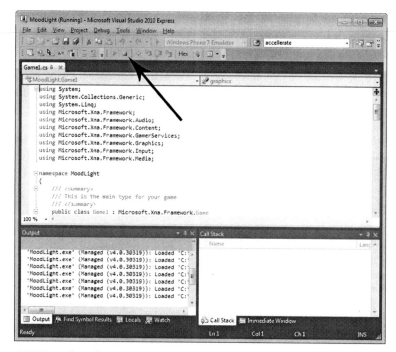

FIGURE 1-7 Stopping a running program.

Storing Games on the Xbox 360 or Windows Phone

Once you've created a game and deployed it to an Xbox 360 or Windows Phone, the game itself remains stored inside the machine for you to load and play later, without the need for a PC to be attached. You can find the games you have created by selecting your Game Library on the Xbox 360 or entering the Xbox Live Games menu on the Windows Phone.

Running the Same XNA Game on Different Devices

You can use a single XNA workspace to hold multiple projects, one for each device you want to target. You will find out more about projects and workspaces in the section "XNA Game Studio Solutions and Projects" in Chapter 4. The following example shows how a Windows PC project can be copied to produce an Xbox 360 project.

Creating a Copy of an XNA Project for Another Device

Start by clicking the MoodLight project in the Solution Explorer of XNA Game Studio so that it is selected. Then choose Create Copy Of Project For Xbox 360 from the Project menu, as shown in Figure 1-8.

FIGURE 1-8 Copying a project.

XNA Game Studio now copies the project and adds the copy to the workspace. This means that there are now two projects in the workspace, as shown in Figure 1-9.

> **Note** It looks as if there are now two copies of everything concerned with the project. This is not actually the case. The copy uses links to the files in the original. This means that changes to the content of one project are reflected in the other.

You can select which of the projects to start by setting one of the projects as the StartUp Project. If you look carefully at Figure 1-9, you see that the Windows version of MoodLight has the name of the project displayed in bold type. This means that it is the project that runs on the Windows machine. To set a project as the StartUp project, you right-click the project and choose Set as StartUp Project from the menu that appears, as shown in Figure 1-10.

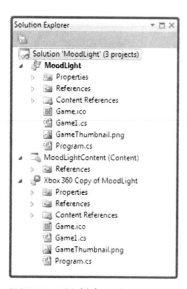

FIGURE 1-9 Multiple projects.

When you click Start Debugging, the project that is selected as the StartUp project is the one that gets to run.

> **Sample Code: Blue Screen of Life** All the sample projects can be obtained from the Web resources for this text, which can be found at *http://oreilly.com/catalog/9780735651579*. The sample projects in the 01 Moodlight Blue Screen folder for this chapter draw a blue screen for you. They are exactly the same as an empty project that you might create. There are versions for Windows PC, Xbox, and Windows Phone. You can open the project by double-clicking the Visual Studio solution (.sln) file in this directory to start Visual Studio.

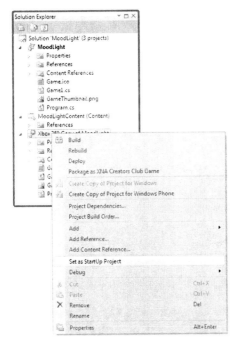

FIGURE 1-10 Selecting the StartUp Project.

Choosing Between Windows Phone and Emulator

If you have created a game that is aimed at the Windows Phone device you can select whether the game runs on the Windows Phone itself or the emulator as shown in Figure 1-11.

FIGURE 1-11 Choosing between Windows Phone Emulator and Windows Phone device.

To deploy to the device it must have been registered as a development device. The phone must be connected to the computer via USB and the Zune software must be running. The phone should not be displaying its lock screen when you try to deploy the program to it.

Conclusion

Actually, you've done quite a lot in this chapter. You've learned about computers, what makes great programmers so easy to get along with, and the difference between C# (the programming language of champions) and XNA (the game development framework of champions). You've also got all of your development tools sorted out, and you are now ready to roll. And you did manage to turn the screen a nice blue color.

Chapter Review Questions

Every chapter in this book has a set of questions at the end, just to test you a little. There are no prizes, but you might find it useful to check that you know the answers to the questions in one chapter before you go on to the next. All the answers are either true or false, and you can find them by reviewing the chapter and looking in the Glossary. The list of answers for all the book's review questions are at the back of the book in Appendix A. No peeking now.

1. The most important thing about being a great programmer is having a big brain.

2. You must have an Xbox 360 to create games with C# and XNA.

3. XNA is a programming language.

4. XNA Game Studio is an IDE.

5. The C# compiler produces an XNA output file.

6. C# is a framework.

7. You need an App Hub membership to run your XNA programs on your Xbox 360.

8. You need an App Hub membership to run your XNA programs on your Windows Phone.

9. The XNA Game Studio Device Center runs your programs on your Xbox 360.

10. The compiler runs your program.

11. The empty project created by XNA Game Studio draws a red screen.

12. It is not possible to use an Xbox 360 gamepad on a PC.

13. To write an XNA game for a Windows Phone, you use a special version of XNA called XNA Phone Home Edition.

14. All the items that make up a game are held together by Visual Studio in a solution folder

Chapter 2
Programs, Data, and Pretty Colors

In this chapter, you will

- Explore how games actually work.

- See how data is stored in a program.

- Discover how colors are managed on computers.

- Find out about classes and methods.

- Write some code that controls color.

- Write some code that makes decisions.

- Create a funky color-changing mood light.

Introduction

You now know how to create a Microsoft XNA program and run it. Your program only turns the screen blue, but you could call it a start. Next, you are going to figure out how game programs are constructed. Then you'll play with colors and find out how XNA stores color information and how C# stores data.

> ### Program Project: A Mood Light
>
> Your first project is going to be a program that turns a display (the bigger the better) into a mood light. These are the things that they have on spaceships, where a chandelier actually would not work very well. Instead, the spaceship will have a panel on the wall that can be set to glow in different colors and brightness levels or perhaps even change color over time. This is probably not a very efficient way of lighting a building—you are using one of the most powerful game consoles ever made to replace a lamp—but it is a fun exercise and may even lead to a game idea or two along the way. You can use the same program to convert your Windows Phone into a multicolored flashlight.

Before going any farther, you need to consider what a game program does. Computer programs in general read data, do something with it, and then send it out. This is true whether the computer is working out company wages or timing the ignition spark in a car engine. Figure 2-1 shows how this works with respect to game programs. The gamepad provides the input data to the game, and the display screen shows the output.

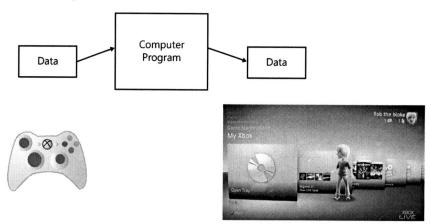

FIGURE 2-1 An Xbox game as a computer program.

Later versions of games might have other inputs and outputs, too; for example, if you are playing on Xbox Live, your console is receiving information about other players in your networked game. For now, start by considering only the output from your game. In Chapter 3, "Getting Player Input," you'll take a look at where the input values come from.

Making a Game Program

To see how a game program can produce a display, you need to look inside one of the C# programs that XNA built. At the end of Chapter 1, "Computers, C#, XNA, and You," you used XNA Game Studio to create a game program. Now you are going to look at this program and discover how it works.

The file that contains the game behavior is called Game1.cs. The name Game1 was generated automatically when the project was created; the .cs part is the *file extension* for C# programs. If you want to look inside this file, start XNA Game Studio and open the file from Solution Explorer. You can find Solution Explorer, shown in Figure 2-2, in the top right corner of the XNA Game Studio screen. If you double-click the name of the file that you want to work with, the file opens in the editing window.

If you look at the content of Game1.cs, which drew that impressive blue screen, you can see how the program works. The program code that XNA Game Studio created when you made an empty game contains the following method:

```
protected override void Draw(GameTime gameTime)
{
    GraphicsDevice.Clear(Color.CornflowerBlue);

    // TODO: Add your drawing code here

    base.Draw(gameTime);
}
```

FIGURE 2-2 Solution Explorer.

A *method* is a named part of a program. In this case, the method has the name Draw (you can ignore the protected override void part for now). All you need to know at the moment is that when XNA wants to draw the screen, it uses this method. You can change what gets drawn by altering the content of this method. At the moment, we just get a blue screen; if you look at the second line of the preceding code, you can see where the blue screen comes from.

Statements in the *Draw* Method

The Draw method contains a block of statements. C# programs are expressed as a series of statements that are separated by a semicolon (;). Each *statement* describes a single action that your program needs to do. There are a number of different kinds of statements; you discover new ones as you learn more about programming. The statements are organized into a single block. A *block* is a way to lump statements together. The start of a block is marked with an open curly bracket character ({) and the end of the block is marked with a closing curly bracket (}). These curly kinds of brackets are sometimes called *braces*. The C# compiler, which is trying to convert the program text into something that can actually run, notices and complains if you use the wrong kind of bracket.

In the preceding code, there is also a *comment*. Comments are ignored by the compiler; they let you put text into your program to describe the program or to remind you to do things. In the preceding code, the comment is a "TODO," which tells programmers that they need to do something. In this case, a programmer must add drawing statements at that position in the program file. The compiler can tell that the text is a comment because it starts with the character sequence //. For instance, look at the following example:

```
// This is a comment. It can be any text.
```

You can add comments anywhere in your program.

> **The Great Programmer Speaks: Comments Are Cool** Our Great Programmer likes comments. She says that a well-written program is like a story in the way that the purpose of each part is described. She says that she will be looking at our code and making sure that we put the right kind of comments in.

From the point of view of changing the color of your screen, the statement that is most interesting is this one:

```
GraphicsDevice.Clear(Color.CornflowerBlue);
```

Clear is a method that is part of XNA. You will see precisely how it fits into the framework later; for now, all you need to know is that the Clear method is given something that describes a color, and the method clears the screen to that color. At the moment, you are sending the Clear method the color CornflowerBlue, and it is clearing the screen to be that color. If you want a different color, you just have to send a different value into Clear:

```
GraphicsDevice.Clear(Color.Red);
```

If you change the color as shown in the preceding line and run the program, you should see that the screen is now set to red.

> **Sample Code: Red Screen of Anger** All the sample projects can be obtained from the Web resources for this text, which can be found at *http://oreilly.com/catalog/9780735651579*. The sample project in the directory "01 MoodLight Red Screen" in the resources for this chapter draws a red screen for you. You could run this when you felt particularly angry. You can change the color that you want to display by changing the colors used in the Draw method; there are some comments in the code to help you with this.

You can set the background color to a range of preset ones, but you can also design colors of your own, which brings us to our first project.

Working with Colors

You have seen that XNA has a set of colors built in, including one with the strange name of Teal (it is actually a rather boring blue/green). However, you want to make your own colors and use these in your program.

Storing Color Values

A particular color is represented by a structure that holds the red, green, and blue intensity values. A *structure* is used to hold a number of related data items in the same way that you might write your name, address, and phone number on a piece of paper. You want to create your own colors, and you need somewhere to store the color values you create. In programming terms, this is called *declaring* a *variable*. Figure 2-3 shows the anatomy of the statement that declares a variable to hold a value that represents a color.

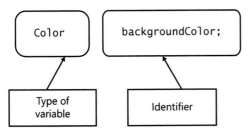

FIGURE 2-3 Declaring a *Color* variable called *backgroundColor.*

The *type* of the variable is set as `Color`. This determines what you can put in your variable. Having seen this declaration, the C# compiler knows that you want to create a location with the name backgroundColor in memory, which can hold color information. In programming terms, the name of a variable is called an *identifier*. The word backgroundColor is an identifier that I've invented. When you create something to use in a C# program, you have to think up an identifier for it. An identifier is made up of numbers and letters and must start with a letter. The identifier should describe what you are going to use the thing for; in this program, you are storing the color that is going to be used for the background, so it can be given the identifier backgroundColor.

Note The C# compiler uses the type of a variable to make sure that a program never tries to do something that would be stupid. The value `Color.Red` is recognized by the compiler as being of type `Color`, and can therefore be placed in a variable of type `Color`. If the programmer wrote some code that tried to put something else in the variable backgroundColor, such as a player name, then the program would fail to compile. This is rather like real life, where an attempt to put an elephant in a camera case would be similarly unsuccessful.

The Great Programmer Speaks: Pick Useful Identifiers Our Great Programmer says that there should be a special place in hell reserved for programmers who create identifiers like X24, or secretMagicCode, or clunk. She says that these tell a reader of the program code nothing about what the variable is being used for. She really likes identifiers like CarSpeed, backgroundColor, and accountBalance.

Setting a Color Value

You now have a variable that can hold the color of your background. At the moment, it is not set to anything useful. So next, you have to write a statement that causes the game program to put a value into this variable. You start by creating a new Color value that contains a particular amount of red, blue, and green. Figure 2-4 shows the anatomy of an assignment that makes a new Color value and then places it in the variable.

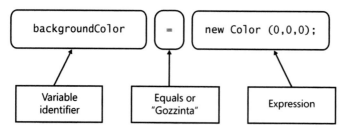

FIGURE 2-4 Assigning a new Color value to backgroundColor.

The thing that is going to be assigned is on the right side of the equals sign. In this case, you are making a new Color value. Don't get this confused with a double-equals that might be used to compare two things. You should regard the equals sign in Figure 2-4 as being what I call a "gozzinta" operator. The value on the right of the equals sign "goes into" the variable on the left. You will investigate how to compare things later in this chapter, in the section "Making a Proper Mood Light." Now that you have your variable, you can use it in the game program:

```
GraphicsDevice.Clear(backgroundColor);
```

The preceding statement calls the Clear method and feeds it the value of backgroundColor. This causes the screen to be cleared to the new color you created. If you put these statements together, you get a game program that contains a backgroundColor variable that is used by the Draw method, which sets it to a value and then clears the screen using it:

```
protected override void Draw(GameTime gameTime)
{
    Color backgroundColor;
    backgroundColor = new Color(0,0,0);
    GraphicsDevice.Clear(backgroundColor);
    base.Draw(gameTime);
}
```

If you want to find out what color you get if you make one with no red, no green, and no blue, you can run a program that uses this Draw method. But I don't think I'm giving too much away when I tell you that this would produce a black screen. The actual color values are given in the order red, green, and blue, and each must be in the range 0 to 255 (you shall learn the reason for this later). By using different values when you set the Color, you can experiment with different displays. The color combinations obey all the rules of color combinations (for light, rather than for paint) that you would expect:

```
backgroundColor = new Color(255, 255, 0);
```

The preceding statement sets backgroundColor to a color value that has the red and green values at maximum, which would be displayed as yellow.

> **Sample Code: Yellow Screen of Peril** The sample project "02 MoodLight Yellow Background" creates a yellow background color and fills the screen with it. You can change the numbers in the Draw method to make any color you like.

Controlling Color

At this point, you can see that we can add C# statements to the Draw method to change what is drawn on the screen. You also know that XNA uses a Color structure to lump together information that describes a particular color and that you can create your own Color variables in the game that contain a specific amount of red, green, and blue. Finally, you have managed to make a program that uses a color variable to set the screen to any color that you like.

Next, you want the light to change color over time, to get a nice soothing mood light effect. This sounds like hard work (and like every great programmer, I really hate hard work), but actually it turns out to be quite easy. To discover how to do this, you have to find how XNA is connected to the game programs that you write. The way this works uses C# classes.

Games and Classes

The game program is actually a *class* called Game1. A class is a collection of abilities (methods) and data (variables) that forms part of a program. You can put as much stuff as you like inside a single class. A class is usually constructed to look after one particular part of a system. Later in this book, in Chapter 14, "Classes Objects and Games," you'll use classes called things like GameSprite. In the commercial world, you might find classes called "Receipt," "Invoice," and "StockItem."

When it created our project, XNA Game Studio gave the game class the name Game1. However, you can rename this if you wish; you will see how to do this later in the book in a section in Chapter 11 named, "Renaming the *Game1* Class."

Classes and Behaviors

A behavior is something that a class can be asked to do. A particular method performs a particular behavior. You have already used the Clear behavior of the GraphicsDevice class. When you use Clear, this causes the code in the Clear method to be obeyed to clear the screen. You don't need to know how Clear works; you just need to know that you can feed it with information to tell it what color you want to use.

Drawing and Updating in Games

The Game1 class provides Update and Draw behaviors (among others) so that XNA can ask Game1 to update the state of the game and draw it on the display. Draw and Update are methods that you provide for use by XNA.

In the programs you have written up to now, you have done all the work in the Draw method. However, this is not really how games should work. The Draw method should do nothing other than draw the display, and the game should be updated by using the Update method. You might be wondering why we have this split between Draw and Update. Why can't Update do everything, including the drawing part?

The answer to this question has to do with the way that games work. It is very important that the game world is updated at constant speed. If Update is called less frequently than it should be, players would find that time in the game goes into "slow motion," which would be very frustrating for them because the game would not respond properly to their inputs to the gamepad. However, a game can usually get away with calling the Draw method less often—all that happens is that the display becomes more jerky as it is redrawn less frequently.

I've played a few games that do this, usually when there are a large number of objects on the screen at the same time. What is happening is that the display is running more slowly, but behind the scenes, the game is being updated properly, so gameplay itself is not affected. If the update and draw behaviors were not separated, it would not be possible to run them at different rates.

Sharing Game World Data Between *Draw* and *Update*

When you create a game, you must create the variables that hold the state of the game itself. In a driving game, this state would include the speed of the car the player is driving, the car position on the track, and the position and speed of the other cars. This could be called the game world data. The game world data that you are going to use in the mood light is the amount of red, green, and blue that defines the color of the light. The present version of Draw is entirely self-contained. It has a *local* variable that is set with the color that is to be drawn:

```
protected override void Draw(GameTime gameTime)
{
    Color backgroundColor;
    backgroundColor = new Color(255,255,0);
    GraphicsDevice.Clear(backgroundColor);
    base.Draw(gameTime);
}
```

Local variables are used when you just want to manipulate some data for a very short time. In this case, the program makes a color value that can be fed into the Clear method. At the moment, the value of backgroundColor is constructed from the values 255, 255, and 0, which give the amount of red, green, and blue in the color. We want to construct the color value from game data values that are set up by the Update method. To make your light work the way that XNA does, the program must store this game data in a place where both the Draw and Update methods can use it. In other words, you need to set up some game world data. Figure 2-5 shows how the Update and the Draw methods are part of the Game1 class, along with the intensity variables that make up the game world.

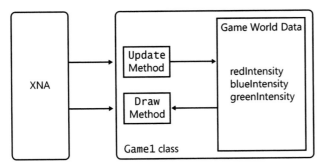

FIGURE 2-5 The Game1 class and XNA.

The job of the Update method is to update the game world data in the game (that is, adjust the intensity values). The job of the Draw method is to use the game world data to draw the display (that is, create a color from these values and clear the screen with it).

The XNA system calls Draw and Update at regular intervals when the game is running. You have already used methods provided by other classes; you know that the Clear method can be called to clear the display to a particular color. We are going to make the Update method set the value of the color to be used, and the Draw method will just draw using that color. Values that are shared among methods in a class are called *members* of the class.

Classes as Offices

You can think of Update and Draw as two people sitting in an office called Game1. Each of them has his or her own telephone and pad of paper for taking notes (local storage). In the middle of the office is a desk (the description of the game world) with bits of paper on it.

Every now and then, Mr. Draw's phone rings, and a voice on the other end of the line tells him that a sixtieth of a second has gone by. Mr. Draw then jumps up, gets the value of the background intensities from the Game World data on the desk in the office, creates a color value on his notepad, and then uses his phone to call Ms. Clear in the GraphicsDevice office down the hall and asks her to clear the screen to that color. She has a set of paint cans and can fill the screen with any color that she is asked to use.

At a similar interval, the Update phone in the Game1 office rings, and a voice tells Mrs. Update that a sixtieth of a second has gone by. She jumps up, goes to the table in the office, and updates the Game World information on the bits of paper. You can see how this would look in Figure 2-6.

The people/methods in our office/classes perform actions for each other, and data is the information that the class stores within itself. When a class wants to use a method, it calls it.

In our first version of the Game1 class, the information on the table is the color that Mr. Draw uses to color the graphics display. You change what happens when the screen is drawn by changing what Mr. Draw does (the content of the Draw method). You change what happens when the game itself is updated by changing what Mrs. Update does (the content of the Update method).

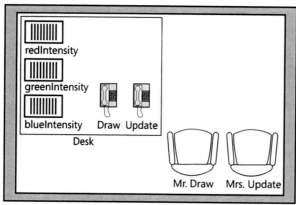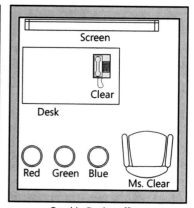

Game1 office   GraphicsDevice office

FIGURE 2-6 The Game1 and GraphicsDevice classes as offices.

Note that no method has to know exactly how the other methods work. Mr. Draw has no idea about cans of paint and displays, but he does know that if he asks Ms. Clear to clear with yellow paint, this results in a yellow screen being drawn. A call of a method is equivalent to calling up someone in an office and asking her or him to perform a task.

Game World Data

The Game World data must be held as part of the class so that the Draw and Update methods can make use of it. For the MoodLight game the data will be the brightness of the red, green, and blue components of the color of the light to be produced.

```
class Game1 {

    // The Game World - our color values
    byte redIntensity ;
    byte greenIntensity ;
    byte blueIntensity ;

    // TODO: Draw method goes here

    // TODO: Update method goes here

}
```

The preceding code declares three variables inside the Game1 class. These are part of the class; they are often called *members* of the class and can be used by any methods that are also members of the class. They have the identifiers redIntensity, greenIntensity, and blueIntensity. You can think of these as separate pieces of paper on the desk in the Game1 office. Figure 2-7 shows how a class can contain members.

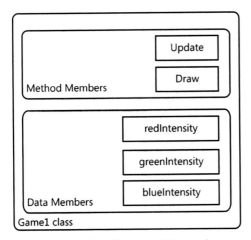

FIGURE 2-7 The Game1 class and its members.

There are two kinds of members: methods (which do something) and data (which hold information). The Game1 class you are working on has both kinds of members; it has the Draw method and the Update method, as well as the three data members, which are going to be used to hold the color values for the changing background. The intensity data members are of type byte.

If you refer back to Figure 2-3, you can see that a declaration is the type of the variable, followed by the identifier. Previously you have declared variables of type Color that can represent a color. Now you are using another type that can represent a numeric value.

Storing Data in Computer Memory

The data for each color intensity is being held in a variable of type byte. The byte type is interesting because it uses 8 bits of computer memory to hold the value that it is trying to represent. Computer memory is actually a huge number of such locations, each of which is 1 byte in size. The Xbox 360 has 512 megabytes of memory. This means that the memory inside the console has about 512 million storage locations, each of which can hold a single byte value. The memory is addressed by number, and the compiler generates a program that uses a particular memory location when it accesses a particular variable. Figure 2-8 shows how this might work. The compiler has decided that blueIntensity is to be held in memory byte number 1003, greenIntensity in memory byte number 1004, and so on.

When the program runs, the statements that work with redIntensity, blueIntensity, and greenIntensity are directed to these locations in memory. Each data type uses a particular amount of computer memory; a byte uses a single memory location. The Color type uses at least 4 bytes of memory; other types can use a lot more. When the program needs to hold a Color value, the compiler allocates a number of adjacent memory locations.

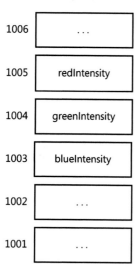

FIGURE 2-8 Storing the color intensity values in memory.

> **Note** In XNA, we never have to worry about precisely where the compiler chooses to put things. These issues are managed automatically and hidden from our programs. In fact, the way things really work is a little more complex than the explanation given, but for now, it is important for you to remember that computer data is held in memory locations of a particular size and that a particular number of memory locations is available for a program to use.

The same memory locations that store data can also be used to hold program instructions. When an Xbox game is running, it might be that half the memory space holds the game program code (the methods) and the other half holds the data that is being used (the variables). When a game is showing the dreaded "Loading" screen, the Xbox is actually transferring program code and data values from the game disk into the memory.

Drawing by Using Our Color Intensity Variables

The color intensity variables that we have created represent the amounts of red, green, and blue that the mood light has. You can use them in your Draw method to create the color to be used to clear the screen:

```
class Game1 {

    // The Game World - our color values
    byte redIntensity ;
    byte greenIntensity ;
    byte blueIntensity ;
```

```
protected override void Draw(GameTime gameTime)
{
    Color backgroundColor;
    backgroundColor =
        new Color(redIntensity, greenIntensity, blueIntensity);
    graphics.GraphicsDevice.Clear(backgroundColor);
    base.Draw(gameTime);
}

// TODO: Update method goes here
```

}

This Draw method looks very much like the previous one, except that it uses member variables to define the color that is created rather than specifying particular values. Note that the assignment to backgroundColor has been spread over two lines. The C# compiler is quite happy with this.

> **The Great Programmer Speaks: Don't Try to Fit Everything on One Line** Our Great Programmer is very keen on sensible program layout. This means not letting program lines extend off the end of the page. She says if a line gets too long, you should break it at a sensible point (not in the middle of an identifier) and then continue to the next line, slightly indented. She has personally checked all the program listings in this book to make sure that the layout meets her exacting requirements.

Updating Our Colors

When the program starts, the values of byte data members are automatically set to 0 and the background color is set to black. If you run a program with the preceding Draw method, you see that the screen just goes black. What you now need to do is take control of the update process and make the colors change over time. When an empty project is created, XNA Game Studio creates a bare-bones Update method that contains a TODO reminding the programmer to add the required code:

```
protected override void Update(GameTime gameTime)
{
    // Allows the game to exit
    if (GamePad.GetState(PlayerIndex.One).Buttons.Back==ButtonState.Pressed)
        this.Exit();

    // TODO: Add your update logic here

    base.Update(gameTime);
}
```

The Update method is rather similar to Draw but has an extra couple of statements in it, one of which starts with the word if. This is the part of the code that decides when the game should end. When you ran your program, you may have noticed that pressing the Back button on the gamepad or on your Windows Phone stops the game. These two statements are the ones that dictate that behavior.

The first statement says, "If the Back button on the gamepad for player 1 (or the Back button on the phone) is pressed, do the next statement," and the second statement says, "Exit the program." Put those together, and you get a behavior that means that when the Update method is called, if the Back button is pressed, the program exits. You are going to spend some time on conditions later, but for now, just remember that if you delete these two lines from your program, it is impossible to stop it via the Xbox gamepad. So don't delete them.

You may be wondering who calls Update and how often. The answers at the moment are "the XNA engine" and "60 times a second." Whenever your game is active, it needs to update the game world. This has to happen repeatedly for a game to be any fun. The XNA engine calls the Update method to give it a chance to perform. In a full-blown game, this involves reading the gamepad, moving all the objects in the game world, checking to see if any have collided, and so on. In the mood light, the Update method just changes the color values that Draw uses to draw the display.

To start with, you are just going to make a mood light that gets steadily brighter over time, so the Update method increases the value of the red, green, and blue intensities by one each time that it is called:

```
protected override void Update(GameTime gameTime)
{
    // Allows the game to exit
    if (GamePad.GetState(PlayerIndex.One).Buttons.Back==ButtonState.Pressed)
        this.Exit();

    // Make each color brighter
    redIntensity++;
    greenIntensity++;
    blueIntensity++;

    base.Update(gameTime);
}
```

The Update method works by using the *++ operator*. An operator is something in the program that tells the compiler that you want to perform an operation on a particular item. In this case, you are using the operator *++* on each of the intensity variables. The item that an operator works on is called an *operand*. Sometimes operators work by combining operands, and sometimes they work on a single operand. The *++* operator works only on a single operand. The Update method uses it on each color in turn so that each color intensity increases by one. This means that each time the Update method is called, the display should get a little bit brighter.

If you run the program with this Update method, you see that the display does get steadily brighter for about four seconds. Then it goes black again. This does not seem right. One of the additions seems to be making the value much smaller rather than increasing it. To understand why this is, you need to take a look at how numbers are stored in computers.

Memory Overflow and Data Values

You have already seen that byte values are actually represented by 8 memory bits. Now you need to understand what this means and the problems that it can cause.

A *bit* is the smallest unit of data that you can have. A bit is either on or off; in other words, it can store just two different values. The two values are often referred to as true or false. Each value is represented by a particular voltage in the memory of the Xbox, but we don't need to worry about that in detail.

Think of a bit as a coin on a table. The coin can be either heads or tails; that is, in one of two possible states. If you put a second coin on the table, the two coins in combination now have four possible states, head-head, head-tail, tail-head, and tail-tail. Each coin that you add to the table doubles the number of possible states (that is, when you add the coin, you can have all the previous states with the new coin on heads plus all the previous states with the new coin on tails).

If you do the math with eight coins, you find that they can occupy 256 different states. So 8 data bits can hold 256 different values. One of these values is 0 (all false or all tails), which means that the largest possible integer value that a byte can hold is 255 (all true or all heads). When the ++ operator tries to increase the value of 255, it will produce the value of 256, which cannot be represented by 8 bits. The addition process would like to set the value of a ninth data bit to 1, so that it can represent the value of 256, but there is no ninth bit to set. So what happens is that the other 8 bits are cleared to zero. This causes the value to wrap around, which means that the value in the byte goes back to 0 again. The result of this is that the screen goes from maximum brightness to minimum brightness in a single step. The technical name for this is *overflow*.

One very important thing to note here is that no error messages are produced. The computer does not "know" that it has done anything wrong. Sometimes if your program does something stupid, you get an error and your program stops. However, in this case, the game does not seem to notice that you have just fallen off the end of a byte and it continues to run. Your program may well do the wrong thing, though. This means that your program has a bug in it. When you create the finished mood light code, you need to make sure that the values never "wrap around" like this.

Note Note that you have not "run out of memory." Rather, the program has tried to put too much information in a single memory location. The Xbox can work with values much larger than 256; it does this by using multiple storage locations to hold a single item. As an example, you have seen that the information to describe a color fills at least four memory locations.

The Great Programmer Speaks: The Computer Doesn't Care   Our Great Programmer finds it very amusing when people say, "The stupid computer got it wrong." She says this is not what happens. What really happened was that the person who wrote the program did a bad job. She has been known to roll around on the floor laughing when people ask her, "But why didn't the computer notice it was wrong?" She knows that the computer really doesn't know or care what a program actually does. The job of the computer is to follow the instructions that the program gives it. The job of the programmer is to write instructions that are correct in every scenario.

Sample Code: Fade from Black   The sample project in the "03 MoodLight Fade Up" directory in the source code resources for this chapter performs the fade up discussed in this section. It then wraps around to black as the values in the bytes overflow.

Making a Proper Mood Light

The fade-up part of the mood light is very good, but you don't want it to suddenly change from white to black each time around. What you would like is for it to fade smoothly up and down. If you were telling Mrs. Update what to do, you would say something like this:

"Make the value of redIntensity bigger each time that you are called. When the value reaches 255, start making it smaller each time you are called until it reaches 0, at which point you should start making it bigger again. Do the same with blue and green."

Mrs. Update would think about this for a while and decide that she needs to keep track of two things for each color: the current intensity value (in the range 0 to 255) and something that lets her remember whether she is counting up or counting down for that color. Then, each time she is called, she can follow a sequence like this:

1. If we are counting up, increase the value of redIntensity.

2. If we are counting down, decrease the value of redIntensity.

3. If redIntensity is 255, change to counting down.

4. If redIntensity is 0, change to counting up.

This is an *algorithm*. It provides a sequence of operations that is used to solve a problem. In this case, we wanted to make the value of redIntensity move up to 255 and down again in steps of 1.

Of course, Mrs. Update is not a person but a C# method, so now we have to convert these steps into C#. The first thing that we need to do is work out what data we need to store. We need the intensity value and also a way of remembering if we are counting up or down. Here's the code that declares the needed variables:

```
// The Game World - our color values
byte redIntensity = 0;
bool redCountingUp = true;
```

You have seen the redIntensity variable before; what you haven't seen is the way that we can set it to 0 when we declare it. The redCountingUp variable is new, though. It is of a new type (C# has hundreds of different types, you'll be pleased to hear). This is the bool type, which is special because it can hold only two possible values: true or false. It allows programs to perform what is called *Boolean algebra*, which consists of calculations involving only the values true and false. Such calculations are usually used to drive decisions along the lines of "If itIsRaining is true and robWillBeGoingOutside is true, I should call the takeMyUmberella method."

In this case, the bool type is perfect because redCountingUp is either true or false and nothing else. The program uses it to make decisions in the Update method so that it can behave according to the data. This ability to make decisions is what makes computers truly useful, in that they can change what they do in response to their situation. To make decisions in your programs, you have to use conditional statements.

Making Decisions in Your Program

You have seen two kinds of statement so far. One calls a method to do something (you use this to call the Clear method), and the other changes the value of a variable (you use this to increase the intensity of your colors). Now you are going to use a conditional construction that can change what the program does depending on the particular situation.

Creating Conditional Statements

Figure 2-9 shows how a conditional construction fits together. Conditional constructions start with the word if. This is followed by a condition in brackets. The condition produces a Boolean result, which can be either true or false. You can use a variable of bool type directly here.

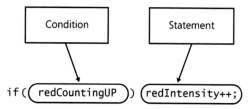

FIGURE 2-9 The *if* condition in action

If the condition is `true` (that is, the variable `redCountingUp` holds the value `true` in this case), the statement following the condition is performed. The result is that when this statement is obeyed, the value of `redIntensity` gets bigger if the program is counting up. The condition can be any value that gives a Boolean result, including this rather stupid code:

```
if (true) redIntensity++;
```

The preceding code is completely legal C# code and compiles with no problem. When the program runs, the condition is true, and the statement increases the red intensity value. This is very stupid code, though, as the test might as well not be there. You could also write the following:

```
if (false) redIntensity++;
```

In this code, the statement following the condition is never obeyed because the condition is always false. This C# code compiles all right, but if you look very closely at the Microsoft Visual Studio display, you might notice that it is trying to tell you something, as shown in Figure 2-10.

Error List					
❌ 0 Errors ⚠ 1 Warning ⓘ 0 Messages					
Description	File	Line	Column	Project	
⚠ 1 Unreachable code detected	Game1.cs	80	24	MoodLight	

Error List   Output   Find Symbol Results

FIGURE 2-10 Compiler warnings.

If the error window in Figure 2-10 is not displayed, you can open it by selecting the View menu and clicking Error List in that menu. Alternatively you can use the key combination Ctrl+W+E.

When the compiler has finished trying to convert your C# source code into a program that can be run on the computer, it tells you how many mistakes that it thinks it has found. There are two kinds of mistakes. An *error* is a mistake that prevents what you have written from being made into a program. Errors are really bad things like spelling identifiers wrong, using the wrong kind of brackets, and the like.

The other kind of mistake is called a *warning*. This is where the compiler thinks you might have done something wrong, but it does not prevent your program from running. Figure 2-10 shows the warning message for a program with a test for (false) in it.

What the compiler is telling you is that it has managed to work out that the statement after the test will never be reached. This is because it is impossible for the value `false` to be true. The compiler is warning you that although the code is legal C# code, what it does might actually not be what you want.

> **The Great Programmer Speaks: Warnings Should Always Be Heeded** Our Great Programmer has very strong opinions on compiler warnings; she reckons that your code should compile with no warnings at all. Warnings usually mean that your solution is imperfect in some way, and you should always take steps to investigate and resolve them.

Adding an *Else* Part

The condition you have created is only half correct. If the program is not counting up, it must make the value of redIntensity smaller. You can use the -- operator to do this, but we need to add extra code to the condition. You need to add an *else* part. Figure 2-11 shows another form of the `if` condition, with the `else` part added.

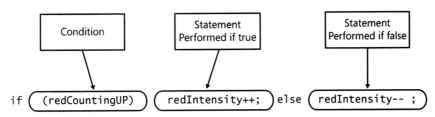

FIGURE 2-11 The *if* condition with an *else* part

The two statements are separated by a new key word, `else`. The new code means that if the program is counting up (that is, redCountingUp is `true`), the value gets bigger, but if the program is counting down (that is, redCountingUp is `false`), the value gets smaller. The `else` part is optional; you must add one only if you need it.

Testing Values

The program must also manage the value in redCountingUp so that when it reaches the upper limit, it starts to count down, and when it reaches the lower limit, it starts to count up again. In other words:

1. When redIntensity reaches 255, set redCountingUp to `false`.

2. When redIntensity reaches 0, set redCountingUp to `true`.

To do this, you need another kind of condition, one that performs a comparison. Figure 2-12 shows how such comparisons are created. This performs the first of these two tests.

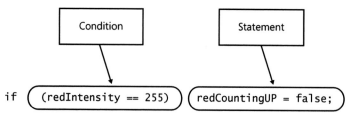

```
if  (redIntensity == 255)   redCountingUP = false;
```

FIGURE 2-12 Performing a comparison using the *if* condition

The key to understanding what is happening is the == comparison operator. When the program evaluates this condition, the values on the left and right of the == operator are compared. If they are the same, the result of the comparison is true, and the statement that follows the condition is performed. If they are different, the result of the comparison is false, and the statement that follows the comparison is ignored.

The sequence == is the comparison operator. It is completely different from the = operator, which we know as the "gozzinta." It is important that you don't get these two confused. Unfortunately, you have both a gozzinta and a comparison taking place in the if statement because you want to put a new value into redCountingUp if the comparison succeeds.

Fortunately, the compiler can usually detect when you use the wrong operator and produce a message. There are other comparison operators that can test to see if one value is greater or less than another; we will use these later. An if statement that uses a comparison operator can have an else part; it is just that we don't need one here. The final code to make our red intensity value move up and down ends up as follows:

```
if (redIntensity == 255) redCountingUp = false;
if (redIntensity == 0) redCountingUp = true;
if (redCountingUp) redIntensity++; else redIntensity--;
```

The program needs a second test to change the direction of the counting when the bottom limit of the intensity value is reached. The tests are performed before the intensity value is updated. This is because when the program starts running we want it to work correctly for any initial value of redIntensity. If the starting value is 255 the program must count down. If the starting value is 0 the program must count up.

Note Pay very careful attention to the three statements shown in this section. Go back and read our original instructions to Mrs. Update and make sure you are absolutely clear how these have been converted into C# statements that perform the job. You will notice that Mrs. Update's original design has had to be changed so that it works with any starting value.

The Completed Mood Light

You now have the code that lets you create a smoothly pulsing mood light:

```
// The Game World - our color values
byte redIntensity = 0;
bool redCountingUp = true;

byte greenIntensity = 0;
bool greenCountingUp = true;

byte blueIntensity = 0;
bool blueCountingUp = true;

protected override void Update(GameTime gameTime)
{
    // Allows the game to exit
    if (GamePad.GetState(PlayerIndex.One).Buttons.Back ==
        ButtonState.Pressed)
        this.Exit();

    // Update each color in turn
    if (redIntensity == 255) redCountingUp = false;
    if (redIntensity == 0) redCountingUp = true;
    if (redCountingUp) redIntensity++; else redIntensity--;

    if (greenIntensity == 255) greenCountingUp = false;
    if (greenIntensity == 0) greenCountingUp = true;
    if (greenCountingUp) greenIntensity++; else greenIntensity--;

    if (blueIntensity == 255) blueCountingUp = false;
    if (blueIntensity == 0) blueCountingUp = true;
    if (blueCountingUp) blueIntensity++; else blueIntensity--;

    base.Update(gameTime);
}

protected override void Draw(GameTime gameTime)
{
    Color backgroundColor;
    backgroundColor =
        new Color(redIntensity, greenIntensity, blueIntensity);
    graphics.GraphicsDevice.Clear(backgroundColor);

    base.Draw(gameTime);
}
```

These versions of Update and Draw produce a program that smoothly fades the screen between black and white.

> **Sample Code: Mood Light** The project in the "04 MoodLight" directory in the source code resources for this chapter contains the Update and Draw methods presented in this section and provides a smoothly changing mood light that goes from dark to light and back again.

A Proper Funky Mood Light

Going from black to white and back is all very well, but it would be nice to have some additional variety to our light. It turns out that this is very easy to achieve. At the moment, the red, green, and blue intensities are all the same values, counting up from 0 to 255 and back down again. This just gives shades of gray. What you want is different combinations and the color intensities going up and down at different times. You can do this by changing the starting values of our intensity values and update directions:

```
byte redIntensity = 0;
bool redCountingUp = true;

byte greenIntensity = 80;
bool greenCountingUp = false;

byte blueIntensity = 160;
bool blueCountingUp = true;
```

Rather than all the colors starting at 0 and counting up, the green value now starts at 80 and counts down, and the blue value starts at 160. This means that instead of just different shades of gray, you now have lots of other colors being presented. This provides a very groovy display. If you change the values in your program to the ones shown in this section, you can get a much more interesting-looking display. You can even try values of your own and see what they look like.

For a much longer-lasting display, we need to change the rate at which the three colors are updated. This is not actually very hard to do, so I've written an "Ultimate Mood Light" that you can take a look at.

> **Sample Code: Ultimate Mood Light**   The project in the "05 Ultimate Mood Light" directory in the source code resources for this chapter contains a new version of Update, which changes the red, green, and blue intensities at different speeds, resulting in a display that never seems to actually repeat (although it does eventually). Look at the code and see if you can understand how it works.

Finding Program Bugs

Your younger brother has been reading this book and typing in the programs on his computer. He has just come and told you that the book is rubbish because the programs don't work. He has written an Update method and is complaining that for him the red value only gets brighter. You ask him to show you the code and you see this:

```
if (redIntensity == 255) redCountingUp = true;
if (redIntensity == 0) redCountingUp = true;
if (redCountingUp) redIntensity++; else redIntensity++;
```

At first glance, it looks fine, and the C# compiler is quite happy that it is legal, but it is obviously not working. There is a bug in the program. Note that the bug is not there because the computer has made a mistake, so the instructions themselves must be faulty. You don't want to bother the Great Programmer, as she seems to be busy playing Halo on her Xbox, so you take a look, bearing in mind something she said recently.

> **The Great Programmer Speaks: Run Programs by Hand to Find Bugs** A good way to find out what a program is doing is to behave like the computer and "run" the program yourself. By working through the statements by hand, keeping track of the variables and making the changes to them that the program does, you can often find out what is wrong.

Your younger brother has actually made two mistakes in copying the program from these pages. See if you can find them by working through the statements.

Figure 2-13 highlights the errors that your younger brother has made.

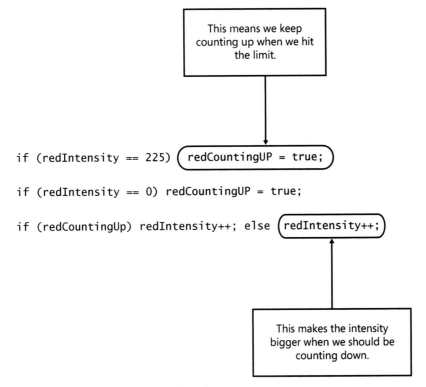

FIGURE 2-13 Finding the errors in the code.

The two errors both have the same effect, they cause the screen to get brighter all the time. If you fixed only one of them the program would still appear broken.

Conclusion

You have learned a lot in this chapter. You now know the fundamentals of C# programs and the XNA framework. You have seen how to identify and create variables that store data and also how to write statements that change the values of these variables. You have seen that the data in a variable is held in a location in memory, which is a certain size and has a particular capacity. If you exceed this, the value does not fit and is damaged.

You know that in C#, programs are broken down into classes, each class having things it can do (methods) and things it can hold (member variables). Classes are like offices, where workers (methods) can be asked to do things. You also know that an XNA game is a particular kind of class that contains an Update method, which is used by XNA to update the state of the game world, and a Draw method, which is used to draw the current state of the game world. You have seen how our programs can be made to make decisions and change what they do, depending on the values of the data they hold.

Chapter Review Questions

Time for another review. Have a go at the questions before you move on. When you learn to program, you find that each step builds on the last, so it is important that you understand what is in this chapter before you move on to the next. Again, all the answers are either true or false, and you can work them out from this chapter and the Glossary.

1. A program is a sequence of variables.
2. Programs are always held in a file called Program.prog.
3. An identifier is a name that we give to something we want to use in our program.
4. Methods tell the computer how to do something.
5. The Draw method updates the game.
6. A block of statements is made of wood.
7. The compiler checks code comments for accuracy and spelling.
8. A Color value is held as a single byte.
9. The type of a variable determines what kind of data can be put into it.
10. A local variable is held inside the class.
11. An identifier is a name built into C# to identify things.
12. A variable has an identifier and a type and holds values that our program wants to work with.

13. A variable of type bool can hold only the values 0 and 1.

14. Conditional statements start with the word when.

15. An if condition must have an else part.

16. An algorithm is like a recipe.

17. The = operator is used to compare two values and test if they are the same.

18. A class holds method members and data members.

19. A good identifier for a class would be PlayGame.

20. A good identifier for a method would be Explode.

21. A byte holds a single bit of data.

22. The ++ operator works between two operands.

23. The C# compiler detects if a variable overflows when the program is running.

24. Boolean values can be either true or false.

Chapter 3
Getting Player Input

In this chapter, you will

- Find out how Microsoft XNA represents the gamepads and keyboards.

- Discover the C# language structures that let us get player input.

- Write some really silly games and scare people with them.

Introduction

You now know the basics of computer game programming. You know that a program is actually a sequence of statements, each of which performs a single action. You have seen that statements are held inside methods, each of which performs a particular task, and that methods are held in classes along with data. The program itself works on data values, which are held in variables of a particular type, and the program can make decisions based on the values that the variables have. (If none of this makes much sense, reread Chapter 2, "Programs, Data, and Pretty Colors," until it does.)

Now you are going to expand your understanding to include how to receive input from the outside world so that games can actually react to what the player does. You shall see that once we have done this, a number of possibilities open up, and you can create some truly silly games, including "Color Nerve," "Mind Reader," "The Thing That Goes Bump in the Night," and "Gamepad Racer."

Program Project: A Mood Light Controller

In Chapter 2, you created a light that changes color over time. I also mentioned that this is the kind of thing that will be used in the starships of the future. A color-changing light is not all that useful for reading books, but it's great for setting moods; what our starship captain really needs is a light that she can set to any color. So now you are going to make a lamp that can be controlled by an Xbox gamepad. The user presses the red, blue, green, and yellow buttons on the gamepad to increase the amount of that color in the light. To make this work, you have to discover how to read the gamepad.

Before you start looking at gamepads, though, you need to decide how the program will actually work. Consider the following statement of C# from the previous mood-light program, which is part of the Update method:

```
if (redCountingUp) redIntensity++;
```

This is one of the tests that controls the intensity of the red part of the color. What it is saying is "If the Boolean value redCountingUp is True, increase the value of redIntensity by 1." The statement is processed each time Update is called (at the moment that is 60 times a second), so this means that if redCountingUp is True, the red intensity of the screen gets progressively brighter over time.

You want to write some code that says, "If the red button on Gamepad 1 is being pressed, increase the value of redIntensity by 1." Then, if the player holds down the button, the screen gets redder. So all you have to do is change this test to read the button on the gamepad, and you can create a user-controlled light easily.

Reading a Gamepad

The gamepads are actually very complex devices. They are connected to the host device either by a universal serial bus (USB) cable or by a wireless connection. As far as you are concerned, the way that programs work with gamepads does not depend on how they are connected. The connection to a gamepad can be used to read the buttons and joysticks and can also be used to send commands to the gamepad—for example, to turn the vibration effect on and off. The Xbox and XNA provide support for up to four gamepads connected simultaneously.

Gamepads and Classes

The gamepad information is represented in XNA by means of a class called GamePadState. The job of this class is to provide the connection between the program and the physical gamepad that the player is holding. To understand how you are going to use this, you have to learn a bit more about how classes work.

You have already seen what a class is in the section "Games and Classes" in Chapter 2. A class contains data (variables that can hold stuff) and methods (code that can do stuff). You can think of a class as an office, with a desk holding the variables and people acting as the methods. Figure 3-1 shows the office plan for the class Game1, which you have seen is the basis of an XNA game.

This class contains some variables on the desk (in this case, the background color intensities) and two methods, which we have called Mr. Draw and Mrs. Update. Each method has a corresponding telephone. Programs can place calls to the telephones to request that the method perform the required task.

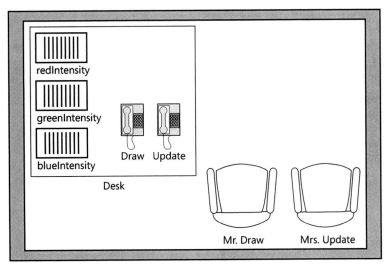

Game1 office

FIGURE 3-1 The Game1 class as an office plan.

> **The Great Programmer Speaks: Classes Are Not Really Offices** Our Great Programmer
> has been reading these notes and finds them quite amusing. She says that classes are not exactly
> like offices, but she thinks that for the purpose of getting an understanding of how programs are
> constructed, it is okay to regard them as such.

When an XNA game starts, the XNA system makes an *instance* of the Game1 class that it then
can ask to Draw and Update. When an instance of a class is created, the instructions for the
methods that it contains are loaded into memory and space is set aside for the data variables
that the instance holds.

The class files that you write give the plans for the class so when the program runs, instances
of each class can be created. In real life, you would make a game office by building a
room, putting a desk and some telephones in the room, and then hiring a Mr. Draw and
a Mrs. Update. The process of making an instance of a class is similar. However, to save
memory, the running program uses only one copy of the method code, which is shared
among all the instances of a class.

> **Note** It is important to remember that this happens when a program runs. The process of
> creating instances of classes is not performed by the compiler. The job of the compiler is to
> convert your C# source code into instructions that the target device runs. By the time that
> your program has control, the compiler has done its job, and the computer is just running the
> machine language output that the compiler produced.

Finding a Gamepad

XNA also looks after a lot of other things when a game is running, one of which is the GamePad class connected to all the gamepads. You don't have to know how the gamepad is actually connected; for all you know, it might use tiny pixies traveling up and down the wires carrying pixie notes written on pixie paper saying, "Master has pressed the Red Button," but then again it might not. Figure 3-2 shows how the GamePad class would look if it were an office.

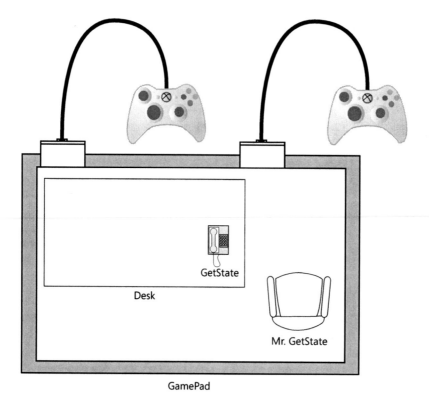

FIGURE 3-2 The GamePad class as an office.

The GamePad class contains a method called GetState, which gets the state of one of the gamepads. When GetState is called, it looks at one of the gamepads, reads its settings, and then sends information back for use in the statement it was called from.

The GetState method is supplied with a parameter that identifies the gamepad to be read. A *parameter* is a way that a call can give information to a method. You have seen these before; in your very first programs, you were passing Color parameters into the Clear method to select the color of the screen that you wanted.

In the case of the GetState method, the parameter identifies the gamepad that you want to read. If you are thinking in terms of offices, you can think of a parameter as part of the instructions that come down the telephone. When the phone rings and Mr. GetState answers it, he is asked, "Get me the state of Gamepad 1." The information about the state of the gamepad is sent back in a GamePadState structure, which is shown in Figure 3-3.

GamePadState	
Buttons	
Green A	ButtonState.Pressed
Red B	ButtonState.Released
Blue X	ButtonState.Released
Yellow Y	ButtonState.Released
Start	ButtonState.Released
Back	ButtonState.Released

FIGURE 3-3 GamePadState structure with the green A button pressed.

You can think of this as a set of items filled in on a form if you wish, but actually it is a C# structure that contains the data members shown in Figure 3-3, as well as some other data.

So, if Mrs. Update wants to know the state of one of the gamepads on the Xbox, she calls the GetState method in the GamePad class and asks, "Can you give me the state of the gamepad for Player 1, please?" Mr. GetState jumps up, fills in a "GamePadState" form, and sends it back to her. Figure 3-4 gives the breakdown of the C# statement that gets the state of a gamepad into a variable of type GamePadState.

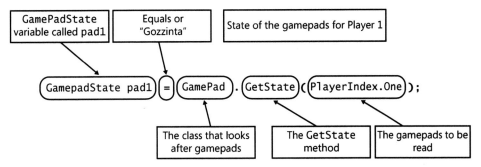

FIGURE 3-4 Getting the status of a gamepad.

Testing the Gamepad Status

Now that you have the status, you can use it in the program to see if a button has been pressed. Figure 3-5 shows the breakdown of the C# statement that will perform the test.

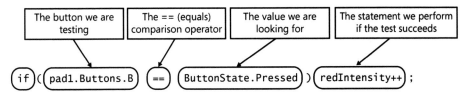

FIGURE 3-5 Testing a button on a gamepad.

This compares the state of the red button B with the value ButtonState.Pressed. If the two are equal, this means that the button is down, and the Update method must make the red intensity bigger. You can then use the same principle to manage the blue and green values, which means that you now have an Update method that looks like the following:

```
protected override void Update(GameTime gameTime)
{
  // Allows the game to exit
  if (GamePad.GetState(PlayerIndex.One).Buttons.Back == ButtonState.Pressed)
    this.Exit();

  GamePadState pad1 = GamePad.GetState(PlayerIndex.One);

  if (pad1.Buttons.B == ButtonState.Pressed) redIntensity++;
  if (pad1.Buttons.X == ButtonState.Pressed) blueIntensity++;
  if (pad1.Buttons.A == ButtonState.Pressed) greenIntensity++;

  base.Update(gameTime);
}
```

The only problem with the Update method described here is that the program doesn't handle the yellow button yet. When the yellow button is pressed, the program needs to increase the green and the red intensities; that is, it must perform two statements if the condition is true. It turns out that doing so is very easy; you can just put the two statements into a block that is controlled by the condition, as shown here:

```
if (pad1.Buttons.Y == ButtonState.Pressed)
{
    redIntensity++;
    greenIntensity++;
}
```

You have seen blocks before; the body of a method (the bit that does the work) is a block. In C# terms, a *block* is a number of statements that are enclosed in curly braces. The code shown here performs both statements if the condition is true because they are in a block controlled by the condition.

> **The Great Programmer Speaks: Blocks Rock** Our Great Programmer tends to use blocks after if conditions even when she doesn't actually need to. She says that it makes the program text clearer, and that it is much easier to add extra statements later if you need to.

If you put the preceding statements into the Update method of one of your earlier Mood Light programs, you get compiler warning messages because the new version of Update doesn't use all the variables that were created for previous versions of the program. To get rid of these warnings, you must delete the statements that create the unused variables. The Great Programmer doesn't like it when programs have variables in them that are not used. She says this looks unprofessional, and I agree with her.

Sample Code: Manual MoodLight All the sample projects can be obtained from the Web resources for this text, which can be found at *http://oreilly.com/catalog/9780735651579*. The sample project in the directory "01 Manual MoodLight" in the resources for this chapter implements the Update method, as shown in this section. You can increase the brightness of the colors on the screen by pressing the buttons on the gamepad.

Game Idea: Color Nerve

Every now and then, we are going to try out a game idea. These start out very simply and then build up to more complicated and interesting games. You can use the Manual MoodLight code to create your first game. The game uses something we saw in Chapter 2. You noticed that if you keep making a value bigger, there comes a point where it won't fit in the memory store allocated for it, and then it overflows. This is what caused the screen to go from bright white to black. However, you can use this to create our first "Very Silly Game."

Color Nerve is a game for two or more players. The players take turns pressing one or more buttons on the gamepad. (The other players must watch carefully to make sure that they actually do press at least one button.) Each player can press as many buttons as he wants for as long as he wants during his turn, but if the screen changes suddenly (because one of the color values has gone from 255 to 0), he is out, and the game continues. The last player left in the game is the winner.

This game can be very tactical. Players can press the buttons for very short times, or at the start of the game, they can show their nerve by holding the buttons down for longer periods, trying to cause problems for the next player. They can also try to work out which color has wrapped around so that they can press that button when it is their turn. The game works very well at parties, any number of people can take part, and the rules are very easy to understand. In Chapter 4, "Displaying Images," you will improve the game to add pictures as well as a plain screen.

Using the Keyboard

XNA works with keyboards as well as with gamepads. You might be surprised to learn that you can plug a USB keyboard into an Xbox 360 and use it just as you'd use the keyboard on the PC. If you want the program to work with the keyboard, you can add code that does this, as shown here:

```
KeyboardState keys = Keyboard.GetState();

if (keys.IsKeyDown(Keys.R)) redIntensity++;
if (keys.IsKeyDown(Keys.B)) blueIntensity++;
if (keys.IsKeyDown(Keys.G)) greenIntensity++;
if (keys.IsKeyDown(Keys.Y))
{
    redIntensity++;
    greenIntensity++;
}
```

Note that the process is very similar to how the gamepad works, but there are slight differences. You don't need to tell the GetState method on the Keyboard which keyboard to read because XNA supports only a single keyboard. The KeyboardState item that is returned from the call is not actually a piece of paper; instead, it is an object that provides methods that the program can use to discover whether a particular key is pressed. Rather than seeing if the state of a button is set to the value ButtonState.Pressed, the program can call the method IsKeyDown. You supply the IsKeyDown method with a parameter that identifies the key you are interested in, as follows:

```
if (keys.IsKeyDown(Keys.R)) redIntensity++;
```

This code is a conditional statement that increases the value of redIntensity if the R key is pressed. The method IsKeyDown returns true if the key is down and false if not. You can, therefore, use it to control the update of the redIntensity value.

Stopping the Game with the Escape Key

The Update method that is created when you make a new XNA game contains a test that checks for the Back button on gamepad 1 and calls the Exit method to stop the game when the Back button is pressed. If you are using a keyboard instead of a gamepad you will not be able to press this button to stop the game. You can add a test for the Escape key on the keyboard. This key is a "control" key, in that it does not actually relate to a printable character, but is designed to signal an action you want the program to take. Other control keys include the Enter key and the Backspace key. You can use the same IsKeyDown method to test for the Escape key.

```
if (keys.IsKeyDown(Keys.Escape)) Exit();
```

This code stops the game when the Escape key is pressed.

Using a Gamepad and a Keyboard at the Same Time

If you want to use a gamepad and a keyboard simultaneously, you have to test for both. This means that the Update method now looks like this:

```
protected override void Update(GameTime gameTime)
{
  GamePadState pad1 = GamePad.GetState(PlayerIndex.One);

  if (pad1.Buttons.Back == ButtonState.Pressed) Exit();
  if (pad1.Buttons.B == ButtonState.Pressed) redIntensity++;
  if (pad1.Buttons.X == ButtonState.Pressed) blueIntensity++;
  if (pad1.Buttons.A == ButtonState.Pressed) greenIntensity++;
  if (pad1.Buttons.Y == ButtonState.Pressed)
  if (pad1.Buttons.B == ButtonState.Pressed) redIntensity++;
  {
    redIntensity++;
    greenIntensity++;
  }

  KeyboardState keys = Keyboard.GetState();

  if (keys.IsKeyDown(Keys.Escape)) Exit();

  if (keys.IsKeyDown(Keys.R)) redIntensity++;
  if (keys.IsKeyDown(Keys.B)) blueIntensity++;
  if (keys.IsKeyDown(Keys.G)) greenIntensity++;
  if (keys.IsKeyDown(Keys.Y))
  {
    redIntensity++;
    greenIntensity++;
  }
  base.Update(gameTime);
}
```

This code is not good because you are doing the same thing twice, just triggered in a different way. The Great Programmer, if she ever saw this, would not be impressed. Fortunately C# provides a way that a program can combine two conditions and then perform some code if either condition is true. This way of combining conditions is called the *OR* logical operator because it is true if one thing or the other is true, and it is written in the program as two vertical bars (||):

```
GamePadState pad1 = GamePad.GetState(PlayerIndex.One);
KeyboardState keys = Keyboard.GetState();

if (pad1.Buttons.B == ButtonState.Pressed ||
    keys.IsKeyDown(Keys.R)) redIntensity++;
```

The *OR* logical operator is placed between two Boolean expressions that can be either true or false. If one or the other expression is true, the combined logical condition works out to be true.

In this code, if the red button is pressed on the gamepad *or* the R key is pressed on the keyboard (or both), the `redIntensity` value increases. This is exactly what you want, and it means that Color Nerve can now be played with the gamepad or the keyboard (or both at the same time). Logical operators are so called because they produce logical rather than numerical results. There are other logical operators that you will use as you create more complex programs.

> **Note** If you find this logical operator stuff hard to understand, just go back to the problem that you are trying to solve. You want the program to perform a statement (`redIntensity++`) if the red key is pressed on the gamepad *or* if the R key is pressed on the keyboard. So you use the *OR* operator (||) to combine the two tests and make a condition that triggers if one or the other condition is true.

> **Sample Code: Color Nerve**   The sample project in the directory "02 Color Nerve" in the resources for this chapter implements the game. You can adjust the colors of the screen by pressing the gamepad buttons or a key on the keyboard.

Adding Vibration

The communication between the gamepad and the game works in both directions. Not only can you read buttons on the gamepad, but also you can send commands to the gamepad to turn on the vibration motors. Again, you don't have to know exactly how these messages are delivered; all you need to know is the features of XNA that are used to control this vibration effect.

This means you can make your Color Nerve game even more exciting by making the gamepad vibrate when the intensity values are getting close to their limits. It is interesting how features like this can enhance even a simple game. You will be using the vibration effect on the gamepads quite a lot in the next few games.

Controlling the Vibration of a Gamepad

The GamePad class provides a method called `SetVibration` that lets a program control the vibration motors:

```
GamePad.SetVibration(PlayerIndex.One, 0, 1);
```

The `SetVibration` method uses three parameters. The first one identifies which gamepad you want to vibrate. The second parameter is a value between 0.0 and 1 that controls the vibration of the left motor. The bigger the number, the more the gamepad vibrates. The third parameter controls the right motor in the same way as the left one. The statement shown here would set the right motor of Gamepad 1 vibrating at full speed. The left motor is the low-frequency vibration, and the right motor is the high-frequency vibration.

If you think of the GamePad class/office having a man called Mr. SetVibration, this means that he would be told which gamepad to vibrate and the settings for the left and right motors. Once the method has been called, the gamepad starts to vibrate, and it keeps vibrating until you call the method again to change its setting. In other words, you can think of the SetVibration method as a switch that can be set to a number of different positions. Initially, both of the gamepad motors are set at 0, which means no vibration.

Testing Intensity Values

The game needs to decide when to turn on the vibration. To do this, it must test the intensity values and turn on the vibration motor if any of them is getting too large. The program can decide to turn on the motors if any of the red, green, or blue intensity values is greater than 220. To do this, the program must test the intensity values as follows:

```
if (redIntensity > 220)
{
    GamePad.SetVibration(PlayerIndex.One, 0, 1);
}
```

This code shows another form of condition. In the previous examples, the conditions have been checking to see if two values are equal. This code tests if one value is greater than another. The greater-than sign (>) is another logical operator. Placed between two values, it returns true if the value on the left is greater than the value on the right and false if not. That is exactly what you want.

Using the preceding code, the gamepad starts to vibrate using the right motor when the red intensity value goes above 220. If you add this code to the Update method in the Color Nerve game, you find that if you increase the red value, the gamepad starts to vibrate. Unfortunately, our program has a bug. When the red intensity value returns to 0, the vibration does not stop. You need to add some code that turns off the motor when the intensity value is less than 220. It turns out that this is very easy to do—you can add an else part to the condition:

```
if (redIntensity > 220)
{
    GamePad.SetVibration(PlayerIndex.One, 0, 1);
}
else
{
    GamePad.SetVibration(PlayerIndex.One, 0, 0);
}
```

The statement after the else is performed if the condition is found to be false. (You can add an else part to any if condition that you create.) This means that when the red intensity value returns to 0, the vibration stops. You can extend the tests using *OR* so that the program tests all the intensity values:

```
if ( redIntensity > 220 ||
     greenIntensity > 220 ||
     blueIntensity > 220 )
{
    GamePad.SetVibration(PlayerIndex.One, 0, 1);
}
else
{
    GamePad.SetVibration(PlayerIndex.One, 0, 0);
}
```

Now the vibration is controlled by all the intensity values. As an improvement to the game, you might want to experiment with different kinds of vibration for different colors, perhaps by using the low-frequency motor as well. This is controlled by the other value in the call of SetVibration:

```
GamePad.SetVibration(PlayerIndex.One, 1, 0);
```

The line of code shown here turns on the low-frequency vibration. You might also want to experiment with the thresholds at which the vibration starts.

The program still has one more problem. If you run it and make the gamepad vibrate, when the program finishes, the gamepad doesn't always stop vibrating. You need to add code that stops the vibration when the game ends. The game stops when the player presses the Back button on the gamepad. The test for this is in the Update method. If the Back button is pressed, the Exit method is called to stop the game:

```
if (GamePad.GetState(PlayerIndex.One).Buttons.Back == ButtonState.Pressed)
    this.Exit();
```

The Exit method removes the game display and shuts the game down in a tidy fashion. What the program must do is turn off the gamepad motors before Exit is called. To do this, the program needs to perform more than one statement if the Back button is pressed, so we need another block:

```
if (GamePad.GetState(PlayerIndex.One).Buttons.Back == ButtonState.Pressed)
{
    GamePad.SetVibration(PlayerIndex.One, 0, 0);
    this.Exit();
}
```

Now, when the player presses the Back button to end the program, the vibration motors are turned off.

The Great Programmer Speaks: When in Doubt, Make Sure Yourself The Great Programmer says that if you are in a situation where you are not sure whether something is always the case, you should add code to remove all possible doubt. Testing the vibration behavior described in this section, I discovered that the gamepad is left vibrating on earlier versions of XNA, but not on some newer ones. To make absolutely sure that the vibration stops regardless of the version of XNA under which your game runs, you should include the code to stop the vibration yourself.

Sample Code: Vibration Color Nerve Game The sample project in the "03 Color Nerve with Vibes" directory in the source code resources for this chapter holds a version of Color Nerve that has the vibration effect enabled.

Game Idea: Secret Vibration Messages

Once you see that it is easy to read gamepad buttons and drive the motors, you can start to have more fun with XNA, particularly with wireless gamepads. You can create mind-reading games where your assistant seems to know exactly what you are thinking. What the audience doesn't know is that both of you are holding Xbox gamepads in your jacket pockets and using them to send signals back and forth using the vibration feature. The code to do this is actually very simple, and you should be able to understand what it does:

```
protected override void Update(GameTime gameTime)
{
    // Allows the game to exit
    if(GamePad.GetState(PlayerIndex.One).Buttons.Back == ButtonState.Pressed)
    {
        GamePad.SetVibration(PlayerIndex.One, 0, 0);
        GamePad.SetVibration(PlayerIndex.Two, 0, 0);
        this.Exit();
    }

    GamePadState pad1 = GamePad.GetState(PlayerIndex.One);
    GamePadState pad2 = GamePad.GetState(PlayerIndex.Two);

    if (pad1.Buttons.A == ButtonState.Pressed)
    {
        GamePad.SetVibration(PlayerIndex.Two, 0, 1);
    }
    else
    {
        GamePad.SetVibration(PlayerIndex.Two, 0, 0);
    }

    if (pad2.Buttons.A == ButtonState.Pressed)
```

```
    {
        GamePad.SetVibration(PlayerIndex.One, 0, 1);
    }
    else
    {
        GamePad.SetVibration(PlayerIndex.One, 0, 0);
    }

    base.Update(gameTime);
}
```

The Update method reads the A button on the gamepad for Player 1. If this is pressed, it turns on the fast vibration motor in the gamepad for Player 2. It then repeats the process the other way, sending signals from Gamepad 2 to Gamepad 1. This gives you a way in which you can send wireless signals from one gamepad to another. Note that both conditions have else parts so that if the button is not pressed, the vibration is turned off.

You could also use this for practical jokes; for example, just leave a gamepad underneath your victim's bed and then wait until he turns the light off and settles down. Then give the vibration a quick blast for the maximum scare factor. Just don't blame me if you never get the gamepad back!

Sample Code: Vibration Messages The sample project in the "04 Mind Reader" directory in the source code resources for this chapter holds a version of the vibration message program. Just remember to use it wisely. The program also turns the display screen black so that it is not obvious that there is a program running.

Game Idea: Gamepad Racer

The final game idea in this chapter is really silly, but it can be great fun. The first thing you need to do is find a large, smooth table. Put a couple of books under the legs at one end so that the table is sloping, not horizontal. If you put a wireless Xbox gamepad at the top of the table and make the gamepad vibrate, it slides down the table toward the other end. You may need to experiment with the angle, but I've found that with care, you can arrange things so that a gamepad takes around 30 seconds to slide all the way down the table with vibration at full power. If you line up four gamepads on the top of the table, players can pick the one they think will win, and then you can race them down the slope.

The code for this game is very simple indeed; the Update method just turns on all the vibration motors in the gamepads:

```
protected override void Update(GameTime gameTime)
```

```
{
    // Allows the game to exit
    if(GamePad.GetState(PlayerIndex.One).Buttons.Back == ButtonState.Pressed)
    {
        GamePad.SetVibration(PlayerIndex.One, 0, 0);
        GamePad.SetVibration(PlayerIndex.Two, 0, 0);
        GamePad.SetVibration(PlayerIndex.Three, 0, 0);
        GamePad.SetVibration(PlayerIndex.Four, 0, 0);
        this.Exit();
    }

    GamePad.SetVibration(PlayerIndex.One, 1, 1);
    GamePad.SetVibration(PlayerIndex.Two, 1, 1);
    GamePad.SetVibration(PlayerIndex.Three, 1, 1);
    GamePad.SetVibration(PlayerIndex.Four, 1, 1);

    base.Update(gameTime);
}
```

The only complication is that when the game ends, you must turn off all the vibrations. Put all the gamepads at the top of the slope and then run the program. Press the Back button on Gamepad 1 to stop the game.

Sample Code: Gamepad Racer The sample project in the "05 GamepadRacer" directory in the source code resources for this chapter holds a version of the Gamepad Racer program.

Note By carefully tuning vibration values it is possible to "sabotage" gamepads so that the same one wins each time. Note that I do not condone such behavior.

Program Bugs

Your younger brother is still trying to learn to program, but he keeps having problems. He claims that this book is faulty because the programs don't work properly when he types them in. He is trying to get the Color Nerve game to work, but every time he runs the program, the yellow intensity gets brighter whether he presses the button or not. You take a look at his program and find the following code in the Update method:

```
if (pad1.Buttons.Y == ButtonState.Pressed ||
    keys.IsKeyDown(Keys.Y)) ;
{
    redIntensity++;
    greenIntensity++;
}
```

This is the only part of the program where the yellow intensity is being increased, and it seems that the condition is being ignored.

This looks perfectly okay, and it seems to compile and run correctly, but it seems to be making the yellow intensity brighter every time. At this point, it is a good idea to look at Microsoft Visual Studio and see if the compiler is trying to tell you anything about the code. Figure 3-6 shows your brother's code after he has compiled it.

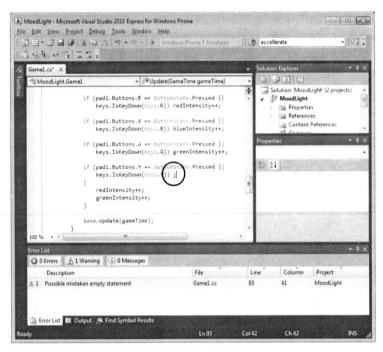

FIGURE 3-6 Visual Studio compiler warning display.

Your attention is drawn to the bottom left corner, where the message "Possible mistaken empty statement" appears. If you double-click this message, you find that the cursor moves to a point just after the if condition (I've drawn a circle around it in Figure 3-6).

The C# compiler is trying to tell us something about this statement. If we go back to the original listing, we find that your brother has added an extra semicolon at the end of the condition. The problem is that this ends the statement controlled by the condition. So if the R button or the R key is pressed or the Dpad is pressed down, the program decides to do nothing (an empty statement) and then goes on and performs the next statements no matter what, leading to the effect that we are seeing. Figure 3-7 shows how this happens.

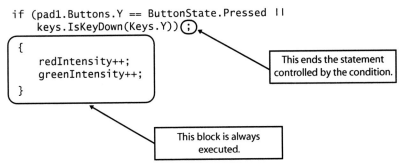

```
if (pad1.Buttons.Y == ButtonState.Pressed ||
    keys.IsKeyDown(Keys.Y))(;)
{
    redIntensity++;
    greenIntensity++;
}
```

This ends the statement
controlled by the condition.

This block is always
executed.

FIGURE 3-7 The effect of an extra semicolon.

You remove the semicolon, the warning goes away, and the program works fine. Your younger brother is now starting to revise his opinion of you and offers to take out the trash that night, even though it is your turn.

The Great Programmer Speaks: Helping Other People Is a Good Plan The Great Programmer has been watching all this with approval. She figures that it is always a good idea to try to help people who are stuck with a problem. Sometimes when a programmer working on uncovering a bug has the chance to explain what is going wrong with a piece of code to an innocent bystander, that can be enough to allow the programmer to work out what is broken. That means you can get a reputation as a fearsome bug fixer just by standing by. Furthermore, seeing what mistakes other people make can give you hints on things that you need to look out for when your programs go wrong. Oh, and sometimes you get your trash taken out for free.

Conclusion

You have learned a lot in this chapter, and you have finally managed to create some games that players can have fun with. You have seen how XNA allows programs to interact with physical devices by calling methods on classes, and we have seen how a program can make decisions on the information that it receives from the devices and use this to make simple (and silly) games.

Chapter Review Questions

No chapter would be complete without a review. So here it is. You should know the routine by now; just decide whether a statement is true or false and look the answers up in Appendix A at the back of the book to find out whether you are a winner or a loser.

1. If a class is an office, a method is a desk.

2. The compiler creates all the instances of classes in a program.

3. An if statement must have an else part.

4. A parameter is used to feed information into a class.

5. The else part of an if statement is always performed.

6. The state of a gamepad is represented in an XNA program by a byte value.

7. The GamePad.GetState method can be used to see if a button is pressed on a gamepad (this is a tough question; you are allowed to look at the chapter to work it out).

8. A block is a number of C# statements enclosed in curly brackets.

9. The C# condition (true || false) means "true or false" and would work out to true.

10. The C# condition (redIntensity > 220) evaluates to true if the value in greenIntensity is greater than 220.

11. The gamepad vibration always turns off automatically when an XNA game stops running.

Part II
Images, Sound, and Text

Chapter 4
Displaying Images

In this chapter, you will

- Find out how the Content Manager lets you add pictures to Microsoft XNA games.

- Discover how pictures are manipulated in game programs.

- Display your pictures on the screen.

- Make a better version of Color Nerve and an even groovier mood light.

Introduction

Your understanding of computers and programs should be coming along nicely by now. You are starting to get a grasp of classes, methods, and data, as well as the C# constructions that let your programs make decisions depending on the values in your variables. You also know how to read information from the gamepad and the keyboard and how to use this information to change what a game does when it runs.

In this chapter, you learn how to use images in your programs, improve Color Nerve so that it lets you use your own pictures, and make an even more impressive mood light.

Program Project: Picture Display

Pictures in games are always nice. XNA provides features that are extremely useful for manipulating images on the screen. Many games use image resources to generate the view that the player sees. In this project, you get XNA to display a picture. Once you have some of your images loaded into your programs, you can see about using them in games. Doing this very simple thing requires a lot of work, including the following steps:

1. You need to get the picture that you wish to draw into your game solution so that it becomes part of the program when it is loaded into the target device.

2. You must add code to the program that fetches the image into the program when it runs.

3. You need to tell XNA where on the screen the image is to be drawn.

4. You go ahead and draw the item.

The good news is that while you're learning how to do this, you're finding out a lot about how games, C#, and XNA work.

Resources and Content

In the early days of computers, a program simply read in numbers and printed out results. Things have moved on a bit since then, and now computer programs can work with images, video, and sound. This is especially useful where games are concerned; a large part of the enjoyment of a game results from an attractive game environment. And sometimes the graphics themselves form part of the game play. If you want to become a game developer, you need to know how these resources are made part of your program. In fact, many programs today have significant graphical content in the form of splash screens, icons, and the like. So the first thing you need to do is get some images and incorporate them into your project. Later, I'll show you how to use other kinds of resources, including fonts (for writing text) and sounds.

Unfortunately, I won't be able to help you create your graphics for use in computer games. I have no artistic abilities whatsoever, although I do know how to use a camera. If you need artistic resources, my advice is to find someone who is good at art and commission him or her to do the drawings for you. The same goes for any music or sounds that you might need.

This means that you can concentrate on what you are supposed to be good at: creating the game itself. This is what professional game developers do. They have a team of programmers who make the game work and a team of artists and sound technicians who work on the sensory aspects of the game. Having said that, you might be good at graphic design as well as programming, in which case you can do both. However, I still advise getting an artist involved, as it helps spread the work around and provides you with a useful sounding board for ideas. It also makes it more fun.

Getting Some Pictures

At this point, you need some pictures. You need to tailor your images to fit the screen of the XNA device you are going to use. The Xbox screen is capable of showing high-resolution images. A high-resolution image is made up of a large number of dots, or pixels. Modern digital cameras can create images that are thousands of pixels in height and width. However, from a game point of view, you want to make the images as small as you can. This reduces the amount of memory they consume and also reduces the work required to move them around the screen. You won't usually need very high resolution for your games, so your pictures need be no more than 800 pixels in each direction. The Windows Phone display is available with two resolutions: 480 x 800 pixels and 320 x 480 pixels. This means that you can use smaller images for XNA games intended to run on this device. You don't need to make your pictures exactly fit on the screens. We shall see later that you can use XNA to scale any size image to fit on any size display.

There are a number of different formats for storing pictures on computers. Your pictures should be in the Portable Network Graphics (PNG), Windows Bitmap (BMP), or Joint Photographic Experts Group (JPEG) format. The PNG and BMP formats are lossless, in that they always store an exact version of the image that is being held. PNG files can also have transparent regions, which is important when you want to draw one image on top of another. The JPEG format is lossy, in that the image is compressed in a way that makes it much smaller, but at the expense of precise detail. The games that you create should use JPEG images for the large backgrounds and PNG images for the smaller objects that are drawn on top of them.

If you have no pictures of your own (which I consider highly unlikely), you can use the ones that I have provided with the sample files for this chapter, but the games will work best if you use your own pictures. Figure 4-1 shows my picture of Jake. I will be using this for my first XNA graphics programs. You can use another picture if you wish.

FIGURE 4-1 Jake.

I have saved the image in the JPEG file format with a width of 600 pixels. If you need to convert into this format, you can load an image using the Microsoft Paint program and then save it in this format. With Paint, you can also scale and crop images if you want to reduce the number of pixels in the image. For more advanced image manipulation, I recommend the program Paint.NET which you can obtain for free from *http://www.getpaint.net/*.

Content Management Using XNA

As far as XNA is concerned, *content* (images, sounds, 3-D models, and video) is what makes games more interesting. XNA treats items of content in the same way that variables are created in programs. XNA can import a content item of a particular type (for example, my file containing a picture of Jake) and give it an identifier. When the game program is running, XNA fetches the game content items as they are requested by name. These content items are sometimes referred to as *assets*. In the same way that a company has assets, such as buildings, machinery, and staff, a game has assets such as sounds and images.

Working with Content Using XNA Game Studio

You use XNA Game Studio to put content into your game. When the finished program is constructed, XNA Game Studio makes sure that the assets are available to your game. The good news is that you don't need to worry about any of this; you need only know how to load assets into XNA Game Studio and get hold of them from within your game programs.

XNA Game Studio Solutions and Projects

You start making a game by creating a brand-new project. I called mine JakeDisplay. You create the project using the New Project dialog box as you've done for all your previous projects. Remember that the project you are creating is either a Windows Game (4.0), an Xbox Game (4.0), or a Windows Phone Game (4.0). You can see this dialog box in use in Figure 1-4 in Chapter 1, "Computers, C#, XNA, and You." Note that the Create Directory For Solution option is selected in this dialog box. Whenever you create a project, you should ensure that this option is selected. This creates a directory structure that contains the program and all the other items that are required to make the game work.

Figure 4-2 shows what is created when I make a new project called JakeDisplay.

FIGURE 4-2 The JakeDisplay solution directory.

However, the file JakeDisplay that you can see in the directory is a solution. This might be confusing. You've used the New Project command in XNA Game Studio and have ended up with a solution. In this case, XNA Game Studio has created a solution called JakeDisplay and then added a single project to that solution. The project is also called JakeDisplay. You can think of a *solution* as a "shopping list" of projects. Figure 4-3 shows how this works. The solution holds a list of the names of project files. Each of the project files holds a list of the names of the files used in that project. Each item on the list is often referred to as a *reference* to that item, in that it tells XNA Game Studio how to get to it.

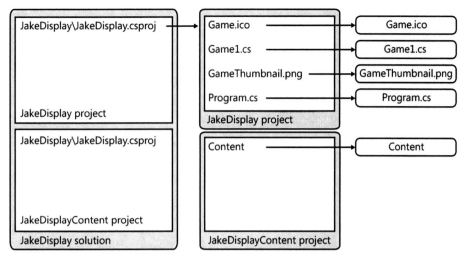

FIGURE 4-3 The JakeDisplay solution.

The solution file holds the name of the JakeDisplay project and the JakeDisplayContent project. The JakeDisplay project file holds the names of the C# files in the project (Game1.cs and Program1.cs) and other resources used by the project. At present, the only two resources are GameThumbnail.png, which is an image used as a thumbnail on the display when the game is stored on the Xbox or Windows Phone, and Game.ico, which is the icon used for the game program file on a Microsoft Windows PC. When you add your image of Jake to the project, you add the name of the file to the JakeDisplayContent project file so that XNA Game Studio knows where to go to get the asset. XNA Game Studio displays the contents of the solution and project files as a diagram in Solution Explorer, as shown in Figure 4-4. Note that the solution file and project files also contain other settings (the Properties and References) that you'll use later.

FIGURE 4-4 JakeDisplay in XNA Game Studio Solution Explorer.

You have already seen that a single game solution can hold projects for deployment to an Xbox, a Windows Phone, or a Windows PC. Sometimes you might want to add more projects to a solution so that you can separate your code into reusable portions or because you want to reuse code that you already separated that way. For example, you might make a project called HighScoreManager, which would be in charge of displaying high-score tables for your game. High scores work the same way in many games, so it makes sense to write the code only once and then use it in those games. You would do this by creating a library project to deal with the high scores and then add this project to the "shopping list" of those projects. However, for now, you simply create games that contain a game project and a content project.

> **The Great Programmer Speaks: Architecture Is Important** Our Great Programmer is very keen on using projects to reuse code. The way she sees it, that way she can get paid several times for writing the same piece of software. When she starts work on a new system, she takes a lot of time to try to structure things into projects so that different parts of the system are in separate projects.

Adding Content to a Project

An XNA Game Studio solution contains references to everything that it uses. To keep things simple, the solution contains two projects. One contains the program code and the other the content that the game uses. Figure 4-5 shows the content of the JakeDisplayContent project directory that XNA Game Studio created for you when you made the new project. At the moment, the directory contains no resource files. It does contain some directories, however. These are where the content items will be placed when they have been prepared for use by the programs themselves.

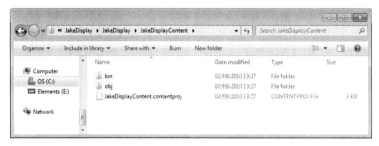

FIGURE 4-5 The contents of the JakeDisplay project directory.

When you add an asset to the JakeDisplayContent project, it is stored in this directory. Figure 4-6 shows the JPEG image of Jake that I used in my Pictures directory. You need to place the picture that you want to use into a directory somewhere on the computer.

You can either use one of the graphics images that are available in the sample projects or create your own picture at this point. Now that you have your graphics resource, you can tell XNA Game Studio to use it. To do this, you need to add the content to the project. Resource references are added by using the Add Existing Item – Content dialog box, which can be opened as shown in Figure 4-7. Start by right-clicking the JakeDisplay project's Content item in Solution Explorer. From the menu that appears, select Add, and then select Existing Item.

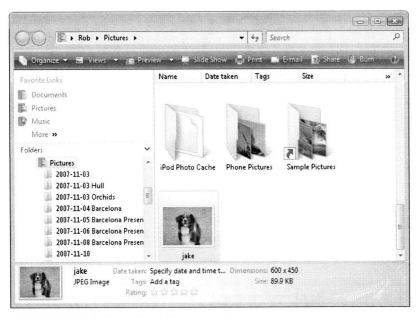

FIGURE 4-6 My Jake image in my Pictures directory.

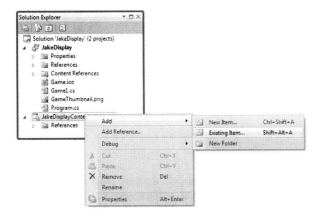

FIGURE 4-7 Opening the Add Existing Item – Content dialog box.

Figure 4-8 shows the dialog box that you can use to select an item to add to the project.

Now you can select the image file that you want to use and click Add to add it. The project now contains the resource. Figure 4-9 shows the resource reference in the project once you've added it. You follow the same process to add other images to a game.

If you want to add more than one image to a project, simply repeat the process. Remember that each image is stored as part of the game program, so the more images you add, the larger your game becomes and the longer it takes to transfer it into the target when it runs.

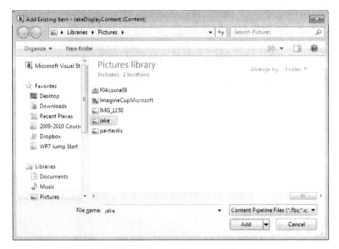

FIGURE 4-8 The Add Existing Item – Content dialog box.

FIGURE 4-9 The JakeDisplay project containing the image resource.

Note The Xbox and Windows PC have plenty of memory in which to store loaded images. However, the Windows Phone device is more constrained in the space that it has available. If you want to store lots of pictures in a game you are writing for the Windows Phone, you can use smaller images (320 x 240 pixels or less) to make sure that you don't run out of space.

Adding Links to Resources

When you add a resource using the process described previously, XNA Game Studio makes a copy of the resource and places the copy in the Content directory of the project. If you want several projects to share a single copy of a resource, you can add a link to it instead. You do this by clicking the down arrow at the right of the Add button in the Add Existing Item dialog box, as shown in Figure 4-10, which allows you to add the resource as a file or as a link.

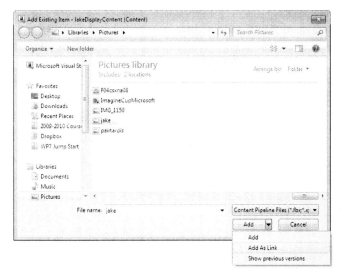

FIGURE 4-10 Adding the Jake image as a link.

Each time XNA Game Studio builds the game, it follows the link to the resource to use it. If the resource is moved or deleted, the build process fails.

The XNA Content Pipeline

The process of feeding resources in at one end and getting a complete game assembly out of the other is a bit like a *pipeline*. In fact, the XNA Framework refers to this part of the game-building process as the Content Management Pipeline.

Using Resources in a Game

You've done a lot of hard work, but your program still can't draw any pictures. If you run the solution that you've created, you get the familiar blue screen. Next, you have to write some C# code that fetches the image resource and draws it on the screen at a particular location.

Loading XNA Textures

Within XNA, images that you want to draw in your games are called *textures*. Textures can be drawn as flat pictures, and they can also be wrapped around 3-D models. You've already seen how to use the XNA Color type, which lets you manipulate color information. Now you'll use another type of XNA data variable so that you can work with your picture as a texture. XNA provides a range of types that are used to deal with textures. The type you'll use is called Texture2D. This holds a texture that you manipulate in two dimensions; that is, it is drawn on the screen as if it were a flat surface.

You use the same program structure that you used for previous games. Members of your game class represent the "game world." These are updated by the Update method and used by the Draw method to draw the output. The game data takes the form of a single variable that holds the texture, as shown here:

```
// The Game World

Texture2D jakeTexture;
```

The Draw method draws this texture on the screen, and you could use the Update method to make the image move around the screen by changing the draw position.

You also can use another method that lets the program take control when the graphics need to be loaded. Figure 4-11 shows how this works. It is a more detailed version of Figure 2-5 in Chapter 2, "Programs, Data, and Pretty Colors," which showed how XNA calls the Draw and Update methods as a game runs. It shows that there is also a LoadContent method that is called by XNA when a game starts running.

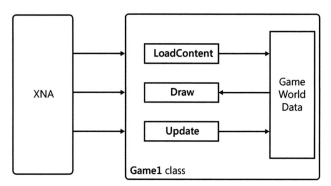

FIGURE 4-11 The Game1 class with the LoadContent method.

You can think of LoadContent as another person in the Game1 office. That person has his or her own telephone. When the phone rings, that person must load all the content and make it ready for use, as follows:

```
protected override void LoadContent()
{
    // Create a new SpriteBatch, which can be used to draw textures.
    spriteBatch = new SpriteBatch(GraphicsDevice);

    // TODO: use this.Content to load your game content here
}
```

In addition to loading the content that the game needs, the LoadContent method also creates a SpriteBatch for the program to use. You will use this later to draw the texture on the screen. You've even been given a comment to tell you where to place the code that loads your texture. This is the place where the program must ask the Content Manager to fetch the texture:

```
protected override void LoadContent()
{
    // Create a new SpriteBatch, which can be used to draw textures.
    spriteBatch = new SpriteBatch(GraphicsDevice);

    jakeTexture = this.Content.Load<Texture2D>("jake");
}
```

When the game starts, XNA calls the LoadContent method to fetch content for use in the game. The method then performs the statement that loads the texture content:

```
jakeTexture = this.Content.Load<Texture2D>("jake");
```

The Load method is a kind of multipurpose tool called a *generic* method. Because it's generic, it can be used to fetch any kind of item, from textures to audio files to 3-D models. You tell Load to fetch a Texture2D by placing the name of the type you want after the method name. You then give the method the asset that you want it to fetch. If you select the Jake.jpg item in Solution Explorer, as shown in Figure 4-9, and then look in the XNA Game Studio Properties pane (which should be in the lower right of the XNA Game Studio window), you can see that the asset name has been taken from the file name of the resource. Figure 4-12 shows the property information for the Jake image resource.

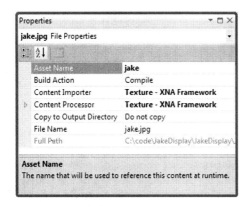

FIGURE 4-12 Jake image resource properties.

This property information tells XNA Game Studio where the image file is located, what to do with the file when the project is built, and the name to use in the program. So, once the LoadContent method has completed, you have a copy of the image in the texture in your game. If the game had lots of different images, you would declare additional `Texture2D` items in your game world and assign them to textures using the `LoadContent` method as well.

If you get the name of the texture wrong, the game program fails in this method, as it is looking for an asset that is not there. The program fails by throwing an *exception*. Figure 4-13 shows the error that is produced if the asset name of a content item is incorrect.

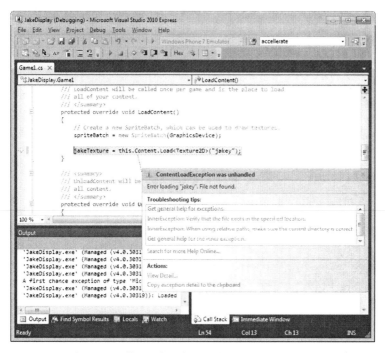

FIGURE 4-13 The texture file not found exception.

Later, you'll find out how to take control when things go wrong like this; for now, you should make sure that the asset name you use in the call of LoadContent matches the name of the content item.

> **The Great Programmer Speaks: Always Worry About Things Going Wrong** Our Great Programmer spends a lot of time worrying about things that might go wrong. She figures that in a commercial application, such as one that might be used in a bank, she has to write at least as much program code to deal with all the potential errors as she writes to perform the actual job. Game programs are probably not as critical as bank code in that, if they go wrong, nobody actually loses any money, but if a game constantly crashes, it will never become popular. Later, you'll see how to make sure that your program fails as seldom as possible.

Positioning Your Game Sprite on the Screen

In computer gaming terms, you can think of the image of Jake as a sprite. A *sprite* is a flat, preloaded image that is used as part of a computer game. Sprites can be large, such as background sky, or smaller, such as spaceships and missiles in a space shooter game. From the point of view of XNA, a sprite is an image resource along with location information that tells XNA where to draw the image. This means that you need a way to tell XNA where on the screen you want to put your sprite. You do this by using yet another XNA type, the Rectangle. This holds information about the position and size of a rectangle. You don't need to worry about how a rectangle works at the moment; you need only know how to create one and set the size and position of it. Figure 4-14 shows how you use a rectangle to express where on the screen you want Jake to be drawn.

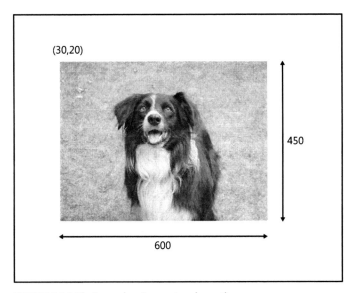

FIGURE 4-14 Placing a drawing rectangle on the screen.

The position of the rectangle is given by the coordinates of its top left corner. You can regard the screen as a piece of graph paper. You express a position on the screen by giving an x coordinate value (the distance across the screen from the left) and a y coordinate value (the distance down the screen from the top). This means that the position with the coordinate of (0, 0) is the top left corner. Note that this is not quite the same as graphs that you may have drawn in the past. In a conventional graph, the y value increases as you go up the page. In computer graphics, the y value increases as you move down the page.

In Figure 4-14, you can see that the top left corner of the Jake sprite is at position (30, 20). This means 30 steps across and 20 down. The units are called pixels. *Pixel*, an abbreviation for "picture element," refers to the smallest dot that can be drawn on the screen. The Xbox can drive displays with a range of different sizes, so the pixel at position (30, 20) may be a different physical distance across the screen, depending on the type of screen being used. Later, you'll find out how to write games that automatically scale themselves to fit any screen.

A rectangle is also used to give the width and height of the sprite. In Figure 4-14, I am drawing the texture in an area that is 600 pixels wide and 450 pixels high. The good thing about this is that I don't have worry about the original size of the image; XNA simply scales the image to fit in a rectangle that size. Later, you'll have some fun modifying the size. The rectangle where Jake is drawn is another item in the game world for the program, as shown here:

```
// The Game World

Texture2D jakeTexture;
Rectangle jakeRect;
```

The actual `Rectangle` you are going to use is created using new:

```
jakeRect = new Rectangle(30, 20, 600, 450);
```

This code sets a `Rectangle` variable to one with the position and dimensions that you need. When the rectangle is created, it is passed the x, y, width, and height values so that these can be held within the rectangle structure. This means that if you ever want to move the image or change its size on the screen, you need to change only one of the values that is held in the rectangle. These values are members of the `Rectangle` structure. In C#, members that hold values are called *fields*.

You can think of a field as a variable that has been declared inside a structure or class. In the case of your `Game1` class, the game world data that you created (for example, the color intensity values for your mood light) are fields of that class. Later, you'll see how to get hold of individual fields inside the `Rectangle` so that you can change its size and position.

The `Rectangle` needs to be created when the game program starts. You could do this in the LoadContent method, but XNA provides another place where it is more sensible, namely, the `Initialize` method. This is called when the game starts up. If all these methods are confusing, think about what happens when you organize a party. This takes a number of steps:

1. Set up the tables and chairs.
2. Fetch the food and drink.
3. Repeatedly play music and dance.
4. Tidy up afterward.

When an XNA game runs, it goes through the same process:

1. Set things up: `Initialize`
2. Load game content: LoadContent

3. Repeatedly update the game and draw the display: Draw and Update

4. Free up all the content: UnloadContent

When the game ends, the XNA system calls the UnloadContent method. You can add statements to that method to release resources explicitly that your game has used, but for now, you can leave this out.

In fact, you need not provide code for all these methods; they are there only so that you can take control at various points of the game's life cycle. The code that you put in the Initialize method needs to create a Rectangle that describes the destination of the draw operations:

```
protected override void Initialize()
{
    jakeRect = new Rectangle(30, 20, 600, 450);
    base.Initialize();
}
```

Sprite Drawing with *SpriteBatch*

You now have all the information about your sprite and are ready to draw it. Next, you need to take control in the Draw method and put your image onto the screen. But before you can do the drawing, you need to take some time out and discover more about how game consoles work.

A modern game console is not one powerful computer; in fact, it is several. Some of these run the game itself, whereas other special graphics processors drive the display. The graphics processor unit (GPU) contains optimized hardware to allow it to update the screen as fast as possible. When the Draw method runs, the method assembles a bunch of instructions for the GPU and sends the instructions into the GPU. The GPU then follows those instructions to put a picture on the screen. Complex games contain many images that may be drawn at several different positions on the screen. It is important that the transfer of the position information and associated images is organized as efficiently as possible. XNA provides a special class called SpriteBatch to batch up a set of sprite-drawing instructions. Your program calls methods on a SpriteBatch variable to get the drawing done. This means that a SpriteBatch needs to be created for the program to use. When XNA Game Studio creates a new project, it adds the statements to the LoadContent method that create a SpriteBatch for you to use. The variable is called spriteBatch.

Note It might look as if you have two items with the same name in your program. However, if you look carefully, you see that the class SpriteBatch starts with an uppercase S, but the spriteBatch variable starts with a lowercase s. This works because the C# compiler considers the case of the letter as significant in an identifier. In other words, your program could have two variables, Fred and fred, and they would not be confused.

Now you can use spriteBatch to draw the sprite. You must tell spriteBatch when you've started drawing sprites and when you've finished:

```
protected override void Draw(GameTime gameTime)
{
    graphics.GraphicsDevice.Clear(Color.CornflowerBlue);

    spriteBatch.Begin();
    spriteBatch.Draw(jakeTexture, jakeRect, Color.White);
    spriteBatch.End();
    base.Draw(gameTime);
}
```

You call methods on the spriteBatch variable to begin the draw process, draw the sprite, and then end the drawing. The Draw method is part of the SpriteBatch class and is given parameters that identify the image to be drawn, the rectangle to place it in, and the color of the light to "shine" on the texture.

> **Note** The game class contains a Draw method, which is used to draw the entire game. The SpriteBatch class also contains a Draw method, which is used to draw textures. Although the methods have the same name and are both involved in the draw process, they actually do different things. However, both are performing a drawing operation in their own way, so it is appropriate for the designers of XNA to call them Draw methods.

If you put a program together with the previously described methods, you can finally run a program that will display an image on the screen.

> **Sample Code: Jake Display** All the sample projects can be obtained from the Web resources for this text, which can be found at *http://oreilly.com/catalog/9780735651579*. The sample project in the 01 JakeDisplay directory in the resources for this chapter draws a picture of Jake.

Figure 4-15 shows the output that you get when you run your program to display Jake on the screen.

If you change the content of the file Jake.jpg, you can make this program display other pictures.

If you run this program on a Windows Phone you will find that the picture is too large to fit on the display. This will not cause XNA to report an error, but not all of the image will be displayed. You can fix this by reducing the width and height of the rectangle to 180 and 120 respectively. This preserves the aspect ratio, but makes sure the image will fit on the screen.

FIGURE 4-15 Displaying Jake on a PC screen.

Filling the Screen

It would be nice if the image that you display could exactly fill the screen. You've used values that let you see the picture, but the picture does not completely cover the display, and if you run the program on differently configured systems, you notice that the picture takes up a different amount of space on the screen. It turns out that filling the screen is easy to do. Your program can ask the XNA environment the width and height of the screen and use this to set the size of the display rectangle, as follows:

```
jakeRect = new Rectangle(
    0,     // X position of top left corner
    0,     // Y position of top left corner
    GraphicsDevice.Viewport.Width,   // rectangle width
    GraphicsDevice.Viewport.Height); // rectangle height
```

I've changed the layout of my call to construct the jakeRect variable. Rather than put everything on one line, I've spread the call out a bit and added some comments. This makes it easier to see what's happening. The code is constructing a Rectangle instance. When you do this, you can feed information into the construction process to set up the value. This particular call is feeding in the position of the top left corner in the form of x and y and the width and height of the rectangle that is required. I can get the width of the screen by using the following code:

```
GraphicsDevice.Viewport.Width
```

This looks a bit scary but is easy to understand. It's rather like the way that we explain where things are. My office is on the third floor of the Robert Blackburn Building on the Hull campus of the University of Hull. You could express this information as follows:

```
HullCampus.RobertBlackburn.ThirdFloor.RobMiles
```

The Hull campus contains a number of buildings, the Robert Blackburn Building contains a number of floors, and so on. You can now find your way to my office by starting at the Hull campus, looking for the Robert Blackburn Building, going to the third floor, and then finding the office with "Rob Miles" written on the door. The identifier is `GraphicsDevice.Viewport.Width`, which means, "Start at the `GraphicsDevice` variable, go to the `Viewport`, and then get the `Width` field from it." The `GraphicsDevice` variable is the Graphics Device manager for your program. It is created by XNA and provides methods and data that you can use in your program (you've already used the `Clear` method to clear the screen). The `GraphicsDevice` contains a `Viewport`, and so on. Part of the skill of using XNA is knowing where these data items are.

Intellisense

You can find your way around the XNA framework by using the *Intellisense* feature, which is part of XNA Game Studio. Whenever you type an identifier into the editor, it finds the variable that the identifier represents and offers you options based on that identifier. These can save you a lot of typing. Figure 4-16 shows how it works. I have just typed the identifier `graphics` followed by the period that separates it from the next item. Intellisense is showing me all the possible items that are available. I can scroll down the list, select the one I want by pressing Enter, and then move on to the next item.

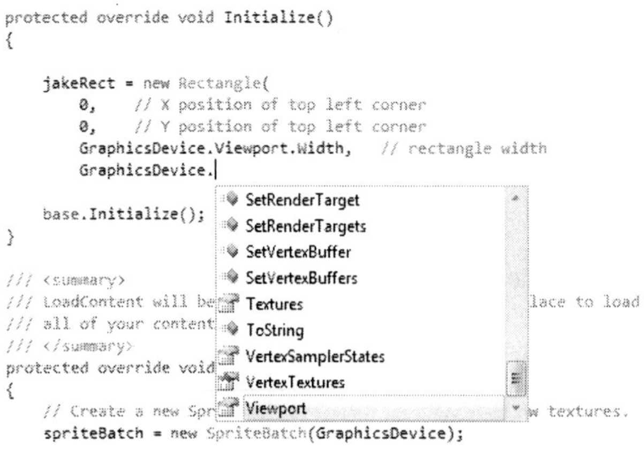

```
protected override void Initialize()
{

    jakeRect = new Rectangle(
        0,      // X position of top left corner
        0,      // Y position of top left corner
        GraphicsDevice.Viewport.Width,   // rectangle width
        GraphicsDevice.|

    base.Initialize();              SetRenderTarget
}                                   SetRenderTargets
                                    SetVertexBuffer
/// <summary>                       SetVertexBuffers
/// LoadContent will be            Textures                lace to load
/// all of your content            ToString
/// </summary>                      VertexSamplerStates
protected override void            VertexTextures
{                                   Viewport                 w textures.
    // Create a new Spr
    spriteBatch = new SpriteBatch(GraphicsDevice);
```

FIGURE 4-16 Intellisense for the Graphics Device manager.

You can move quickly up and down the list of items by typing the first few letters of the name of the selection you want. Intellisense also shows you brief help snippets about the items that you can select. It makes writing programs much easier and reduces the amount you have to remember. The Great Programmer doesn't think she could write programs without it.

> **Sample Code: Jake Full Screen** The sample project in the 02 Jake Full Screen directory in the resources for this chapter draws a picture of Jake that completely fills the screen.

> **Note** If you are using an Xbox that is connected to a TV, you might notice that not all the picture is visible. This is because TVs use an "overscanned" display, where only the middle part of the picture is displayed. I'll describe how to fix this in Chapter 11 in the section "Dealing with Display Overscan." You'll also find that if the shape of your picture does not exactly match that of the screen, the image appears stretched. I'll discuss these problems of "aspect ratio" in Chapter 11 in the section "Drawing and Aspect Ratios."

Game Idea: Color Nerve with a Picture

Now that you can display pictures, you can improve your Color Nerve game and display a picture rather than a blank background. This makes the game much more fun, especially if a familiar picture is used.

The key to this is the way that you select the color you want to use to "light" any sprite that you draw:

```
spriteBatch.Draw(jakeTexture, jakeRect, Color.White);
```

When drawing this image, I used a white light so that the colors look natural. You can use any color of light, and XNA processes the image accordingly. If you want the image to be drawn more dimly, you can draw with the color gray; if you want to tint the image, you can simply change the color. You can use any color that you can create to tint your sprite, as follows:

```
protected override void Draw(GameTime gameTime)
{
    Color textureColor;
    textureColor = new Color(redIntensity,greenIntensity,blueIntensity);

    spriteBatch.Begin();
    spriteBatch.Draw(jakeTexture, jakeRect, textureColor);
    spriteBatch.End();

    base.Draw(gameTime);
}
```

Rather than using white as the drawing color, this version of Draw uses the color it creates based on the red, green, and blue intensity values.

> **Sample Code: Jake Color Nerve** The sample project in the 03 Image Color Nerve directory in the resources for this chapter is a version of Color Nerve that uses the picture of Jake.

You can use the same principle to make a picture mood light; this works especially well if you use a black-and-white image or one with really strong colors in it. You can also make a picture recognition game here, where the aim of the game is to be the first one to recognize a picture as you slowly make it brighter.

> **Sample Code: Image MoodLight** The sample project in the 04 Image MoodLight directory in the resources for this chapter is a version of the ultimate mood light that uses an image background. The image contains a pattern of blocks of different colors. One interesting challenge is to try to work out which of the blocks is white (only one of them is).

Conclusion

You have learned a lot in this chapter. You've seen how you can add graphical resources to XNA projects and use them in your game programs. You've also found out how images are positioned and drawn on the screen in XNA.

Chapter Review Questions

Just in case you thought you were having too much fun, here's a chapter review to bring you back down to earth. You can look up the answers in Appendix A.

1. The C# compiler manages images.

2. In an XNA program, an image can be held in a texture.

3. XNA uses the LoadContent method to load the graphics images onto the display.

4. A sprite is a small, pixie-like creature who lives with the fairies.

5. The SpriteBatch class is used to batch up sprites before they are drawn.

6. There is no need to add any code to the Initialize method to make an XNA game work.

7. A Rectangle has a Width field that specifies how wide it is.

8. The XNA system can store only one image at a time.

9. A pixel is a measure of screen size.

10. The origin of the XNA drawing operations is the top left corner of the display area.

11. PNG images would be good for background images in a game.

12. It is impossible to find out how wide the screen is from an XNA game program.

Chapter 5
Writing Text

In this chapter, you will

- Discover how text is drawn using Microsoft XNA.
- Add some font resources to your XNA program.
- Draw some funky text.
- Create the biggest clock you've ever seen.
- Find out how to fake 3-D images.

Introduction

Your programming skills are really coming along. Your programs can store different kinds of numbers, do things with them, and even make decisions. You also know how to add image assets to your games and place them on the screen.

In this chapter you find out how to use some XNA features to make your games even better. Then you can move on to create fully formed games. The first thing you want to do is add some text output so that your games can talk to the players.

Program Project: Giant Clock

The Xbox, the Windows Phone, and the PC each has a clock inside, so each device always knows the date and time. You can use this feature to turn the entire display into a digital clock.

Text and Computers

In the early days of computers, the appearance of text that you could print was limited by the shapes built into a mechanical printer. Later, dot-matrix, laser, and inkjet printers came along, giving high-resolution graphical displays that could draw any character design you wanted. XNA programs are capable of drawing very high-resolution images, and you can use this ability to display text.

Text as a Resource

Before you can start drawing text using XNA, you need to understand just how computers manage character designs. The design of the shape of the characters is described in a *font* file. Microsoft Windows provides a very large number of these font files. The shape of the text that you are reading now is described in a font called "Segoe."

The font file gives the shape of each of the characters. When a character shape is needed for either printing on paper or drawing on the screen, the font data is used to draw this shape at the required size. To get an XNA program to display text in a particular font, you need to add a reference to that font file to the program project. You then use the XNA Content Management System to bring the font into the program for use when you want to draw text.

Creating the XNA Clock Project

You create the project (called `BigClock`) using the New Project dialog box as you've done for all your previous projects. You can see this dialog box in Figure 1-4 in Chapter 1, "Computers, C#, XNA, and You." Note that the Create Directory For Solution option is selected in this dialog box. Whenever you create a project, you should ensure that this option is selected.

Adding a Font Resource

Figure 5-1 shows how to add a new resource to a game project. In Solution Explorer, right-click the Content item in the `BigClockContent` project (not the BigClock project), then select Add, New Item.

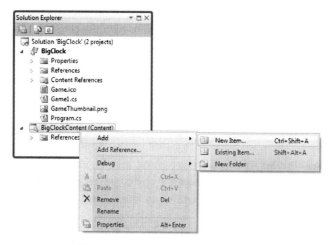

FIGURE 5-1 Adding a new item.

You can add a number of different kinds of new items to a project. Figure 5-2 shows the dialog box that lets you select the kind of item you wish to add.

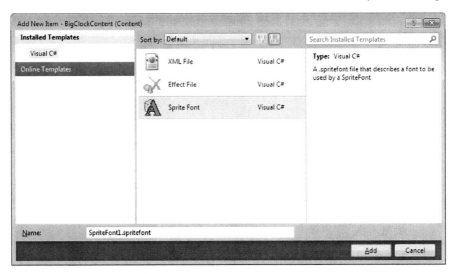

FIGURE 5-2 Selecting a new item.

The range of items that you can add to your project depends on how many other Microsoft Visual Studio components you have installed. You might have more items available than those shown in Figure 5-2. If you select the Sprite Font item, you can create a sprite font reference. When you do this, you find that XNA Game Studio has filled in the Name information at the bottom of the dialog box with SpriteFont1.spritefont. This is the name that you use within your program to refer to this item of font content. We are going to use this for now, but in later games, you might want to change it to a name that has a bit more meaning.

When Visual Studio builds the BigClockContent project, it reads an existing font on your Windows PC to build the SpriteFont that is used when the game runs. When a new font resource is created, it is initially set to use a font called Kootenay, which is supplied with XNA Game Studio.

You can use a different font if you want, but if the name you give does not match a font that's installed on your computer, you won't be able to build your program because the Content Manager will be unable to find the requested item.

You can have more than one font in your game if required, but you need to add each font that you want to use as another resource. Remember, though, that adding extra fonts makes your output program bigger because the character designs need to be made part of the program. The name that you give must match a font available on the computer that's being used to build the game because the XNA Content Manager uses the font file on the host computer to build the sprite design for use in your XNA program.

Figure 5-3 shows the font item in Solution Explorer in XNA Game Studio as added to the project. If you select this item in Solution Explorer and open it by double-clicking it, you can see that it's a file describing the font that's to be used in your program.

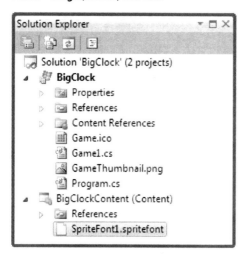

FIGURE 5-3 The font reference in the BigClockContent project.

> **Note** It's important you understand what's happening here. When you add a resource to a project, you simply add a reference to the item that you want to use. You can think of the reference as an item on a shopping list. Just like an item on a shopping list would remind you to buy a new toothbrush the next time you were shopping, a resource reference tells the Content Manager that a certain resource must be fetched when the program is to be built.

When the project is built, the Content Manager follows the reference to the required item and then adds it to the program that's being built. The purpose of the resource information is to tell the Content Manager what to retrieve and how to use the resource in the project.

This reference file is not written in C#, nor is it plain text. It's written in a format called *Extensible Markup Language (XML)*.

The XML File Format

A markup language is used to describe things. It contains the names of these things and information about them. As its name indicates, XML is extensible, so you can use it to describe just about anything. As an example, a snippet of XML that describes a high score might look as follows:

```
<?xml version="1.0" encoding="us-ascii" ?>
<highscore game="Breakout">
  <playername>Rob Miles</playername>
  <score>1500</score>
</highscore>
```

This high score information is for the Breakout game; it shows the name of the player and the score the player reached. The format of the lines and the way that the open bracket (<)

and close bracket (>) characters are used to denote the names of the values and the values themselves are defined in the XML standard. The first line of the snippet identifies which version of XML you're using for the rest of the data. The nice thing about XML is that it's easy for non-computers to understand the content, and it's a very well-established way in which computer software can exchange information.

In the case of your font, the XML tells the Content Manager the name of the font to fetch, the size of the font, whether it's to be drawn as bold or italic, and other font-related information. You don't need to worry too much about what's in this file at the moment, but you can take a look if you wish. Later, you'll edit the content of this file to change the size of the characters that are drawn.

Loading a Font

The Content Manager fetches a font and make it available for use in a very similar way to the images that you've used before. Each character design is delivered to your program as a little image that the Draw method displays on the screen. For your clock, the game world consists of a variable called font, which is of type SpriteFont. This holds a reference to the font the program will have loaded. SpriteFont is another XNA type (there are many more). Your SpriteFont will hold information about a font that the Content Manager loads for you. You can declare the variable for the game world as follows:

```
// Game World
SpriteFont font;
```

The font can be loaded in the LoadContent method:

```
protected override void LoadContent()
{
    // Create a new SpriteBatch, which can be used to draw textures.
    spriteBatch = new SpriteBatch(GraphicsDevice);

    font = Content.Load<SpriteFont>("SpriteFont1");
}
```

At this point, you might be experiencing déjà vu or at least think you've seen this code before. The pattern is the same as when you loaded your images, and even the name of the method is the same. However, this time you're using the generic Load method to fetch a SpriteFont rather than a Texture2D element. There is some strong programming magic at work here, but fortunately you don't need to worry about this at the moment; all you need to know is that the Load method gets whatever type it is asked to fetch. Later, you'll create some games that contain textures, fonts, and sounds, and for each type, the Load method behaves in an appropriate manner.

Drawing with a Font

Now that you have your font, you can draw with it. Remember that when you used the textures in Chapter 4, "Displaying Images," you used a Rectangle to tell the Draw method where to place the texture. However, when drawing text, you don't do this. Instead, you use a *vector*, which tells the Draw method where on the screen to start. "Vector" is a fancy word that means "direction and distance." You're using the 2-D (x and y value) version of the vector. Games that work in 3-D space use values of x, y, and z (where z is the depth value).

A 2-D vector is given as two coordinates: the x value and the y value. It's a bit like a treasure map that pirates used. A pirate would say, "Start ye at the Old Oak Tree and take ye twenty paces East and thirty paces South, and there ye shall find my treasure chest." The vector says, "Start at the origin and move 20 units across and 30 units down." If you think about it, this means that a vector indeed specifies a direction so that a very smart pirate could work out that she could "cut corners" and get to the treasure more quickly by moving in the appropriate direction. Figure 5-4 shows how this would work, with a line showing the direct path to Blackbeard's treasure.

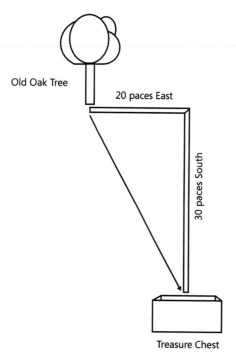

FIGURE 5-4 Vectors and directions to a pirate treasure.

In a text-drawing program, you're using a vector like a coordinate in that it specifies the top left corner of the text you're about to draw. You feed it into the DrawText method as follows:

```
protected override void Draw(GameTime gameTime)
{
    graphics.GraphicsDevice.Clear(Color.CornflowerBlue);

    Vector2 textVector = new Vector2(20, 30);

    spriteBatch.Begin();
    spriteBatch.DrawString(font, "Hello World", textVector, Color.Red);
    spriteBatch.End();

    base.Draw(gameTime);
}
```

You've placed the top left corner of the text at the spot 20 pixels across the screen and 30 pixels down. The text that you're writing is the famous string "Hello World," which is, by one of the laws of the universe, what your first program that prints text should say. In a C# program, you enter a string as a sequence of characters enclosed in double quotation marks. You're printing the text in Red. If you run this program, you get the display shown in Figure 5-5.

FIGURE 5-5 "Hello World" on the big screen.

Although it is perfectly okay to make your first program print something other than "Hello World," I take no responsibility for any misfortune that you suffer as a result of offending the programming gods in this way.

Sample Code: "Hello World" All the sample projects can be obtained from the Web resources for this text, which can be found at *http://oreilly.com/catalog/9780735651579*. You can make your "Hello World" program by creating an empty project, adding the font reference, and then adding the game world section and the **LoadContent** and **Draw** methods described in this and the preceding section. If you don't want to do that, you can load the sample project in the 01 Hello World directory in the resources for this chapter, which writes "Hello World" on the screen. Either flesh out your own BigClock solution or just open the 01 Hello World project to continue with the rest of the chapter.

Changing the Font Properties

The program works all right, but you really wanted something larger than this small text. It is possible to scale text sprites, but at the moment it's easiest to get larger text simply by changing the XML in the SpriteFont resource file. This also means that if anybody asks you what you were doing today, you can say, "Oh, I hand-coded some XML," which should impress them a bit. To get hold of the file that describes the font, open it by double-clicking it in Solution Explorer for the BigClock project. Figure 5-6 shows which item to select.

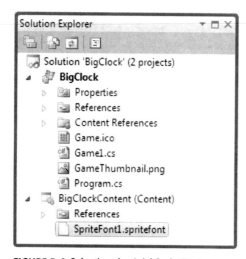

FIGURE 5-6 Selecting the Arial SpriteFont resource.

The left window in XNA Game Studio changes to show you the XML that describes the font to be loaded. The font and the size of the text are set as shown here:

```
<!--
Modify this string to change the font that will be imported.
-->
<FontName>Kootenay</FontName>
```

```
<!--
Size is a float value, measured in points. Modify this value to change
the size of the font.
-->
<Size>14</Size>
```

You can change the name of the font that you want to use and the size of the font by adjusting the items shown in bold in this code. You can also adjust the style and the spacing between letters. You can change FontName to select any font installed on your computer (but personally, I really like Kootenay). Use Control Panel in Windows to find out what fonts are available. Make sure you type the name correctly, including spaces and capital letters. You need to adjust the font size depending on the font design that you select. I've found that a font size of 100 gives nice large text using the Kootenay font on an Xbox or a Windows PC screen. If you are using a Windows phone a size of 30 works well.

Getting the Date and Time

You can now display text on the screen in a variety of sizes and fonts. You could use this to write a program that simply displays messages on the screen. Next, you need a way to determine the correct time for the clock in your program to display. The PC, the Windows Phone, and the Xbox have internal clock hardware that is used by some games to change the way they play so that, for example, if it's dark outside, it's dark in the game as well. To accomplish this, the XNA Framework must provide a way of finding the date and time.

The date and time values are held in a special structure called DateTime. You already know that XNA provides types that are tailored to different needs. You've seen the Color type, the Texture2D type, and the SpriteFont type, to name a few. The DateTime type holds all the information about the date and time of a particular instance. The structure is not part of XNA as such; rather, it's part of the Microsoft .NET Framework, which provides resources to all C# programs. Thus, when you want to manipulate dates and times in a C# program running on a Windows operating system, you can do it in exactly the same way.

For your clock, you need a DateTime structure that's set to the current date and time. It turns out that DateTime provides a property that creates one for you. A *property* is a value or setting that an object in a C# program can expose for you to use. You've already seen these; when you used Color.CornflowerBlue, you were asking the Color structure to give you a color that represents that shade of blue. You use DateTime.Now in the same way. Later, when you start using structures and classes to design more complicated game programs, you'll get more of an insight into how all this works. For now, you simply get a DateTime value that holds the current time and use that to drive your clock, as follows:

```
DateTime nowDateTime = DateTime.Now;
```

The Now property of the DateTime structure is always set to the current date and time. This works by taking values from an internal hardware clock, which means that after a while, the value will be out of date. In fact, you could use a DateTime variable to record the time at which the game was started.

Once you have your DateTime variable, you can ask it to do things for you. One thing it can do is give you a string that contains the time in text form:

```
DateTime nowDateTime = DateTime.Now;
string nowString = nowDateTime.ToLongTimeString();
```

These two statements create a variable of type DateTime, which holds the current date and time, and then use this to create a string. A string does exactly what you would expect, it holds a string of text. The DateTime structure contains a method with the identifier ToLongTimeString. You know that objects contain methods; this method has the job of converting the date and time information inside the object into a string that you can put on the screen in text form. In fact, DateTime provides several methods that you can use (see Table 5-1).

TABLE 5-1 **Some *DateTime* String Methods**

Method Call	Output
ToLongTimeString()	20:23:55
ToShortTimeString()	20:23
ToLongDateString()	16 March 2009
ToShortDateString()	16/03/2009
ToString()	16/03/2009 20:23:55

We have previously considered different types in C# as offices. You can think of these methods as a number of different people sitting in the DateTime office, all of whom have their own telephone and can be asked to deliver an appropriately formatted string of text. You can call any of these methods to get a string of text that describes the value being held by the variable nowDateTime. You can use them to add the date and time to your clock if you wish.

Note The precise format of the date and time produced depends on the *localization* of your system. Most software products are configured to display the date and time in a manner in keeping with the country where they are being used. The previously given samples are for a Windows PC used in England. Yours might look slightly different.

Putting all this together, you can create a version of the Draw method that displays the current time on your screen:

```
protected override void Draw(GameTime gameTime)
{
    graphics.GraphicsDevice.Clear(Color.CornflowerBlue);

    DateTime nowDateTime = DateTime.Now;
```

```
        string nowString = nowDateTime.ToLongTimeString();
        Vector2 nowVector = new Vector2(50, 400);

        spriteBatch.Begin();
        spriteBatch.DrawString(font, nowString, nowVector, Color.Red);
        spriteBatch.End();

        base.Draw(gameTime);
    }
```

I've changed the name of the vector to nowVector to better describe what it is used for. I've put the clock in the upper-left hand corner of the screen. You can experiment with different fonts, sizes, and positions.

> **Sample Code: Big Clock**   The sample project in the 02 Big Clock directory in the resources for this chapter contains an XNA Game Studio solution for the program in this section.

Because the Draw and Update methods are called automatically for you by the XNA environment, the clock is repeatedly redrawn with the up-to-date time.

Making a Prettier Clock with 3-D Text

At the moment, your clock is very boring; it just displays the time in red on a blue background. You can make the text more interesting by changing the way that you draw the time. This kind of multiple drawing is performed a lot in computer games.

Drawing Multiple Text Strings

One way to make the display more interesting is to draw different-colored versions of the text at slightly different positions on the screen:

```
protected override void Draw(GameTime gameTime)
{
    graphics.GraphicsDevice.Clear(Color.CornflowerBlue);

    DateTime nowDateTime = DateTime.Now;
    string nowString = nowDateTime.ToLongTimeString();
    Vector2 nowVector = new Vector2(50, 400);

    spriteBatch.Begin();

    spriteBatch.DrawString(font, nowString, nowVector, Color.Red);

    nowVector.X = nowVector.X + 4;
    nowVector.Y = nowVector.Y + 4;
```

```
spriteBatch.DrawString(font, nowString, nowVector, Color.Yellow);

spriteBatch.End();

base.Draw(gameTime);
}
```

This version of the Draw method is very similar to the original, except that DrawString is now called twice, first drawing in red and then in yellow. In between the draw operations, the values of the X and Y properties of the position vector are increased by 4 using the following statements:

```
nowVector.X = nowVector.X + 4;
nowVector.Y = nowVector.Y + 4;
```

Figure 5-7 shows how this works. The thing on the right side of the "gozzinta" is an *expression*. This generates a result that is then placed in the destination.

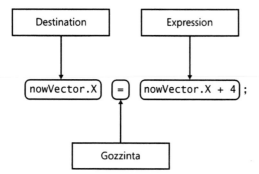

FIGURE 5-7 A statement that evaluates an expression and updates the value for a variable.

The sequence of instructions that the compiler creates to work out the statement is as follows:

1. Fetch the value of the X property of nowVector.

2. Add 4 to it.

3. Store the value back in the X property of nowVector.

The effect of adding 4 to the X and Y properties is to move the drawing position for the text across and down the screen. Figure 5-8 shows the result of these changes.

FIGURE 5-8 A more interesting time display.

From this, you can see that when you draw on the screen, the images are laid on top of each other in the order they are drawn. The red version of the time string is overwritten by the yellow one. The nice thing about this approach is that it gives a good 3-D effect. The human eye interprets the darker color as being in the "background," making the letters appear to pop out of the display. However, the 3-D effect is not quite perfect. The image in Figure 5-9 is an enlargement of part of the text and shows that the red part is not actually "solid"; instead, it's simply a layer drawn behind the yellow one.

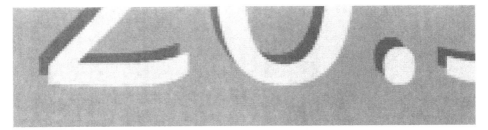

FIGURE 5-9 A zoomed-in detail of the overwritten text.

If you want the 3-D effect to be perfect, you need to draw lots more red versions to "fill in the gaps." You could do this by simply copying the code four times, but perhaps you remember reading somewhere that computers are supposed to make life easier, and this doesn't feel very easy at all. What you really want to do is perform a block of statements a given number of times, and it turns out that C# provides a way to do this: it's called the for loop construction.

Repeating Statements with a *for* Loop

A program can do three things as it runs. It can perform a single action (a statement), it can make a choice of what to do (a condition statement), or it can repeat something (a loop construction). It might surprise you to learn that with these three programming constructions, you could write any program. You've seen how to write statements and conditions; now you need to discover how to create a loop. With a loop, you need to write the drawing instructions only once, and the loop construction then performs them as many times as you like:

```
spriteBatch.Begin();

int layer;
for (layer = 0; layer < 4; layer++)
{
    spriteBatch.DrawString(font, nowString, nowVector, Color.Red);
    nowVector.X++;
    nowVector.Y++;
}

spriteBatch.DrawString(font, nowString, nowVector, Color.Yellow);

spriteBatch.End();
```

This code performs four drawing operations with the red color. The code in the block controlled by for is repeated a given number of times. When the loop finishes, the final DrawString puts the yellow version on top of all the red ones. Note that the yellow DrawString is not repeated four times because it is not inside the block of code controlled by the for loop.

The loop itself is controlled by the three items in brackets that follow the key word for. These are shown in Figure 5-10. Each of the three items is used to manage the behavior of the loop.

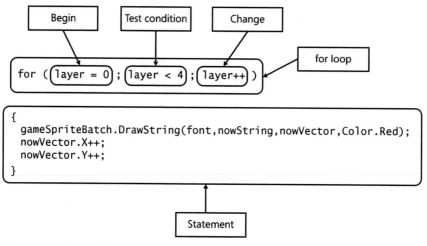

FIGURE 5-10 How a *for* loop is constructed.

- **Begin**   This is a statement that is obeyed when the loop starts. In this example, you're using an integer variable called `layer` to count each of the layers that you're drawing, and the loop must set this to zero at the beginning.

- **Test Condition**   The condition controls when the loop finishes. It can be either `true` (the loop continues) or `false` (the loop ends). The condition in your loop is `layer < 4`. You might not have seen the < operator before; it performs a "less-than" comparison between the two operands. If the item on the left is less than the item on the right, the result of the comparison is `true`. If the item on the left is not less than the item on the right, the result of the comparison is `false`. C# provides a range of different comparison operators.

- **Change**   Each time the statements in the loop are completed, the change is performed. In this case, the change statement `layer++` makes the value in `layer` 1 larger each time. After the change has been performed, the test condition is evaluated to see whether the statements controlled by the loop are to be executed again.

The C# compiler has the job of producing the machine instructions that perform the loop when the program runs. The precise sequence that's followed by the code that the compiler produces is as follows:

1. Perform the Begin statement to start the loop.
2. Perform the Test and finish if the test is false.
3. Perform the statement in the loop body.
4. Perform the Change statement.
5. Return to step 2.

> **Sample Code: 3-D Big Clock** The sample project in the 03 3D Big Clock directory in the resources for this chapter contains an XNA Game Studio solution that uses a for loop to draw multiple versions of the time.

Other Loop Constructions

C# also provides two other loop constructions, called do – while and while. These are not actually vital, in that you can always get the looping behavior that you want by using an appropriately designed for loop, but they can be useful in situations where you don't want to go to the trouble of creating a for loop construction. You can find out more about these kinds of loops and when they would be useful in the glossary in the do – while entry.

Fun with *for* Loops

You can test your understanding of the for loop behavior by looking at some for loops and trying to work out what they would do. For instance, look at this one:

```
for (layer = 0 ; layer > 4 ; layer++)
```

There's a mistake in this statement, but it's rather hard to spot. The mistake is that the test is now layer > 4. The > character means "greater than." This means that the test is now true only when the value of layer is greater than 4. Because the initialization sets the value of layer to 0, this condition is never true. The result is that the code in the statement controlled by the loop is never performed. Now look at this statement:

```
for (layer = 0 ; layer < 4 ; layer--)
```

There's another mistake here. The less-than character (<) is in the correct place, but rather than increasing the value of layer each time around, the change makes layer smaller by using the -- operator each time. This means that the value of layer never becomes greater than 4, so the loop never ends. The result is that your program appears to "get stuck" at this point.

You can write code to request this as follows if you really want a loop that goes on forever:

```
for (layer = 0 ; true ; layer--)
```

Simply putting the value true in the position of the condition causes the loop to never stop. If you're wondering what would happen if you ran a loop like this, you can try it if you like, but I can save you the trouble. If you run either of these never-ending loops, you eventually get the message shown in Figure 5-11. This is the message that XNA displays when it runs out of memory.

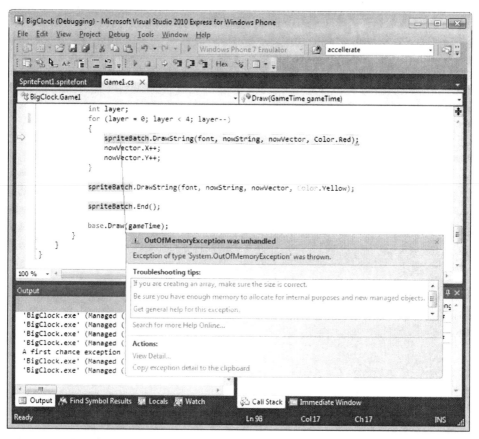

FIGURE 5-11 Out-of-memory error message.

The reason you get this message is that each time the DrawString method is called in the body of the loop, it uses a small amount of memory to record what is drawn. If you call the method a large number of times, it eventually uses up all the memory available for this purpose, and the memory allocation part of XNA throws an exception when it is asked for memory it doesn't have. The good news is that this doesn't cause any damage, but it does cause serious damage to your credibility.

One of the nice things about loops is that you can get a lot more work done by the computer simply by changing the values that cause them to stop. For instance, look at this code:

```
for (layer = 0; layer < 40 ; layer++)
```

This version of the loop draws 40 red time values before putting the yellow one on top. It gives rise to the rather funky display shown in Figure 5-12.

FIGURE 5-12 Funky time.

This is nice, but you can do even better. You can make the display even more funky by using some other drawing tricks that XNA provides.

Creating Fake 3-D

Lots of the graphics in games are faked. Rather than make something 3-D, a game programmer makes something that looks 3-D but turns out to be much easier to program. In this section, you make some 3-D text, but without using any complicated rendering or models (although you can do this kind of thing if required). You use only two principles:

- Things that are 3-D have shadows.
- Things that have the light shining directly on them look the brightest.

This means that you need to draw your text in three stages. First, you draw the shadows, then the "sides" of the text, and finally the top layer of the text. This seems like a lot of work, but, as Figure 5-13 shows, I think it's worth the effort.

FIGURE 5-13 3-D text that "jumps" out of the screen.

Creating Shadows Using Transparent Colors

The first part of the text that you want to draw is the shadow at the back. You draw your picture from the back forwards and use the fact that each time you draw, you add to what's already there. You use another feature of XNA drawing: colors that cause things to be drawn slightly transparent (that is, with part of the background showing through). By drawing transparent colors on top of each other, you can get a nice blurry effect, as done in the following code:

```
Color nowColor = new Color(0,0,0,20);
for (layer = 0; layer < 10 ; layer++)
{
    spriteBatch.DrawString(font, nowString, nowVector, nowColor);
    nowVector.X++;
    nowVector.Y++;
}
```

This code is very similar to the previous code that draws the 3-D text except that it creates the value for nowColor in a slightly different way. The Color is constructed from four values rather than three:

```
Color nowColor = new Color(0,0,0,20);
```

The first three values give the intensity of red, green, and blue, which you've set to 0 because you're drawing in black. The fourth gives the transparency of the color. In graphical terms, this is often called the *alpha* channel value. The bigger the number, the less the background shows through. Just like your color intensity values, the transparency value can range from 0 (completely transparent) to 255 (solid color). If you don't give a transparency value, the Color is created as solid.

A value of 20 means that a lot of the background shows through the color that you draw. Figure 5-14 shows the display produced by drawing 10 times using a transparent black value. Note that because each of the drawing positions is slightly different, you get a blurring effect.

FIGURE 5-14 Creating a shadow using transparent colors.

This works rather well in that the text is nicely blurred around the edges, as a shadow would be. Now you know one way video games achieve blur. They can do it by repeatedly drawing the same scene in slightly different positions.

The next part of the drawing process uses the same technique you've used before, except that you use slightly different colors. The complete drawing method follows.

```
protected override void Draw(GameTime gameTime)
{
    graphics.GraphicsDevice.Clear(Color.CornflowerBlue);

    DateTime nowDateTime = DateTime.Now;
    string nowString = nowDateTime.ToLongTimeString();
    Vector2 nowVector = new Vector2(50, 500);
    int layer;

    spriteBatch.Begin();

    // Draw the shadow
    Color nowColor = new Color(0, 0, 0, 20);
    for (layer = 0; layer < 10; layer++)
    {
        spriteBatch.DrawString(font, nowString, nowVector, nowColor);
        nowVector.X++;
        nowVector.Y++;
    }

    // Draw the solid part of the characters
    nowColor = Color.Gray;
    for (layer = 0; layer < 5; layer++)
    {
        spriteBatch.DrawString(font, nowString, nowVector, nowColor);
        nowVector.X++;
        nowVector.Y++;
    }

    // Draw the top of the characters
    spriteBatch.DrawString(font, nowString, nowVector, Color.White);
    spriteBatch.End();

    base.Draw(gameTime);
}
```

This produces the display shown in Figure 5-13.

> **Sample Code: 3-D Shadow Clocks** The sample project in the 04 3D Shadow Clock directory
> in the resources for this chapter contains an XNA Game Studio solution that shows the 3-D time
> over a blue background. If you want to draw the time over a picture, you can take a look at the
> solution in the 05 3D Picture Clock directory, which draws the same clock over a picture of Jake.
> Finally, if you want to see the time over your mood light, look at the solution in the 06 3D Clock
> MoodLight directory.

Drawing Images with Transparency

Something else that's useful is that if you draw an image using a color that has a
transparency value, the image is drawn transparently. This is how game programmers get
pictures to fade slowly onto the screen. The image is repeatedly drawn with different levels of
transparency to make it slowly appear over a background.

Conclusion

In this chapter, you've learned how to add font resources to your programs. You've also gained a bit of insight into how 3-D effects can be created from 2-D images. You've also seen how you can use the for loop construction to repeat code a particular number of times.

Chapter Review Questions

At the risk of being somewhat predictable, the chapter ends with another set of true-false problems.

1. A font describes the color of the text to be printed.

2. An XNA game can use only one font to draw text.

3. The Content Manager creates your fonts.

4. A resource in an XNA project is a reference to an item that must be included in the game file when the program is built.

5. XML stands for Xbox Machine Language and is used to design the font graphics.

6. A vector describes a direction and distance of movement.

7. The first program you write that can print should display "Hello Mum".

8. The Xbox requires a network connection to load the date and time.

9. Dates and times are printed the same all over the world.

10. The DateTime structure holds the value of a particular date and time.

11. A property of an object cannot be used outside that object.

12. You can call the ToString method on an object to ask the object to supply a text description of itself.

13. A for loop construction always runs forever.

14. The C# code for (layer = 0; layer < 4; layer++) would repeat five times.

15. After a loop controlled by the C# code for (layer = 0; layer <= 10; layer++) has completed, the value in layer would be 10.

16. The C# code for (layer = 4; layer < 0; layer++) would repeat zero times.

17. The C# code for (layer = 4; layer > 0; layer++) would repeat infinite times.

18. Colors can be made "transparent."

Chapter 6
Creating a Multi-Player Game

In this chapter, you will

- Discover how to detect and use individual button-press events in a game.
- Learn how to create and debug a complex program.
- Write one of the only 16-player games for the Xbox in the world.

Introduction

Now that you can write programs that process data, read input from the gamepad, and display text and graphics, you can move on to create some proper games. The first games that you are going to create are simple to use and play, but are great fun, particularly if you have large numbers of people around to play them. While you create the behaviors for the games, you also learn some more C# constructions that can be used in later games.

> ### Game Idea: Button-Bashing Mob
>
> One very popular and easy-to-create game is one where a player has to repeatedly press a button as quickly as possible. Players compete against each other, and the winner is the one who can press their button the most in a given time. Because each gamepad has four buttons and the Xbox can support four gamepads, up to 16 players can take part, for maximum button-bashing fun.

Creating the Button-Bash Game

To get started, you need to create an empty project called ButtonBash. This project needs to be able to display text. The best way to do this is to create a new project and then initialize and load the font as for the Big Clock application in Chapter 5, "Writing Text." Set the size of the font to 30 in the `SpriteFont1.spritefont` file that you create.

To create the game, you first build a program that counts and displays the presses of a single button on the gamepad. Then you can scale up the program and use more buttons. This is a very common programming technique. "Make a button-bashing game for 16 players" sounds a bit daunting, but "Make a program that counts how many times the B button on gamepad 1 is pressed" is something you can probably do.

> **Note** To complete this program, you are going to take two things that you already know how to do (read buttons on the gamepad and display messages on the screen) and use these abilities to create a game called Button Bash. You do this sort of combining a lot in programming; in fact, you can think of writing programs as stringing a set of behaviors together to get the required result.

Button-Bash Game Data

Your program needs to keep track of the number of times the button has been pressed. You can use an integer to hold the value as follows:

```
// Game World
int count;
```

The value of an int variable in C# can go over 2,000,000,000. It's unlikely that anyone who is not Superman could press a button that number of times in a minute.

Starting the Button-Bash Game

The game is started by the player pressing the Start button on the gamepad to zero the counter. The program handles this in the Update method:

```
protected override void Update(GameTime gameTime)
{
    // Allows the game to exit
    if (GamePad.GetState(PlayerIndex.One).Buttons.Back == ButtonState.Pressed)
        this.Exit();

    GamePadState pad1 = GamePad.GetState(PlayerIndex.One);

    if (pad1.Buttons.Start == ButtonState.Pressed)
    {
        count = 0;
    }

    base.Update(gameTime);
}
```

This program builds on the gamepad reading code that you wrote in Chapter 3, "Getting Player Input." It creates a GamePadState variable called pad1 and then tests to see if the Start button has been pressed on it. When the Start button is pressed, the conditional statement in the Update method sets count to 0.

Displaying the Button-Bash Count Value

As the game is being played, it must display the current number of presses on the screen for the player to see. You can use a variant of the Draw method in the Big Clock program to display the value in count:

```
protected override void Draw(GameTime gameTime)
{
    graphics.GraphicsDevice.Clear(Color.CornflowerBlue);

    string countString = count.ToString();
    Vector2 countVector = new Vector2(50, 400);

    spriteBatch.Begin();

    spriteBatch.DrawString(font, countString, countVector, Color.Red);

    spriteBatch.End();

    base.Draw(gameTime);
}
```

Running this program gives you what you expect: the value 0 displayed on the screen.

Counting Button Presses

Now you need to add the statements to the Update method that count the number of times that the B button has been pressed:

```
if (pad1.Buttons.B == ButtonState.Pressed)
{
    count++;
}
```

This seems to be what you want; if the condition is true because the button has been pressed, the counter is incremented.

> **Sample Code: Broken Button Bash**   All the sample projects can be obtained from the Web resources for this text, which can be found at *http://oreilly.com/catalog/9780735651579*. The sample project in the 01 Broken Button Bash directory in the resources for this chapter contains a Microsoft XNA Game Studio solution that contains a program that uses the Update method described in this section to implement a test button-bashing program.

You might have gathered from the example title "01 Broken Button Bash" that this won't work. This is because the Update method is called 60 times a second. If you hold down the button, you find that each time Update is called, the value of count gets one bigger, so the score goes up at a rate of 60 times a second. This is impressive (and might be the basis of other games in the future), but it won't give you the game you want.

Detecting Changes in the Button Position

You need to find a way of detecting when the state of the button changes from the up to the down position. Your program must increase count only when this happens, not when the button is simply being held down. Figure 6-1 shows the sequence of events when the button is pressed. The Update method is being called at regular intervals. At some point, the B button is pressed. This means that when Update is called the first time in the illustration, it detects that B is up, and the second time it is called, it detects that B has been pressed.

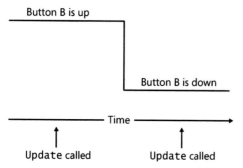

FIGURE 6-1 Time line for Update calls and the B button.

This means that the Update method must perform a test along the lines of "If the button was up last time and is down this time, now the counter must be increased." The Update method needs to know the state of the button the last time Update was called. It can then test to see if the button state has changed since it was called the last time. You can declare a GamePadState variable to hold this value and create an Update method as follows:

```
GamePadState oldpad1;

protected override void Update(GameTime gameTime)
{
    // Allows the game to exit
    if (GamePad.GetState(PlayerIndex.One).Buttons.Back == ButtonState.Pressed)
        this.Exit();

    GamePadState pad1 = GamePad.GetState(PlayerIndex.One);
    if (pad1.Buttons.Start == ButtonState.Pressed)
    {
        count = 0;
        oldpad1 = pad1;
    }

    if ( oldpad1.Buttons.B == ButtonState.Released &&
         pad1.Buttons.B == ButtonState.Pressed )
    {
        count++;
    }

    oldpad1 = pad1;
    base.Update(gameTime);
}
```

The variable oldpad1 holds the previous state of the gamepad; at the end of the method, you store the current pad state in it. The test for the change makes use of the *AND (&&)* logical operator. Only if the previous state of the button was up *AND* the current state is down is the count value increased. You've already seen the *OR (||)* logical operator, which causes a condition to be true if one or the other condition is true (or both are true). The *AND* operator is used in the same way but produces a true result if the conditions on each side of it are both true. When the player presses Start to begin the game, the value of oldPad1 is set to the current pad state, so that only changes to the gamepad after Start is pressed are registered.

> **Note** This code is quite simple, but you need to understand exactly how it works. Make sure that you can follow what is going on: the way that Update is called 60 times a second and the way the method makes a copy of the previous gamepad settings at the end of each call.

If you had a *really* fast player who could press and release a button in less than a sixtieth of a second, your program would not detect this, as the up-and-down changes would occur between two calls to the Draw method.

Level and Edge Detectors

The code in the previous section is an edge detector in that it detects a change from one state to another. This is the kind of code that you would use to detect when a game player selects an option or presses a switch. Up until now, you have used the buttons as level detectors in that only whether a button is up or down has been significant. When you design the controls for a game, you need to decide what kind of input you're using for the control. If you're creating a driving game, you'd use a level-based signal to control whether the accelerator was pressed and perhaps an edge-triggered signal to control the gear selections made by the player.

> **Sample Code: Working Button Bash** The sample project in the 02 Working Button Bash directory in the resources for this chapter contains an XNA Game Studio solution that contains a program that counts the presses for button B.

Constructing the Complete Game

Now that you know how to make edge detectors, you can go on and create the button-counting code for all 16 buttons in the game. The best way to organize these is to track and examine each controller in turn. For each controller, you need some variables to hold information about the gamepad and the buttons:

```
// Gamepad 1
GamePadState pad1;
GamePadState oldpad1;
int acount1;
int bcount1;
```

```
int xcount1;
int ycount1;

Vector2 apos1 = new Vector2(150, 250);
Vector2 bpos1 = new Vector2(200, 200);
Vector2 xpos1 = new Vector2(100, 200);
Vector2 ypos1 = new Vector2(150, 150);
```

The top two variables hold the gamepad states. The pad1 variable holds the state of the gamepad during a call of Update. The oldPad1 variable holds the value from the previous call of Update. Then there are counters for each of the buttons on the gamepad. Finally, there are four vectors that position the counters on the screen. The code that runs in the Update method is a variation on the edge detector that you saw previously but is extended to handle all the buttons on the gamepad:

```
pad1 = GamePad.GetState(PlayerIndex.One);

if (pad1.IsConnected)
{

    if (pad1.Buttons.Start == ButtonState.Pressed)
    {
        acount1 = 0;
        bcount1 = 0;
        xcount1 = 0;
        ycount1 = 0;
        // repeat for the other three gamepads
    }

    if (oldpad1.Buttons.A == ButtonState.Released &&
        pad1.Buttons.A == ButtonState.Pressed)
    {
        acount1++;
    }

    if (oldpad1.Buttons.B == ButtonState.Released &&
        pad1.Buttons.B == ButtonState.Pressed)
    {
        bcount1++;
    }

    if (oldpad1.Buttons.X == ButtonState.Released &&
        pad1.Buttons.X == ButtonState.Pressed)
    {
        xcount1++;
    }

    if (oldpad1.Buttons.Y == ButtonState.Released &&
        pad1.Buttons.Y == ButtonState.Pressed)
    {
        ycount1++;
    }

    oldpad1 = pad1;
}
```

This code makes use of the IsConnected property of the GamePadState structure. This property is true only if the gamepad is active, meaning that the program updates the values for the gamepad only when it is connected. Now that you have the game behavior working, you need to add the display part of the game code in the Draw method: This is the code for gamepad 1. A similar sequence of statements will be required for the other three gamepads.

```
spriteBatch.Begin();

if (pad1.IsConnected)
{
    spriteBatch.DrawString(font, acount1.ToString(), apos1, Color.Green);
    spriteBatch.DrawString(font, bcount1.ToString(), bpos1, Color.Red);
    spriteBatch.DrawString(font, xcount1.ToString(), xpos1, Color.Blue);
    spriteBatch.DrawString(font, ycount1.ToString(), ypos1, Color.Yellow);
}

spriteBatch.End();
```

This code uses the vectors that were set up at the beginning of the program to position the count values in the correct place on the screen. The code also draws the counters only if that gamepad is connected.

> **Sample Code: Button Bash**   The sample project in the 03 Multi Player ButtonBash directory in the resources for this chapter contains an XNA Game Studio solution that contains a program that you can use to play 16-Player Button Bash.

Code Design

If you look at the sample program, you notice that there's a lot of repetition. The same code is used four times in a row, once for each gamepad. In addition, the statements for each gamepad are fundamentally similar. It turns out that you can use more advanced features of C# to make this program much smaller and easier to understand. However, the game works well, and the more people who take part, the more fun it is. Simply begin the game by pressing Start on gamepad 1, and then all the players must bash their particular button as many times as possible in a certain amount of time. This turns out to be a test of stamina as much as anything else. Later, you might return to this code and add an automatic clock to time the games.

> **The Great Programmer Speaks: Make Sure You Can Test Your Code**   The Great Programmer has been looking at the code that you've been writing. She notices that your program is quite long and reckons that she could do the job with fewer statements. But because your game works and she enjoys playing it, she thinks it's a good solution. However, she's worried about one thing. The only way that the program can be tested completely is by using four Xbox gamepads. If you don't have four gamepads on hand, you can't prove that all the counter and display code works properly. In many of the programs that she has written, it's been very difficult to test parts of the code, particularly the bits that deal with errors. She therefore thinks that you need to work out a way that you can test the program without needing to have all the hardware present. I will show you how to do that next.

Adding Test Code

If you have four gamepads, you can simply connect them and play the game. However, if you have only one, you need a way to use it to test the code for the other gamepads as well. The simplest way to do this is to copy the state of gamepad1 into the other gamepads during the Update method:

```
pad2 = GamePad.GetState(PlayerIndex.Two);

// test code - copy the value of pad1 into pad2
pad2 = pad1;

if (pad2.IsConnected)
{
    // code for gamepad 2
}
```

The test code copies the value of pad1 into pad2. This means that the button presses on this gamepad are now copied onto the counters for this pad, too. If you also copy this information into the other two gamepads, you can test the code for all of them with only a single gamepad. Figure 6-2 shows you the display produced by a test version of the program. I found some faults in my original positioning of the counter displays by using this program on a PC with only one Xbox gamepad attached.

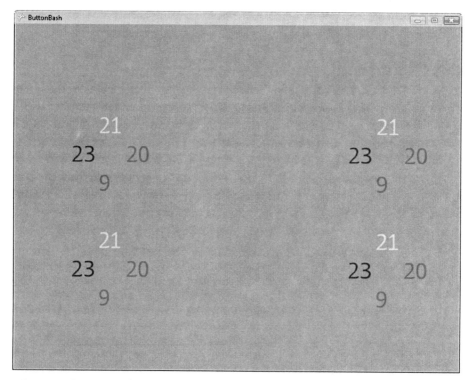

FIGURE 6-2 Test gamepad counter displays.

Once the code has been tested, it's important that these tests are removed from the program. It turns out that C# provides a mechanism called *conditional compilation*, which lets you ask the compiler to ignore parts of a program. This provides a way that you can mark statements of program code that are to be ignored and that do not become part of the program when it is built, but that you can keep around for testing when you later update your code.

To understand what's going on here, you have to take the lid off the compiler and find out a bit more about how it works. The job of the compiler is to take the C# statements that you write and convert them into machine instructions for the Xbox, PC, or Windows Phone. The compiler opens the source file on the computer that holds your C# and reads it a line at a time. It finds all the variables, makes sure they are used correctly, looks for all the statements, and generates low-level instructions that are to be used when the program runs.

The part at the very front of the compiler that reads in the C# file is called the *preprocessor*. If you built a machine to make apple pies, you'd have to have a part at the front that peeled the apples, discarded any rotten ones, and got them ready for cooking. The preprocessor does this peeling job for the compiler. It takes the program source, removes all the comments (which the compiler should not see), discards blank lines and empty space, and passes on clean statements. However, the C# compiler preprocessor can also be told to do things to the source that it sees:

```
#if test
          // test code - copy the value of pad1 into pad4
          pad4 = pad1;
#endif
```

Commands to the preprocessor have a # at the start of the line and are called *directives*. What the previous statements say to the preprocessor is, "If the test symbol has been defined, pass on the following statements to the rest of the compiler; otherwise, ignore them." The statements to be passed on are between the #if and the #endif directives.

If you want to switch these lines on, you simply need to define the test symbol at the top of the source file as follows:

```
#define test
```

If the test symbol has been defined, all the test statements are compiled into the main program. Deleting the #define directive keeps the designated statements from being compiled.

> **Sample Code: Button-Bash Test**   The sample project in the 04 Button Bash Test directory in the resources for this chapter contains an XNA Game Studio solution that contains a program that you can use to test the button-bashing program with only one gamepad.

If you use XNA Game Studio to open the code file Game1.cs in the 04 Button Bash Test sample project, you see that the test code is "live." If you go to the top of Game1.cs and delete the #define line, you see that all the code controlled by the test symbol goes light gray in the editor to indicate that this code is no longer live. If you run the program, it now works with four gamepads as it should.

> **Note** It's very important that you understand what's happening here. The program is not making a decision what to do when it runs; this decision is taking place when the program itself is built. If the symbol is not defined, the statements are not even part of the machine language program itself.

You can create as many symbols as you like, so if you wanted to, you could turn on and off different parts of the program. This is one of the ways that game manufacturers make "demo" versions of their games. Some game levels are compiled conditionally in the source so that they can make a limited version of the program just by recompiling with some of these symbols missing. Note that the test is not perfect, for example if your program was displaying the count for gamepad 1 in place of the count for gamepad 2, this would not be detected by this test. You would have to think of a different kind of test behavior to detect this fault.

> **The Great Programmer Speaks: Remember to Charge for Testing** The Great Programmer is one of the most expensive programmers you'll ever meet. She charges a lot of money for her work. But her customers are happy to pay because they know they are getting a properly tested program and they never get any nasty surprises. She says that if you're asked how much a job will cost and how long it will take, you must make sure that you include the time it will take you to test your solution, as well as the time it will take to actually write the program that does the job. She's very careful to include the cost of these parts of the work in her prices, and her software is always very well tested and works the first time, so she makes the big bucks.

Conclusion

In this chapter, you've discovered how to detect edges on button presses and how to use this to create a good party game. Finally, you've seen the importance of testing and found a mechanism, conditional compilation, that makes testing easier.

Chapter Review Questions

Perhaps the world will end with a set of review questions. I'm not sure about that actually, but I am sure that this chapter does. As usual, say whether these statements are true or false.

1. Only the start button can be used as edge triggered.

2. You need to have the previous state of the gamepad if you want to detect an edge.

3. Edge-triggered inputs work only if the button is held down.

4. Conditionally compiled code is discarded when the program runs.

5. The preprocessor produces the output file from the compiler.

Chapter 7
Playing Sounds

In this chapter, you will

- Find out how to prepare sounds for inclusion in Microsoft XNA projects.

- Incorporate sounds into XNA.

- Play the sounds from within your programs.

Adding Sound

Now that you can display pictures and text, it's time to make some noise. Then you can set about making a proper gaming experience for your players. You add sound to a game in the same way as you add other resources. You can even grab your favorite sound sample and drop it into the XNA Game Studio project as you did for the graphics resources (remembering to respect copyrights, of course).

If you want even more control over the sounds that your game makes, you can use something called the Microsoft Cross-Platform Audio Creation Tool (XACT) to create the library of sounds that you want to use, insert the library into your game, and then create a sound engine in the game program to play those sounds at the appropriate times. This facility is very powerful, but it can be confusing to use, so we use simple sound playback in this chapter.

> **Program Project: Drum Pad**
>
> The first program you are going to build creates a very simple drum kit that is controlled from a gamepad. Each button is assigned a different drum sound, enabling you to use your console to play the drums.

Creating the Drum Pad Project

You create the project (called DrumPad) using the New Project dialog box as you've done for all your previous projects. You can see this dialog box in use in Figure 1-4 in Chapter 1, "Computers, C#, XNA, and You."

Capturing Sounds with Audacity

You start with a few drum sounds. The samples that I used were captured using the microphone input in my notebook to record live drum sounds. I used a program called

Audacity, which you can obtain for free from *audacity.sourceforge.net*. This program captures live sound and provides a graphical interface that you can use to select portions of recordings and export them as .wav files. Figure 7-1 shows a wave form that has been captured and a portion marked off to be exported.

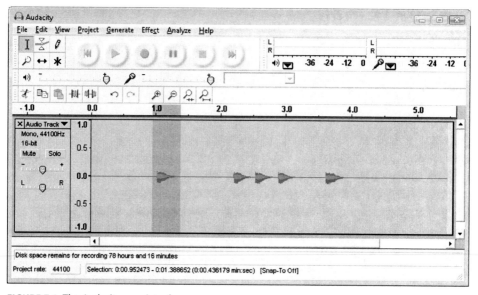

FIGURE 7-1 The Audacity user interface.

Each time you click the round, red, record button in the controls at the top of the screen, a new track is recorded. Before you start recording, you should select the format of the sound that you are going to capture. The quality of a sound recording is controlled by the sample rate and the resolution of each sound sample. You need to be careful when recording sounds because the higher the quality of the sound, the more disk space and memory that the sample takes up. I have found that a sample rate of 44,100 hertz (Hz) and 16-bit resolution gives high-quality sounds that do not take up too much memory. You can select these by clicking the item on top of the track as shown in Figure 7-2, where the sample rate is being selected. The resolution is set using the Set Sample Format item immediately above the Set Rate option on the menu shown.

Once you have selected a sound quality setting, it is used for any future recordings. If you are recording very long sounds, such as background music, you might decide to reduce the quality so that the sound files are smaller.

Note that with sound samples, as with other assets in your game, you must be careful to observe copyright laws. Although it's very tempting to use parts of songs or TV shows as in-game sounds, you need to make sure that you don't get into trouble for doing this.

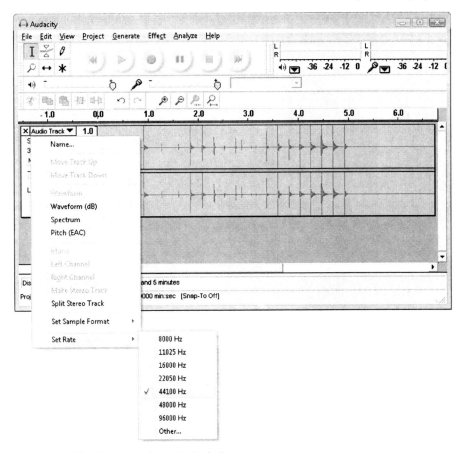

FIGURE 7-2 Selecting a sample rate in Audacity.

Sounds and File Types

When I finished with the drums, I had some sound files that were .wav files. Today, you're more likely to have heard of .mp3 or .wma files when storing sound. In these files, the sound information is compressed so that it takes up less space in your music player. The XNA Framework can play simple sound effects from .wav files. Later in this chapter, in the section "Playing Songs using the *MediaPlayer* Class," you find out how to create an XNA program that plays complete songs from .mp3 or .wma files.

Storing Sounds in Your Project

Sounds are just another item of content, along with images and fonts. You add them to your project in the same way. Start by right-clicking the Content folder in XNA Game Studio, then select Existing Item from the Add option, as shown in Figure 7-3.

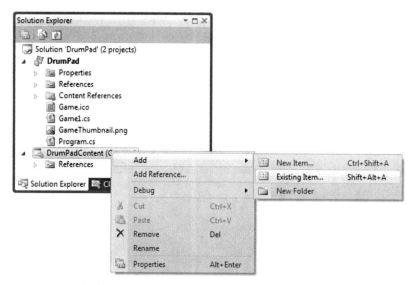

FIGURE 7-3 Adding items to the Content folder.

This causes the Add Existing Item - Content dialog box to appear. You can then navigate to the folder on your system containing the sound files and open them as shown in Figure 7-4. Note that you can select multiple items in this dialog box if you want to add more than one thing at a time.

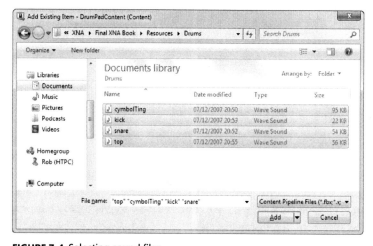

FIGURE 7-4 Selecting sound files.

Note If you've installed any programs that work with sound files, you might find that your .wav files have different icons. The ones in Figure 7-4 are associated with Windows Media Player on my computer.

Once the files have been added to the game project, the Content Manager transfers them into the game and makes them available to the game program.

> **Resources: "Drum Sounds"**   All the sample projects and content resources can be obtained from the Web resources for this text, which can be found at *http://oreilly.com/ catalog/9780735651579*. You can find the drum samples in the resources directory for this chapter. Before you hit the drums, remember that sounds might be faint on your PC but play loudly through your Xbox, or vice versa.

Using Sounds in an XNA Program

Now that you have the files, you can get them into a form that can be used in your XNA program. You follow the same pattern you have used twice before now, with fonts and images:

- Create a variable to hold the loaded content.

- Set the variable in the LoadContent Method.

- Use the resource in the game.

The variable type that you are going to use is SoundEffect. This represents a sound that you want to play. You need four of these variables, as you are giving our player four drum sounds to play:

```
// Game World
SoundEffect kick;
SoundEffect cymbolTing;
SoundEffect snare;
SoundEffect top;
```

Once you have the variables, you now need to load them from the Sounds folder in the content for this game:

```
protected override void LoadContent()
{
    // Create a new SpriteBatch, which can be used to draw textures.
    spriteBatch = new SpriteBatch(GraphicsDevice);

    kick = Content.Load<SoundEffect>("kick");
    cymbolTing = Content.Load<SoundEffect>("cymbolTing");
    snare = Content.Load<SoundEffect>("snare");
    top = Content.Load<SoundEffect>("top");
}
```

This code sets the SoundEffect variables with the samples that they are going to play.

Playing Sounds

Now you're at the point where you can play sounds in your program. You are going to make a program that plays different drums by pressing different buttons on the Xbox gamepad. The sound should be produced when the button is pressed. You can use the edge detection code from Chapter 6, "Creating a Multi-Player Game," to detect when to play the sounds:

```
// Current state of the gamepad during the Update
GamePadState pad1;

// Old gamepad state. XNA initializes this to all
// buttons not pressed. After the first call of Update
// this holds the previous gamepad state.
GamePadState oldpad1;

protected override void Update(GameTime gameTime)
{
    pad1 = GamePad.GetState(PlayerIndex.One);

    if (pad1.IsConnected)
    {
        // allow the game to exit when back is pressed
        if (pad1.Buttons.Back == ButtonState.Pressed)
        {
            this.Exit();
        }

        // test if A has been pressed since the last Update
        if (oldpad1.Buttons.A == ButtonState.Released &&
            pad1.Buttons.A == ButtonState.Pressed)
        {
            snare.Play();
        }
    }

    // record the current gamepad state for the next
    // call of Update
    oldpad1 = pad1;

    base.Update(gameTime);
}
```

This version of Update plays the "snare" sound when the A button is pressed on gamepad 1. It does this by calling the Play method provided by a SoundEffect object. You can expand this code so that each of the buttons on the controller plays one of your four sound effects.

> **Sample Code: 01 DrumPad** The 01 DrumPad project in the resources for this chapter contains all the .wav files. It makes a different drum sound when each of the buttons is pressed. If you want to use your own sounds with this project, simply replace the .wav files in the Content folder with yours and rebuild the XNA Game Studio project.

If you play with the sample project, you find that you can get several versions of a given sound sample playing at the same time if you press the buttons very quickly.

Playing Background Music

You can also use the XNA sound system for playing background music. The technique described here can also be used for engine noise or background sounds for a particular location. Unlike the sounds you've used so far, you want the music to repeat when it finishes playing, and you'd also like a way to stop and start the music from within your program. The actual music file is a .wav file like all the other sounds, but it might be somewhat larger. It is loaded into the game project in the same way as the other sounds you saw earlier.

If a sound can be played successfully the Play method returns the Boolean value true, which your program can test in a condition.

```
if (snare.Play())
{
    // if we get here the sound was played successfully
}
```

This can be useful if your game makes a very large number of sounds. The hardware in your Windows PC, Xbox, or Windows Phone has only a limited number of audio channels, and if the program tries to play too many sounds at the same time it will run out of hardware to play them on. The good news is that you will have at least 32 channels to use, meaning your game can play up to 32 sounds at the same time.

Creating a

A drum makes a sound only when you hit it. However, in games you'll also need sounds that play continuously, or when the player stops and starts them. As an example, you might need to play a sound for the engine in a car. This sound will play all the time the engine is running. We are going to make a game that plays a shooting sound as long as a gamepad button is held down. You can use this code to make engine sounds, or anything else that needs continuous sound playback. To do this, we'll create a playing sound effect and then make calls from our game to control the sound playback.

The *SoundEffectInstance* Class

If you want to control something, it is very useful if that thing has a handle. Sound effects are just like this. When you use the Play method described earlier, the sound is played until the end of the sample is reached. If we want to control sound playback, our game must create a "handle" object that is connected to the playing sound. The game can then call methods on this handle object to control the sound playback. The XNA class that is used to control a playing SoundEffect is called SoundEffectInstance because it will be controlling the playback of a sound effect. The game world for the raygun program will consist of the sound effect and the instance used to control it.

```
// Game World
SoundEffect shootSoundEffect;
SoundEffectInstance shootSoundEffectInstance;
```

The game will load the sound effect using the Content Manager as usual, and it will then ask the sound effect to create an instance of the sound:

```
protected override void LoadContent()
{
    // Create a new SpriteBatch, which can be used to draw textures.
    spriteBatch = new SpriteBatch(GraphicsDevice);

    shootSoundEffect = Content.Load<SoundEffect>("shootSound");

    shootSoundEffectInstance = shootSoundEffect.CreateInstance();
}
```

The CreateInstance method is provided by the SoundEffect class to allow a game to reserve a sound channel and connect a handle to it. Note that this method does not cause the sound to start playing. It is rather like being given a remote control to a TV. Now that we have the remote, we can use it to control the device.

Controlling a Sound Effect Instance

With our remote control, we can make our sound play. It turns out that a SoundEffect instance value is more useful than just a remote control in that it can also tell the game about the status of the sound. We can therefore make a game that starts playing the sound effect only if it is not playing already:

```
protected override void Update(GameTime gameTime)
{
    // Allows the game to exit
    if (GamePad.GetState(PlayerIndex.One).Buttons.Back == ButtonState.Pressed)
        this.Exit();

    pad1 = GamePad.GetState(PlayerIndex.One);

    if (pad1.Buttons.A == ButtonState.Pressed)
    {
        if (shootSoundEffectInstance.State != SoundState.Playing)
        {
            shootSoundEffectInstance.Play();
        }
    }
    else
    {
        shootSoundEffectInstance.Stop();
    }
    base.Update(gameTime);
}
```

This Update method will start playing the sound effect instance if the A button on the game-pad is pressed. It will also stop the sound if the button is released. This code is actually rather clever, in that it when the sound effect finishes playing (which causes the state to become stopped) it will automatically restart it. Note that we are using button A to provide a level rather than an edge, and therefore the program does not need to detect when the button is pressed, merely whether it is up or down.

> **Sample Code: 02 RayGun**   The 02 RayGun project in the resources for this chapter contains a program that repeats a sound sample as long as the A button is held down on the gamepad.

Changing Instance Properties

The preceding code makes the sound repeat by restarting playback when it stops. This works, but it means that the game has to keep checking to see if the sound has finished playing. There is a much easier way of making a sound repeat: we can just set the repeating property of the sound to true:

```
shootSoundEffectInstance.IsLooped = true;
```

The IsLooped property controls whether or not the sound plays repeatedly. It is normally set to false, which means that the sound will play once and then stop. If this property is set to true, the sound will repeat forever.

You can also modify the Pitch and Pan properties of a playing sound. Changing the pitch of a sound makes it higher or lower, and you can set the pitch value between –1 (half the original pitch) and +1 (double the original pitch). This is very useful if you want to make it sound like an engine is speeding up. The Pan value lets you move the sound between the left and right speakers. It can be set between –1 (hard left) and +1 (hard right). We can easily use the values from the gamepad thumbsticks to let us move our raygun sound around and change its pitch. We will find out more about the thumbsticks in Chapter 12, "Games, Objects, and State."

```
shootSoundEffectInstance.Pitch = pad1.ThumbSticks.Left.Y;
shootSoundEffectInstance.Pan = pad1.ThumbSticks.Left.X;
```

> **Sample Code: 03 RayGun**   The 03 RayGun with pitch and pan project in the resources for this chapter contains a program that repeats a sound sample as long as the A button is held down on the gamepad. You can use the left thumbstick to change the pitch of the sound and also move it from left to right.

Sound Bugs from Your Younger Brother

Your younger brother is quite keen on a raygun of his own and rushes off to create this program. However, he is soon back complaining that the program is faulty because "It goes wrong when I run it." You try the program, and sure enough, you get the screen shown in Figure 7-5.

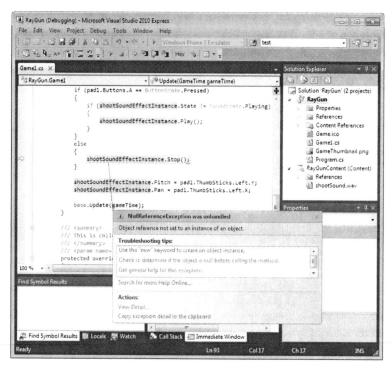

FIGURE 7-5 Throwing a NullReferenceException.

The reason for this is quite simple. Some types in C# are managed by reference. This means that a variable of this type is actually a reference to an object in memory. When you use the variable, the program follows the reference to the object it refers to and uses that object. A reference that is null is not set to refer to an object, so any attempt to follow this reference causes the program to fail. If a program tries to follow the shootSoundEffectInstance reference before it has been set to refer to an object, it is trying to go nowhere. This infringement is picked up by the system running our program, and the program is stopped at this point. The program should work OK, so there must be something missing from the version that your younger brother has entered. You remember that the SoundEffectInstance value should have been set in the LoadContent method. You take a look there and find that your younger brother has left out that statement:

protected override void LoadContent()

```
{
    // Create a new SpriteBatch, which can be used to draw textures.
    spriteBatch = new SpriteBatch(GraphicsDevice);

    shootSoundEffect = Content.Load<SoundEffect>("shootSound");


}
```

The missing line is shown in the preceding code in bold. It is the one that creates the handle to the sound effect the program wants to control. If this statement is not performed, the value of shootSoundEffectInstance remains set to null, which means that an attempt to find an object on the end of it will result in an exception that stops our program.

The good news is that this kind of problem is detected when the program runs and does not cause the Xbox, Windows Phone, or Windows PC running the program to crash. Similar mistakes with other programming languages can sometimes result in the famous "Blue Screen of Death" appearing.

Checking for Null References

It is actually possible for a program to fail with a null reference if the CreateInstance method is unable to allocate a sound channel to play our sound effect. This would only happen if we were playing lots of sounds. If CreateInstance can't find a channel to play the sound, it will return a null value to indicate that more sounds cannot be played at the moment. A completely bomb-proof game would test the value returned to make sure that an instance had been created.

```
if (shootSoundEffectInstance == null )
{
    // if we get here, the sound cannot be used
}
```

We can create a different version of the test to check that the sound effect instance has been created before we use it. This uses a new operator, !=, which means "not equal to."

```
if (shootSoundEffectInstance != null )
{
    // if we get here, we can use the sound
}
```

If we protected all use of the variable with tests like these, we would make sure that our program never crashed due to the value being set to null.

The Great Programmer Speaks: Sometimes you should check your references. Our Great Programmer reckons that sometimes a program should check that a reference has been set up before you try to use it. In the case of a game, it is not usually a problem if it fails for no reason (although players might not like this). However, in really important programs it is important to know if something you asked for has been delivered.

The XACT Audio Tool

If you have the time, you can explore some of the more powerful features of XNA sound generation, including using the XACT audio tool, which is supplied with the XNA Framework. This is a professional standard game sound creation program that can be used to create very impressive sound effects, including automatic random selection of different sounds for a particular event and changing the pitch and volume of sounds as they play.

Playing Songs Using the *MediaPlayer* Class

The sounds you have played so far have been created using SoundEffect values. These are intended for use in games, where the game program needs to be able to play the sounds quickly in response to game events. However, sound effects are not the best way to play longer sound samples, such as songs, because the sound data takes up too much program memory. Instead, you can use the media-playing features of XNA, which let your games use compressed .mp3 and .wma files as background music.

Up until now, you have used .wav files in your games. You have created these files using the Audacity program. However, any sound files that you have on your computer are unlikely to be held in this format. Instead, you will probably find that your files are either .mp3 or .wma files. These hold the sound in a compressed form that takes up less storage space. XNA is not able to use .mp3 or .wma files as content for sound effects, but it does have the ability to play such files using the MediaPlayer class.

The MediaPlayer class provides a Play method that is used to start playback of a particular Song value. You can load a song as you would any other item of content.

```
// Game World

// Song to be played by the MediaPlayer class
Song music;


protected override void LoadContent()
{
    // Create a new SpriteBatch, which can be used to draw textures.
    spriteBatch = new SpriteBatch(GraphicsDevice);

    music = Content.Load<Song>("music");
}
```

The music item in the Content folder is an .mp3 file. This can be added into the game solution in exactly the same way as the drum sound samples.

It is very easy to control the playback of a song using the MediaPlayer class. The code here will use the A button to start/resume playback and the B button to pause it:

```
pad1 = GamePad.GetState(PlayerIndex.One);

if (pad1.Buttons.A == ButtonState.Pressed)
{
    if (MediaPlayer.State == MediaState.Paused)
    {
        MediaPlayer.Resume();
    }

    if (MediaPlayer.State == MediaState.Stopped)
    {
        MediaPlayer.Play(music);
    }
}
if (pad1.Buttons.B == ButtonState.Pressed)
{
    if (MediaPlayer.State == MediaState.Playing)
    {
        MediaPlayer.Pause();
    }
}
```

The MediaPlayer class provides a property called State that your program can use to determine whether or not it is presently playing a song.

> **Sample Code: 04 MusicPlayer** The 04 MusicPlayer project in the resources for this chapter contains an XNA project and an .mp3 music file. The music playback can be started/resumed with button A and paused with button B.

When you run this program, you will notice that the first time you press button A to start the music there is quite a delay before the tune starts to play. This is because the media player has to open the media file and start playing it. The SoundEffect class uses sound samples that are held in memory and can play them instantly. You should use the media player only for background music and not when you need instant response.

Conclusion

This has been an interesting chapter. You've seen how to capture sounds and store them on your computer. You've also discovered how to use XNA to make sounds and play music.

Chapter Review Questions

And now the ever-popular review. Some people say that for some things in life, there are no right answers. Well, I think that for these questions, there is—namely, true or false.

1. Sound in an XNA program is managed by the Content Manager.

2. Games can use .mp3 files for sound.

3. You have to copy your sound files onto your target device by hand.

4. You can play only one sound at a time in an XNA program.

5. The Play method loads a sound effect into memory.

6. The Play method does not return anything useful.

7. A null reference refers to a null object.

Chapter 8
Creating a Timer

In this chapter, you will

- Find out how your program can measure the passage of time.
- Create a multi-player reaction game.
- Use C# arrays to allow the program to determine who won.

Making Another Game

You are now going to use your knowledge of Microsoft XNA and C# to create another game. This builds on the party theme that you explored in Chapter 6, "Creating a Multi-Player Game," where you created a button-bashing game.

> ### Game Idea: Mob Reaction Timer
>
> In this game, you test the reactions of your players. Each player is in charge of one button on a gamepad. The game plays a sound, and the player who presses his or her button the soonest after the sound starts playing wins. Anyone who presses the button before the sound starts playing is out.

You need to use a timer variable to keep track of time and a variable for each player to measure the reaction time of that player. Those variables are declared in the following code:

```
// Game World

int timer;

// Gamepad 1 scores
int ascore1;
int bscore1;
int xscore1;
int yscore1;
```

These are the variables for the timer and the first gamepad. The timer starts counting up from zero when the sound plays. Each time that XNA calls the Update method, the value in timer is increased by one and the program checks to see if the player has pressed his or her button. If the button has been pressed, the value of the timer is copied into the score variable for that button. The player with the lowest value is the winner. The first problem we have to solve is how to start the game. If the sound is produced as soon the game begins, the player who starts the game has an obvious advantage. One way to make this work is to make

131

the timer a negative number when the game starts and increase it each time Update is called. When it reaches the value 0, the sound is played and the game starts counting. Figure 8-1 shows how this works.

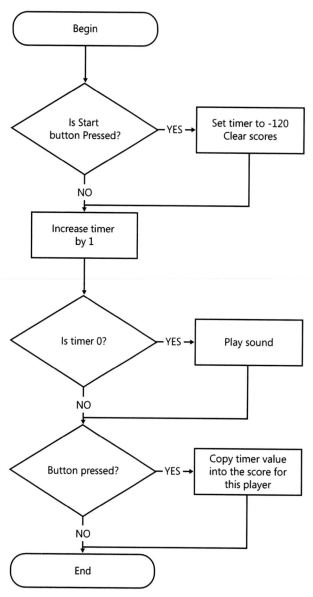

FIGURE 8-1 Flow diagram for a reaction timer.

Each time Update is called, the flow in Figure 8-1 is performed. If the Start button is pressed, the timer variable is set to –120. Each time Update runs, the value in timer is made one bigger. When timer reaches zero, the sound is played. When a button press is detected, the program copies the current value of timer into the score for that button. If a player presses a button before the sound has been played, he or she has a negative `timer` value. The player who gets the smallest positive value is the winner. The game world variables for this game will include the game timer variable along with the scores for each gamepad and the sound effect that is used to play the sound.

```
// Game World

// Display font
SpriteFont font;

// Game Timer
int timer;

// Game world sounds
SoundEffect dingSound;

// Gamepad 1
GamePadState pad1;
GamePadState oldpad1;
int ascore1;
int bscore1;
int xscore1;
int yscore1;
```

Each time that `Update` is called it must perform the actions shown in the flowchart, as shown in the following code:

```
protected override void Update(GameTime gameTime)
{
    pad1 = GamePad.GetState(PlayerIndex.One);

    if (pad1.Buttons.Back == ButtonState.Pressed)
    {
        this.Exit();
    }

    // start a new game
    if (pad1.Buttons.Start == ButtonState.Pressed)
    {
        timer = -120;
        ascore1 = 0;
        bscore1 = 0;
        xscore1 = 0;
        yscore1 = 0;
    }

    // update the timer
    timer++;

    // play the sound at the start of the game
    if (timer == 0)
    {
        dingSound.Play();
    }
```

```
    // if A is pressed copy the timer
    if (oldpad1.Buttons.A == ButtonState.Released &&
        pad1.Buttons.A == ButtonState.Pressed)
    {
        ascore1 = timer;
    }

    // repeat for buttons B, X and Y

    oldpad1 = pad1;
    // repeat for gamepads 2, 3 and 4

    base.Update(gameTime);
}
```

You should look carefully at this method because, although it is not very large, it is somewhat complicated. Remember that the Update method is called 60 times a second, so when the Start button is pressed and timer is set to –120, this means that there is a 2-second delay before the sound plays. The code runs and works well. In fact, I'm rather proud of it. Unfortunately, it has a rather nasty bug in it.

> **Sample Code: 01 Broken Reaction Timer Game** All the sample projects can be obtained from the Web resources for this text, which can be found at *http://oreilly.com/ catalog/9780735651579*. The 01 Broken ReactionTimer project in the resources for this chapter contains a version of the game using the Update method from this section. Have a go with it and see if you can find the bug.

Reaction Timer Bug

You first notice the bug in the program when you find that your younger brother is beating everyone at the game. He seems to have amazing reflexes. Or he is cheating. It turns out to be the latter. He has noticed that although you get a negative (and therefore invalid) score if you press your button before the sound plays, you can press the button again later and have another go. What he does is press the button up and down very rapidly until he hears the sound and then stops. This usually results in him winning.

If you look at the code in the Update method, you find that there's nothing to stop a naughty player from pressing his or her button lots of times. There's no penalty for pressing the button before the sound plays because the player can just press the button again. You've designed the game without allowing for the fact that players might cheat and seem to have reckoned without your younger brother.

You need to change the program to fix the problem. At this point, you're doing proper programming. You've used an *algorithm* that gives a set of steps to make the game work, but you've found that it's faulty in some circumstances. Therefore, you need to either improve your solution or find a better one.

Because I wrote the first version, I'm going to start by asking you to work out what is going wrong. This might seem a little unfair, but I'm going to give you some help by suggesting things that might be the cause. Pick the one you think is the most sensible and then read on.

1. The problem occurs because you're not detecting when the player releases the button as well as when it's pressed.

2. The problem occurs because you should be using level detection on the buttons, not edge detection.

3. The problem occurs because you should register only the first press of the button.

4. The problem occurs because you need to reset the gamepad after it's been read.

If you look carefully at the flow diagram in Figure 8-1 and the code, you can simulate these ideas to see which makes the most sense. If this feels a bit like solving a puzzle, you're very close to what this part of programming is all about. If you get stuck trying to solve a programming problem, the best thing to do is to go back and consider what you're trying to achieve. What you must not do is just add lines of code in the hope that one of them fixes the problem.

Your younger brother is winning by pressing his button more than once. Because you can't physically stop him from doing this, you have to find a way to prevent later button presses having any effect on the score of the player. From the previous list, option 3 is the best one to try. So the problem now becomes: How can you tell if the button has been pressed more than once? Take a look at the flowchart and try to decide what the program could test to decide if this is the first or second time that the button has been pressed in a game.

It turns out that this is easy. The program works by copying the value of the timer into the score for each player. When the Start button is pressed, the program loads zero into the score values for each of the players. The very first time the player presses his or her button, the zero is replaced with a time value. Next time he or she presses the button, the score is not zero, so you should not update this value. The following code implements this fix:

```
// if A is pressed and ascore1 is 0 copy the timer
if (oldpad1.Buttons.A == ButtonState.Released &&
    pad1.Buttons.A == ButtonState.Pressed && ascore1 == 0)
{
    ascore1 = timer;
}
```

The program now contains a condition that tests whether the score is zero and sets the score only if it is. If the score is not zero (that is, the button has already been pressed), then the score is not stored.

> **Sample Code: 02 Fixed ReactionTimer** The 02 Fixed ReactionTimer project in the resources for this chapter contains a mended version of the game using the Update method as fixed in this section.

Finding Winners Using Arrays

Your younger brother is now rather cross with you. The update means that he can't always win at the game anymore, and this has upset him somewhat. So he has taken to claiming that the game is rubbish anyway "because it doesn't tell you who won."

Unfortunately, he has a point. When the game finishes, the players must look at the screen and decide who the winner is. This doesn't seem right, bearing in mind that computers are supposed to make our lives easier. So now you have to work out a way of deciding who has the winning score. Any scores less than or equal to zero must be ignored because those players either pressed their buttons before the sound played or never pressed their buttons at all. Of the remaining scores, you want the one with the lowest value. You could write some complicated code like this:

```
if ( ascore1 > 0 )
{
    if ( ascore1 < bscore1 && ascore1 < xscore1 && ascore1 < yscore1 )
    {
        // if we get here button A of Gamepad 1 has won
    }
}
```

This code works only for the A button of gamepad 1. The first `if` statement checks to see if the score is greater than zero. If it is, the second condition is evaluated. This is a rather complicated `if` statement that checks to see if the score for the A button is less than the score for the other buttons on the gamepad. If the score is less than all of them, that button is the winner. You need to write three other conditions for the other buttons on the gamepad. This is a lot of work, and it gets even worse when you consider the possibility of four gamepads.

Creating an Array

What you need is a way of working through a list of scores using your program. In C#, a variable that holds a list of values is called an *array*. The type of values that you want your array to hold are integers, and it is "one-dimensional," in that it has only one list of values. Arrays can be declared and initialized just like any other C# variable:

```
int[] scores = new int[4];
```

This declares an array variable called `scores` that can refer to one-dimensional integer arrays and makes it refer to a new 4-element array instance. This would let the array hold the score values for the four buttons on gamepad 1.

You can think of an array as a row of numbered boxes, each of which can hold a single value. A single "box" in an array is called an *element*. Figure 8-2 shows how this works.

The size of the array is set when you create it. In the previous code, you made an array with four elements. If you want a different size, you simply change the 4 to a different number.

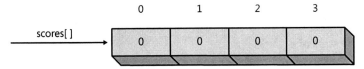

FIGURE 8-2 An array reference and an array instance

> **Note** You may have noticed that I'm talking about "array instances" and that arrays are created using the key word new. I have used these terms before when I was talking about objects. This means that arrays are implemented in C# as objects, and you can ask them to do things for you. Later in this chapter, you'll see how you can use array properties and methods to make your life easier.

Using Data in an Array

Now that you have your array, you need to be able to get a hold of individual elements. If you take a look at Figure 8-2 again, you see that each element has a number above it. This is called the *subscript* or *index* of that element in the array. You can regard a subscript as telling the computer how far "down" an array to go to get to the element that is required. In this respect, array elements are similar to house numbers on a street (except that no houses have the number zero). To use a particular element in an array, you simply give the subscript of the element that you want. The following code shows how this works. The value of the subscript is enclosed in square brackets:

```
if (oldpad1.Buttons.A == ButtonState.Released &&
     pad1.Buttons.A == ButtonState.Pressed && scores[0] == 0)
{
    scores[0] = timer;
}
```

This C# code works in the same way as the original code, except that it uses the first element in the array, scores[0], instead of a variable called ascore1. You can use scores[1] as bscore1, the score for the B button on gamepad 1 and so on.

At this point, it doesn't seem that creating an array has made life much easier; you've only found a quick way of declaring more than one variable. However, the real power comes when you use variables in your array subscripts, as follows:

```
for ( int i = 0; i < 4 ; i++ )
{
    scores[i] = 0;
}
```

This is a for loop construction that takes the value of i from 0 to 3 (remember that when the value of i reaches 4, the test "i less than 4" fails and the loop stops). The value of i is used as a subscript for the array access. This means that the first time around the loop, the statement will set scores[0] to zero. The next time around the loop, the assignment statement works on scores[1], and so on, up until the end of the array. This is how you'd set the scores array elements to zero at the start of a game.

> **Note** The previous code uses an additional C# feature of the for loop that lets you declare the counter variable (in this case, a variable called i) in the loop itself. This variable exists only for the duration of the loop, being local to the for loop block. The Great Programmer thinks this is the right thing to do here, as you need the variable only for the duration of the loop block.

In this case, you want to work with only four elements, so the code doesn't look that much shorter than your original. However, if you needed to set 1,000 values, the code would contain the same statements, except that you'd change the limit value so that i goes up to 999.

> **Note** If you have a mind like your younger brother, at this point you'll be wondering what would happen if you tried to use silly subscript values like scores[101]. Your younger brother would no doubt be hoping that this would cause the computer to crash or, better yet, allow access to secret memory locations. The boring answer is that if you step outside what are called the *bounds* of an array, your program is stopped in its tracks by an exception because this is just not allowed to happen in a proper language like C#. This form of naughtiness was not always detected in older computers, however, and was once one of the standard ways that a virus program could attack a system.

Scanning an Array

Now you need to use an array to help you find the best score. Figure 8-3 shows a typical arrangement of the values.

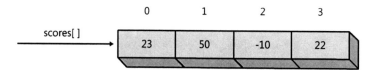

FIGURE 8-3 Sample scores

You now need to write some C# to work through the array and find the best score. At this point, you have a problem. If I ask you, "Which element in Figure 8-3 has the winning time in it?" you would glance at the page and say, "The element with subscript 3." And you'd be right. The problem is that you won't necessarily be able to tell me precisely how you worked it out. You simply looked along the row, and that number was the smallest number that wasn't negative. It was obvious.

Unfortunately, you can't say to the C# compiler, "Look along the row and find me the winner." You need to set things out in simpler and much more boring steps. The program must look at each element in turn and see if it wins. At any given point in the process, the program would have an idea of the best result it has seen so far. If it sees a value that is better, it now has a new winner, and so on.

If you think about it, this is what people really do, particularly if they are working through 1,000 numbers instead of only a few. In that case, you would take care to remember the best result that you had seen so far as you went through and probably write it down on a piece of paper. With all this in mind, consider the following code:

```
int winningValue = 120;
for (int i = 0; i < 16; i++)
{
    if (scores[i] > 0)
    {
        if (scores[i] < winningValue)
        {
            winningValue = scores[i];
        }
    }
}
```

This code uses a variable called winningValue to hold the smallest value it has seen so far. It starts by setting it to a large value that is guaranteed not to be a winner. It then compares winningValue with each element in the array in turn. If the element is smaller than the current smallest value, it sets winningValue to the new value. Before it tests winningValue, the code makes sure that the count is a valid one (in that the button must have been pressed). At the end of the pass through the loop, the variable winningValue has the value of the winning score.

Now that you know the winning score, you can write some code to display the winner:

```
string winnerName;

if ( scores[0] == winningValue )
{
    winnerName = "Gamepad 1 button A";
}

if ( scores[1] == winningValue )
{
    winnerName = "Gamepad 1 button B";
}
```

This code selects the winning string for the A and B buttons on gamepad 1. The string winnerName is set with the name of the winning button and gamepad and can be displayed on the screen at the end of the game. You could write more statements for each of the other buttons and gamepads.

Note You need to make sure that when you check the buttons, you set the correct elements in the array; otherwise, the wrong names are displayed.

Using an Array as a Lookup Table

The previous code produces a string that contains the name of the winning gamepad and button. But you still need to perform all those conditional statements to decide the string to display. You do have a way to make your life easier, though, and it starts by finding out the position in the array of the winning score. Here's code that does that:

```
int winningValue = 120;
int winnerSubscript = 0;
for (int i = 0; i < 16; i++)
{
    if (scores[i] > 0)
    {
        if (scores[i] < winningValue)
        {
            winningValue = scores[i];
            winnerSubscript = i;
        }
    }
}
```

This is the same loop as before, but you now have a variable called winnerSubscript that holds the position in the array of the winning value. Note that the program copies the value of i into the winnerSubscript when it finds a new winning value. Remember that when you find a new winning value, the variable i holds the subscript in the array where that value is stored.

Now that you have the subscript value of the winning score, you can use it in another array to find the string that describes that player. The array is set up as shown in Figure 8-4.

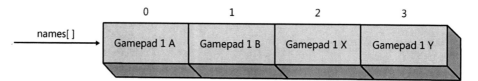

FIGURE 8-4 A player lookup table.

This is an array of strings of text. There is an element in the array for each of the buttons on gamepad 1, and the names are lined up with the buttons that are tested. Now, to get the description of the winner, you simply need to look up the name in your table:

```
winnerName = names[winnerSubscript];
```

You need to have a way of setting up the lookup table with the correct strings. C# provides a way that you can create an array and set the initial values in it:

```
string[] names = new string[] {
    "Gamepad 1 A",
    "Gamepad 1 B",
    "Gamepad 1 X",
    "Gamepad 1 Y"
};
```

This creates an array with the preset values that you specify. Note that you don't need to tell C# how long the array is because the compiler can work this out automatically.

Displaying the Winner

You now have code that you can use to display the winner. Now you need to work out how to add this to the program. A good time to display the winner would be two seconds after the sound was produced, which is when the timer value reaches 120. By then, all the players should have pressed their buttons. The following code does that:

```
protected override void Update(GameTime gameTime)
{
    pad1 = GamePad.GetState(PlayerIndex.One);

    if (pad1.Buttons.Back == ButtonState.Pressed)
    {
        this.Exit();
    }

    // start a new game
    if (pad1.Buttons.Start == ButtonState.Pressed)
    {
        for (int i = 0; i < 16; i++)
        {
            scores[i] = 0;
        }
        winnerName = "";
        timer = -120;
    }

    // update the timer
    timer++;

    // play the sound at the start of the game
    if (timer == 0)
    {
        dingSound.Play();
    }
```

```
// if A is pressed and scores[0] is 0 copy the timer
if (oldpad1.Buttons.A == ButtonState.Released &&
    pad1.Buttons.A == ButtonState.Pressed && scores[0] == 0)
{
    scores[0] = timer;
}
// Repeat for other buttons and gamepads

if (timer == 120)
{
    int winningValue = 120;
    int winnerSubscript = 0;
    for (int i = 0; i < 16; i++)
    {
        if (scores[i] > 0)
        {
            if (scores[i] < winningValue)
            {
                winningValue = scores[i];
                winnerSubscript = i;
            }
        }
    }

    if (winningValue != 120)
    {
        winnerName = names[winnerSubscript];
    }
    else
    {
        winnerName = "**NO WINNER**";
    }
}

base.Update(gameTime);
}
```

This version of Update works out the winner two seconds after the sound has been played. It places the name of the winner in the variable winnerName, which can then be displayed in the Draw method. When the game is started, the winnerName is set to an empty string so that the name appears only when it has been calculated.

There is one further improvement to this code, which is that if all the players have pressed their buttons before the sound, no one wins. The program checks to see if the winningValue has been changed by the search for the best time. If no value better than 120 was found, it means that everyone pressed their button too early. As a result, the program displays "**NO WINNER**".

Sample Code: 03 ReactionTimer with Winner Display The 03 ReactionTimer with Winner Display project in the resources for this chapter contains a fully working version of the game that displays the winner.

Conclusion

In this chapter you've created another party game, discovered how to measure time and trigger events. You've also started to work with arrays as a means of allowing your programs to work much more effectively with collections of data.

Chapter Review Questions

And now yet another popular set of review questions. Just remember that there is nothing like knowing what you know. Prove it by saying whether these statements are true or false.

1. The C# code `int[] scores;` creates an array that could hold four integers.
2. An array can hold any type of data.
3. An array is an object.
4. The first element in an array has the subscript 1.
5. It doesn't matter if your array subscript values are out of range.

Chapter 9
Reading Text Input

In this chapter, you will

- Discover how the keyboard works in Microsoft XNA.

- Use enumerated types.

- Use arrays and references.

- Work with strings of text.

- Create a message board program.

Using the Keyboard in XNA

The Xbox itself does not have a keyboard, but you can plug any Universal Serial Bus (USB) keyboard into an Xbox and it will work. XNA programs use the keyboard in the same way whether they are running on an Xbox or a Microsoft Windows PC. In this chapter, you explore how you can use the keyboard in your XNA games. At the same time, you find out more about how C# programs can manipulate text.

Program Project: Message Board

The next program you make won't be a game as such, but rather an extension to one of your earlier programs. You create a message board that can be used to display text for all to see. You can use this to tell people where you are. (Really cool kids might have one on the outside of their bedroom door to show when they are free/busy and leave helpful messages for parents like "Please clean.") Or you could use it in the living room on the big-screen TV to avoid talking to people.

Creating the Message Board Project

You can use an earlier project, the BigClock project in the 06 3D Clock MoodLight folder in the resources for Chapter 5, "Writing Text," as the starting point of your message board. This provides a clock (which would be a nice thing to have on the message board) and also has the code that lets you display text on the screen.

Registering Key Presses

You've used the keyboard before in the Color Nerve game in Chapter 3, "Getting Player Input." You used it alongside the gamepad as follows:

```
GamePadState pad1 = GamePad.GetState(PlayerIndex.One);
KeyboardState keys = Keyboard.GetState();

if (pad1.Buttons.B == ButtonState.Pressed ||
    keys.IsKeyDown(Keys.R))
{
    redIntensity++;
}
```

This code increases the intensity of the red part of your color if the B button on the gamepad is pressed or the R key is pressed on the keyboard. The IsKeyDown method is provided with a parameter that tells it which key to test for. If that key is pressed down, the method returns true. By calling IsKeyDown with different parameters, you can check to see if particular keys are pressed. This is particularly useful in a game situation because a player might be holding down several keys at once, such as holding down an arrow key to move a spaceship as well as pressing the spacebar to fire a weapon.

The previous code is using inputs in a *level*-sensitive mode in that so long as the R key is held down, the intensity value increases. However, you've seen that this is not always how you want to use inputs. Sometimes you want them to be *edge-triggered* so that you register an event only when something changes. You used edge-triggered events to detect button presses to create the button-bashing games in Chapter 6, "Creating a Multi-Player Game," and also in the reaction timer game in Chapter 7, "Playing Sounds." For a keyboard to be useful, it must be edge-triggered; you want to know only when the key changes from up to down. You can't just say that a key has been pressed if IsKeyDown says it's down at any particular time.

There are two reasons that you can't do this. The first is that if you test the keyboard 60 times a second, your program might decide that a particular key has been pressed 60 times a second. The second reason is that when people type, they often press several keys at once. When I type the word "the," I find that as I press the "h" character, I still have the "t" held down. This is called "rollover," and hardware designers have been dealing with this ever since keyboards were first used on computers. So you need to write some kind of keyboard edge-triggered code.

> **Note** At this point, it's worth mentioning that reading text from a keyboard in XNA is a lot trickier than reading text in other programming environments. This is because in XNA, the keyboard handling is really designed for playing games.

Note In conventional programming, there are commands that let you read in a line of text that the user enters. If you write programs using other frameworks to run in the Windows environment, you can request that a method be called each time the user presses a key. However, you're using XNA, so you just have to live with this. The only good news is that this does provide a good way to learn some fundamental programming principles along the way.

Detecting When Keys Are Pressed

You can detect a key being pressed by comparing the current state of the keyboard with the state it had previously. If a key is shown as being in the down position and it was previously up, this means that it must have been pressed, and you need to register it. You could do this on an individual key basis as follows:

```
if (keyState.IsKeyDown(Keys.R) && oldKeyState.IsKeyUp(Keys.R))
{
    // if we get here the key R has just been pressed
}
```

This code tests to see if the R key has just been pressed. The variable `oldKeyState` holds the previous state of the keyboard, and the variable `keyState` holds the current state. The problem with this approach is that you would need to perform this test for every single key on the keyboard, which would take a while to write. Fortunately, there's a slightly easier way to do this. The KeyboardState structure provides a method called `GetPressedKeys` that gives you an array of the keys that are currently pressed. You've seen arrays before; you made one to hold the score values of the reaction timer game in Chapter 8. This time, the array is being used to allow a method to return a set of answers, each of which identifies a key that is currently pressed. The elements in the array are of type Keys.

Note There is potential for confusion here. You can use a key on a keyboard to type a character. In this case, the word *type* means the action of typing. However, within the C# language the type of a variable determines what the variable can be used for.

The Keys Type

Part of the fun of programming is deciding the best way to store the things that a program must work with. You've seen that you can use the byte type to hold small integer values (in the range 0 to 255) and the int type to hold integer values in a wider range. We have also seen that XNA provides a variety of types that can hold game-specific things like textures and colors. The designers of XNA needed a way to represent a key on the keyboard so that programmers can write programs that react to a particular key being pressed. You've already used values of type Keys in your programs; Keys.R is used in the previous code to ask IsKeyDown to test whether the R key is being pressed.

Enumerated Types

The Keys type is a kind of type that I haven't discussed yet. It's an *enumerated type*. The word *enumerate* means to "count" or "number" items. Enumerated types are created by programmers when they need only a particular range of values to represent something. When the XNA team realized they needed to store information about a particular key on the keyboard, they could have used numbers (for example, they could have decided that *A* was 65, *B* was 66, and so on). However, they decided to create an enumerated type instead.

An enumerated type is one where the programmer defines the range of possible values that variables of this type can have and creates names for each of these values. Possible keys on a keyboard include the letter keys, A to Z, and the digit keys, 0 to 9, as well as the left and right Shift keys, the Enter key, and the Esc key, so the Keys type has a value for each of these.

> **The Great Programmer Speaks: Enumerated Types Are Useful** The Great Programmer is a big fan of enumerated types. She says that if you create a type that can have only certain values, it reduces the chances of your program doing silly things. As an example, she says that if you had a game that was either in Attract mode (nobody playing), Play mode (game in progress), or High Score mode (entering the high-score value), it makes very good sense to represent these states with a variable that can have only one of those three values. You could use an integer to store this and remember that 0, 1, and 2 mean the three different states, but this would not stop a malicious programmer (or your younger brother) putting "97" in there and causing the program to do strange things.

The Keys enumeration does not include separate values for capital (uppercase) A and little (lowercase) a. It just represents the key itself. Your program needs to check if the A key and a Shift key are being pressed at the same time. If they are, the user is typing an uppercase A.

Working with Arrays, Objects, and References

The GetPressedKeys method returns an array of Keys values. Each element in the array describes a key that is presently pressed. The more keys that are pressed, the more elements are in the array. Figure 9-1 shows how such an array might look.

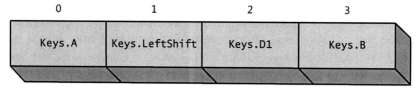

FIGURE 9-1 A sample *Keys* array.

From the illustration, you can see that when the method was called, the A key, the left Shift key, the digit 1, and the B key are all pressed down. This means that to determine which keys have been pressed on the keyboard, you need to work through the array of key information supplied by the GetPressedKeys method. However, before you write the code to do this, it's time to take a detour into how arrays and objects work together and consider what the GetPressedKeys method actually gives you.

Values and References

Up until now, you've treated all objects equally. You've used byte, string, Texture2D, double, Color, SpriteBatch, and lots of other kinds of objects in your XNA programs and treated all of them in the same way. You know that different objects hold different amounts of data and that this data is held inside the object in *fields*. You also know that objects expose *properties* that you can use to access the values of the fields in the object and that objects also have *methods* that you can use to ask an object to do something for you. You can *declare* variables of these types, give them *identifiers*, and assign values to them using the = operator. Sometimes you need to use the key word new to create instances (for example, for SpriteBatch), and sometimes you don't (for byte). Now is the time to improve your understanding of how objects are organized in memory. You need to consider the difference between *value* and *reference* types.

An array is a type that's managed by *reference*. It's very important that you understand how references work in C# programs. The Great Programmer reckons that you can't call yourself a proper programmer unless you understand how references work, and you need to consider this now. A reference is a kind of variable that refers to something. It doesn't hold any data; rather, it refers to the object in memory that contains the data. If you wanted an array that could hold four Keys values, you would write the following:

```
Keys[] pressedKeys;
pressedKeys = new Keys[4];
```

The first statement creates an array reference called pressedKeys. The second statement makes an array that can hold four Keys values. These are two separate actions. When they are complete, you have an array reference that has been made to refer to a particular four-element array of Keys that is sitting in memory somewhere. At the moment, the pressedKeys reference is the only way that you can locate and use that four-element array.

Arrays as Offices

If you want to go back to the office scenario, you can think of an array as an office, as shown in Figure 9-2.

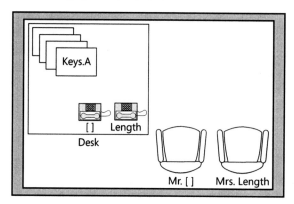

Array office

FIGURE 9-2 The Keys array as an office.

The office holds the usual desk with the properties on it and the telephones for the behaviors that the object can support. The array type exposes a property called Length that's used to find out how many elements there are in the array. When the Length phone rings, Mrs. Length gets up, gets the number of array elements on the property table, and tells the caller the result as follows:

```
int keyCount = pressedKeys.Length;
```

This code shows how the Length property is used. If the pressedKeys reference refers to the array you created previously, the keyCount integer would be set to 4.

There's also another strange-looking property called [ ] in your array office. This is how elements are accessed. Mr. [ ] provides access to the pile of elements on the table. He is given the subscript value and then counts down the pile of elements on the table to get to the one that you want. If you give the subscript 0, you get the top one; the subscript 1 gets you the one below that; and so on. Mr. [ ] can read values off the array elements and also can write new values at the appropriate place in the pile. The following code shows how Mr. [ ] is used:

```
pressedKeys[0] = Keys.R;
```

It would cause him to put the value Keys.R in the element on the top of the pile.

You can think of a reference to an object as the phone number that you use to call to the people in that office. When a new instance of a class is created, it's as if you built an office, put in a desk and telephones, and hired a staff member for each behavior. Each telephone is identified with the phone number of the office, followed by an extension for the behavior in the object that you want to contact. So you could use 123435.Length to get a hold of Mrs. Length in office 12345. Of course, in reality, a reference is the place in memory where the object is stored rather than a telephone number, but the principle is the same. When you're given a reference, all you're told is how to get hold of something. The following code would create a new array and then set pressedKeys with the "telephone number" of that array:

```
pressedKeys = new Keys[4];
```

The only way that you can get hold of this array is by using pressedKeys to locate it. If the pressedKeys variable is destroyed or overwritten, the object might as well not exist, as you have no way of getting in touch with it. This is the same as if you met someone wonderful at a party and failed to get their telephone number. If you can't get to an object, it might as well not be there.

Say Hello to the Garbage Collector

Within C#, there's a special mechanism for getting rid of objects that might as well not be there. The *garbage collector* process has the job of looking for objects that do not have anything referring to them and removing them from memory. Memory allocation is an important part of programming, and you need to be careful not to make too much work for the garbage collector. An inexperienced programmer could write the following C# code:

```
Keys[] pressedKeys ;
pressedKeys = new Keys[100];
pressedKeys = new Keys[200];
```

This is very stupid code. It's completely legal and would compile and run, but it's still very stupid because the 100-element array that was created in the second statement is immediately made useless in the third, where pressedKeys is made to refer to another, larger array. This is like building a brand-new office and then destroying the only copy of the telephone number that could be used to contact it. The garbage collector would eventually notice that the array object had no references referring to it and would destroy it, but until this happened, a large chunk of memory would be unusable.

The Great Programmer makes sure that when she writes a program, it does not repeatedly create and destroy objects in this way; as a result, her software runs quickly and uses only the minimum amount of memory.

Using References and Values

You can see that reference variables are quite different from "ordinary" variables that simply hold values. It's important that you understand the difference. A reference variable holds the "telephone number" of an instance of an object. A value variable holds a particular value, for example:

```
int myAge;
myAge = 21;
```

These statements declare an int variable called myAge and set it to the rather optimistic (in my case) value of 21. You can think of myAge as a piece of paper with space to write a single integer value on it. When a value is assigned to the variable, it's equivalent to writing a new number on the paper. If I assign the value in myAge to another int variable, the value on the paper is copied across:

```
int myAge;
myAge = 21;
int tempAge;
tempAge = myAge;
```

You now have a new int variable called tempAge. This has the value 21 written on it because that's the value that was copied from the myAge variable. In other words, when you work with value types, you're copying values from one piece of paper to another. Changing the value written on one piece of paper does not change the value on another:

```
tempAge++; // this will not change the value in myAge
```

If the value in tempAge is increased by 1, it now holds the value 22, but myAge still has the value 21.

However, consider what happens when the program performs assignments using references:

```
Keys[ ] pressedKeys ;
pressedKeys = new Keys[100];
Keys[ ] oldKeys;
oldKeys = pressedKeys;
```

The oldKeys variable is a reference that can refer to an array of Keys. If I set oldKeys equal to pressedKeys, it means that it refers to the same object as pressedKeys does. In other words, it contains the same office phone number. Whether you use oldKeys.Length or pressedKeys.Length, you get the same Mrs. Length on the end of the line. So you can see that the following statements both set the element at the start of the same array:

```
oldKeys[0] = Keys.X;
pressedKeys[0] = Keys.Y;
```

First, the element is set to X; then it is set to Y. At the end of these two statements, both oldKeys[0] and pressedKeys[0] contain Y.

An object managed by reference doesn't have a name; rather, it's identified only in terms of the things that are referring to it. You should never say "the array called oldKeys"; you can say only "the array that oldKeys is currently referring to." During the lifetime of the oldKeys reference, it could be made to refer to many different arrays.

Why Do We Have References and Values?

You might be wondering why the designers of C# have bothered with value and reference types. All they have done so far is make programming more confusing in that assignment statements can assign either references or values. Look at this code:

```
x = y;
```

This statement could mean, "Make the reference x refer to the same thing that y refers to," or it could mean, "Take the value in y and copy it into x." Without knowing what types x and y are, you can't decide. However, references are very useful in programs. As an example, consider the Texture2D type. You've used this in your programs to store an image you might want to draw. The image might be very large, in which case a Texture2D instance would take up a lot of memory. Because of this, textures are managed by reference. If I want to give someone my texture, I'll pass them a reference to it. In a game, you often want to do this because you can use the same texture to draw lots of objects. In a space shooter game, each of the identical aliens that are attacking your spaceship could be drawn using the same texture. Value types, on the other hand, are small and copies can easily be passed between different parts of a program.

References and *GetPressedKeys*

Up until now, you've been using value types and reference types without worrying too much about the difference, but as you write more complicated games, you need to deal with both kinds. In Chapter 14, in the section "References," you'll revisit the way that value and references are used when you design some data types of your own; for now, the important thing to remember is that an array is a type that is managed by reference, and that what you get back from GetPressedKeys is a reference to an array.

Displaying Keys

You start your message board off by writing a program that displays the keys that are presently being held down on a keyboard. The Update method sets a message string in the game world that the Draw method puts up on the screen for everyone to see. The code in the Update method must look through the array of pressed keys and add a description of each key to the message string as follows:

```
// Game World
string messageString;

protected override void Update(GameTime gameTime)
{
    KeyboardState keyState = Keyboard.GetState();
```

```
// Allows the game to exit by pressing the Esc key
if ( keyState.IsKeyDown(Keys.Escape) )
{
    this.Exit();
}

// Get the pressed keys and display them
Keys[] pressedKeys;
pressedKeys = keyState.GetPressedKeys();
messageString = "";
for (int i = 0; i < pressedKeys.Length; i++)
{
    messageString = messageString + pressedKeys[i].ToString() + " " ;
}

base.Update(gameTime);
}
```

The first part of the method sets messageString to an empty string. Then the string
representation for each Keys item in the array is added to the end of the message. You've
used the ToString method before when you converted dates and times into strings for your
clock. ToString asks an object to provide a string of text describing the information it holds.
When you call ToString on an instance of a Key, it should tell you what key it is. The string
that is built in the Update method is displayed by the Draw method:

```
protected override void Draw(GameTime gameTime)
{
    graphics.GraphicsDevice.Clear(Color.CornflowerBlue);

    Vector2 messageVector = new Vector2(50, 100);

    spriteBatch.Begin();
    spriteBatch.DrawString(font, messageString, messageVector,
                           Color.White);
    spriteBatch.End();

    base.Draw(gameTime);
}
```

This Draw method simply draws the messageString on the screen. Figure 9-3 shows the
output of the program if the Caps Lock key, the A key, and the left Alt key are held down.

> **Sample Code: Key Viewer** All the sample projects can be obtained from the Web resources
> for this text, which can be found at *http://oreilly.com/catalog/9780735651579*. The KeyViewer
> project in the 01 KeyViewer directory in the resources for this chapter contains a program that
> uses the Draw and Update methods described in this section to display the keys that are being
> pressed on the keyboard. Note that different hardware is able to support different numbers of
> keys being held down at the same time.

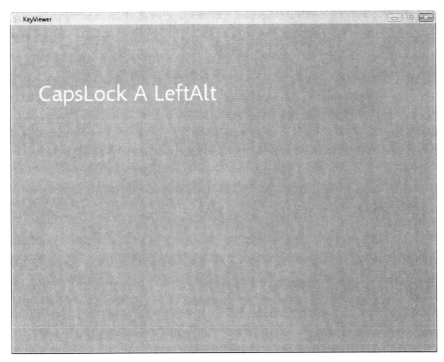

FIGURE 9-3 Drawing level-detected key presses on the screen.

Detecting Key Presses

As you see with the KeyViewer program, the name of the key that is pressed is displayed so long as the key itself is held down. However, as we found with the gamepad, you want to register a key press only when you see a key change from up to down. You detect such changes by comparing the present state of the keyboard with the previous state. Figure 9-4 shows how this might work. It shows the oldKeys that were previously pressed and the pressedKeys that are presently pressed. Your program must decide which key has just been pressed.

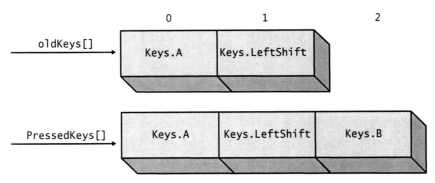

FIGURE 9-4 Detecting key presses.

If you look at Figure 9-4, you can see that the key that must have just been pressed is the B key. The A key was already pressed, as was the left Shift key. You need to find a sequence of operations that can work this out. This means that it is time to create another *algorithm*.

When faced with a situation like this, I think that it's a bit like being a detective. A detective arrives at the scene of a crime, looks at the evidence, and then tries to build up a sequence of events that explains everything that has been found. A programmer has some information that comes in from which he or she must produce the desired output by a process that he or she needs to devise. If you have a problem like this, it's often useful to set out what you know and what you want to find out and then try to find a way of getting one from the other.

In this case, in the input side, you have a list of keys that were pressed before and a list of keys that are pressed now.

The output that you want is any keys that have been pressed since you last looked. If you think about it for a while, you can come up with a way to tell which keys have just been pressed:

"Any keys in the list of keys that are pressed now that are *not* in the list of keys that were pressed before are ones that have just been pressed."

You can test this by applying it to the keys in Figure 9-4. Both the A key and the left Shift key are in the oldKeys array and the pressedKeys array. However, the B key is only in the pressedKeys array, so it must have just been pressed down. At the moment, your solution does not give you any steps to follow; what you need to do now is convert it into a proper algorithm. Initially, you can write this in English; then you can convert it into C# code.

"Take each value in pressedKeys in turn and check to see if it occurs in oldKeys. If you don't find the value in oldKeys, that key must have been pressed since you last looked."

You know that to work your way through an array, you need to use a for loop of some kind. In this case, you need to put one for loop inside another because you need to look through the oldKeys array for each of the values in pressedKeys. This is called "nesting" the for loops and is a very common programming technique:

```
// String we are going to display - initially an empty string
string messageString = "";
// the keys that were pressed before - initially an empty array
Keys[] oldKeys = new Keys[0];

protected override void Update(GameTime gameTime)
{
    KeyboardState keyState = Keyboard.GetState();

    // Allows the game to exit by pressing the Esc key
    if (keyState.IsKeyDown(Keys.Escape))
    {
        this.Exit();
    }
```

```
    // the keys that are currently pressed
    Keys[] pressedKeys;
    pressedKeys = keyState.GetPressedKeys();

    // work through each key that is presently pressed
    for (int i = 0; i < pressedKeys.Length; i++)
    {
        // set a flag to indicate we have not found the key
        bool foundIt = false;

        // work through each key that was previously pressed
        for (int j = 0; j < oldKeys.Length; j++)
        {
            if (pressedKeys[i] == oldKeys[j])
            {
                // we found the key in the previously pressed keys
                foundIt = true;
            }
        }
        if (foundIt == false)
        {
            // if we get here we didn't find the key in the old keys, so
            // add the key to the end of the message string
            messageString = messageString + pressedKeys[i].ToString();
        }
    }

    // remember the currently pressed keys for next time
    oldKeys = pressedKeys;

    base.Update(gameTime);
}
```

This version of Update takes each key in the pressedKeys array and searches the oldKeys array to see if that key is in there. If it doesn't find the key, it adds a description of the key to the message string. I've added quite a few comments (the lines that start with //) that should make the code easier to understand. Note that I am using a bool variable called foundIt to record whether a key has been found when the old key array is searched. If this flag is not set during a search, that key value is not present in the old array and must be a new key. The message string itself is drawn in the same way as it was in the previous program.

Don't worry if you find this code confusing at first; just remember the problem that it is trying to solve. The program has two lists of keys, an old list and a new list. It is trying to detect new arrivals (that is, those who are in the new list but not in the old one). You would use the same algorithm if you were in charge of greeting people arriving at a party. Every now and then, you would look around and try to spot any new faces that you hadn't seen before. If you were organized, you would keep a list of those people you have seen, and then look out for people not on that list. If you look at the code, you should find that it is doing exactly that.

> **Sample Code: First Message Display** The MessageBoard project in the 02 First Message
> Display directory in the resources for this chapter contains a program that uses the Update method
> from this section to build and display a message from the keys that are pressed on the keyboard.

If you look closely at the code in Update, you find that at the end of the method, the value of
oldKeys is set to refer to the pressedKeys array so that the next time that Update is called,
it will have some old keys to check against. However, the very first time that Update is called,
there are no old keys. This problem has been solved by making oldKeys refer to an empty
array when the variable is declared:

```
// the keys that were pressed before - initially an empty array
Keys[] oldKeys = new Keys[0];
```

This declaration creates the oldKeys array reference and makes it refer to an array that
contains zero elements. The program must do this because the Update method uses this
reference to find the list of the keys that were pressed before. It turns out that this is a problem
only if there is a key pressed the very first time that Update is called, which is not normally the
case. However, I am confident that your younger brother would soon find this mistake.

> **The Great Programmer Speaks: Testing Is Vital** Our Great Programmer reckons that
> good testers are worth their weight in gold. She might not include your younger brother in this
> category, but she does say that people who are good at breaking programs are very valuable.
> You might not think of asking the question, "I wonder what would happen if we ran the program
> with a key already held down?" but it is useful if someone tries this before the program is actually
> given to customers. The Great Programmer even goes as far as rewarding people who find faults
> in her programs so that she can identify and fix mistakes before they become faults. When you
> start thinking about selling your games (and App Hub now makes this viable), it is useful to find
> a bunch of people like your younger brother and offer them a free soda for every new bug they
> find in the program.

Using *Break* to Improve Performance

The program that you've written works fine, but it's not as efficient as it could be. There's an
additional feature of C# that you can use to improve it. The C# language provides a key word
called break that you can use to abandon the execution of a loop. When you're searching
through oldKeys to see if it contains a key that is currently pressed, as soon as you find a
match, you need not look any further. You can use the break key word to break out of the
search loop, as shown in bold type here:

```
// work through each key in that was previously pressed
for (int j = 0; j < oldKeys.Length; j++)
{
    if (pressedKeys[i] == oldKeys[j])
```

```
    {
        // we found the key in the previously pressed keys
        foundIt = true;
        // no need to look any further
        break;
    }
}
```

If the program reaches the break instruction, it abandons the loop and continues running at the statement after the loop.

Decoding Key Characters

You can now detect individual key presses, which is nice. However, at the moment, the text you get from the keys is not as useful as you might like. The letter keys seem to work okay, but keys like Shift and the spacebar do not produce the output you want. Figure 9-5 shows what happens if you try to type in "Hello World." When you press Shift to get the uppercase characters, this is registered as a key, and the spacebar key doesn't work properly, either.

FIGURE 9-5 Some problems with typed text.

What you need to do next is decode the keys into more useful strings. If you get the value Keys.A, you'd like to have "A," and so on. You could use a large number of if statements to do this, but C# provides a better way of doing this, called a switch statement:

```
string keyString = ""; // initially this is an empty string
switch (pressedKeys[i])
{
    // digits
    case Keys.D0:
        keyString = "0";
        break;
    case Keys.D1:
        keyString = "1";
        break;
    // rest of digits here


    case Keys.A:
        keyString = "A";
        break;
    case Keys.B:
        keyString = "B";
        break;
    // rest of alphabet here

    // punctuation characters
    case Keys.Space:
        keyString = " ";
        break;
    case Keys.OemPeriod:
        keyString = ".";
        break;
}
```

The switch statement selects a particular case based on the value of a *control expression*. In this case, the control expression is pressedKeys[i], the value of the key you've discovered has just been pressed. Depending on this value, the code sets a string called keyString to the appropriate text. Once the string has been set, the code uses the C# break key word, causing the program to exit from the switch statement. You've seen break before when you used it to exit from a for loop. You can also use it to exit from a switch statement.

If the value in the control expression does not match any of the cases, the statement has no effect. The switch statement does not make anything possible that you couldn't do with a large number of if statements, but it does make programming easier in some situations.

Using the Shift Keys

If you use the previous code to decode your keys, you have a usable text reader, but at the moment, it doesn't use the Shift keys properly, so every letter that is typed is in uppercase.

However, it turns out that it's easy to fix this by adding the following code after your switch statement:

```
if (keyState.IsKeyUp(Keys.LeftShift) &&
    keyState.IsKeyUp(Keys.RightShift))
{
    keyString = keyString.ToLower();
}
```

I'm quite proud of this code. It tests the state of the two Shift keys on the keyboard. If both Shift keys are in the up position, the string that has been pressed is converted into the lowercase version of that text. This works because the string type provides a method called ToLower that provides a lowercase version of the string, which turns out to be exactly what you want. ToLower is clever in that it has no effect on characters other than letters, such as numbers and punctuation.

You could expand this code to allow the user to type in the shifted versions of the number keys. You could also create a flag variable to keep track of the Caps Lock key.

Editing the Text

The string type provides a huge number of methods that can be used to get a hold of processed versions of the string. It provides one called ToUpper, which produces a version of the string containing all uppercase letters; it also provides a method that can be used to chop out a certain number of characters from the string. You can use this to provide your user with simple text editing, as follows:

```
if (pressedKeys[i] == Keys.Back)
{
    if (messageString.Length > 0)
    {
        messageString = messageString.Remove(messageString.Length - 1);
    }
}
```

If the user presses the Back key, this code removes a key from the end of the messageString. It does this by using the Remove method, which removes characters from the end of the string. Remove is told the position to start removing from, so I give it the length of the string minus 1 to remove the last character. The code also checks to see if the length of the string is zero because if the string has zero length, there's nothing to remove.

The final enhancement that you need to add is the ability to take a new line in our string so that the user can create messages that are more than one line in size. A string can contain special *control characters* that control the layout of the text. The most useful of these is the newline character, which instructs whatever is processing the string to take a new line. It turns out that the DrawString method that you use to draw the text on the screen takes a new line when it sees this character in a message, so all you need to do is convert the Enter key (which users press when they want a new line on the display) into a newline character. The convention in C# strings is that a control character is preceded by the backslash character (\). The following `case` is added to your `switch` statement to convert the Enter key into a string that causes `DrawString` to take a new line:

```
case Keys.Enter:
    keyString = "\n";
    break;
```

C# provides other special formatting characters, but for now, you use only the newline character.

Sample Code: Message Board Program   The MessageBoard project in the 03 Full Message Display directory in the resources for this chapter contains a program that uses the previously mentioned code to implement a message display with a changing color background, 3-D text, and a clock.

Figure 9-6 shows the fully featured message board in action. The clock is always drawn on the line beneath the text.

FIGURE 9-6 A message board with clock.

You can experiment with the sample code for the Message Board program. You could try using different sizes of text to create different kinds of displays.

Conclusion

You now have a way that users can type text into your XNA program. This can be the basis of some interesting games, as you'll see in later chapters. You've also started to look at how data is stored and structured in C# programs and at the difference between value and reference types. You've used a new program structure, the switch statement, that lets a program select among a number of different options depending on the value of a particular expression. Finally, you've taken a look at the things you can do with strings.

Chapter Review Questions

And now the ever-popular chapter review. The questions are different, but the range of answers is still the same: true or false.

1. In XNA, a keyboard can register only one key at a time.

2. The Keys type holds a string.

3. There are separate Keys values for uppercase A and lowercase a.

4. The Keys type is an enumerated type.

5. A reference gives the location of an object in memory.

6. It's not possible for two references to refer to the same object in memory.

7. The garbage collector runs only when a program has finished.

8. The break key word causes your program to stop.

9. A switch statement is used to turn off the power to the computer.

10. The string class provides a method to produce an uppercase version of itself.

11. It's not possible to add two strings together.

Part III
Writing Proper Games

Chapter 10

Using C# Methods to Solve Problems

In this chapter, you will

- Use image manipulation to write a game you might like to play.
- Discover how to create and use your first C# methods.
- Take a look at test-driven development.
- Make some mistakes and discover how to fix them.

Introduction

Your programming skills are coming along. Your programs can store different kinds of numbers, do things with them, and even make decisions. You also know how to add image assets to your games and display them on the screen.

Now you create a game based on the image manipulation. To make your life easier, you create some C# methods of your own, and you also look at a development technique called *test-driven development*.

Playing with Images

In Chapter 4, "Displaying Images," you discovered how to load images into your programs. Now you can start to have some fun with them. Up until now, the image drawing that you performed simply displays a texture on the screen in the same place each time the Draw method is called. It would be really nice to be able to move the picture around the screen and maybe even zoom in on it. You might even find that these abilities give you an idea for a game.

Zooming In on an Image

When you wrote your image display program, you created a variable called jakeRect of type Rectangle. This rectangle was the destination of the draw action. The size of the rectangle was set to the full screen in the Initialize method, as follows:

```
protected override void Initialize()
{
    gameSpriteBatch = new SpriteBatch(graphics.GraphicsDevice);
    jakeRect = new Rectangle(
```

```
    0,    // X position of top left hand corner
    0,    // Y position of top left hand corner
    GraphicsDevice.Viewport.Width,    // rectangle width
    GraphicsDevice.Viewport.Height); // rectangle height

    base.Initialize();
}
```

When the Draw method ran, it drew the image texture in the jakeRect rectangle:

```
protected override void Draw(GameTime gameTime)
{
    graphics.GraphicsDevice.Clear(Color.CornflowerBlue);

    gameSpriteBatch.Begin();
    gameSpriteBatch.Draw(jakeTexture, jakeRect, Color.White);
    gameSpriteBatch.End();

    base.Draw(gameTime);
}
```

Now you change the way that the picture is drawn by changing the values in jakeRect as the program runs. XNA can resize the picture for you so that you can move and scale your picture very easily. You start by adding the following Update method to the display program:

```
protected override void Update(GameTime gameTime)
{
    // Allows the game to exit
    if (GamePad.GetState(PlayerIndex.One).Buttons.Back == ButtonState.Pressed)
        this.Exit();

    jakeRect.Height++;
    jakeRect.Width++;

    base.Update(gameTime);
}
```

Each time the Update method is called, the width and height fields of the rectangle are increased by one. These fields are the data members inside the rectangle that represent the rectangle dimensions. You get a hold of a field in an object by giving the identifier of the variable a period character (.) and then the name of the field you wish to use. Remember that this is the rectangle that describes where you want Jake to be drawn, so changing the size of this rectangle changes the size of the image on the screen.

Microsoft XNA does not care about the fact that you're "drawing off the screen" and simply shows you the part of the picture that fits on the screen. Figure 10-1 shows what the screen looks like after a program using this Update method has been running for a few seconds.

If you leave the program running a very long time, it only zooms in on a particular blade of grass, but it does show how you can change the way that images are placed on the screen.

FIGURE 10-1 Stretching Jake

Sample Code: Jake Zoom All the sample projects can be obtained from the Web resources for this text, which can be found at *http://oreilly.com/catalog/9780735651579*. The sample project in the 01 Jake Zoom directory in the resources for this chapter draws a picture of Jake and then slowly zooms in on it.

Game Idea: Super Zoom Out

You can use this zooming ability to create a game. Rather than starting with a picture and then zooming in on it, you could start with a zoomed image and slowly pull back (zoom out) to reveal more and more of the picture. The first person to correctly identify the picture wins the game. This game is quite fun, particularly if the images are ones that are familiar to the players.

Creating a Zoom-Out

The starting point of the game should be an enormous drawing rectangle that you reduce in size as the game continues, causing more and more of the image to be visible.

Updating the Drawing Rectangle

To make this work, you need to change the way that you set up the `Rectangle`, which describes the part of the image that you'll draw. Here's the code for that:

```
protected override void Initialize()
{
    gameSpriteBatch = new SpriteBatch(graphics.GraphicsDevice);
    jakeRect = new Rectangle(0, 0, 6000, 4500);

    base.Initialize();
}
```

This creates a rectangle that's 6,000 pixels wide and 4,500 pixels high, or 10 times the original image size and much bigger than the screen. Figure 10-2 shows the effect of using a rectangle like this. If you use this rectangle to control the draw process, the image is too large to fit on the display, so it shows only the upper-left corner.

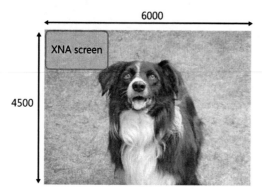

FIGURE 10-2 Jake in "Zoom"

The program then reduces the width and height of the rectangle each time `Update` is called:

```
protected override void Update(GameTime gameTime)
{
    // Allows the game to exit
    if (GamePad.GetState(PlayerIndex.One).Buttons.Back == ButtonState.Pressed)
        this.Exit();

    jakeRect.Height--;
    jakeRect.Width--;

    base.Update(gameTime);
}
```

The idea of this `Update` is that each time it's called, the width and height fields of the rectangle are reduced by one. This decreases the amount of zoom, meaning that more of the picture will be visible.

> **Sample Code: Jake Display Bad Zoom**   The sample project in the 02 JakeDisplay Bad Zoom
> Out directory in the resources for this chapter displays a zoomed-in image of Jake and then uses
> the Update method from this section to zoom out.

If you run the program, you find that although the zoom-out idea is a good one, the way it
behaves is not quite what you want. Figure 10-3 shows what happens after you've run this
program for a while.

FIGURE 10-3 Zooming out Jake, a first attempt

More of the picture is visible, but it seems to have been stretched for some reason.
To understand what's happening, you need to think first about what you set out to do.

1. You wanted to display only part of the image on the screen. This allows you to show
   only part of the image so that the player has to guess what the picture is.

2. To achieve this, you made the draw rectangle enormous by multiplying its width and
   height by 10 so that only part of the drawn image was visible on the screen.

3. You then created an Update method that reduces the width and height of this rectangle by
   one each time it is called so that the amount of image in the screen increases progressively.

4. You've noticed that as this program "zooms out" of the image, it no longer looks right.

The problem is that each time you reduce the width and height, you're reducing them by the same amount (that is, both the width and the height get smaller by one). Figure 10-4 shows the path followed by the lower-left corner of the Jake image if you repeatedly reduce the width and height of the picture by one each time.

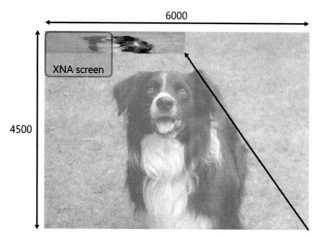

FIGURE 10-4 Zoom path behavior

The path does not follow the diagonal of the image; instead, it moves up too quickly and scrunches the height of the picture. This happens because you're reducing the height and width by the same amount each time. Because the picture is not as high (4,500) as it is wide (6,000), the height is "used up" more quickly, leading to a scrunched picture.

You can fix the problem by reducing each value by a percentage each time rather than by a particular value. For example, if you wanted to reduce the picture size by 1 percent, you would take 45 (1 percent of 4,500) off the height and 60 (1 percent of 6,000) off the width. This sounds a bit complicated, so let's ask the Great Programmer for advice.

The Great Programmer Speaks: Break Complicated Things Down   The Great Programmer thinks that it's always a good idea to break more complicated things down into smaller chunks using methods. She says there are three reasons to do this:

- It makes the programming simpler.

- Perhaps you can find someone else to do that task (or maybe a method already exists to do that).

- You might end up with methods that you can use in other parts of your program.

In this case, you want to reduce the sizes by a particular percentage, so a good starting point is a method that works out percentages.

Because the Great Programmer is never wrong, you now have to find out how to use methods to help you solve your problem.

Creating a Method to Calculate Percentages

A method is a block of code that does something for you. Each method has an identifier that you use to refer to the method when you call it.

Putting a Method into Your Game Class

You've seen methods many times before. Mr. Draw and Mrs. Update are methods that were written by the XNA team for you to use. Now you create a method of your own. This means that you need to provide a name (identifier) for the method and a way that the method can tell you the result. You also need to provide a list of instructions for the method to use when it's asked to run. Figure 10-5 shows how this might work. You've given the method the name getPercentage, and Mr. getPercentage now has a chair and a telephone in the Game1 office.

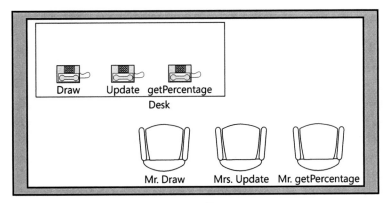

Game1 office

FIGURE 10-5 A new member of the *Game1* class

When the getPercentage telephone rings, Mr. getPercentage jumps up and answers it. He is told the number and the percentage required. He then needs to work out the answer, write it down on a piece of paper, and have the value sent back to the caller. The details of what information is passed into the method (the telephone call) and the result it delivers (what's written on the piece of paper) are written in C# as the method *header*. The details of what the method does is called the method *body*. Figure 10-6 shows how this would apply to a method called getPercentage.

This is not a very good getPercentage method in that it doesn't work out the result, but it does show how a C# method is made up of a header and a body.

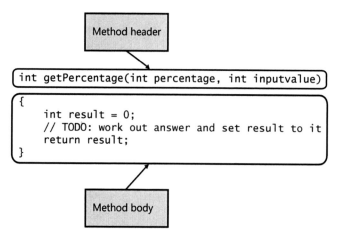

```
int getPercentage(int percentage, int inputvalue)
{
    int result = 0;
    // TODO: work out answer and set result to it
    return result;
}
```

Method header

Method body

FIGURE 10-6 A *getPercentage* method header and body.

The *method header* gives the identifier for the method, what type of result it returns, and the number and type of any parameters. A *parameter* is used to feed information into a method. It's how you told the Clear method the color to use when the screen was cleared way back in Chapter 1, "Computers, C#, XNA, and You." Once the compiler has the header of a method, it knows what the method "looks like" in that it can create the code to use the method. This description of a method is often called the *signature* of the method. The getPercentage method accepts two integer parameters and returns an integer result. When you create a method, you decide the type and number of the parameters that the method needs to do its job. Some methods have many parameters; others have none. The Initialize method does not accept any parameters; it's simply called to initialize the game program and does not need to be told anything.

The method header is followed by the method body, a block of statements that perform the task for which the method was created. The body can be a very large number of statements or only one or two. If the method delivers a result (which your getPercentage method needs to do), then the body must contain a statement that returns a value of the type specified in the method header. Once the compiler has the body of the method, it knows what statements need to be performed when the method is called. I've put a TODO in the place where the calculation needs to go. You haven't seen the return statement before, but it's the key word return, followed by the value the method is to send back to the caller.

Calling a Method

You've called methods many times in your programs. You use the getPercentage method as you would any other, but you need to make sure that you supply the right kinds of parameters, as follows:

```
height = height - getPercentage(1, height);
```

This line of code would use getPercentage to reduce the value of the variable called height by 1 percent. When a method call is made, the program does a number of things in sequence:

1. It makes a note of where it is in the program so that it can come back to the right place when the method finishes.

2. It gets the values of any parameters and sets them up for the method to use.

3. It jumps into the method body and performs the statements in the method body.

4. At the end of the method body, or when it reaches a return statement, it goes back and delivers whatever value was expected.

5. Then the program continues running at the statement following the method call.

Note You need to make sure that you call the method correctly. If you don't give the expected number of parameters, or one of them is not the correct type of data, the C# compiler shows you the errors and refuses to make a program that you can run.

Returning Nothing Using *void*

The getPercentage method must return a value, but sometimes a method need only perform a task. The Draw and Update methods are like this. Although they're given parameters to work on, they don't return an answer for the caller to use. Methods that don't return a result are given the return type void. This tells the compiler that the method does not deliver any information to the caller:

```
protected override void Draw(GameTime gameTime)
{
    graphics.GraphicsDevice.Clear(Color.CornflowerBlue);

    // game draw behavior here
    base.Draw(gameTime);
}
```

Methods that don't return anything don't have to contain a return key word to deliver a result. Instead, they return when the program reaches the end of the statements in the method body. Don't worry about the meaning of the protected and override key words.

If you want a method to return before the end of the method block, you can use the `return` key word to cause a return at that point. If the method returns a value, the `return` key word must be followed by an expression that delivers a value of the required type.

It's up to you whether a method you create returns a value. Most of the methods that I write do return something, usually whether or not the method has worked correctly.

Creating a *getPercentage* Method

At this point, you know how to create methods. Now you need to make one that works for you. You started with an "empty" `getPercentage` method:

```
int getPercentage(int percentage, int inputValue)
{
    int result = 0;
    // TODO: work out answer and set result to it
    return result;
}
```

This code shows how the method works, and this compiles and runs. However, because it always returns 0, it won't do what you want. You need to add statements to the method body to get it to behave as you want.

Testing a Method

At this point, you've created a version of `getPercentage` that doesn't work properly, and this seems a bit silly. The Great Programmer tells you that it's quite sensible to create "broken" methods like this; you can use them to decide what the method looks like and then go back and fill in the statements later. You can also use them to write tests, as follows:

```
protected override void Draw(GameTime gameTime)
{
    if ( getPercentage(10, 800) == 80 )
    {
        graphics.GraphicsDevice.Clear(Color.Green);
    }
    else
    {
        graphics.GraphicsDevice.Clear(Color.Red);
    }
    base.Draw(gameTime);
}
```

This code is a test of the `getPercentage` method that turns the screen green if a call of the method works and red if it doesn't. Programmers usually use better ways to perform these tests, but it demonstrates the principle. This is a version of a professional development technique called *test-driven development*.

> **The Great Programmer Speaks: Test-Driven Development Is the Best Way to Write Programs** The Great Programmer likes test-driven development even more than she likes shoe sales, which is to say, a lot. She says that creating tests and then writing program statements that pass the tests is a very good way to develop software. But she warns that you should design your tests carefully.

Designing Tests for *getPercentage*

You could easily write a version of getPercentage that would pass the previously mentioned single test:

```
int getPercentage(int percentage, int inputValue)
{
    return 80;
}
```

This method would pass the one test that you've created but would not be a very good way to work out percentages. It does highlight a very important point, though: A test can prove only that a particular fault is not present. It can't prove that there are no faults in the code at all. The test that you wrote checks that your method could work out that 10 percent of 800 is 80. Even the original method that always returned 0 would work whenever you tried to work out 0 percent of something or any percentage of 0. If programmers claim that their code is "fully tested," usually what they really mean is that they can't think of a reason it shouldn't work, and this is not quite the same thing.

Testing computer programs is really difficult. If you want to test a design for a bridge over a river, you simply make a test bridge and put increasingly heavy things on it until it breaks. Then you know the heaviest thing that can go across that kind of bridge. Where computers are concerned, it doesn't work like this. A computer program might work with one value and then fail with another, slightly different one.

The good news (for most of you at least) is that your programs won't ever do anything that could be called "mission critical." However, if you end up writing programs for a living, you should take testing very seriously. It's what separates the Great Programmers from the merely good programmers.

I've come up with some C# code that gives your method a reasonable workout. It is not a particularly comprehensive test, but it will do for now:

```
protected override void Draw(GameTime gameTime)
{
    if ( (getPercentage(0,      0) == 0)  &&   // 0 percent of 0
         (getPercentage(0,    100) == 0)  &&   // 0 percent of 100
         (getPercentage(50,   100) == 50) &&   // 50 percent of 100
         (getPercentage(100,  50) == 50) &&    // 100 percent of 50
         (getPercentage(10,  100) == 10) )     // 10 percent of 100
```

```
    {
        graphics.GraphicsDevice.Clear(Color.Green);
    }
    else
    {
        graphics.GraphicsDevice.Clear(Color.Red);
    }
    base.Draw(gameTime);
}
```

Note that I'm using the *&& (AND)* operator to combine a bunch of conditions. You've seen the || *(OR)* condition before. I used to test if one thing *or* another was true. The && condition lets me test if one thing *and* another is true. I want all the calls of getPercentage to work before I show the green screen. If any one of them fails, the && condition returns false, and you'll get a red screen. This is not a very sensible way to manage large numbers of tests because if you get a red screen in this scenario, you have difficulty working out which test has failed. However, the principle is an important one. The objective now is to create a version of getPercentage that passes all the previously mentioned tests.

Creating the *getPercentage* Method Body

You now have a design for the method header and a set of tests for the method, so now you must create the method body. You could make it work like this:

1. Calculate the fraction of the amount that you want (this is the percentage divided by 100; in other words, 50 percent would give you 50/100, which is a half).

2. Multiply the incoming amount by this fraction to create the result.

The getPercentage method that uses this technique looks like the code shown here:

```
int getPercentage(int percentage, int inputValue)
{
    int fraction = percentage / 100;

    int result = fraction * inputValue;

    return result;
}
```

First, you work out the fraction; then you do the multiplication. The / operator can be applied between two *operands* (things that operators work on) and performs a division. The * operator is applied in the same way but performs multiplication.

Remember that when the method runs, the parameters percentage and inputValue are set to the values that they have in the call of the method:

```
int test;
test = getPercentage (10, 800);
```

The previous call would be performed with percentage set to 10 and inputValue set to 800:

```
int fraction = 10 / 100;
int result = fraction * 800;
```

If you plug the figures in and do the sums by hand, the result comes out fine. When you use this version of the method, though, you get a red screen, which is not good. Something is broken, and you need to fix it.

> **Sample Code: Percentage Test** The sample project in the 03 Percentage Test directory in the resources for this chapter implements the Update method presented in this section. You won't ever use this project as the basis of a game, but you do use it to investigate the problems that you're having with the getPercentage method.

Debugging C# Programs

By now, you've probably started to wonder if zooming is worth all this effort. You've done lots of work and found out about methods, parameters, tests, and other stuff, but you have a red screen for your trouble. The good news is that the techniques you're learning are how all programs are written. The process of failing to get a picture of Jake to zoom properly is teaching you a lot about how programs are constructed. But now you need to learn some more things about how C# programs work and how to debug them.

Debugging with Breakpoints

You know that your program isn't working because the screen goes red when it runs. That means that at least one of the tests is failing. However, at the moment, you don't know which of the conditions is wrong. It would be really nice if you could stop the program and take a look at the values to see what's going on at that point. Fortunately, using the magic of XNA Game Studio you can do this by setting a breakpoint.

A *breakpoint* is a way of marking a particular statement in your program and saying to XNA Game Studio "When the program reaches this statement, pause it and let me take a look at stuff." This makes your game stop, so you use breakpoints not when you're playing the game, but only for debugging. Breakpoints are easy to set; you simply open the C# file in XNA Game Studio and click on the left margin in the position shown in Figure 10-7. XNA Game Studio highlights the line in brown, and a brown dot appears against the line. You want to stop the program when it has calculated a percentage, so the return statement is a good one to put the breakpoint on.

You can set lots of breakpoints in a program. The program stops at each one when it gets to that statement. Real programmers call this "hitting a breakpoint," so I suppose we should, too.

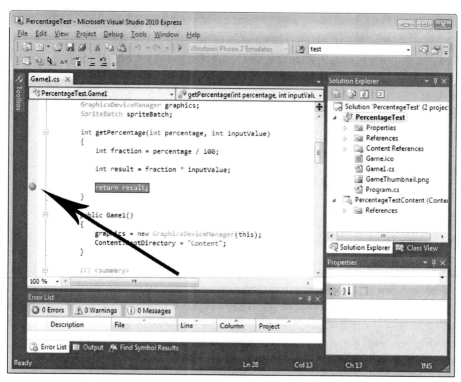

FIGURE 10-7 Setting a breakpoint in XNA Game Studio.

Hitting a Breakpoint

If you now run the program, you see that when it gets to the line that you've marked as a breakpoint, it stops. This works whether you're using a PC, an Xbox, or a Windows Phone for the development. This is impressive as a technical feat in that when you're using the Xbox or Windows Phone, you're controlling the program remotely from XNA Game Studio but I guess that today it's okay to take these things for granted. When your program hits the breakpoint, it stops and gives you the display shown in Figure 10-8.

Viewing Variables

Now that the program has stopped, you can look at the values of the variables and see what's gone wrong. This is very easy to do; you simply rest the mouse pointer over the identifier of the variable in the code that you're interested in. A box pops up and tells you the value in that variable, as shown in Figure 10-9, where I placed the cursor over the `fraction` variable.

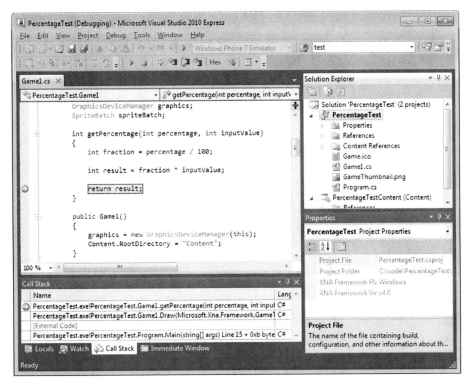

FIGURE 10-8 Hitting a breakpoint in XNA Game Studio.

```
      int result = fraction * inputValue;

      return result;
   }
                    result 0
```

FIGURE 10-9 Viewing a variable value in XNA Game Studio.

You can rest the cursor over any variable in the method to find out what it holds. If you do this the first time that the breakpoint is hit, all the values for `fraction`, `inputValue`, and `percentage` are 0. This is exactly what you'd expect. The very first call of `getPercentage` is as follows:

```
if ( (getPercentage(0,     0) == 0) & // 0 percent of 0
```

For these input values, the method is working correctly in that 0 percent of 0 is 0. It must be one of the later calls of `getPercentage` that's failing. This means that you need to run the program a bit further to find the problem. You can do this by pressing the green arrow in the program controls in the top left corner, as shown in Figure 10-10.

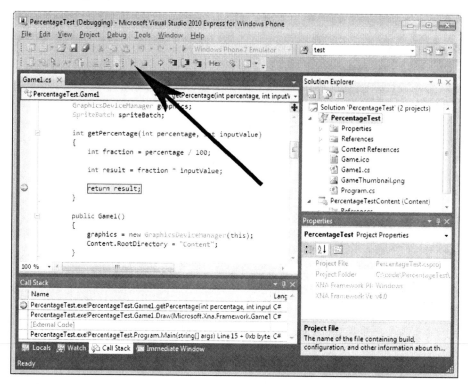

FIGURE 10-10 The continue button in the program controls

The program runs and hits the breakpoint again. This is the second call of getPercentage, which has been asked to work out 0 percent of 100. You can use the debugger to view the result value again, and you find that it is 0, which is correct. So you need to continue the program again. This time, you stop the third call of getPercentage, where you're trying to work out 50 percent of 100. This should work out to be half of 100, or 50. But when you use the debugger, you find that the result that's being calculated has the value of 0, which is wrong. If you dig a little further, you find that the value of fraction is also 0. This looks like the problem. If fraction is 0, when you work out the calculation fraction * inputValue, you get 0 because anything multiplied by 0 is 0. So you need to take a close look at how you calculate the value of fraction:

```
int fraction = percentage / 100;
```

The problem has to do with the int type, which is used to hold integer values. An integer does not have any fractional part. When you try to work out 50 / 100, which should work out to 0.5 or a half, there's no place in the variable fraction to put this. Integers are used to store values that do not have any fractional part. It's reasonable to use them to count pixels because there's no such thing as half a pixel as far as the display is concerned. C# is quite happy to divide an integer by an integer, but it always produces an integer result when it does this, throwing away the fractional part.

However, for your program, you need to manipulate numbers that have that fractional bit; otherwise, the program won't work. Such numbers are called *real* or *floating-point* numbers. Therefore, you need a new type of data storage that can hold this type of number.

Using Floating-Point Numbers in C#

C# provides a variety of number storage options. For this task, you need to use the float type, which can hold floating-point numbers. These are so called because they have a decimal point that can "float" up and down the number, depending on the value being held.

A floating-point number is capable of holding the 0.5 value that you need to store. So you change the type of the fraction variable to float in your method:

```
int getPercentage(int percentage, int inputValue)
{
    float fraction = percentage / 100;

    int result = fraction * inputValue;

    return result;
}
```

However, when you try to build this method, things go horribly wrong. You now get an error message, as shown in Figure 10-11, because your program no longer compiles. The compiler has found something wrong with the code that you've written, and it can't produce an output program that runs.

FIGURE 10-11 Build error message dialog box

This is quite often how programming is. You think you've found the answer to the problem, you put in the fix, and the problem promptly gets worse. The Great Programmer can tell many tales of bugs that she's found and fixed, and she has lots of experience with this kind of thing. She also has some good advice at this point.

The Great Programmer Speaks: Don't Let It Get to You When you get to a snag like this, don't panic. It's probably a good time to go off and get a cup of coffee, walk the dog, do 20 pushups, or do whatever else to relax. The important point to remember is that you will find an answer to the problem, you will make it work, and you will understand what's going on.

People tell me things like "I spent five hours last night trying to fix a bug in a program," as if that is supposed to impress me. Not so. If you can't fix it after an hour or so, you should go and do something else. It doesn't matter what that thing is; just don't think too hard about the problem while you do it. When you come back to the code, it's amazing how many times you can then fix the bug in an instant, as if the back of your brain has been working away on the problem, and suddenly up pops the answer for you.

The Compiler and C# Types

In this case, you're having problems because you don't know all about how C# works and what the compiler is having trouble with. If you go back and look at your method now that you have the error, you see that XNA Game Studio is trying to tell you something about the program. Some parts of the code are underlined in wavy blue lines. This indicates that the compiler is flagging some aspect of these statements for your attention. If you rest the cursor over the offending text, a message pops up that describes what the compiler has determined is wrong. Figure 10-12 shows what happens if you do this on your broken version of getPercentage.

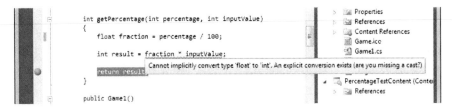

FIGURE 10-12 Compilation errors in getPercentage

The compiler is saying "Cannot implicitly convert type 'float' to 'int'. An explicit conversion exists (are you missing a cast?)." This is a technically correct description of the problem, but the compiler might as well be saying "Cannot put pizza in briefcase, but I can chop off a slice so it fits if you like" for all that this means at the moment. To understand what's going on, you need to get into the compiler and work out what the problem in the code really is.

The compiler has the job of converting the C# that you've written into instructions that the computer can perform. Consider a C# statement that performs an addition:

```
greenIntensity++;
```

This statement increases by one the value of the variable greenIntensity. The compiler might produce a sequence of machine code statements a bit like this:

1. Fetch the value of greenIntensity from memory.

2. Add 1 to this value.

3. Store the result in the greenIntensity memory location.

So you can think of a compiler as somewhat of a translator, only rather than converting from English to French, it's converting from C# into machine instructions. At the same time, the compiler tries very hard to stop a programmer from doing stupid things. In this case, it's telling you that your program might lose data as it is. If you try to put a floating-point value (with a fractional part, say, the value 2.9) into a variable of type int (which doesn't have support for the floating bit), you are in danger of losing information. The line of code that you're looking at does just that:

```
int result = fraction * inputValue;
```

From your knowledge of math, you know that that if you multiply an integer value (inputValue) by a floating-point value (fraction), the result is a floating-point value. When you move that into the result, you're moving a floating-point value into an integer, which results in data loss. In programming terms, this is called *narrowing*. You're moving values from a data type with a wide range of values (floating point) into a type with a narrower range of values (integer). This is rather like trying to sail a high-masted sailboat under a low bridge. There's a danger that something might get chopped off in the process. You'd be heading for exactly the same trouble if you tried to put the value of an integer variable into a byte. The C# compiler has been designed to look for situations like this, where data might be lost by mistake, and to refuse to perform the conversion automatically.

Compilers and Casting

When the compiler sees a statement that narrows a value, it produces the error message, "Cannot implicitly convert type 'float' to 'int'." What it's saying is that the compiler won't produce output steps that perform the conversion unless you explicitly ask it to. This is because it thinks you might have made a mistake when you combined these two types.

The next part of the message gives you some more help. "An explicit conversion exists (are you missing a cast?)." This means that the compiler can perform such a conversion, but you need to use a cast to request that the action be performed. A *cast* is where you ask the compiler to produce code that converts a value from one type to another. You're saying, "We know what we're doing, so trust us on this and let the conversion take place." The cast you want looks like this:

```
int result = (int)(fraction * inputValue);
```

A cast is the name of the type you want (in parentheses). It precedes the value to be cast, which in this situation is the entire sum, which I've also put in parentheses. Now the compiler is quite happy to perform the narrowing since you've said that it's okay to do so.

Note that not all casts work. You can't convert from a Color to an int by using a cast because the compiler hasn't been told how to generate code to do this. For casting from floating point to integer, though, the compiler knows just what to do. It generates code to throw away the fraction and put the integer part into the destination. This means that if what you are casting were 0.999999, the destination would be set to 0, something you might need to watch out for later. So, after all that, you now have a new, improved version of the method:

```
int getPercentage(int percentage, int inputValue)
{
    float fraction = percentage / 100;

    int result = (int)(fraction * inputValue);

    return result;
}
```

This version of the method compiles, so you can now run the program with your bug fix. And you get your red screen again—which seems very unfair.

Expression Types

At this point, you might be thinking that programming is not for you. Nothing seems to work. You started off trying to draw a picture on the screen. You got that working and decided to do some zooming, only to find that you need to do some serious messing about to make the picture stay the same shape. And it still doesn't work. If you put in some breakpoints and do some more digging, you'll find that the problem occurs when you work out the fraction:

```
float fraction = percentage / 100;
```

Even though you're storing the result of the division in a floating-point variable, for some reason the calculation is generating a result of 0 when you divide 50 by 100. You can blame the compiler again for this one. The compiler has the job of converting operators like / (divide) into the instructions that perform the division. There are two kinds of division: those that produce an integer result and those that produce a floating-point result. If the compiler sees an expression that divides an integer by another integer, it performs the integer division even if the result is being put into a floating-point variable.

There is actually method in this madness. You want your programs to run as fast as possible, and calculating the fractional portion of the result takes extra time, so it makes sense not to do the full division if you don't need to. However, you need to force the compiler to perform floating-point division, and the way you do that is to turn one of the things in the calculation into a floating-point value. You can do this by casting again:

```
float fraction = (float) percentage / 100;
```

This forces the compiler to regard the percentage variable as floating point so that it uses a floating-point division to get the correct result. This means that your getPercentage method now looks like this:

```
int getPercentage(int percentage, int inputValue)
{
    float fraction = (float) percentage / 100;

    int result = (int)(fraction * inputValue);

    return result;
}
```

If you put this into your program and run it, you find that you have a green screen. This means that this version of the method seems to work with the tests that you've created. So at this point, you can feel very pleased with yourself. You show your code to the Great Programmer. She wrinkles her nose, sits down at the keyboard, and types this:

```
int getPercentage(int percentage, int inputValue)
{
    return (inputValue * percentage) / 100;
}
```

This works fine as well and is much simpler than your version, which is annoying. However, both methods work okay, and unless you're performing many thousands of calls to your method, the user won't notice the difference between yours and the Great Programmer's. And anyway, you learned a lot writing your method, so there. The Great Programmer even has a point about this.

The Great Programmer Speaks: Don't Get Upset with Other Programmers If you end up writing programs for a living, you'll come up against programmers who are better than you (who you copy) and worse than you (who you help). It's important not to get upset when another programmer suggests a better way of doing something, finds something wrong with your code, or says something stupid. My experience has been that I am wrong as often as I am right, and the nicer I am about these situations, the more people want to work with me. Try to work in an "egoless" way if you can; it makes everyone happier in the long run. That's not to say that you shouldn't argue your corner when you think your ideas or opinions are the best way forward, but if the argument goes against you, accept this in good grace. In any project, what you're really working toward is a "happy ending." There are many ways you can get to the ending—just make sure that you get there happy.

Sample Code: Working Jake Zoom Program The sample project in the 04 Working Jake Zoom directory in the resources for this chapter uses the GetPercentage method that the Great Programmer wrote for us. It steadily zooms out of a picture of Jake. It is by no means a perfect program, though, because the picture gets smaller than the screen size and eventually stops zooming.

Stopping the Zoom

You need to find a way to stop the zoom when the image is the same size as the screen. It turns out that this is quite easy. You need only change the size of the sprite rectangle while it's wider than the screen. You've already seen that you can use the `Width` property of the device viewport to determine this value, so you simply need to add a condition as follows:

```
if (jakeRect.Width > graphics.GraphicsDevice.Viewport.Width)
{
    jakeRect.Width =
        jakeRect.Width - getPercentage(1, jakeRect.Width);
    jakeRect.Height =
        jakeRect.Height - getPercentage(1, jakeRect.Height);
}
```

The program now stops zooming, reducing the height and width of the drawing rectangle at the appropriate time.

Zooming from the Center

The zoom that you have at the moment starts off as zoomed in on the upper-left corner of the image. This is because when you create `jakeRect`, you set its position to (0, 0), which is the upper-left corner of the screen. Figure 10-13 shows what's happening. The upper-left corner of the image is being displayed because the rectangle is positioned at the upper-left corner of the display area.

FIGURE 10-13 Zooming in on the upper-left corner of the image.

If you want to zoom in on the center of the image, you need to move the upper-left corner of the draw rectangle up and to the left, as shown in Figure 10-14, moving the display area into the middle of the image. Remember that XNA draws only the part of the rectangle starting at coordinate position (0, 0) and extending to the width and height of the screen's display area.

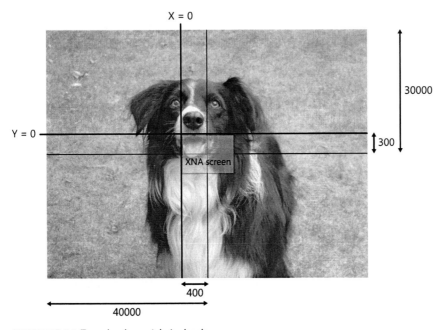

FIGURE 10-14 Zooming in on Jake's cheek.

The thin lines on Figure 10-14 show both the center of the image of Jake and the center of the display area. To get the center of the image lined up exactly with the center of the display area, you must move the X (horizontal) position of the upper-left corner of the rectangle 40,000 (half the image width) to the left and then 400 (half the screen width) to the right. You then need to do the same thing with the Y (vertical) position. For the method to work properly, it has to know the width of the texture that is to be used, so all the work must be performed in the LoadContent method, as follows:

```
protected override void LoadContent()
{
    // Create a new SpriteBatch, which can be used to draw textures.
    spriteBatch = new SpriteBatch(GraphicsDevice);

    jakeTexture = this.Content.Load<Texture2D>("jake");

    int displayWidth = GraphicsDevice.Viewport.Width;
    int displayHeight = GraphicsDevice.Viewport.Height;

    int scaledWidth = jakeTexture.Width * 10;
    int scaledHeight = jakeTexture.Height * 10;
```

```
jakeRect = new Rectangle(
    -(scaledWidth / 2) + (displayWidth / 2),
    -(scaledHeight / 2) + (displayHeight / 2),
    scaledWidth, scaledHeight);
}
```

To make this code clearer, I've created some extra variables that hold the width and height of the scaled image and the width and height of the display area. Note that you can make a number (or an expression) negative simply by putting a minus sign in front of it.

Now that you've put the viewing rectangle in the center of the screen, you need to move the draw position each time you scale the image. It turns out that if the width of the rectangle changes by X-amount, the position of the upper-left corner must move to the right by half of X to keep the rectangle centered with respect to the display area. The code to do this is as follows:

```
int widthChange = getPercentage(1, jakeRect.Width);
int heightChange = getPercentage(1, jakeRect.Height);
jakeRect.Width = jakeRect.Width - widthChange;
jakeRect.Height = jakeRect.Height - heightChange;
jakeRect.X = jakeRect.X + (widthChange / 2);
jakeRect.Y = jakeRect.Y + (heightChange / 2);
```

This code works out the change in width, updates the width and height of the rectangle, and then moves the X and Y positions of the rectangle to keep the drawing centered correctly. To get a good understanding of what's happening here, you can try some values and sketch some diagrams based on Figure 10-14. I often find it very useful to draw out what needs to happen on graph paper (that's how I worked out what the previous code must do).

> **Sample Code: Broken Jake Center Zoom Program** The sample project in the 05 Broken Jake Center Zoom directory in the resources for this chapter uses the code given so far in this section to zoom out of the picture and keep it in the center. The name doesn't particularly inspire confidence, though, and when you run it, you find that it doesn't work properly.

The problem with this zoom program is that although it works fine, when the zoom finishes, the image is not lined up properly with the display. If you add some breakpoints and do some digging, you find that the X and Y draw positions, which should be 0 when you've fully zoomed out of the image, still hold negative values at the end of the zoom. The problem lies with the following two statements:

```
jakeRect.X = jakeRect.X + (widthChange / 2);
jakeRect.Y = jakeRect.Y + (heightChange / 2);
```

You know that you want to move these positions by half the change in the width and height. Unfortunately, you're dividing integers. This means that you can get only an integer result; in other words, if the width change were 101, the change to the value of X would be 50, not 50.5. This calculation is repeated many times, and eventually this lack of precision leads to an answer that's incorrect. The only way to solve this problem is to change the data type you're using to hold all the values. Rather than using the integer values that are stored in the jakeRect, you need to create floating-point variables and use them instead. Floating-point values have a fractional part, meaning that they are better for representing a smooth transition from one coordinate to another. Here are the updated variable declarations:

```
float displayWidth;
float displayHeight;
float rectWidth;
float rectHeight;
float rectX;
float rectY;
```

These variables are set up by the LoadContent method. The new variables are used in all the calculations and are transferred into the jakeRect to position the drawing as follows:

```
float widthChange = getPercentage(1, rectWidth);
rectWidth = rectWidth - widthChange;
rectX = rectX + (widthChange / 2);

float heightChange = getPercentage(1, rectHeight);
rectHeight = rectHeight - heightChange;
rectY = rectY + (heightChange / 2);

jakeRect.Width = (int)rectWidth;
jakeRect.Height = (int)rectHeight;
jakeRect.X = (int)rectX;
jakeRect.Y = (int)rectY;
```

> **Sample Code: Float Jake Center Zoom Program** The sample project in the 06 Float Jake Center Zoom directory in the resources for this chapter uses floating-point values to keep track of the size and position of the draw rectangle. Note that it also contains a floating-point version of getPercentage.

It's not uncommon for games—and indeed other programs—to have problems with the precision of numeric calculations. The float and double data types provided by C# can hold numbers to very high levels of precision, but you need to remember that updates to the variables in games may take place many millions of times a second. Errors in values that build up over time, sometimes called *cumulative errors*, are something that programmers often need to address.

Conclusion

This has been another very busy chapter. You began with a simple idea for a game and then got diverted into program design and structure. You made your first simple method, which worked on numbers that you gave it and returned a result. You also looked at the test-driven programming technique, which you can use to make sure the methods you create work correctly. Finally, you saw how to manage the draw position of an item on the screen and discovered why game programs need to use values stored to high levels of precision.

Chapter Review Questions

If chapter reviewing is what you want to do, you've come to the right place. See if you can outperform a penny with heads for true and tails for false.

1. You use an XNA Rectangle to draw a texture on the screen.

2. Only the creators of XNA are allowed to make methods.

3. Methods are created inside classes.

4. The body of a method is made up of C# statements.

5. Methods must return a result.

6. A method can contain only one return.

7. A method must have at least one parameter.

8. The C# compiler automatically fills in the value of any missing parameters when a method is called.

9. Test-driven development means that you do all the testing when the program is finished.

10. You can set breakpoints only when your program is not running.

11. The C# compiler automatically converts a float value into an int value.

12. The C# compiler lets you move an integer into a double precision variable.

13. A cast requests that data be converted from one type into another.

14. You can cast a string into an integer.

Chapter 11
A Game as a C# Program

In this chapter, you will

- Find out how Microsoft XNA games are actually C# programs.

- Start to create a game from the contents of a grocery bag.

- Make your game display fit correctly on the screen.

- Get the first components of a game running.

Introduction

At the moment, you know quite a lot about how XNA works and how to use C# language constructions to control the facilities that XNA gives you. You have created games by investigating what you need to do inside the game class to get the effects that you want on the screen. Now it's time to step back a little and consider how the XNA Framework and the C# language fit together and just what a C# program is. This helps you understand how to construct games of your own and also how you can make programs other than games. If you like, you can think of this as "lifting the hood" on the C# process and looking at how the engine and transmission work underneath. You consider what makes up a C# program and how it is started and given control.

To do this, you create a brand-new game from scratch, using the contents of a grocery bag. You start by creating some simple game behaviors and then combine them until you get something that might be fun to play.

> ### Game Idea: Bread and Cheese
>
> Game ideas are tricky things. The way I see it, there are two ways that you can make a great game:
>
> You can wake up one morning with the idea perfectly formed in your head and then sit down and write the game program. Alternatively, you can start off playing with a few pieces of program code and then tinker with them until you get something interesting.

You take the second approach for your game, using as your inspiration the contents of a grocery bag. The Great Programmer has been out getting some food and has come back with some bread, some cheese, some tomatoes, and a green pepper. She wonders if you might like to use these things in your game. She suggests that you get the cheese bouncing around the screen, maybe add the bread as a bat to hit the cheese around, and see where this takes you. For now, you decide to call the game BreadAndCheese and to find a use for the tomatoes and peppers later.

Creating Game Graphics

In a large-scale game development, you have the graphics created for you by the art department, but for this one, we are going to do all the work ourselves. I created the graphics for the game by taking a well-lit picture of each item against a white background. I then cut the central image out of the picture and pasted it onto a transparent background (see Figure 11-1). To do this, I used a free graphics editing program called "Paint.NET," which can be downloaded from *www.getpaint.net*. I then ate the cheese on the bread, and it was delicious. If you want to do something similar to create your game objects, it's very easy. You could use model cars, candy, toy soldiers, or anything else that's easy to photograph. When you take the pictures, ensure that the objects are as evenly lit as possible; ideally, take the pictures outside on a cloudy day. If you have a friend who is good with a camera, you might like to ask your friend to give you a hand.

FIGURE 11-1 Your game objects.

You add these images to the project in the same way that you added Jake to your first image-drawing program in Chapter 4, "Displaying Images."

Projects, Resources, and Classes

You start by making a new game project using XNA Game Studio and call the project BreadAndCheese. Before you go any further, it's worth spending some time discovering how an XNA program fits together and actually gets to run. You can use this knowledge to tidy up your solution and allow you to understand better how C# programs are structured.

XNA Game Studio Solutions and Projects

You know that when you make a new project, XNA Game Studio creates a solution, a project, and some C# class files. Figure 11-2 shows how these appear in Solution Explorer. Some programmers call a solution a *workspace,* but I am going to use the word *solution* throughout this book.

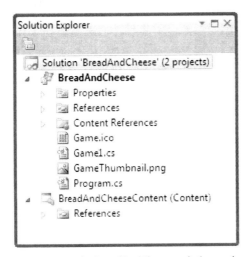

FIGURE 11-2 The BreadAndCheese solution and projects

In Chapter 4, you saw that when you create a new project, you get a new solution as well. An XNA Game Studio solution can contain a number of projects. Each project brings together C# program source files and resources. A brand new game solution contains two projects. One of these is the game code and the other is the content, such as images, sounds, and so on, that the game uses.

Projects and Folders

Whenever you write a program, you need to consider how things will be organized. At the moment, all the files related to a particular game program are stored in a single directory in the file store of the PC. You should be familiar with using directories, or *folders* as they are sometimes called. Microsoft Windows provides folders for your documents and pictures so that you can group documents and pictures together easily. When XNA Game Studio creates a new XNA project, it makes a new folder that holds all the information for a particular solution. This folder contains other folders, reflecting the way that XNA Game Studio organizes things.

Because you're about to add a whole bunch of image files to the BreadAndCheese project, it makes sense to put these all together in a particular place in the content project. You can get XNA Game Studio to create such a location. You create an images folder and put all the images into it. When you add sound to the game, you can then put all the sounds in a different place, thus keeping everything nice and tidy.

> **The Great Programmer Speaks: Tidy Is Good** If you take a peek at the Great Programmer's desk, you might notice what a mess it is. There are bits and pieces everywhere, used concert tickets, old photos, and even the occasional stuffed toy. However, if you look inside the organization of her projects, you find everything perfectly tidy, with images in graphics folders, sounds in audio folders, and all items having a name that reflects exactly what it is used for. She reckons she does not have time to keep her desk tidy (and actually doesn't particularly want to), but she knows that keeping her project and resource files well organized pays huge dividends when she needs to find something important.

Figure 11-3 shows how you can use XNA Game Studio to create a new content folder. Start by right-clicking the Content item in the BreadAndCheeseContent project in the Solution Explorer and find your way to the New Folder option as shown.

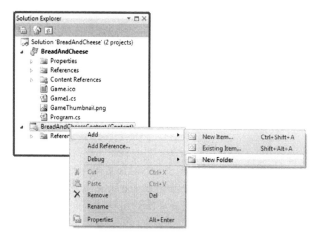

FIGURE 11-3 Creating a new content folder in XNA Game Studio

XNA Game Studio creates a new folder with the original name New Folder. You can overtype this with a more appropriate name; I'd suggest Images. Once you've created the new directory, it takes its place in Solution Explorer for the project, as shown in Figure 11-4.

FIGURE 11-4 The new Images folder in Solution Explorer

This has created a new directory, and the next step is to get your image files and put them into that directory. You can do this in exactly the same way as you added the picture of Jake in Chapter 4, only rather than adding them to the Content directory, you can add them to the Images directory instead. Figure 11-5 shows how this should appear once two image files have been added.

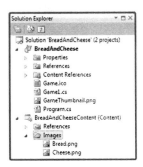

FIGURE 11-5 An Images folder with Bread and Cheese images in it

The Content Manager needs to be told to look in the folder for the resource when it tries to load it. This means that the name of the folder holding the resource must be used when it is loaded, as shown in the LoadContent method here:

```
protected override void LoadContent()
{
    // Create a new SpriteBatch, which can be used to draw textures.
    spriteBatch = new SpriteBatch(GraphicsDevice);

    breadTexture = Content.Load<Texture2D>("Images/Bread");
    cheeseTexture = Content.Load<Texture2D>("Images/Cheese");
}
```

The name of the folder is given, separated from the asset name by the forward slash / character. It is perfectly possible to create folders inside folders, so that you could have a folder inside Images that contained backgrounds, another that contained enemy sprites, and so on. The Great Programmer thinks this kind of organization is a really good idea. It is particularly useful if you have different teams working on the same game project and you don't want to have problems with name clashes.

The Game Program Files

Now that you know how best to organize the assets in a game, it is time to take a look at the program files that XNA Game Studio has created for you.

You're already familiar with the Game1.cs file, which contains the program that provides all the game behaviors, including the Update and Draw methods. However, this is not where your program starts running. To discover how this happens, you need to look in the Program.cs source file.

The Program.cs File

The Program.cs file is created automatically by XNA Game Studio when you make a new game project. You don't have to change this file, but the Great Programmer (who is at the moment rather cross because I seem to have eaten all the cheese that she bought) reckons that you really should know how programs work if you're going to call yourself a programmer. If you take a look at the Program.cs file in XNA Game Studio, you find that it's quite small:

```
using System;

namespace BreadAndCheese
{
#if WINDOWS || XBOX
    static class Program
    {
        /// <summary>
        /// The main entry point for the application.
        /// </summary>
        static void Main(string[] args)
        {
            using (Game1 game = new Game1())
            {
                game.Run();
            }
        }
    }
}
#endif
```

The job of the C# code in this file is to create an instance of the game class and then start the game running. A C# program is started by the call to the program's `Main` method. You can see the `Main` method in the `Program` class shown previously, but there are also some words that you have not seen before, and now you must consider what they mean.

> **Note** You may notice that this code uses conditional compilation to ensure that the Program class is only created for XBOX and WINDOWS systems. We first saw conditional compilation in Chapter 6 in the section, "Adding Test Code". There we used conditional compilation to allow us to add test code to our programs and then switch this test code off when we create the final program. The reason for the use of conditional compilation here is that the Windows Phone operating system starts XNA games in a slightly different way. For the rest of this section we are going to consider the way that Xbox and the Windows PC do things.

Namespaces and Programs

At the top of the Program.cs file, there's the statement that tells the compiler to use the `System` namespace:

```
using System;
```

The word `using` has two meanings in C#. In this statement, it's used as a *compiler directive*. In other words, it's a message to the compiler and doesn't directly generate machine language instructions for the program the compiler is creating. You use directives to tell the compiler what to do. In this case, you want to tell the compiler to use the `System` namespace.

A *namespace* is a space where names have meaning. You can think of it as a directory of services. The `System` namespace contains descriptions of lots of classes provided by .NET that you might want to use in your program. You've already used one class from the `System` namespace; the `DateTime` class is described there. You used this to obtain the current time for the clock, as described in the section entitled "Getting the Date and Time," in Chapter 5, "Writing Text."

Whenever you use a name that the compiler hasn't seen before, it looks in all the namespaces that it has been told about to see if it can find a resource that matches that name. If the name is found, the compiler generates code that uses that resource. If the name is not found, the compiler states that it doesn't know about the item. As an example, consider what would happen if your program contained the following statement:

```
dateTime d;
```

The statement is intended to create a DateTime variable, but the name has not been typed correctly. When the program is compiled, this statement produces the following compilation error:

```
Error   1       The type or namespace name 'dateTime' could not be found (are you missing a
using directive or an assembly reference?)
```

The compiler is saying that it can't find anything called dateTime. It even suggests that you might need to add a using directive to identify the namespace that holds this item. (Of course, in this case it is wrong, in that you have misspelled something, rather than forgotten to tell the compiler where to look for it—but at least the compiler is trying to help).

As far as programmers are concerned, a namespace is a way they can make sure that when they invent an identifier for an object, it's unique in their namespace and won't be confused with an identically named resource in any other namespace. In fact, the next line of Program.cs sets up a namespace for your solution:

```
namespace BreadAndCheese
{
    // Program class in here
}
```

XNA Game Studio automatically creates a namespace to hold all your classes. The namespace is given the same name as the solution. If other C# programmers want to refer to the Game1 class that is in your namespace, they could insert using BreadAndCheese at the top of their program source files. If you use two namespaces that contain a class with identical names, the compiler asks you to use the fully qualified form of the name, as in this example:

```
BreadAndCheese.Game1 myGame = new BreadAndCheese.Game1();
```

A *fully qualified* name includes the namespace in which the object is declared, followed by the name of the class required.

A namespace can contain other namespaces, so programmers can build a tree of namespaces that can be used to hold different categories of resources. The designers of XNA have created several namespaces that describe resources you've used in your programs. The using directives at the top of Game1.cs include the following:

```
using System;
using System.Collections.Generic;
using System.Linq;
using Microsoft.Xna.Framework;
using Microsoft.Xna.Framework.Audio;
using Microsoft.Xna.Framework.Content;
using Microsoft.Xna.Framework.GamerServices;
using Microsoft.Xna.Framework.Graphics;
using Microsoft.Xna.Framework.Input;
using Microsoft.Xna.Framework.Input.Touch;
using Microsoft.Xna.Framework.Media;
```

The features of XNA that you've used are described in appropriate namespaces; for example, the Texture2D class is described in the Microsoft.XNA.Graphics namespace.

> **Note** It's important to remember that the namespace information is used by the compiler to identify the resources that are to be used. The resources themselves are loaded and used when the program runs and your solution must have a reference to them. A solution contains a list of references that it is using; you can see the References folder in Figure 11-2, just above the Content folder.

You'd create namespaces of your own if you wanted to use some classes in more than one solution. For example, you might create some classes that deal with high scores in a game. For this, you might create a HighScores namespace that stores and displays a high-score table.

Static Classes and Methods

The next line in Program.cs describes a class called Program:

```
static class Program
{
    // content of the class goes here
}
```

The class has been made static. You haven't seen the word static before, but it means "always there." In the programs you've written up until now, you've had to create instances of classes using new. When a class is made static, it means that there's always one and only one instance of that class present when the program is running. When a C# program starts up, before the code that you've written is given control, any static classes are created automatically. This means that there's no need to ever create an instance of the Program class by using new because it's always there when your program starts.

The next line of the program declares a method called Main in the Program class:

```
static void Main(string[] args)
{
    // content of the Main method goes here
}
```

The Main method has also been made static. This is because it must exist before your program begins to run. When you run a C# program, the operating system loads the program file into memory, creates all the static classes, and then finds and calls the Main method. One and only one of the classes in a program must contain a Main method so that the operating system knows where to start. Imagine you misspell the name of the method, for example you write the following:

```
static void main(string[] args)
{
    // content of the Main method goes here
}
```

The compiler produces an error message saying that the program cannot be started, as follows:

```
Program 'BreadAndCheese.exe' does not contain a static 'Main' method suitable for an
entry point
```

The compiler is trying to make an executable output (one that can be run as a program), and if the Main method isn't present, it literally doesn't know where to start the program.

Making Methods Static

Methods are made static so that they can be used without needing to have an instance of the class present. Static methods can be ones that are used to perform a particular task and are not part of a class instance. The getPercentage method that you created in Chapter 10, "Using C# Methods to Solve Problems," could be made static because it simply works out a calculation and returns the result.

Main Method Parameters

When the Main method is called to start the program, it's provided with a parameter called args, which is an array of strings. This parameter gives the Main method any arguments that have been supplied to the program when it starts. An argument is a way of giving a program instructions when it runs. If a program is run from the command prompt (in other words, you type in a command to make the program run), you can provide arguments simply by typing them after the program command. For example, the Windows command del (for delete) is followed by a list of arguments that give the names of the files that are to be deleted, like this:

```
del notes.txt oldImage.png
```

In this case, a program that implements the delete behavior is provided with two strings, which are the names of two files to be deleted. Because XNA games are usually started from within Windows or directly by the target device, you won't be providing arguments to the Main method, so you can ignore these parameters.

The C# *Using* Statement

The Program.cs file contains a second use of the keyword using. This is a bit confusing because I've just described using, but this is a different use of the same keyword. Previously, you saw that using was a directive to the compiler meaning, "Look in here if you want to find out about something." Once you get inside the C# program itself, however, the word has a different meaning: "Use this object and then dispose of it when you are finished." It's a way of explicitly telling the run-time system how long you need an object. You've seen that the garbage collector is continuously searching for objects that it can remove from memory. If you want to speed up this process and make sure that an object is disposed of as soon as the program has finished with it, an object should be used within a block of code following a using statement.

As an example, consider how you'd use a class called HugeObjectUsedForSums in this program:

```
using ( temp = new HugeObjectUsedForSums() )
{
    // do things with temp to work out the answer
}
```

You need to make an instance of HugeObjectUsedForSums to perform some calculations, after which you want it removed as quickly as possible. The previous code does this. As soon as the program leaves the block following the using statement, the system knows that temp is no longer required, and the resources that it uses can be recovered.

The *Main* Method in an XNA Game

In an XNA game, the job of the Main method is to create an instance of the Game1 class and then make it run. Look at the following code:

```
static void Main(string[] args)
{
    using (Game1 game = new Game1())
    {
        game.Run();
    }
}
```

The designers of XNA wanted to make sure that the instance of the game class created to run the game is destroyed as soon as it's no longer needed, so they place it within a block of code after a using statement.

The Run method runs your game. When Run is called, it calls the Initialize and LoadContent methods and then repeatedly calls the Update and Draw methods. When the game finishes, the Run method ends, the game class is destroyed, and the program finishes.

Renaming the *Game1* Class

The Great Programmer doesn't like using the names that XNA Game Studio creates. She suggests that rather than calling the game class Game1, you might want to call it something else, perhaps BreadAndCheeseGame. This make it easier for other people to understand what your program does. At the moment, the Game1 class is held in a file called Game1.cs. The C# language doesn't insist that the file and the class it holds have the same name, but it would seem sensible to make the two names line up.

You can rename the Game1.cs file from within XNA Game Studio. One way to do this is to right-click the filename in Solution Explorer and select Rename from the menu that appears, as shown in Figure 11-6.

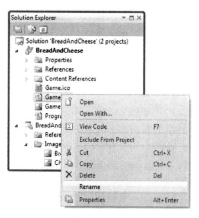

FIGURE 11-6 The Rename command for a source file.

When you select Rename, you can type a new name, as shown in Figure 11-7.

FIGURE 11-7 Renaming a class file.

You need to make sure that you don't remove the ".cs" from the end of the filename. This is the filename extension, and it is how XNA Game Studio and the rest of Windows know that the file contains a C# program. One really nice feature of XNA Game Studio is that when you finish typing the new name and press Enter, the dialog box shown in Figure 11-8 appears.

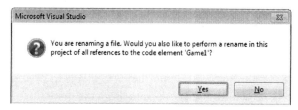

FIGURE 11-8 Renaming a class globally.

XNA Game Studio detects that you're renaming the file and offers to rename the class throughout all your files for you. To accept this useful offer, you simply click OK, and the Game1 class is now renamed BreadAndCheeseGame in all your source files. This renaming process is a lot subtler than you might think. The class is renamed in the BreadAndCheeseGame.cs file and also where it's used in the Program.cs file.

> **The Great Programmer Speaks: Refactoring Is Good** What you've done is called "refactoring," which means changing the code you've written to make it better. If you find that a block of statements needs to be made into a method, you can use the refactoring support in XNA Game Studio to do this for you. If you invent a better name for a variable than the one that you originally came up with, you also can use XNA Game Studio to change the name for you. Before we had tools like XNA Game Studio, it was very difficult to do this, so programmers tended to be stuck with bad decisions made at the beginning of a project. Today, it's very easy to make these changes. The Great Programmer is very keen on refactoring; she says that as you write a program, your understanding of the problem improves, and you'll need to make these changes.

You can access the refactoring support in XNA Game Studio by selecting the item you want to refactor and right-clicking the selection. You can then select Refactor from the menu that appears. Of course, you can rename only the items that you've created yourself; for example, it would not be sensible to try to rename the Update method.

Creating Game Objects

Now that you have a good understanding of your classes and how a game program fits together, you can start making objects to be used in your game. You begin with the graphical items to be drawn on the screen. To start, you draw the cheese and make it move, and then you implement the bread bat.

Sprites in Games

Graphical objects in a game are often called *sprites*. A sprite can be a very small image, such as a spaceship viewed from far away, a missile, or a piece of cheese. It can also be very large. The background of your screen can be a single sprite. Sprites have graphical content and a position on the screen. Your sprites are drawn with a particular texture and have a position specified by a rectangle, as follows:

```
// Game World
Texture2D cheeseTexture;
Rectangle cheeseRectangle;
```

When the game starts, you load the texture from the image content, set the size of the draw rectangle, and draw the texture using techniques that we first saw in Chapter 4. Your finished game will contain a great many sprites.

Managing the Size of Game Sprites

Owners of Xbox consoles can choose from a variety of screen-size and screen-resolution settings. They can also select between standard and wide screen shapes. Your game must work correctly on any of these sizes and give the player the same game-play experience on each. If you do this correctly, it should even be possible to play the game properly on the Windows Phone screen. This means that your game must automatically set the size of the objects that you draw, depending on the display in use. The game must also adjust the speed at which the objects in the game move; otherwise, a game that works on a small TV might be unplayable on a large display.

You've seen in the section entitled "Filling the Screen" in Chapter 4 that you can get the dimensions of your screen from the display adapter viewport properties. However, getting a hold of these is a rather laborious process, so you create two data fields in your game that hold these values for you to use. The best place to set these variables is in the `Initialize` method, which is called once when your game first starts running:

```
// Display settings
float displayWidth;
float displayHeight;
```

```
protected override void Initialize()
{
    displayWidth = GraphicsDevice.Viewport.Width;
    displayHeight = GraphicsDevice.Viewport.Height;
    base.Initialize();
}
```

Working with Floating-Point Values and Integers

The previously mentioned `displayWidth` and `displayHeight` variables have been declared as floating-point, although the display properties themselves are integers. This is because all your calculations involving the width and height of items need the fractional part that floating-point variables give you, so that they are sufficiently accurate.

However, all the properties of your display rectangle are integers, so you need to convert these floating-point values into integers when you want to position the sprites. You know that you can use casting to convert from one type to another, but you also need to allow for the fact that casting always truncates; in other words, if the floating-point input were 1.99999, it would still be converted to 1, which would be inaccurate. You can make sure that the converted value is as accurate as possible by adding 0.5 to the floating-point value before you truncate it so that 1.99999 would turn into 2.4999 and then be truncated down to 2. You can see this in action in the `scaleSprites` method later in this chapter.

Double Precision Floating-Point Values

C# and XNA can use two different types to hold floating-point values. One of these is called float and holds a number with seven digits of precision. This means it could hold the mathematical constant pi (an endless decimal) as 3.141593. The other is called double. It uses twice as much memory to hold each value and is good for around 16 digits of accuracy, and could hold pi as 3.14159265358979. Very high levels of precision can be important in video games because values are being updated thousands of times a second, so errors accumulate quickly. For the purpose of your game, you can use floating-point variables. However, you need to remember that when you give a real number value (one with a decimal point) in the program text, the C# compiler assumes that it's a double precision one. This means that the following statement causes a compilation error:

```
float pi = 3.14159;
```

This is because 3.14159 is compiled as a double precision value, and you know that the C# compiler reacts badly when you perform an action that might result in a loss of data (which is what could happen if you put a double value into a float variable). There are two ways around this: you can cast the double value to floating-point, or you can change the value in the program to be a floating-point value, as shown here:

```
float pi = 3.14159f;
```

Putting the letter "f" after a decimal value tells the compiler that you're writing a floating-point value, not a double precision value.

Drawing and Aspect Ratios

When an image is drawn, you need to be careful to preserve its *aspect ratio*. The aspect ratio of an image is the ratio of the width to the height. For your cheese, this is just about one because the texture is square, but for your bread, it's quite different. Figure 11-9 shows the effect of getting the aspect ratio wrong when you draw the bread bat.

Correct Aspect Ratio

Distorted Aspect Ratio

FIGURE 11-9 The effect of aspect ratio on drawing.

The bread has an aspect ratio of around 4 to 1; in other words, it is around four times as wide as it is high. The program can get the aspect ratio of the original image from the dimensions of the texture:

```
float aspectRatio =
    (float) cheeseTexture.Width / cheeseTexture.Height;
```

The program can now use the aspect ratio to calculate the correct height of a sprite given the width that we want it to have.

> **Note** The variable `aspectRatio` is being declared and used in the program to hold a value that is going to be used in one particular part of the code. This is called a *local variable* because it is used in only one place in the code and has no need to be visible anywhere else.

Sprite Sizing

Next, you need to decide how large to make the cheese sprite. This depends on the game you're creating. Do you want to have a big cheese or a little cheese? In some games, the objects change size as the game progresses so that you can start with large sprites and then reduce their size and increase their speed to make the game more challenging. You think that having the cheese take up around one-twentieth of the screen width would work well, but you're not sure. You ask the Great Programmer for advice because it was her cheese that you used for the game.

> **The Great Programmer Speaks: Flexibility Should Be Designed into Your Programs** The Great Programmer has no idea what size cheese makes a good game. She suggests that you have no idea either. Therefore, you need to make sure that when you create the game, you make it as easy as possible to change the size of the cheese and all the other game sprites. Your program could use variables to represent the scale values, so that rather than using the literal value of one-twentieth (0.05) to represent the fact that you want the width of the cheese to be one-twentieth of the screen, you use a variable called `cheeseWidthFactor` instead. Then you can easily change the value everywhere it's used just by changing the value of `cheeseWidthFactor`. Your program could also use methods. If you create a method called `scaleSprites`, you can then call it to perform the scaling. If you decide that you need to change the size of the sprites during the game, you simply need to call this method again.

With these points in mind, you create a method called `scaleSprites` and some variables to hold the width factors. You can call the `scaleSprites` method from `LoadGraphicsContent` when the cheese texture has been loaded. It sets the size of the draw rectangle to match the display you're using, as follows:

```
void scaleSprites()
{
    cheeseRectangle.Width = (int)((displayWidth * cheeseWidthFactor) + 0.5f);
    float aspectRatio = (float) cheeseTexture.Width / cheeseTexture.Height;
    cheeseRectangle.Height = (int)((cheeseRectangle.Width / aspectRatio) + 0.5f);
}
```

This scaleSprites method performs the required calculations. Note that you need to use casting to convert the floating-point results into integers that can be used to set up the cheeseRectangle.

Moving Sprites

Now that you have your cheese sprite, you need to make it move. You use two floating-point variables to hold the draw positions and two more floating-point variables to hold the speed at which the cheese is moving:

```
float cheeseX;
float cheeseXSpeed;
float cheeseY;
float cheeseYSpeed;
```

Each time that Update is called in your game, you update the X and Y properties of cheeseRectangle, causing the cheese to be drawn in a different position and so appear to move:

```
protected override void Update(GameTime gameTime)
{
    // Allows the game to exit
    if (GamePad.GetState(PlayerIndex.One).Buttons.Back==ButtonState.Pressed)
        this.Exit();

    cheeseX = cheeseX + cheeseXSpeed;
    cheeseY = cheeseY + cheeseYSpeed;
    cheeseRectangle.X = (int)(cheeseX + 0.5f);
    cheeseRectangle.Y = (int)(cheeseY + 0.5f);
    base.Update(gameTime);
}
```

Each time this Update is called, it adds the speed values to the current position of your cheese, causing it to appear to move across the screen. It's important that the cheese appears to move at the same speed on every kind of game display, so you need to calculate appropriate values for cheeseXSpeed and cheeseYSpeed. You know that the Update method is called 60 times a second. If cheeseXSpeed were set to one-sixtieth of the width of the screen, this would mean that the cheese would take around a second to cross the screen.

If you want your cheese to take around 2 seconds to cross the screen, the position of the cheese must change by half that (1/120 of the screen) each time. At this point, you remember what the Great Programmer said. She said that you should make important values into variables so that they are easy to change. With that in mind, you modify the scaleSprites method to calculate speed values as well as sizes:

```
float cheeseWidthFactor = 0.05f;
float cheeseTicksToCrossScreen = 200.0f;

void scaleSprites()
{
    cheeseRectangle.Width = (int)((displayWidth * cheeseWidthFactor) + 0.5f);
    float aspectRatio = (float) cheeseTexture.Width / cheeseTexture.Height;
    cheeseRectangle.Height = (int)((cheeseRectangle.Width / aspectRatio) + 0.5f);

    cheeseX = 0;
    cheeseY = 0;
    cheeseXSpeed = displayWidth / cheeseTicksToCrossScreen;
    cheeseYSpeed = cheeseXSpeed;
}
```

The interval between calls of Update is sometimes called a "tick." The variable cheeseTicksToCrossScreen sets the number of ticks that the cheese takes to move across the screen. The larger this number, the slower the cheese moves. It turns out that 200 ticks is a reasonable number. Note that the value of cheeseYSpeed has been made the same as cheeseXSpeed. This means that the cheese moves at 45 degrees down the screen rather than along the diagonal of the screen.

> **Sample Code: Moving Cheese** All the sample projects can be obtained from the Web resources for this text, which can be found at *http://oreilly.com/catalog/9780735651579*. The sample project in the 01 Moving Cheese directory in the resources for this chapter draws a piece of cheese that flies down the screen and vanishes off the bottom.

Windows Phone games are updated 30 times a second. This is to reduce the loading on the processor and save power. If you want your games to run at the same speed on a Windows Phone your speed calculations must allow for this. You can use the pre-processor symbol WINDOWS_PHONE to select code that can deal with this problem. You will find out more about this in Chapter 19.

Bouncing the Cheese

What you really want to do is have the cheese bounce around the screen. To do this, you need to reverse the direction of movement of the cheese when it reaches the edge. This is what happens when things bounce. To reverse a direction of movement, you simply need to multiply the speed value by –1. You can use the size of the screen and the size of your draw rectangle to determine when you've reached an edge:

```
if (cheeseX + cheeseRectangle.Width >= displayWidth)
{
    cheeseXSpeed = cheeseXSpeed * -1;
}

if (cheeseX <= 0)
{
    cheeseXSpeed = cheeseXSpeed * -1;
}
```

This code performs two tests. The first one checks to see if the cheese has gone off the right of the screen. If the X position plus the width of the cheese is greater than the width of the display, it's time for the cheese to change direction. If the X position is less than or equal to 0, the cheese must change direction again. You need to perform the same tests for the Y movement so that you can get your cheese to bounce properly.

> **Sample Code: Bouncing Cheese** The sample project in the 02 Bouncing Cheese directory in the resources for this chapter draws a piece of cheese that bounces around the screen.

Dealing with Display Overscan

The previously mentioned sample program runs correctly on the Xbox or a desktop PC. However, some Xbox owners find a game based on this code rather hard to play. If they're using an older display device or a TV screen, they complain that the cheese goes off the screen at the edges. This is because TV displays use what is called *overscan*. Figure 11-10 shows the problem. The cheese has managed to disappear almost completely from the TV picture.

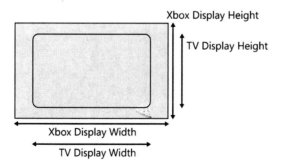

FIGURE 11-10 A drawing extending off the visible screen.

The problem arises because a TV does not show the entire Xbox display; it shows only a central region. This is because glass TV tubes cannot be made to align precisely with the edge of the picture they are showing, so TV signals have an area of overscan where program makers must be careful not to put important parts of a scene. If you let your game objects go into the overscan area, there's a danger that players won't be able to see them, and this would be very bad for game play.

The amount of overscan (in other words, the amount of the display that you lose) varies from one display to another. It's usually expressed as a percentage, perhaps 10 percent or 20 percent. The bigger the number, the greater the amount of screen that's lost. You need to calculate the range of the available screen coordinates that you can use to place items on display if you want them to be visible. You can do this when you set up the scaling values, and you can use a floating-point version of your getPercentage method from Chapter 10 to help you, as follows:

```
// Display settings
float displayWidth;
float displayHeight;
float overScanPercentage = 10.0f;
float minDisplayX;
float maxDisplayX;
float minDisplayY;
float maxDisplayY;

float getPercentage(float percentage, float inputValue)
{
    return (inputValue * percentage) / 100;
}

private void setupScreen ()
{
    displayWidth = graphics.GraphicsDevice.Viewport.Width;
    displayHeight = graphics.GraphicsDevice.Viewport.Height;
    float xOverscanMargin =
        getPercentage(overScanPercentage, displayWidth) / 2.0f;
    float yOverscanMargin =
        getPercentage(overScanPercentage, displayHeight) / 2.0f;

    minDisplayX = xOverscanMargin;
    minDisplayY = yOverscanMargin;

    maxDisplayX = displayWidth - xOverscanMargin;
    maxDisplayY = displayHeight - yOverscanMargin;
}
```

The setupScreen method is called by the Initialize method when the game starts running. It calculates the width and height values based on a particular overscan percentage. It does this by working out the margins required around the screen and then creating maximum and minimum values for the X and Y coordinates. It also provides the game with minimum and maximum values, which can be used to place the cheese on the screen at the start of the game and also in the code that bounces the cheese. Look at the following:

```
if (cheeseX + cheeseRectangle.Width >= maxDisplayX)
{
    cheeseXSpeed = cheeseXSpeed * -1;
}

if (cheeseX <= minDisplayX)
{
    cheeseXSpeed = cheeseXSpeed * -1;
}
```

This code uses the new boundary values to ensure that the cheese never leaves the visible part of the screen.

> **Sample Code: Overscan Bouncing Cheese** The sample project in the 03 Overscan Bouncing Cheese directory in the resources for this chapter draws a piece of cheese that bounces around the screen and stays within a 10 percent overscan boundary.

You now have some bouncing cheese that provides the same gaming experience on any platform. You can now take any image of yours and make it bounce around the screen. In the next chapter, you'll add the bread bat and start hitting the cheese about with it.

From a gameplay point of view, it is best that objects in your games do not do things like bounce off the very edge of the screen. Even if you are writing games for the Windows Phone, which uses an LCD panel and does not use overscan, you should still add margins around the edges.

Conclusion

In this chapter, you've learned a lot. For the first time, you've taken a look at how a game application is structured. You've seen how it's spread over more than one class and how the Program.cs file gets the game running. You've also learned the meaning of some more C# key words. Now you know how one program can be given information provided from another by means of the using compiler directive. You've seen how the static key word can make methods and classes that are created when your application runs without your needing to explicitly create them, and you've looked at the Main method, which is how C# programs are started. You completed your investigation into how C# programs work with a look at the using key word. You moved on to creating your game and found out how to ensure that games work correctly on different types, sizes, and resolutions of the display device. Then you created a sprite and got it moving around the visible portion of the display.

Chapter Review Questions

If you're thinking that you're due for another chapter review about now, you're right. As usual, true or false?

1. Images for use in games must be bought from a special XNA image bank.

2. An XNA Game Studio project contains a solution.

3. You need to create your own Program.cs file to run your programs.

4. The Program.cs source file does not contain your game program.

5. Namespaces are used in a program to locate resources.

6. The main method is called to start the program.

7. If something is made static, it means it can't be moved around in memory.

8. The C# using statement is provided to help the garbage collector work more effectively.

9. The cast from floating-point to integer value automatically rounds up values with a fractional value greater than 0.5.

Chapter 12
Games, Objects, and State

In this chapter, you will

- Discover a better way to structure your programs.
- Add some bread that you can use to bash the cheese around on your screen.
- Give yourself some targets to hit the cheese at.

Introduction

You have the basis of a little game at the moment. You know how to place objects on the screen and manage their movement. You also know how to make sure that the games you create work with different display sizes and resolutions. In this chapter, you develop the game play further, add some more sprites, and create a game that has proper game-play.

Adding Bread to Your Game

You can continue working on the 03 Overscan Bouncing Cheese sample code that you were using in Chapter 11, "A Game as a C# Program." You need to add some bread to your game. The bread will be the bat that the player uses to hit the cheese around the screen. You think that tomatoes might make good targets, but first you need to get the bread working.

You need to store all the same information about the bread as you do about the cheese. It has a position, a texture, and a speed. The only difference is in the Update behavior. Whereas the cheese travels in a particular direction each time it's updated and bounces off the edges of the playing field, the bread is controlled by one of the thumbsticks on gamepad 1. In the game, you need to store the same information for the cheese and bread, so you could go ahead and create all the class member variables for them as follows:

```
Texture2D cheeseTexture;
Rectangle cheeseRectangle;
float cheeseX;
float cheeseXSpeed;
float cheeseY;
float cheeseYSpeed;
float cheeseWidthFactor = 0.05f;
float cheeseTicksToCrossScreen = 200.0f;

Texture2D breadTexture;
Rectangle breadRectangle;
float breadX;
```

```
float breadXSpeed;
float breadY;
float breadYSpeed;
float breadWidthFactor = 0.05f;
float breadTicksToCrossScreen = 200.0f;
```

This code simply has a copy of all the cheese variables, but renamed for bread. However, from a programming point of view, this is not really the best way to do it. The Great Programmer would certainly not approve. She doesn't like it when you have lots of separate variables all relating to one thing. She reckons that all the information about a particular item should be grouped together in one place. There should be a "cheese group" and a "bread group."

You've seen this "grouping together" in Microsoft XNA ever since you started writing programs. For example, you know that XNA holds Color information in the form of a structure with fields that represent the red, green, and blue intensities of a particular color. For your bread and cheese, you'd like to group all this information together in the same way.

Using a Structure to Hold Sprite Information

C# provides a kind of object called a *structure* to allow programmers to group things together. Structures are like classes, in that they can contain methods and data, but they are managed by value. You found out about values and references in the section entitled "Working with Arrays, Objects, and References," in Chapter 9, "Reading Text Input." The fact that structures are managed by value makes them ideal for holding small lumps of data that we want to treat as a whole. You can design a structure that holds all the information about a sprite on the screen as follows:

```
struct GameSpriteStruct
{
    public Texture2D SpriteTexture;
    public Rectangle SpriteRectangle;
    public float X;
    public float Y;
    public float XSpeed;
    public float YSpeed;
    public float WidthFactor;
    public float TicksToCrossScreen;
}
```

Each of the items in the structure is a field. If you compare the fields of the structure GameSpriteStruct with the variables you used in the original bouncing cheese program, you find that it holds all the information you need for a sprite: the texture, the rectangle in which to draw the sprite, the current position of the sprite, the speed at which the sprite moves, and the size and speed settings. Once you've created this structure, you can declare variables of this type for use in your game:

```
GameSpriteStruct cheese;
GameSpriteStruct bread;
```

When you declare a GameSpriteStruct variable, you get a structure that contains all the fields grouped together in it. You can then use the fields in the structure as follows:

```
cheese.SpriteTexture = Content.Load<Texture2D>("Images/Cheese");
bread.SpriteTexture = Content.Load<Texture2D>("Images/Bread");
```

These statements set the textures for the bread and cheese to ones loaded from images placed in your project content. You can get hold of any of the fields in your structure by following the name of the structure variable with a period (.) and then the name of the field. This works because you've made the fields *public*. If you look back to the declaration of GameSpriteStruct, you see that each field has the C# keyword public in front of it. Words placed in front of fields like this are called *modifiers*. There are a number of different modifiers in C#; public is an "access modifier," in that it determines the level of access to a field. Fields marked as public can be used by code outside the class or structure. You can make fields private so that code in methods outside the class or structure can't read or write the value in the field. For now, though, public fields are fine because they are easy to use and you don't have any particular need for security. Now that you have your bread and cheese structures, you can set the values in them:

```
void scaleSprites()
{
    cheese.TicksToCrossScreen = 200.0f;
    cheese.WidthFactor = 0.05f;

    cheese.SpriteRectangle.Width =
        (int)((displayWidth * cheese.WidthFactor) + 0.5f);
    float aspectRatio =
        (float)cheese.SpriteTexture.Width / cheese.SpriteTexture.Height;
    cheese.SpriteRectangle.Height =
        (int)((cheese.SpriteRectangle.Width / aspectRatio) + 0.5f);
    cheese.X = minDisplayX;
    cheese.Y = minDisplayY;
    cheese.XSpeed = displayWidth / cheese.TicksToCrossScreen;
    cheese.YSpeed = cheese.XSpeed;

    bread.WidthFactor = 0.15f;
    bread.TicksToCrossScreen = 120.0f;

    bread.SpriteRectangle.Width =
        (int)((displayWidth * bread.WidthFactor) + 0.5f);
    aspectRatio =
        (float)bread.SpriteTexture.Width / bread.SpriteTexture.Height;
    bread.SpriteRectangle.Height =
        (int)((bread.SpriteRectangle.Width / aspectRatio) + 0.5f);
    bread.X = displayWidth / 2;
    bread.Y = displayHeight / 2;
    bread.XSpeed = displayWidth / bread.TicksToCrossScreen;
    bread.YSpeed = bread.XSpeed;
}
```

This version of scaleSprites sets the width, height, speed, and initial position of the bread and the cheese sprites. It makes the bread take up slightly more of the width of the screen and allows it to move a bit faster than the cheese. The ScaleSprites method also sets the initial position of the bread at the middle of the screen and places the cheese at the top left corner of the display area.

Using the Gamepad Thumbsticks to Control Movement

You've decided that the player will control the bread and use it as a bat to hit the cheese. To make the bread move, you need to add some statements to the Update method. This turns out to be very easy. The Xbox gamepad has two thumbsticks that can be used to control games. These generate floating-point values that you can use to direct the movement of the bread bat. Figure 12-1 shows the range of values that the thumbstick produces. If it's pushed all the way to the left, it will generate −1.0 for the X value. If it's pushed halfway to the left, it will generate −0.5. If the thumbstick is left in the center, the X and Y values are zero.

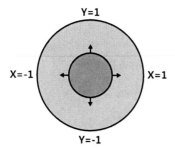

FIGURE 12-1 Thumbstick values.

You've used the GamePadState structure before to read the state of buttons on a gamepad. It also provides a ThumbSticks property that contains two vectors (one for each thumbstick) that allow your program to read the current thumbstick values. In Chapter 17 we will find out how to use the accelerometer in the Windows Phone to control gameplay.

To get the amount of movement of the bread, you simply need to take the values from the left thumbstick and multiply them by the speed values for your bread sprite. The farther the thumbstick is moved, the bigger the values and the faster the bread moves across the screen:

```
GamePadState gamePad1 = GamePad.GetState(PlayerIndex.One);
// Allows the game to exit
if (gamePad1.Buttons.Back == ButtonState.Pressed)
    this.Exit();

// Move the bread

bread.X = bread.X + (bread.XSpeed * gamePad1.ThumbSticks.Left.X);
bread.Y = bread.Y - (bread.YSpeed * gamePad1.ThumbSticks.Left.Y);
bread.SpriteRectangle.X = (int)bread.X;
bread.SpriteRectangle.Y = (int)bread.Y;
```

This code is placed in the Update method and updates the position of the bread rectangle according to the setting of the left thumbstick. Note that the code must subtract the speed value from the Y coordinate. This is because the Y coordinate goes down the screen, with 0 at the top. If the speed value was added to the Y coordinate, the bread would go down the screen when the thumbstick is moved up, making it harder to control. This version of the bread movement does not restrict the bread to the screen, so it is possible for the player to move the bread right off the screen.

> **Sample Code: Bread and Cheese** All the sample projects can be obtained from the Web resources for this text, which can be found at *http://oreilly.com/catalog/9780735651579*. The sample project in the 01 Bread and Cheese directory in the resources for this chapter draws cheese bouncing around the screen and a bread bat that you can move around the screen with the left thumbstick. It works very well, and the feeling of control that you get is very impressive for such a simple program. The bread doesn't yet interact with the cheese; you'll add that later.

Improving Programs Using Methods

The Great Programmer has just been around and has taken a look at your code. She purses her lips when she sees something she doesn't like, and she's doing that now. The bit of code she doesn't like is the scaleSprites method where you set up the bread and cheese sprites:

```
void scaleSprites()
{
    cheese.TicksToCrossScreen = 200.0f;
    cheese.WidthFactor = 0.05f;

    cheese.SpriteRectangle.Width =
        (int)((displayWidth * cheese.WidthFactor) + 0.5f);
    float aspectRatio =
        (float)cheese.SpriteTexture.Width / cheese.SpriteTexture.Height;
    cheese.SpriteRectangle.Height =
        (int)((cheese.SpriteRectangle.Width / aspectRatio) + 0.5f);
    cheese.X = minDisplayX;
    cheese.Y = minDisplayY;
    cheese.XSpeed = displayWidth / cheese.TicksToCrossScreen;
    cheese.YSpeed = cheese.XSpeed;

    bread.WidthFactor = 0.15f;
    bread.TicksToCrossScreen = 120.0f;

    bread.SpriteRectangle.Width =
        (int)((displayWidth * bread.WidthFactor) + 0.5f);
    aspectRatio =
        (float)bread.SpriteTexture.Width / bread.SpriteTexture.Height;
    bread.SpriteRectangle.Height =
        (int)((bread.SpriteRectangle.Width / aspectRatio) + 0.5f);
    bread.X = displayWidth / 2;
    bread.Y = displayHeight / 2;
    bread.XSpeed = displayWidth / bread.TicksToCrossScreen;
    bread.YSpeed = bread.XSpeed;
}
```

For a start, she reckons that the name is no longer correct. The method doesn't only scale the sprites; it also sets their initial position on the screen and their speed of movement. So you promise to go through and change the name of the method, using the Refactor technique you used in Chapter 11. The next thing she doesn't like to see is the same piece of code repeated. Rather than perform exactly the same sequence of statements for the bread as for the cheese, she suggests that you make a method called setupSprite that sets up a sprite. You then call this for every sprite you want to set up. You know that you'll have tomato sprites later, so this seems like a sensible, time-saving plan. You can pass the setupSprite method parameters that give it all the information it needs to work on, so you begin to write the method:

```
void setupSprite(
    GameSpriteStruct sprite,
    float widthFactor,
    float ticksToCrossScreen,
    float initialX,
    float initialY)
{
    sprite.WidthFactor = widthFactor;
    sprite.TicksToCrossScreen = ticksToCrossScreen;
    sprite.SpriteRectangle.Width = (int)((displayWidth * widthFactor) + 0.5f);
    float aspectRatio =
        (float)sprite.SpriteTexture.Width / sprite.SpriteTexture.Height;
    sprite.SpriteRectangle.Height =
        (int)((sprite.SpriteRectangle.Width / aspectRatio) + 0.5f);
    sprite.X = initialX;
    sprite.Y = initialY;
    sprite.XSpeed = displayWidth / ticksToCrossScreen;
    sprite.YSpeed = sprite.XSpeed;
}
```

The method is given the sprite to set up, along with the width factor, the time taken to cross the screen, and the initial start position of the sprite. You can then set up the cheese and bread by making two calls of the method:

```
void setupSprites()
{
    setupSprite(cheese, 0.05f, 200.0f, minDisplayX, minDisplayY);
    setupSprite(bread, 0.15f, 120.0f, displayWidth / 2, displayHeight / 2);
}
```

This looks much neater, and you're really pleased with the code that you've written. You feed all your setup values into the method call, and it calculates the content of the gameSpriteStruct that needs to be set up. The only problem is that it doesn't work. The method call doesn't seem to have any effect on the bread or cheese sprite value.

Value and Reference Parameters

It turns out that your program doesn't work because the parameters in your method are passed by *value*. A parameter is the means by which you can pass information into a method.

When a method is called, the value given in the call is copied into the parameter. This means that when code in a method assigns a value to the parameter, the copy is changed, but not the original. In other words, the statement `sprite.X = initialX;` changes the value of a copy of the `GameSpriteStruct` that was supplied as a parameter. When a method ends, all the parameter copies are discarded, and the updated values are lost.

Passing value parameters into method calls is fine when you want to tell a method something, but it is less useful when you want the method to change the parameter. To make the method useful, you need to find a way of pointing the method at the variable you want it to change. It turns out that you have a way to do this, and you've seen it before. The device you'll use is called a *reference*. If you give the method a reference to the thing you want it to change, it can follow the reference and make changes to your actual bread and cheese objects rather than to copies. In Chapter 9, in the section entitled "Working with Arrays, Objects, and References," you discovered that some variables are managed by value and some by reference. C# structures are managed by value, which is why the values of the cheese and bread sprites get copied when the method is called. To tell C# to manage a particular parameter as a reference, you need to change the header of the method:

```
void setupSprite(
    ref GameSpriteStruct sprite,
    float widthFactor,
    float ticksToCrossScreen,
    float initialX,
    float initialY)
{
    // method goes here
}
```

The `ref` modifier before the `GameSpriteStruct` parameter in the method header tells the compiler to pass a reference to the parameter's location in memory rather than copying a value stored in that memory location. You also need to use the `ref` modifier, as shown here in bold, when you make a call to the method:

```
setupSprite(ref cheese, 0.05f, 200.0f,
            minDisplayX, minDisplayY);
setupSprite(ref bread, 0.15f, 120.0f,
            displayWidth/2, displayHeight/2);
```

Now, when `setupSprite` runs, it is given the values of the rest of the parameters that it needs to work with and a reference to the `GameSpriteStruct` object that needs to be changed. You don't need to change any code in the body of the method itself; the compiler makes sure that the instructions it produces follow the reference and update the correct values in memory rather than updating a copy of the values.

> **Sample Code: Bread and Cheese with Setup Method** The sample project in the 02 Bread and Cheese with Setup Method directory in the resources for this chapter uses a `setupSprite` method to set up the sprites.

Handling Collisions

You have a bread bat and some cheese, and you can move the bread around the game and chase the cheese, but nothing happens when you hit the cheese with the bread. You now need to add the interaction between these two sprites. The first thing the game needs to do is detect when the bread and the cheese collide. The best way to do this is to use the rectangles that define the size and position of the two sprites on the screen. When these two rectangles intersect (that is, both of them cover the same part of the screen), it means that a collision has taken place. Figure 12-2 shows how this works.

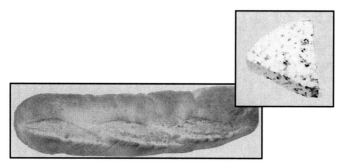

FIGURE 12-2 A sprite collision.

What you need is a method that you can use to detect when this happens. Fortunately, the designers of XNA have provided just such a method using the Rectangle type. The method, called Intersects, is used as follows:

```
if (cheese.SpriteRectangle.Intersects(bread.SpriteRectangle))
{
    // we have a collision
}
```

You call the Intersects method on one rectangle and feed it the other one to compare with it. It returns true if the two rectangles intersect. Note that in the previous code, it is necessary to get the rectangle value of the bread and cheese sprites.

Making the Cheese Bounce off the Bat

Now that you can detect when the cheese and the bread collide, you need to make the cheese "bounce" off the bat. Because the bread is horizontal, it makes sense to bounce the cheese up and down the screen so that whenever the cheese hits the bat, it reverses its movement in the Y direction. The code to achieve this is very simple; you do the same thing with the YSpeed as you do when the cheese hits the top or bottom of the game region:

```
if (cheese.SpriteRectangle.Intersects(bread.SpriteRectangle))
{
    cheese.YSpeed = cheese.YSpeed * -1;
}
```

This code can be placed at the end of the Update method to cause the cheese to bounce off the bat.

> **Sample Code: Cheese and Bread Bat** The sample project in the 03 Cheese and Bread Bat directory in the resources for this chapter lets players hit the cheese up and down the screen with the bread bat.

Strange Bounce Behavior

When you run the game, you find that it works well, and you can guide the cheese around the screen successfully. However, you make the mistake of letting your younger brother have a go, and he's soon complaining that there's a bug in your game. Sometimes the cheese gets "stuck" on the bread. You ask him to show you what happens, and it turns out that he's right. It seems to happen when the bread is moving when it hits the cheese. The cheese travels along the bread, vibrating up and down as it moves. After some thought, you work out what's causing the problem. Figure 12-3 shows what's happening.

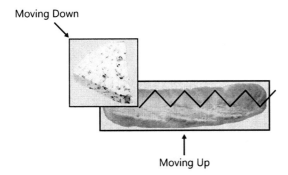

Moving Down

Moving Up

FIGURE 12-3 Cheese that gets stuck on the bread.

When the cheese rectangle and the bread rectangle intersect, the program reverses the direction of movement of the cheese. Normally, this means that the next time the position of the cheese is updated, it moves away from the bread, and the rectangles no longer intersect. However, if the cheese is moving down and the bread is moving up when they collide, the cheese goes so far "in" to the bread that, even after the cheese has been updated, the bread and cheese rectangles still intersect. If this is the case, the Update method reverses the vertical direction of movement of the cheese, causing the cheese to move back into the bread. This continues as the cheese moves along the bread, following the path shown in Figure 12-3, until it finally escapes off the end. There are a number of ways you can solve this problem:

1. When the cheese collides with the bread, the program could stop detecting collisions for a while, giving the cheese a chance to move clear of the bread. To implement this, you need to add a variable to count a certain number of ticks after the collision and not allow collisions until after that number of ticks.

2. The program could move the cheese away from the bread after a collision so that the two sprite rectangles no longer intersect at the next update. To implement this, you need to know which direction the cheese is moving so that you can move it appropriately.

3. You could change the rules of the game and tell the player about this special trick shot where a skillful player can send the cheese in a particular direction by making it stick to the bat in this way. This would require no additional programming at all.

The important thing to remember is that because you own the game universe, including what you say the game is supposed to do, you can change the rules to suit what your program does. The Great Programmer doesn't have this freedom; usually she's paid a large sum of money to create a solution that does what the customer wants. However, quite a few games have turned out the way they are because of the way the programmer made them work or because of a bug that turned out to make the game more fun. In this case, you decide to use the third approach and tell your younger brother that the game is meant to work like that, and he has found a secret feature.

Strange Edge Behavior

Your younger brother is now very pleased with himself and with you. He is pleased with you for making a game that rewards clever play and pleased with himself for finding this new trick in the game. However, this doesn't last long because he soon comes back and tells you that he's found a proper bug in the game. He can make the cheese go right off the screen and not come back. You ask him to show you, and sure enough, if he uses the bread to chase the cheese right to the top of the screen, he can send the cheese right off the screen. This is definitely a bug, and you can't pass it off as a feature.

Debugging a Running Program

One of the great things about XNA Game Studio is that you can stop the game and take a look at what's happening. Once you've persuaded your younger brother to make the problem happen, you can put a breakpoint into the program and stop it so that you can look at the values of the variables. You can do this even as the program is running, either on the Xbox, Windows Phone, or Windows PC. You've used breakpoints before in the section entitled "Creating a Method to Calculate Percentages," in Chapter 10, "Using C# Methods to Solving Problems," where you were debugging the getPercentage method. Now you use them again to find out how your cheese is escaping from the screen.

You can put a breakpoint in the Update method by clicking next to the line at which you want it to stop. XNA Game Studio indicates that a breakpoint has been set by highlighting the line, as shown in Figure 12-4.

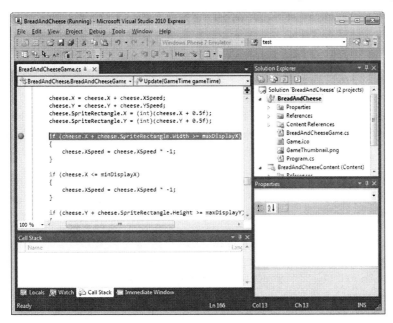

FIGURE 12-4 Adding a breakpoint to the program.

The next time the program reaches this statement, it stops, and XNA Game Studio enters debugging mode. You can then look at the values of the variables to see what's going wrong. You did this in Chapter 10 as well. You add the breakpoint, and the program stops at that line. When you take a look at the values in the cheese sprite, you find that the X coordinate value is fine, but the Y coordinate is –50, which is very wrong. The cheese Y coordinate should never get as low as this because the direction of the cheese movement should reverse when it reaches an edge. You take another look at the code that does this, and it looks sensible:

```
if (cheese.Y <= minDisplayY)
{
    cheese.YSpeed = cheese.YSpeed * -1;
}
```

If the cheese Y value becomes less than the minimum it's allowed to have, the direction of movement is reversed to bring it back onto the screen. The program does this by multiplying the speed of the cheese by –1, which made perfect sense when you wrote it. You take a look at the cheese.YSpeed and find that for the size of the screen you are using it has been calculated as 4. This means that next time the cheese is updated, the Y position of the cheese will be changed to –46 (which is still much lower than it's supposed to be). The result is that the same condition triggers again, reversing the direction of the YSpeed and sending the Y position of the cheese back to –50. So the cheese remains forever off the screen, dancing backward and forward just out of view. The problem happens because the bread collision testing is performed after the cheese has been made to bounce when it hits the edge of the screen, so if the cheese repeatedly bounces off the bread when it's on the edge of the screen, it can be made to vanish like this.

There are a number of ways you can fix this bug. You can stop the bread from going too close to the edges so that it can't harass the cheese like this, or you can fix the bouncing problem of the cheese. You can't really say that this behavior is a feature, although you could create a completely different game where the aim was to push all the objects off the screen, perhaps something called "Herd the Cheese" or "Sweep the Table." However, you decide to fix the problem.

The problem lies with the use of multiplication by –1 to change the direction of movement. If the next update brings the cheese back into the required range, then all is well, but if by some mischance it doesn't, you get the dancing behavior that you've just uncovered.

The best way to fix this is to set the direction of movement of the cheese explicitly to the one in which you need it to go. Rather than bouncing, where you simply reverse the sign of the speed value, you should say, "If the cheese Y position is less than the limit, then make the movement positive so that this always brings the cheese back onto the screen." Even if the cheese Y position remains less than the limit next time, the movement will still be correct and result in the cheese heading in the right direction.

This turns out to be easy. You can use a method called Abs, which is provided by .NET. The Abs method is held in the Math class and returns the absolute value or magnitude of a number. The absolute value of a number is simply its value, if the number is zero or positive, or the opposite of its value if the number is negative. For example, the absolute value of –4 is 4. The Math class provides a number of static methods (which are always available) for use in your programs. The Math class is in the System namespace, so you can use it without having to add any using directives to your program. The code to deal with the Y position of the cheese ends up looking like this:

```
if (cheese.Y + cheese.SpriteRectangle.Height >= maxDisplayY)
{
    cheese.YSpeed = Math.Abs(cheese.YSpeed) * -1;
}

if (cheese.Y <= minDisplayY)
{
    cheese.YSpeed = Math.Abs(cheese.YSpeed) ;
}
```

If the cheese is too high, you make it move downward. If the cheese is too low, you make it move upward. Now there's no way the cheese can get stuck off the screen.

Unfortunately it is still possible to move the bat off the screen, To solve this, you have to add code to limit the movement of the bread.

> **Sample Code: Absolute Cheese Bouncing** The sample project in the 04 Absolute Cheese Bouncing directory in the resources for this chapter has the updated cheese bouncing behavior so that the cheese cannot be forced off the screen.

Adding Tomato Targets

Your younger brother has become adept at balancing the cheese on the bat, but he wants something to aim at, so now's the time to provide some targets. You decide to use tomatoes for this, so you need to add them to your program. You want to have lots of tomatoes, so you need to create an array of GameSpriteStruct instances to hold all of them:

```
Texture2D tomatoTexture;
GameSpriteStruct[] tomatoes;
int numberOfTomatoes = 20;
```

These are the fields that you have to create to hold tomato information. Note that although I've created an array reference called tomatoes, I haven't yet created the array itself. You'll load the tomato texture from your image into a single Texture2D object which will be loaded with the rest of the content for the game:

```
protected override void LoadContent()
{
    // Create a new SpriteBatch, which can be used to draw textures.
    spriteBatch = new SpriteBatch(GraphicsDevice);

    cheese.SpriteTexture = Content.Load<Texture2D>("Images/Cheese");
    bread.SpriteTexture = Content.Load<Texture2D>("Images/Bread");
    tomatoTexture = Content.Load<Texture2D>("Images/Tomato");
    setupSprites();
}
```

Textures are classes, and are managed by reference, not value, so each of your tomatoes contains a reference to the same tomato texture:

```
void setupSprites()
{
    setupSprite(ref cheese, 0.05f, 200.0f, minDisplayX, minDisplayY);
    setupSprite(ref bread, 0.15f, 120.0f, displayWidth / 2, displayHeight / 2);
    tomatoes = new GameSpriteStruct[numberOfTomatoes];

    float tomatoSpacing = (maxDisplayX - minDisplayX) / numberOfTomatoes;

    for (int i = 0; i < numberOfTomatoes; i++)
    {
        tomatoes[i].SpriteTexture = tomatoTexture;
        setupSprite(
```

```
        ref tomatoes[i],
        0.05f,  // 20 tomatoes across the screen
        1000,   // 1000 ticks to move across the screen
        minDisplayX + (i * tomatoSpacing), minDisplayY);
    }
}
```

The setupSprites method creates the tomatoes array and contains a for loop that works through each tomato sprite and sets its size and position. Your first version of the game has the tomatoes evenly spaced in a line along the top of the screen. To make this work, the method uses a local variable called tomatoSpacing that's set to the width of the display divided by the number of tomatoes that you're using in the game. Note that you're following the advice of the Great Programmer in that it is very easy to change the number of tomatoes in the game; you need only change the value of one variable.

At the moment, you won't be making the tomatoes move, so the Update method only needs to copy the X and Y positions of the tomato into the rectangle for that sprite:

```
for (int i = 0; i < numberOfTomatoes; i++)
{
    tomatoes[i].SpriteRectangle.X = (int)tomatoes[i].X;
    tomatoes[i].SpriteRectangle.Y = (int)tomatoes[i].Y;
}
```

The last thing you need to do is add the code to draw all the tomatoes. This is placed in the Draw method as follows:

```
protected override void Draw(GameTime gameTime)
{
    graphics.GraphicsDevice.Clear(Color.CornflowerBlue);

    spriteBatch.Begin();
    spriteBatch.Draw(cheese.SpriteTexture, cheese.SpriteRectangle, Color.White);
    spriteBatch.Draw(bread.SpriteTexture, bread.SpriteRectangle, Color.White);
    for (int i = 0; i < numberOfTomatoes; i++)
    {
        spriteBatch.Draw(tomatoes[i].SpriteTexture,
                    tomatoes[i].SpriteRectangle, Color.White);
    }

    spriteBatch.End();

    base.Draw(gameTime);
}
```

The Draw method contains another for loop that draws each of the tomatoes in turn. Figure 12-5 shows the display produced with your 20 tomatoes along the top.

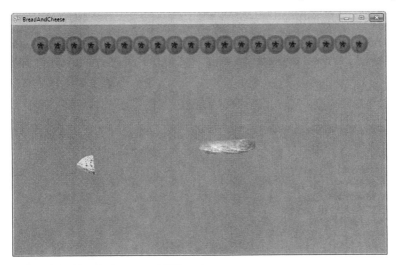

FIGURE 12-5 Bread, cheese, and 20 tomatoes.

Sample Code: Adding Tomatoes The sample project in the 05 Adding Tomatoes directory in the resources for this chapter draws 20 tomatoes along the top of the screen.

Windows Phone Image Sizes

When you write a game for the Windows Phone you need to remember that it is more restricted in the size of the programs it can accept. You also need to bear in mind that the programs themselves may be distributed to customers via the cellphone network. The smaller your games the less time they will take to arrive and the less they will cost to transfer. Up until now I have been using quite high resolution images of the bread, tomatoes, and cheese. However, these images have been so large that if we add too many our games will become very large. (And the phone screen is so small that images made up of fewer pixels are quite acceptable anyway.) For this version of the game I have re-sized the textures so that they look acceptable on the Xbox and Windows PC without taking up too much memory. When you create game resources you must be careful to make sure that the images you produce are of the appropriate size and resolution.

Tomato Collisions

The idea of the game is that when the cheese hits a tomato, the tomato vanishes. This means that you need a way of making the tomatoes disappear. You can't make them vanish as such, but you can decide not to draw them.

Controlling Sprite Visibility

The game must have some way of deciding when a particular sprite shouldn't be drawn. This turns out to be easy; you need only add an extra field to the GameSpriteStruct structure:

```
struct GameSpriteStruct
{
    public Texture2D SpriteTexture;
    public Rectangle SpriteRectangle;
    public float X;
    public float Y;
    public float XSpeed;
    public float YSpeed;
    public float WidthFactor;
    public float TicksToCrossScreen;
    public bool Visible;
}
```

The Visible field is set to true if the sprite is to be drawn on the screen.

Setting the Initial Visibility State

The initial value of Visible can be set by the setupSprite method, which is now given an additional parameter that is used to set the initial visibility of the sprite:

```
void setupSprite(
    ref GameSpriteStruct sprite,
    float widthFactor,
    float ticksToCrossScreen,
    float initialX,
    float initialY,
    bool initialVisibility)
{
    // original setup code here
    sprite.Visible = initialVisibility;
}
```

Initially, it's set to true for all the tomatoes, the cheese, and the bread in the setupSprites method:

```
void setupSprites()
{
    setupSprite(ref cheese, 0.05f, 200.0f, 200, 100, true);
    setupSprite(ref bread, 0.15f, 120.0f, displayWidth / 2, displayHeight / 2, true);

    tomatoes = new GameSpriteStruct[numberOfTomatoes];

    float tomatoSpacing = (maxDisplayX - minDisplayX) / numberOfTomatoes;

    for (int i = 0; i < numberOfTomatoes; i++)
    {
        tomatoes[i].SpriteTexture = tomatoTexture;
        setupSprite(
```

```
            ref tomatoes[i],
            0.05f,  // 20 tomatos across the screen
            1000,   // 1000 ticks to move across the screen
            minDisplayX + (i * tomatoSpacing), minDisplayY,
            true  // initially visible
            );
    }
}
```

This setupSprites method also sets the initial position of the cheese a bit further into the screen so that it does not initially collide with any tomatoes.

Using the *Visible* Field When Drawing

You use the value of the Visible field when you draw the sprites in the Draw method:

```
for (int i = 0; i < numberOfTomatoes; i++)
{
    if (tomatoes[i].Visible)
    {
        spriteBatch.Draw(tomatoes[i].SpriteTexture,
                        tomatoes[i].SpriteRectangle, Color.White);
    }
}
```

Only tomatoes that have the Visible field set to true are drawn on the screen. To make a tomato vanish, you simply set its Visible property to false. You do this in the Update method:

```
for (int i = 0; i < numberOfTomatoes; i++)
{
    if (tomatoes[i].Visible)
    {
        if (cheese.SpriteRectangle.Intersects(tomatoes[i].SpriteRectangle))
        {
            tomatoes[i].Visible = false;
            cheese.YSpeed = cheese.YSpeed * -1;
            break;
        }
    }
}
```

The for loop looks through all the tomatoes and tests to see if any of the tomato rectangles intersect with the cheese. If it finds an intersection, it sets the Visible property of the tomato to false and then reverses the direction of the cheese movement to make it "bounce" off the tomato it has just destroyed. Once it has removed one tomato, it stops looking for any more because the break statement causes the for loop to end at that point. This is important because otherwise, the cheese might collide with and destroy more than one tomato at a time, making the game too easy.

> **Sample Code: Tomato Killer** The sample project in the 06 Tomato Killer directory lets a player steer the cheese around the screen and use it to destroy tomatoes.

Conclusion

You're now starting to make games that look like "proper" ones. You're building your understanding of how C# lets you structure the data in your programs so that it's easier to work with. You've also discovered how to use references so that methods can change the content of variables passed as parameters, and you've found another use for the XNA Game Studio debugger.

Chapter Review Questions

Here's the twelfth chapter review. You know the procedure by now: true or false?

1. Structures are held in fields.

2. Structures let programmers group things together in their programs.

3. Structures are managed by reference.

4. Making a member of a class public stops code in other classes from using that item.

5. The absolute value of a number is always negative.

6. By default, parameters to a C# method are passed by copying their values into the method.

7. You can't put a breakpoint in a running program.

8. The Abs method is static, so you don't need an instance of the Math class to use it.

9. You can't change the name of a method once you've created it.

Chapter 13
Making a Complete Game

In this chapter, you will

- Finish off the game play in your game.

- Add some features to make the game more exciting.

- Discover how to improve the structure of the game program itself.

- Find out how to use state machines to add a title screen to the game.

Introduction

You can now create programs with all the behaviors required to create a "proper" game. You know how to place objects on the screen and manage their movement. You also know how to make sure that the games you create work on different display sizes. You can also display text and produce sounds. In this chapter, you develop the game play further, add some more sprites, and create a game that has proper game-play states.

Making a Finished Game

You now have the basis of a single-player tomato-killer game. The game play is simple—you use the bread to steer the cheese around at the tomatoes—but even your younger brother, who is easy to amuse, quickly finds it boring. Thus, you need to add some additional game-play elements: scores, survival, and progression.

Adding Scores to a Game

Even a simple game can be made addictive by adding a score component. It gets even more interesting when you add a high score so that the player always has something to beat. The game score is another integer variable that's set to 0 when the game starts and increases each time a tomato is killed. You've decided that tomatoes are worth 10 points, so each time the cheese crashes into a tomato, the score goes up by 10. The code that manages the cheese and tomato collisions is in the Update method:

```
if (cheese.SpriteRectangle.Intersects(tomatoes[i].SpriteRectangle))
{
    cheese.YSpeed = cheese.YSpeed * -1;
    score = score + 10;
    tomatoes[i].Visible = false;
    break;
}
```

You could make the game even more interesting by making the value of the tomatoes change over time so that the longer the player takes to destroy them, the less they're worth, but for now, you'll simply give the player 10 points for every tomato destroyed.

Drawing Text in the Game

Now that you have a score value to display you need some code to write it on the screen so that the player can see it increasing. The best way to do this is to create a general-purpose method for drawing text. You can then use the method to draw text whenever you need to display a message. The method needs to be given the text to be displayed, the position of the text, and the color of the text. It uses a font resource that is loaded by LoadContent and draws using the spriteBatch that is set up by the game:

```
void drawText(string text, Color textColor, float x, float y)
{
    int layer;
    Vector2 textVector = new Vector2(x, y);

    // Draw the shadow
    Color backColor = new Color(0, 0, 0, 20);
    for (layer = 0; layer < 10; layer++)
    {
        spriteBatch.DrawString(font, text, textVector, backColor);
        textVector.X++;
        textVector.Y++;
    }

    // Draw the solid part of the characters
    backColor = new Color(190, 190, 190);
    for (layer = 0; layer < 5; layer++)
    {
        spriteBatch.DrawString(font, text, textVector, backColor);
        textVector.X++;
        textVector.Y++;
    }

    // Draw the top of the characters
    spriteBatch.DrawString(font, text, textVector, textColor);
}
```

The drawText method is the same code you used to draw the clock in Chapter 5, "Writing Text." However, it's been packaged as a method that you can use whenever you want to put text onto the screen. It is supplied with the string to be displayed, the color of text that's required, and the position on the screen to draw it. The font that is to be used must have been loaded by the LoadContent method. To draw the score on the screen, you simply need to call the drawText method within the Draw method:

```
protected override void Draw(GameTime gameTime)
{
    graphics.GraphicsDevice.Clear(Color.CornflowerBlue);
```

```
        spriteBatch.Begin();
        spriteBatch.Draw(cheese.SpriteTexture, cheese.SpriteRectangle, Color.White);
        spriteBatch.Draw(bread.SpriteTexture, bread.SpriteRectangle, Color.White);
        for (int i = 0; i < numberOfTomatoes; i++)
        {
            if (tomatoes[i].Visible)
            {
                spriteBatch.Draw(tomatoes[i].SpriteTexture,
                            tomatoes[i].SpriteRectangle, Color.White);
            }
        }

        drawText(
            "Score : " + score.ToString(),
            Color.White,
            minDisplayX,
            maxDisplayY - 50);

        spriteBatch.End();

        base.Draw(gameTime);
    }
```

This Draw method draws all the game objects and then puts the score on last. This means that the score values are shown "on top" of all the other game items. You can call the drawText method several times if you want to draw multiple messages.

Adding Survival

At the moment, the player is under no particular pressure during the game. If the player makes a mistake, it doesn't cost anything. You need to add some bad news to the game. Later, you could add deadly peppers and killer tangerines, but for now, just cause the player to lose a life if the cheese hits the bottom of the screen. The life counter is just another variable in the game. There seems to be a tradition in computer games that you always start with three lives and that each time something bad happens, you lose a life. When you have no lives left, your game ends. The Update method contains the code that checks for the cheese hitting the bottom of the screen; you need only add some code that updates the life counter when this happens. The life counter must be reduced only when the player has some lives left, so the program must test for this, as follows:

```
if (cheese.Y + cheese.SpriteRectangle.Height >= maxDisplayY)
{
    cheese.YSpeed = Math.Abs(cheese.YSpeed) * -1;
    if (lives > 0)
    {
        lives--;
    }
}
```

Next, you need to stop the game from continuing when the number of lives reaches 0. The best way to do this is to exit from the Update method after you've moved the cheese but before you update the bread and look for tomatoes to collide with. This code uses the fact that C# lets a program return from a method at any point during the method:

```
protected override void Update(GameTime gameTime)
{
    . . .
    // code to move the cheese and update the life counter
    . . .
    if (lives <= 0)
    {
        return;
    }

    . . .
    // Code to update the bread position
    // Code to check for the cheese hitting the tomatoes
    . . .
}
```

The effect of this code is that when all the lives are used up, the cheese continues bouncing around the screen, but the score does not change, and the player is unable to control the bread.

You need to display the number of lives left alongside the player score. You can do this by adding this information to the string displayed by Draw:

```
protected override void Draw(GameTime gameTime)
{
    . . .
    // Code to clear the screen and draw the game elements
    . . .

    drawText(
        "Score : " + score.ToString() + " Lives : " + lives.ToString(),
        Color.White,
        minDisplayX,
        maxDisplayY - 50);

    . . .
    // Code to finish off the Draw method
    . . .
}
```

Adding Progression

Once the player has killed all the tomatoes, your game becomes very boring in that there's nothing left to do. Many games are built around the idea of successive levels, with each one being progressively more difficult than the last. The task of the player is to survive as long as possible, building up the highest score possible before all the lives are used up. One way you can achieve progression is by redrawing the tomatoes each time all of them have been destroyed. To make the game more difficult, you can redraw them lower down the screen so that the player has less time to react with each passing level.

To achieve this, you need to detect when all the tomatoes have been destroyed. One way to do this is to use a flag that's set when a tomato is found, as shown in the following code:

```
bool noTomatoes = true;

for (int i = 0; i < numberOfTomatoes; i++)
{
  if (tomatoes[i].Visible)
  {
    noTomatoes = false;
    if (cheese.SpriteRectangle.Intersects(tomatoes[i].SpriteRectangle))
    {
        cheese.YSpeed = cheese.YSpeed * -1;
        score = score + 10;
        tomatoes[i].Visible = false;
        break;
    }
  }
  tomatoes[i].SpriteRectangle.X = (int)tomatoes[i].X;
  tomatoes[i].SpriteRectangle.Y = (int)tomatoes[i].Y;
}

if (noTomatoes)
{
  resetTomatoDisplay();
}
```

The noTomatoes flag is set to false if a visible tomato is found in the list. If the loop completes and noTomatoes is still true, the program must call the resetTomatoDisplay method to put the tomatoes back on the screen again. The method moves the tomato draw height down the screen and then uses a loop to update the draw height of each tomato and make the tomato visible again:

```
void resetTomatoDisplay()
{
    tomatoHeight = tomatoHeight + (displayHeight * tomatoStepFactor);

    if (tomatoHeight > tomatoHeightLimit)
    {
        tomatoHeight = minDisplayY;
    }

    for (int i = 0; i < numberOfTomatoes; i++)
    {
        tomatoes[i].Visible = true;
        tomatoes[i].Y = tomatoHeight;
    }
}
```

The resetTomatoDisplay method cannot move the tomatoes down the screen indefinitely; otherwise, they would eventually fall off the bottom of the display. To prevent this, the method imposes a limit on how far down the screen tomatoes can be drawn. Once this limit is reached, the tomatoes are moved back to the top of the screen again. The limit value is set when the game starts, in the method that sets up the tomatoes:

```
void setupTomatoes()
{
    tomatoHeight = minDisplayY;
    tomatoHeightLimit = minDisplayY + ((maxDisplayY - minDisplayY) / 2);
    tomatoes = new GameSpriteStruct[numberOfTomatoes];
    float tomatoSpacing = (maxDisplayX - minDisplayX) / numberOfTomatoes;

    for (int i = 0; i < numberOfTomatoes; i++)
    {
        tomatoes[i].SpriteTexture = tomatoTexture;
        setupSprite(
            ref tomatoes[i],
            0.05f,  // 20 tomatos across the screen
            1000,   // 1000 ticks to move across the screen
            minDisplayX + (i * tomatoSpacing), minDisplayY,
            true  // initially visible
        );    }
}
```

> **Sample Code: Bread and Cheese Game** All the sample projects can be obtained from the Web resources for this text, which can be found at *http://oreilly.com/catalog/9780735651579*. The sample project in the 01 Bread and Cheese Game directory in the resources for this chapter is a fully working version of the game. Use the bread bat to hit the cheese at the tomato targets. When you've destroyed a complete row, the tomatoes are all redrawn. If you let the cheese hit the bottom of the screen, the life counter is reduced. Once all three lives have been used up, you cannot control the bread, and the score does not update.

Figure 13-1 shows a Bread and Cheese game in progress. This game is actually quite easy to play; it would be interesting to see how much better it would be made by adding a clock that timed the disposal of each level, or some additional forms of player jeopardy.

> **Note** There are some game-play issues with this design that your younger brother might notice, particularly the way that after a level is redrawn, the cheese often collides instantly with one of the tomatoes and gets above the tomato row, bouncing about and making a huge score. If you decide that this is a problem, there are a number of ways you could fix it. I'll leave it to you to sort it out.

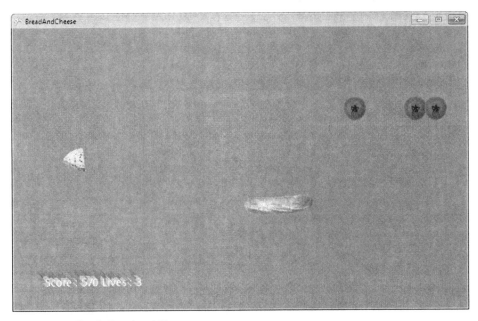

FIGURE 13-1 Simple Bread and Cheese game.

Improving Code Design

In Chapter 11, "A Game as a C# Program," in the section entitled "Renaming the *Game1* Class," you changed the name of the class to one that better reflects the game that's being created. Now you consider other ways that your programs can be better structured. At the moment, you haven't given much thought to the structure of the game program itself. When you have needed extra code, you simply added it where it seemed to do the job. However, this is not very good design practice.

It's much easier if code is structured into well-defined areas. If you think about it, all the cheese, bread, and tomato game elements are used in the same way. The game program performs a number of fundamental actions with these elements during a game:

1. The game elements are set up at the beginning of the game.

2. The game elements are updated during the game.

3. The game elements are drawn during the game.

At the moment, these actions are performed in a piecemeal fashion in the game methods that perform these tasks. However, it makes very good sense to bring the code for each element together so that they're easier to manage. Rather than having bits of behavior for all the elements in the Update method, you can change the Update method so that it instead calls a method for each game element type:

```
protected override void Update(GameTime gameTime)
{
    gamePad1 = GamePad.GetState(PlayerIndex.One);

    if (gamePad1.Buttons.Back == ButtonState.Pressed)
        this.Exit();

    updateCheese();

    if (lives <= 0)
    {
        return;
    }

    updateBread();

    updateTomatoes();

    base.Update(gameTime);
}
```

The same pattern could be used in the Setup and Draw methods. Note that these changes won't make the game program run more quickly (in fact, the method calls slow things down very slightly), but it makes things much easier for the programmer, as shown next. You might remember that the process of tidying up a program like this is known as refactoring. You first saw this in Chapter 11, where you changed the name of elements in your game to better reflect what they were used for. XNA Game Studio provides some useful refactoring features to help you organize your program and perform refactoring.

Refactoring by Creating Methods from Code

The refactoring support in XNA Game Studio makes it easy to create a method from a block of statements. First, you need to highlight the statements to be placed in the new method. Then right-click the block of code to bring up the Context menu, select Refactor, and then select Extract Method from the Refactor menu, as shown in Figure 13-2.

The Extract Method dialog box now appears, as shown in Figure 13-3. Enter the name of the method to be created and click OK.

XNA Game Studio creates a method with the name you've entered, puts the selected code into the method, and places a call to the method where the code used to be. You could have performed all these tasks yourself, but the automation makes it much easier.

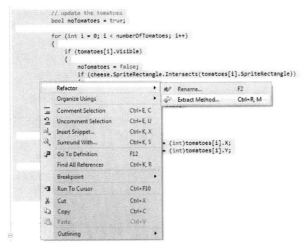

FIGURE 13-2 Opening the Extract Method dialog box.

FIGURE 13-3 Creating a method.

Note If the statements that you have extracted use variables that are local to the block of code from which the statements were taken, you will find that extracting a method stops your program from compiling correctly. You would need to fix the problem by declaring parameters for the new method and passing the variables as arguments.

Refactoring by Changing Identifiers

Frequently it's necessary to change identifiers as a program is developed. This happens because the purpose of the variables and methods changes as you gain a better understanding of the problem you're solving. At the start of the development, you created a method called setupSprites, which set up all the sprite settings for the elements in the game. However, this method now has other responsibilities; it must also set the score and life counters. If the purpose of a method changes, you should make sure to change the name of the method to reflect its purpose. This means that the name of the method should change to setupGame. The refactoring support in XNA Game Studio makes this easy. To rename an identifier, right-click the identifier you want to rename and select the appropriate refactoring command, as shown in Figure 13-4.

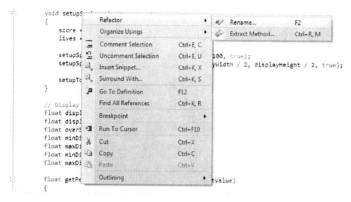

FIGURE 13-4 Selecting the rename operation.

The Rename dialog box now appears, as shown in Figure 13-5. You can type in the new name of the method and select options to control the renaming process. If you've created comments or text strings that refer to the method, you can ask XNA Game Studio to update these, too.

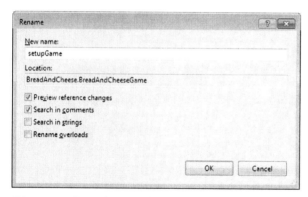

FIGURE 13-5 Renaming a method.

By default, the Preview Reference Changes check box is selected so that you are given a chance to see the names that are about to be changed, as shown in Figure 13-6. You can control which changes are to be made by selecting the check box next to each change.

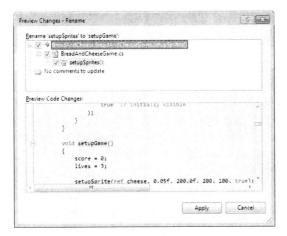

FIGURE 13-6 Previewing name changes.

When you click OK, the changes that you have requested are applied, and the program source code is updated. When renaming items, you must be careful that you don't break your program. Figure 13-7 shows the warning that XNA Game Studio displays if it detects that you're about to rename something that's used in other parts of the program.

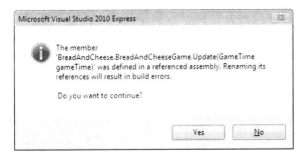

FIGURE 13-7 Warning of invalid name changes.

If you ignore this warning and perform the changes anyway, it's very likely that you'll prevent your program from compiling. The good news here, though, is that you can always use the Undo command in XNA Game Studio to remove the changes that you've made. Figure 13-8 shows where the command is on the Edit menu; you can also invoke it by pressing the left looping arrow on the toolbar or by using the key combination Ctrl+Z or Alt+Backspace.

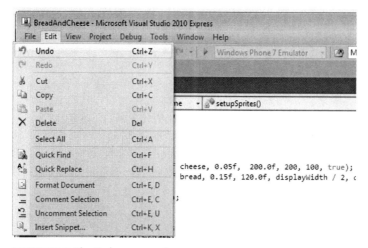

FIGURE 13-8 The Undo command.

Creating Code Regions

Another way to make program listings easier to understand is to use regions. A region is an area of the code that you can expand or collapse. For example, you can expand or collapse the view of your code by clicking on the plus (+) or minus (−) signs at the top of a method. You can also create regions that can be expanded or collapsed by enclosing related code in #region compiler directives, as shown in Figure 13-9. This shows a region around the collapsed methods that were created to manage the tomatoes in the game.

```
#region Tomato code and data

Texture2D tomatoTexture;
GameSpriteStruct[] tomatoes;
int numberOfTomatoes = 20;
float tomatoHeight;
float tomatoStepFactor = 0.1f;
float tomatoHeightLimit;

private void loadTomatoContent() {...}

void resetTomatoDisplay() {...}

void updateTomatoes() {...}

void drawTomatoes() {...}

#endregion
```

FIGURE 13-9 Creating code regions.

Regions can be placed inside other regions to make it easier for other programmers to find their way around your programs.

Creating Useful Comments

You've seen that Microsoft Visual Studio provides a feature called *Intellisense* when you're writing a program. When you're typing a statement that contains a method call, the structure of the method call is described to you automatically using Intellisense. Some of this information is obtained from specially formatted comments that have been added to the method itself. You first saw comments in Chapter 2, "Programs, Data, and Pretty Colors." They provide a way that you can leave notes in your program that the compiler ignores. If you give comments in a particular format, they can be used by the compiler to provide Intellisense to other programmers. As an example, consider the drawText method. Each of the parameters has a particular purpose, and you can add comments to describe them:

```
/// <summary>
/// Draws text on the screen
/// </summary>
/// <param name="text">text to write</param>
/// <param name="textColor">color of text</param>
/// <param name="x">left edge of text</param>
/// <param name="y">top of text</param>
void drawText(string text, Color textColor, float x, float y)
{
    // Draw statements
}
```

The comments are formatted so as to provide XNA Game Studio with Intellisense information so that now when you start coding a call of the method, the extra information is displayed. Figure 13-10 shows how the information is displayed when a call of drawText is being coded.

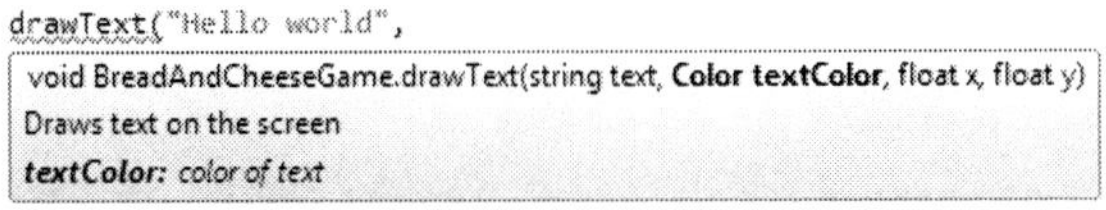

FIGURE 13-10 Using Intellisense comments.

The structure of the Intellisense comments has to be exactly right; otherwise, no help is displayed. You can create these by hand, or you can use XNA Game Studio to create a template for you to fill in. To obtain the template, you type three forward slash (/) characters in succession in the editor immediately above the item to which you wish to add the comment.

> **The Great Programmer Speaks: A Great Program Is a Work of Art** The Great Programmer reckons that, just as there is artistry in the design of a bridge or other great engineering work, well-written code is a thing of beauty. She regards code that uses properly chosen identifiers and appropriate methods and that is broken down into regions as being as worthy of admiration as any other work of art. She always tries to make sure that her code looks good.

> **Sample Code: Refactored Bread and Cheese Game** The sample project in the 02 Refactored Bread and Cheese Game directory in the resources for this chapter is a refactored version of the game. From the player's point of view, it's exactly the same. However, if you look at the source code of this program, you find that the code has been organized into a set of methods and separated into regions. You should find it much easier to locate particular items of code in the source file.

Adding a Background

At the moment, the game is played on the blue background that is provided by XNA. This is okay, but it doesn't look very special. To improve things, you could add a texture that's drawn behind the game. You can do this by following the same pattern that was used for the other graphics items. The set of background methods shown in this next code block match those that are provided for the bread, cheese, and tomatoes. You need only put calls to the following methods into the appropriate game methods, and you have a game with an attractive background image:

```
#region Background code and data

GameSpriteStruct background;
private void loadBackgroundContent()
{
    background.SpriteTexture =
            Content.Load<Texture2D>("Images\\Background");

    background.SpriteRectangle =
        new Rectangle(
            (int) minDisplayX, (int) minDisplayY,
            (int) (maxDisplayX - minDisplayX),
            (int) (maxDisplayY - minDisplayY)
        );
}
private void updateBackground()
{
}

private void drawBackground()
{
    spriteBatch.Draw(background.SpriteTexture,
        background.SpriteRectangle, Color.White);
}

#endregion
```

The background texture is drawn in an area that fills the playfield. This makes it easier for the player to determine when the cheese is going to bounce.

Note that there's an updateBackground method, but it is empty at the moment. Later, you might want to make the background flutter in the breeze or change color as the player approaches the high score. Leaving the method blank makes it easy to add code to do this.

> **Sample Code: Bread and Cheese with Background** The sample project in the 03 Bread and Cheese with Background directory in the resources for this chapter is a version of the game with a rather snazzy tablecloth in the background.

The use of this technique makes it much easier to add new elements to the game program. It also makes it easier to swap one element for another. If other programmers wanted to create a different type of background, you could tell them what methods they would need to provide, and then their code would plug directly into the game code. In later chapters, you will see ways to make genuinely "pluggable" software components that can be added to a game easily.

Adding a Title Screen

At the moment, the game starts when you run the program and then finishes when the last life has been used up by the player. This is not how real games work. If you watch a real video game, you might notice that it has an "attract" mode, where it shows a screen intended to entice the player into playing the game. You can create a simple version of this by adding a title screen like the one shown in Figure 13-11.

FIGURE 13-11 A tasteful title screen.

This screen is displayed when the game is not active. You create a title, `GameSpriteStruct`, and all the associated methods in the same way as you created a background earlier in this chapter.

Games and State

To make the title screen appear correctly, the program must manage the *state* of the game. The best way to do this is to create an enumerated type that has values to represent the states that the game can occupy. You first saw enumerated types in Chapter 9, "Reading Text Input." Each of the possible keys that the keyboard can generate is represented by a value of the enumerated type Keys. You create an enumerated type to hold the state of the game. This type has only two values, representing a state when the title screen is displayed and a state when the game is being played. Once the type has been created, you can make a variable of that type to hold the state of the game, setting it initially to the title screen state as follows:

```
enum GameState
{
    titleScreen,
    playingGame
}

GameState state = GameState.titleScreen;
```

If there are only two states the program can occupy, you might think that this is overkill. You could have just used a Boolean type, perhaps called gameActive, and make it true to indicate a game in progress and false to indicate that the title screen should be displayed. However, you might decide later to add other game states, perhaps one where the high-score table is displayed. This enhancement is easier to implement if you use an enumerated type instead of a Boolean type because you simply need to add a new value to the enumerated type to represent this state.

Using the State Values

The state variable in the game controls what happens in the Draw and Update methods. When the game is in the title screen state, the title screen needs to be drawn. When the game is in the playingGame state, the background, cheese, bread, and tomatoes need to be drawn. The following code accomplishes this:

```
protected override void Draw(GameTime gameTime)
{
    spriteBatch.Begin();

    switch (state)
    {
        case GameState.titleScreen:
            drawTitle();
            break;
        case GameState.playingGame:
            drawBackground();
            drawCheese();
            drawBread();
            drawTomatoes();
            drawScore();
            break;
```

```
    }

    spriteBatch.End();

    base.Draw(gameTime);
}
```

The Update method in the game contains a similar switch construction that would be used to
select the appropriate behavior:

```
protected override void Update(GameTime gameTime)
{
    gamePad1 = GamePad.GetState(PlayerIndex.One);

    if (gamePad1.Buttons.Back == ButtonState.Pressed)
        this.Exit();

    switch (state)
    {
        case GameState.titleScreen:
            updateTitle();  // changes state to playingGame when A pressed
            break;
        case GameState.playingGame:
            updateCheese(); // changes state to titleScreen when game ends
            updateBread();
            updateTomatoes();
            break;
    }

    base.Update(gameTime);
}
```

Building a State Machine

Now that you've identified the states that the game occupies, you need to consider what
causes the game program to move from one state to another. In professional programming,
this is shown using a state diagram, as shown in Figure 13-12.

A state diagram shows the entry point (the black filled-in blob) and then arrows that show
transition from one state to another. Some of the arrows have "guard conditions" on them
that identify things that must happen for the transition to take place. The diagram shows
that when the game starts, it moves into the "Title Screen" state, and then, if the A button is
pressed, it moves into the "Playing Game" state. Once the player has no lives left, it moves
back onto the title screen.

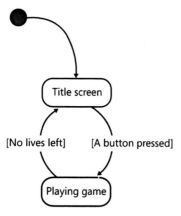

FIGURE 13-12 A game state diagram.

State diagrams are useful in showing how a program behaves. They tell the programmer that at certain points, the program must behave in a certain way; for example, in the previous game state machine, there's no need to test the A button when the player is playing the game. State diagrams are used often in games when game items have a range of possible states. Once you've identified the states, you need to create some methods that manage the transition from one state to another. You need one method to start the game and one that's called when the game is over. The methods must set up all the variables as required and then change the state of the game. Look at the following code:

```
#region Game state management

void startGame()
{
    score = 0;
    lives = 3;
    startCheese();
    startBread();
    startTomatoes();
    state = GameState.playingGame;
}

void gameOver()
{
    if (score > highScore)
    {
        highScore = score;
    }
    state = GameState.titleScreen;
}

#endregion
```

The startGame method clears the score, sets the number of lives left to three, and begins the game. It also calls a method for each of the game elements to reset it to a known position before the game starts running. This makes sure that the bread is sensibly placed on the screen and the cheese isn't so near the edge that the player loses a life as soon as the game starts, which wouldn't be very fair.

The gameOver method updates the high score if it's been beaten and then puts the game back to the titleScreen state. Now all you need to do is call these methods at the appropriate times to change the states in the game state machine. When the player presses the A button, the game must call the startGame method. The test for this should be placed in the updateTitle method, which updates the title screen:

```
if (gamePad1.Buttons.A == ButtonState.Pressed)
{
    startGame();
}
```

A game ends when the last life is used up. The test for this should be placed in the updateCheese method:

```
if (cheese.Y + cheese.SpriteRectangle.Height >= maxDisplayY)
{
    cheese.YSpeed = Math.Abs(cheese.YSpeed) * -1;
    lives = lives - 1;
    if (lives <= 0)
    {
        gameOver();
    }
}
```

Sample Code: Bread and Cheese with Title Screen The sample project in the 04 Bread and Cheese with Title Screen directory in the resources for this chapter is a version of the game that operates using a state machine to provide a title screen.

Many games show different displays during their "attract mode." It's easy to get your game to do this by making the program change from one state to another over time. The game code can do this by counting the number of times that titleUpdate has been called and then moving to another state when the counter reaches a particular value.

The Great Programmer Speaks: State Machines Are a Great Way to Write Programs The Great Programmer uses state machines a lot in her code. They let her programs "remember" where they are so that they can respond correctly when an event happens. She starts off by working out what states her program must occupy and identifying the events that cause the states to change. Once she has done this and drawn her state diagram, she can go ahead and write the code.

Conclusion

At last, you've created what might be regarded as a finished game. It has some rough edges and is rather simple to play, but it should keep your younger brother quiet for an hour or so. You've seen how the way a program is structured and laid out in the source file can have a huge impact on how easy it is to work with the code. You've also discovered some fundamentals of game program behavior by finding out how a state machine can be used to manage the operation of a game.

Chapter Review Questions

I don't know a better way to end a chapter than with some review questions. I really don't.

1. A program returns from a method only when it reaches the end of that method block.

2. Refactoring is how you change the type of the variables.

3. Method names can't be changed once a program has been written.

4. Each code region in a program is stored in a separate source file.

5. Intellisense information is retrieved from code regions.

6. A state machine can have only two possible states.

Chapter 14
Classes, Objects, and Games

In this chapter, you will

- Find out about making programs using software objects.

- Learn some software engineering terms and what they mean when we write programs.

- Use objects to add some new elements to our game easily.

Introduction

In this chapter, you learn something about the craft of programming and how writing a good solution to a problem is all about organization. You also see how a well-organized program is simple to extend and modify, and how to create software components that make it possible to create code mashups very easily.

The Great Programmer is very keen on this chapter. You might not be quite so enthusiastic, but it has to be said that objects do make software construction much easier. The whole of Microsoft XNA is built around objects, so to get a complete understanding of how the framework fits together, you really have to know about objects and how a system is built using them.

Design with Objects

We have seen that if we want to store a block of information about a particular item, we can bring all this together in a structure. We used this technique when we created the GameSpriteStruct structure in Chapter 12, "Games, Objects, and State." Structures are useful, but we would like to be able to solve other problems when we create large programs:

- We want to make sure that a given item in our program cannot be placed into an invalid state; that is, we don't want to have tomatoes that can be positioned off the display screen.

- We want to be able to separate a large system into distinct and isolated parts that can be developed independently and made to work together; that is, we want to get one team of programmers working on game backgrounds, another on the cheese, another on animated bread, and so on.

- We want to make sure that the effort involved with making new types of game elements is as small as possible; that is, if we decide to introduce a new "killer tomato" we want to be able to make use of the existing tomato code as much as we can.

To do all these things, we are going to have to start to consider programs from the point of view of object-based design. This section should come with some kind of a health warning along the lines of "Some of these ideas might hurt your head a bit at the start." But the following points are also very important:

■ Objects don't add any new behaviors to our programs—we know just about everything we need to know to write programs when we know about variables, statements, loops, conditions, and arrays.

■ Objects are best regarded as a solution to the problem of design. They let us talk about systems in general terms. We can decide which objects we need and then go back and refine how the objects actually do their tasks once we have decided how they fit together.

You can write just about every program that has ever been written just by using the technologies that we have seen so far. But objects allow you to work in a much nicer way. And so you are going to have to get the hang of them, like it or not.

An Object Refresher Course

At this point, it is probably worth reminding ourselves what a software object is. An object is a collection of data (fields) and behaviors (methods) that a programmer creates for a particular purpose. An XNA game is an object. It contains data such as the GraphicsDevice (which describes the display system our game can use) and methods such as Draw (which provides the draw behavior for the game). You have created the beginnings of an object with your GameSpriteStruct structure, which brings together information about an item to be displayed on the game screen.

In this chapter, you find out what makes a full-fledged object and how systems are designed using them. To learn how objects can be used in the design and construction of a game, you rebuild the Bread and Cheese game program, this time using objects. Then, in the payoff at the end, you find out how easy an object-based design makes it to add a new game element in the form of the "deadly pepper," which provides a new hazard for the player to deal with. You learn some of the software engineering principles that the Great Programmer seems to know, and how they can be used to improve the design of the game program.

Cohesion and Objects

Cohesion is a term used by software engineers to express how "together" an object is. A "together" object is a bit like those people who are always very organized and always have everything sorted. If you went camping with a "together" object, you would find that it would always know what to do and have the tools with it to do the job. It would not be the one borrowing a can opener from the people in the tent next door so that it could open the can of beans for breakfast. It would have a "can opener" behavior built in, along with everything else it needed to be able to do.

The GameSpriteStruct type is not very "together"; all the data inside it has been made public so that the outside world can get hold of its contents and use the values. Although this has been quite convenient, it is not the best way to create reliable programs. At the moment, it is possible for any code to access the value of SpriteRectangle that the GameSpriteStruct uses to position itself on the screen. This means that a naughty programmer could change the location of the sprite to a random place, which is not good. This would be even more dangerous if you were designing objects to hold bank account information, where you want to protect the account balance and control how money is paid in and out.

Creating a Cohesive *BatSpriteStruct*

Rather than having one generic type of sprite structure, you must now think about each kind of sprite in turn. You can start with the bat, which in the previous game was drawn as a piece of bread. Once you make a bat sprite, you have something that can be moved around the screen by the player. This might come in very handy in any game you might create later that needs any kind of bat. What you want is a BatSpriteStruct that can look after itself and keep its internal data private. It should be able to behave as a bat, and it should not be possible for other programs to upset this behavior. To do this, you need to protect the data inside the bat object, so that programs outside can't see or change the values that control how the bat behaves.

Protecting Data Inside Objects

The C# language provides a means by which data in an object can be made private, so that only methods inside the object can access the data. Of course, once the data has been made private, it is impossible for the outside world to use the data to interact with the bat, so you must add some public behaviors (methods) so that the bat can be asked to do things. Public members of a class can be used by code in any other class. When creating objects with high cohesion, the data in the object should be private and the methods should be public. You select whether or not a member is private or public by putting the appropriate C# keyword in front of the class member when you declare it. From now on you will take care to make sure that only members of a class that need to be used by other classes are made public, and that all other members are made private.

BatSpriteStruct Behaviors

The early part of the design of an object focuses on what it needs to do. Then you can consider the data that the object needs to hold to perform the required actions. There are four things we want the bat to be able to do for our game:

- **Load its content**   Load the texture to be used to draw the object itself on the screen.

- **Start a new game**   Set up the rectangle for drawing the bat and set the initial position and speed at the start of a game.

- **Update itself**   Update the bat position during the game.

- **Draw itself**   Draw the bat at its required position.

There might be other methods that we need later, but these are a start. You can create a method for each of these actions. If this looks like you are taking the different methods out of the regions that were set up when we refactored the program and putting them inside the bat object, that is exactly what you are doing. The methods that make a bat behave like a bat are now being moved into a bat structure. These methods work on data held privately inside the object, so that any code outside the bat is not able to put it in the wrong place on the screen by directly changing the member variables that hold its position:

```
struct BatSpriteStruct
{
    private Texture2D spriteTexture;
    private Rectangle spriteRectangle;
    private float x;
    private float y;
    private float xSpeed;
    private float ySpeed;

    public void LoadTexture(Texture2D inSpriteTexture)
    {
        spriteTexture = inSpriteTexture;
    }

    public void StartGame(
        float widthFactor,
        float ticksToCrossScreen,
        float inDisplayWidth,
        float initialX,
        float initialY)
    {
        spriteRectangle.Width = (int)((inDisplayWidth * widthFactor) + 0.5f);
        float aspectRatio =
            (float)spriteTexture.Width / spriteTexture.Height;
        spriteRectangle.Height =
            (int)((spriteRectangle.Width / aspectRatio) + 0.5f);
        x = initialX;
        y = initialY;
        xSpeed = inDisplayWidth / ticksToCrossScreen;
        ySpeed = xSpeed;
    }

    public void Draw(SpriteBatch spriteBatch)
    {
        spriteBatch.Draw(spriteTexture, spriteRectangle, Color.White);
    }

    public void Update()
    {
        GamePadState gamePad1 = GamePad.GetState(PlayerIndex.One);
        x = x + (xSpeed * gamePad1.ThumbSticks.Left.X);
        y = y - (ySpeed * gamePad1.ThumbSticks.Left.Y);
        spriteRectangle.X = (int)x;
        spriteRectangle.Y = (int)y;
    }
}
```

This is all that is needed to make a working bat. The world outside the bat knows it only by the methods it exposes, and everything about how the bat works is hidden inside and can't be damaged by the outside world.

Objects and Encapsulation

Another software engineering term we can use at this point is *encapsulation*, the approach where everything relating to a particular part of a system is placed in a single object. If you think about it, this is how a lot of appliances work. Your MP3 player contains a computer and some very complicated software, but as far as you are concerned, it just has buttons that you press to select music tracks and play them. You don't know (or even care) how it works internally. You just know which buttons to press to get sound out.

Users of the bat sprite can work the same way. They don't need to know how the bat manages internal state, what variables it contains, or how the methods actually work, they just know what each method does and how to use it. Any game can now contain a `BatSpriteStruct` value and call the methods at the appropriate points to add a bread bat to the game.

> **Sample Code: Bat Sprite Structure** All the sample projects can be obtained from the Web resources for this text, which can be found at *http://oreilly.com/catalog/9780735651579*. The sample project in the 01 Bat Sprite Structure directory in the resources for this chapter contains a `BatSpriteStruct` structure that implements a self-contained bat. This is then used to provide a bread bat that can be steered around the screen.

The next step is to consider how the bread bat can be made to work with other objects to create a working game.

> **The Great Programmer Speaks: Cohesion Is Good** The Great Programmer is going to be talking a lot in this chapter. She really likes cohesion. She likes the way that the bat is now "master of its own destiny." There is no chance that any other part of the program can affect the behavior of the bat. They have to use the four methods described in this section to drive it, and they cannot damage the data inside it. She could give this implementation of the bat to a customer knowing that they could not break it, which for her is a very good thing.

Coupling Between Objects

Now that you have a bat object, you need to connect it to the other game objects. You start with the cheese object, which is acting as the ball in the game and needs to be able to find the location of the bat so that it can make the ball change direction when it hits the bat. Software engineers like the Great Programmer call this kind of object linkage *coupling*. She carefully manages the amount of coupling in her programs because a lot of coupling in a program is bad. If all the objects in a program are coupled together, this makes it much harder to change one component because you have to worry about how the change might affect everything else.

This is a bit like organizing a party. The more people you have to organize, the harder it is to find a free evening. If you are inviting (coupled to) only one or two people, then you can sort out things like the date of the party really quickly. However, if you have lots of friends, and they have lots of friends that they want to bring, too, it can be very hard to agree on a date.

The fewer objects that are coupled, the easier it is to manage change in a program. It is also easier to manage change if the way that the objects are coupled is restricted to a few well-defined connections. Rather than letting the ball structure have access to all the data inside the bat, it makes sense for the bread bat to provide a method that lets the ball ask if it has collided with it. If this is the only form of communication between the ball and the bat, any other changes to them (for example, an animated trail of crumbs behind the bread bat) can be added without fear of changing the way this part of the game works. Good program design is all about making sure that the amount of coupling between different program elements is as small as possible.

> **The Great Programmer Speaks: Proper Design Is Vital** This all sounds like a lot of work. Your game seems to be getting more complicated for no good reason. You make this point to the Great Programmer, who just shrugs and starts up a copy of "Halo Wars" on her Xbox. She gets to a point where her forces are attacking an enemy base. The screen is alive with troops, spartans, warthogs, and gunfire. Then she pauses the game and reminds you that the program behind the scenes must be keeping track of every battlefield element, every vehicle, character, bullet, and flash of light. There must be hundreds of different objects on the screen, all interacting with each other and doing their own thing to make up the game world. A team of programmers must have worked on these objects, with one group doing the vehicles, another the characters, a third the bullets, and so on.
>
> She tells you that if the objects in the game were not carefully organized, it would have been impossible to create the game program. She reckons that modern computer games are among the most complicated software around, and so you need to use these techniques to make sure that the programs are properly structured and the development can be managed across a team of people.

Creating a Link Between the Bread Bat and the Cheese Ball

You will implement the coupling between the bat and ball by providing a method in the BatSpriteStruct. The method is called CheckCollision:

```
public bool CheckCollision(Rectangle target)
{
    return spriteRectangle.Intersects(target);
}
```

Next, the ball has to be provided with a way that it can find the bat sprite when the game is running. The best way is to provide the Update method in the cheese with a reference to the BreadAndCheeseGame game object that represents the running game. The ball can then get hold of data items in the game, including the bat sprite. This link also allows the ball to tell the game itself that lives have been lost if the ball hits the bottom of the display. This information is provided as a parameter to the call of Update in the ball.

```
public struct BallSpriteStruct
{

    // ...
    // All the other members for the ball
    // ...

    /// <summary>
    /// Update the ball position. Handle collisions with the bat.
    /// </summary>
    /// <param name="game">Game the ball is part of</param>
    public void Update(BreadAndCheeseGame game)
    {
        x = x + xSpeed;
        y = y + ySpeed;

        // Set the sprite rectangle to the new position
        spriteRectangle.X = (int)(x + 0.5f);
        spriteRectangle.Y = (int)(y + 0.5f);

        // Check to see if the ball has hit the bat
        if (game.BreadBat.CheckCollision(spriteRectangle))
        {
            // bat has hit the ball.
            ySpeed = ySpeed * -1;
        }

        // Other updates here
    }

    // ...
    // Rest of ball members
    // ...

}
```

When the game is running, the ball can now check for collisions with the bat and behave correctly when it hits it. When the game calls the Update method in the ball, it needs to provide a reference to the game object. C# provides a key word called this, which allows an object to get hold of a reference to itself, shown in bold here:

```
// Update method for the BreadAndCheeseGame
protected override void Update(GameTime gameTime)
{
    GamePadState gamePad1 = GamePad.GetState(PlayerIndex.One);

    if (gamePad1.Buttons.Back == ButtonState.Pressed)
        this.Exit();

    BreadBat.Update(this);
    CheeseBall.Update(this);

    base.Update(gameTime);
}
```

The this key word means "a reference to me." When used within the BreadAndCheeseGame class, it means the currently executing instance of the game class. This is exactly what the ball needs, so that it can get the bat variable out of the game and use it to check for collisions. The ball can also use this reference to tell the game when a life has been lost because the ball has hit the bottom of the screen.

Designing Object Interactions

It is important to manage carefully what each of the game objects is responsible for, what it needs to interact with, and what it needs from what it interacts with. There are several objects in our game, and for each of them, you need to work out what methods it needs to have and who uses them. You can draw these out in tables like Table 14-1.

TABLE 14-1 Methods in *BatSpriteStruct*

Method	Description	Users
LoadTexture	Loads the texture into the bat	BreadAndCheeseGame
StartGame	Calculates the bat size and positions it for the start of the game	BreadAndCheeseGame
Draw	Draws the bat	BreadAndCheeseGame
Update	Updates the bat	BreadAndCheeseGame
CheckCollision	Checks for collision with the bread bat	Ball

This looks very much like the list of bat methods we saw earlier, but there is now the additional method to check for collisions. This table tells us what objects the bat interacts with. For example, you can see that the design of the game does not need the bat to interact with the tomatoes. You can make changes to the bat behavior without affecting how the tomato works, and vice versa.

Software designers draw up tables like these when they are trying to decide what each thing in a system should do. I'm not suggesting that you should create such tables every time you write a program, but they do help you think about the way your solution should be structured.

Objects and Messages

The bat object is one of the simplest ones, but some of the objects need to change the state of the game. Every time the ball hits the bottom of the screen, it needs to tell the game that a life has been lost, and when the ball hits a tomato target, this causes the game score to increase. This makes the game itself a kind of "fourth object," after the bat, ball, and tomato targets. Table 14-2 lists methods for a game object.

TABLE 14-2 **Methods in *BreadAndCheeseGame***

Method	Description	Users
LoseLife	Lose a life	Ball
AddToScore	Adds a value to the score	Ball

The ball object needs to use a reference to the game it is part of, so that it can call methods in the game to send these messages. When the ball is updated, it is given such a reference so that it can call the methods at the appropriate times.

Messages and Organization

At this level, designing a program sounds a lot like an organizational problem, and it is. Consider the example of a ship: The captain gives orders to the mate to set sail in a particular direction. But the captain must also respond to messages from those on the ship. The captain tells the lookout to scan the horizon for pirates. If the lookout spots a suspicious ship, the lookout calls out to the captain, who sends out further orders to the crew to prepare to repel boarders.

A good programmer must be able to work out what each object needs to do and how the objects communicate to create a solution. Note that there is never just one way to structure a program. If you look at my design, you find that the cheese ball does most of the work (you might want to call it the "Big Cheese," I suppose—but I won't) but it is perfectly possible to organize everything around another game object if you wish. The Great Programmer says that there are only two kinds of solutions—those that work and those that don't—and that everything else is just detail. In this, I'm inclined to agree with her.

> **Sample Code: Bread and Cheese Sprite Structures** The sample project in the 02 Bat and Ball Sprite Structures directory in the resources for this chapter contains a `BatSpriteStruct` structure that implements a self-contained bread bat and BallSpriteStruct that implements the cheese. This does not implement all the game play (there are some tomatoes missing) but it does have all the behaviors for the bat, ball, and other game objects. A full table of all the objects and how they interact is also included in the directory.

Container Objects

We now have a very well-organized game that is not complete. The ball and the bat interact properly, but there are presently no tomato targets to aim at. Actually, it turns out that "No Tomatoes" is the punch line of one of my favorite jokes ("What is red and not there?"), but this is not going to help in terms of getting a game that is worth playing. We now need to investigate how we can create tomato target objects and add them.

When adding tomatoes to the game, we have to ask ourselves whether the game should work with individual tomato targets or whether it should work in terms of a collection of them. From the point of view of the game, it makes very good sense to regard the whole row of targets as a single item. The row has to manage things like deciding when the last target has been destroyed, and it makes sense for all this behavior to be hidden from the game itself. The game just calls the Update and Draw behaviors for the row, as it would any other object in the game.

The fact that there are lots of targets inside this object does not affect the game at all. You can use this technique to good effect whenever a game of yours needs to manage lots of related items. Many games have "waves" of attacking aliens, and putting them all in a single collection like this makes them much easier to manage. Table 14-3 lists methods for a target collection.

TABLE 14-3 Methods in *TargetRowStruct*

Method	Description	Users
LoadTexture	Loads the texture for use on the targets	BreadAndCheeseGame
StartGame	Calculates the texture size and positions all the targets for the start of the game	BreadAndCheeseGame
Draw	Draws all the visible targets	BreadAndCheeseGame
Update	Updates the targets and redraws the row if no targets are left	BreadAndCheeseGame
CheckCollision	Checks for collision with the cheese and hides the target that was hit	Ball

These methods look very similar to the ones supplied by the bat sprite, although the way that they are used is slightly different.

The next block of code shows the data that TargetRowStruct stores for a row of tomato targets. The texture is stored once for the entire row, and there is an array of rectangles that holds the position on the screen of each of the targets. This illustrates another common game technique: the same texture is used for a large number of game objects. There is also an array called TargetVisibility, which is used to keep track of which targets in the row are visible. This controls the draw process and is also used to decide when a row needs to be restored and redrawn at the end of a level:

```
public struct TargetRowStruct
{
    private Texture2D targetTexture;
    private Rectangle[] targets;
    private bool[] targetVisibility;

    private int numberOfTargetss;
    private float targetWidth;
    private float targetHeight;
    private float targetStepFactor;
    private float targetHeightLimit;
}
```

> **Sample Code: Bat, Ball, and Targets** The sample project in the 03 Bat, Ball and Targets
> directory in the resources for this chapter contains a version of the game that is nearly playable.
> You can direct the bread bat around the screen and use it to send the ball toward the targets,
> which vanish when they are hit. When the last target is destroyed, the whole row is redrawn
> correctly.

Perhaps the most interesting thing about this sample program is the Draw method:

```
protected override void Draw(GameTime gameTime)
{
    GraphicsDevice.Clear(Color.CornflowerBlue);

    spriteBatch.Begin();

    BreadBat.Draw(spriteBatch);
    CheeseBall.Draw(spriteBatch);
    TomatoTargets.Draw(spriteBatch);

    spriteBatch.End();

    base.Draw(gameTime);
}
```

This Draw method is now tiny. All the responsibility for the draw behaviors has been
delegated to the objects in our game. If we add more game objects, we can use the same
mechanism.

Background and Title Screen Objects

The final two objects that are needed for the game are the background and title screen.
These are actually very similar, in that they are both just textures that must be drawn over the
entire screen. However, the title screen is slightly different in that it has an Update behavior
that checks for the player pressing the A button. When the player presses the A button, the
game needs to start, which means that the BreadAndCheeseGame object must provide a
method that can be called to get the game going. Here's the title screen's Update method:

```
public void Update(BreadAndCheeseGame game)
{
    if (game.GamePad1.Buttons.A == ButtonState.Pressed)
    {
        game.StartGame();
    }
}
```

This is the Update method for TitleSpriteStruct. It is provided with a reference to the
game from which it reads the gamepad settings. If the gamepad has the A button pressed,
the StartGame method is called to get the game going.

> **Sample Code: 04 Bread and Cheese** The sample project in the 04 Bread and Cheese directory in the resources for this chapter contains a version of the game that is fully playable. It works in exactly the same way as the one you developed in the previous chapter, but the Great Programmer prefers to play this version because it is structured better.

At first glance, it looks very similar to the original code, but there are some important changes. All the components could be taken out and used in other games. If you think another game you're developing would be improved by a row of targets or some bouncing balls, you can add the objects and connect them into the Draw and Update behaviors of the game easily.

You have started to build a library of items that can be reused for different games. It now looks a lot easier to make an XNA version of tennis because you have the ball and bat components ready-made. However, reusing components isn't quite as easy as you might like, and we do seem to have a lot of code duplication, in that every structure we have made contains the same LoadTexture method. You might be wondering if there is an easier way to arrange the game objects, and it turns out there is. At this point, we have to leave behind structures and start to work with classes. But first we have to consider how classes and structures differ.

Classes and Structures

In C#, classes and structures are two different kinds of object. They can both hold data fields and contain methods. However, there are some crucial differences between the two. One is that structures are managed in terms of *value,* whereas classes are managed in terms of *reference.* We first discovered these terms in the section entitled "Working with Arrays, Objects, and References," in Chapter 9, "Reading Text Input." Now it is time to understand how they really work and how to use them.

Creating and Using a Structure

We have already seen how to make a structure in C#. The BackgroundSpriteStruct structure was created to hold information about the background display in our game. This is the simplest display element in the game; it just displays the tablecloth texture behind our game sprites:

```
public struct BackgroundSpriteStruct
{
    private Texture2D spriteTexture;
    private Rectangle spriteRectangle;

    public void LoadTexture(Texture2D inSpriteTexture)
    {
        spriteTexture = inSpriteTexture;
    }
```

```
    public void SetRectangle(Rectangle inSpriteRectangle)
    {
        spriteRectangle = inSpriteRectangle;
    }

    public void Draw(SpriteBatch spriteBatch)
    {
        spriteBatch.Draw(spriteTexture, spriteRectangle, Color.White);
    }
}
```

Once the structure has been set up, the program can declare variables of this type:

```
public BackgroundSpriteStruct Background;
```

This sprite contains the texture for the background. Later in the program, the sprite is set with the size of the rectangle it is going to use to draw:

```
// fill the visible area with the background texture
Background.SetRectangle(
    new Rectangle(
        (int)minDisplayX, (int)minDisplayY,
        (int)(maxDisplayX - minDisplayX),
        (int)(maxDisplayY - minDisplayY)
    ));
```

This statement creates a `Rectangle` that fills the playable area of the screen and sets this as the one that is used by the background texture when it draws itself.

Creating and Using an Instance of a Class

We can make a tiny change to the C# code shown previously by converting the background sprite to a class:

```
class BackgroundSpriteClass
{
    // rest of object just as before
}
```

The game element information is now being held in a class rather than a structure. You might think that we can now use a `BackgroundSpriteClass` value in exactly the same way as the structure version, but this does not work. The program compiles correctly, but when we try to run it, the following exception is thrown:

```
System.NullReferenceException was unhandled
```

What is going on? To understand what is happening, you need to know what is performed by this statement:

```
BackgroundSpriteClass Background;
```

It looks like the declaration of a variable called Background. But in the case of a class, it is not what it seems. What you actually get when the program obeys the statement is a new reference variable called Background. This reference variable is allowed to refer to instances of the BackgroundSpriteClass. You can think of a reference a bit like a luggage tag, in that it can be tied to something with a piece of rope. Figure 14-1 illustrates this concept.

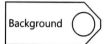

FIGURE 14-1 The Background reference variable as a luggage tag.

A program uses a reference by following the rope to the object it is tied to. When we used arrays in Chapter 9, we had the idea of arrows that "point" at the object. A tag tied with a piece of rope is a slightly more accurate way of describing what is happening. The thing to remember is that when you create a reference, you don't actually get one of the things that it refers to, you just get a tag. When the program runs and tries to follow the reference to get to an object, it fails, because the reference does not actually go anywhere. A reference is initially set to the value null, which we first saw in Chapter 9 in the section entitled "References and *null*." As we saw then, following a null reference results in a program failing.

You can solve this problem by creating an instance of the class and then connecting our tag variable to it. The best place to do this is in the Initialize method of the game:

```
protected override void Initialize()
{
    setScreenSizes();

    Background = new BackgroundSpriteClass();

    // Other initialization stuff here

    base.Initialize();
}
```

This part of the method creates an instance of the BackgroundSpriteClass class and makes the reference variable Background refer to it. We have seen this new key word before. We use it to create arrays. This is because an array is actually implemented by a class, and so we use new to create it. When we create the instance, we actually connect the tag to an object in memory, as shown in Figure 14-2.

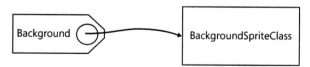

FIGURE 14-2 The *Background* reference variable connected to a *BackgroundSpriteClass* instance.

References

We now have to get used to the idea that if we want to use classes, we have to use references. The two come hand in hand and are inseparable. Structures are useful, but for real object-oriented satisfaction, you have to have a class, and that means that we must manage our access to a particular instance by using references to it. Actually, this is not that painful in reality, in that just about all the time you can treat a reference as if it really was the object, but you must remember that when you hold a reference, you do not hold an instance—you hold a tag that is tied onto an instance.

Multiple References to an Instance

Perhaps another example of references would help at this point. Consider the following code:

```
BackgroundSpriteClass Background = new BackgroundSpriteClass ();
BackgroundSpriteClass temp = Background;
temp.SetRectangle(
    new Rectangle(
        0, 0,   // position of rectangle
        800, 600 // size of rectangle
    ));
```

The question is: What is the resulting value of the rectangle in Background? If we draw a diagram like the one in Figure 14-3, the answer becomes clearer.

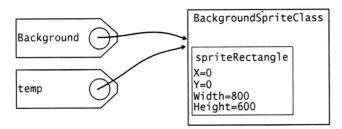

FIGURE 14-3 Multiple references to a single *BackgroundSpriteClass* instance.

Both of the tags refer to the same instance of BackgroundGameSprite. This means that any changes that are made to the object that temp refers to also are reflected in the one that Background refers to because they are the same object. This indicates a trickiness with objects and references. There is no limit to the number of references that can be attached to a single instance, so you need to remember that changing the object that a reference refers to will change that instance from the point of view of other references to the same object.

No References to an Instance

Just to complete the description, we need to consider what happens if an object has no references to it, as in the following:

```
BackgroundSpriteClass Background = new BackgroundSpriteClass ();
Background.SetRectangle(
    new Rectangle(
        0, 0,    // position of rectangle
        100, 200 // size of rectangle
    ));
Background = new BackgroundSpriteClass ();
Background.SetRectangle(
    new Rectangle(
        0, 0,    // position of rectangle
        800, 600 // size of rectangle
    ));
```

This code makes a BackgroundSpriteClass instance, sets the rectangle to a particular value, and then makes another BackgroundSpriteClass instance and sets the rectangle of that one to a different value. The question is: What happens to the first instance? Again, this can be made clear with a diagram such as Figure 14-4.

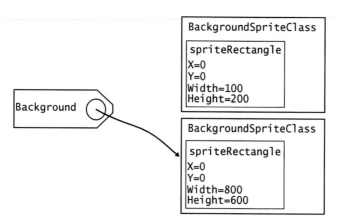

FIGURE 14-4 No references to a *BackgroundSpriteClass* instance.

The first instance is shown "hanging" in space, with nothing referring to it. As far as using data in the instance is concerned, it might as well not be there. When your program is running, a special process called the *garbage collector* has the job of finding such useless items and disposing of them. You first saw the garbage collector in Chapter 9 in the aptly named section "Say Hello to the Garbage Collector"; now you know the full reference-powered truth about how the process works.

Why Bother with References?

References don't sound much fun at the moment. They seem to make it harder to create and use objects and can be the source of much confusion. So why do we bother with them?

To answer this, we can consider the Pacific island of Yap. The currency in use on this island is based around 12-foot-tall stones that weigh several hundred pounds each. The value of a "coin" in the Yap currency is directly related to the number of men who died in the process of bringing the rock to the island. When the residents pay someone with one of these coins, they don't actually pick it up and give it to the person. Instead, they just say, "The coin in the road at the top of the hill is now yours." In other words, they use references to manage objects that they don't want to have to move around.

That is why we use references in our programs. A program can load textures, sounds, and other large objects and they can be left sitting in memory. If a method needs to be given a particular object to work with (for example, if a large sound effect needs to be played), the method can be supplied with a reference to the sound to be used. A downside with using references is that whenever a program wants to use an actual value, it needs to follow the reference to get to the item. This can slow a program down slightly.

Value and Reference Types

We know that everything in C# is an object and that objects can contain methods and data fields. We also know there are two kinds of objects: those managed by value and those managed by reference. Objects managed by value include all the low-level data types such as `int`, `float`, and `double`, along with slightly more complex XNA data types such as `Color`. Any object created as a C# `struct` is also managed by value. By default, whenever a program does something with an object that is managed by value, the *value* of that object is used. The assignment operation copies the value of a variable from one to another. Value types are used in situations where you are working with small amounts of data (for example, numeric values), and the effort of following references would slow things down.

Objects managed by reference include large and complex types such as the `SoundEffect` and `Texture2D` items in an XNA game. The reference assignment makes the variable being assigned to refer to the same object as the source. Whenever a program does something with an object that is managed by reference, a *reference* to that object is used. This means that large objects can be used within a program without the effort of actually copying their contents around in memory.

Should Our Game Objects Be Classes or Structures?

Classes are objects that are managed by reference. Structures are objects that are managed by value. Up to now, we have used structures because we like the way that they can combine data and behaviors and we don't need to use new to make them; but now, classes are starting to look interesting. We have come to an important question. What should we do with our game objects? Should they be value types (structures) or reference types (classes)? We have reached that high spot of many films and TV shows, the courtroom scene. This is where the prosecutor and the defendant do battle to decide the outcome—should the hero walk free or go to jail? So, without further ado, let's present the case for both sides, with you as the judge.

Game Objects Should Be Structures Managed by Value

First, we have the case for game objects as structures. The case here looks pretty clear-cut. Value types are a good idea when the objects don't hold much data, your program makes heavy use of them, and you want to have lots of them in memory. The objects in our game are actually quite small, only a few tens of bytes in size, and a game could have hundreds, perhaps thousands of them on the screen at once. All the game objects are updated and drawn 60 times a second, and so they are used a lot. This would be much quicker if the program didn't have to waste time following references to find each one.

At this point, the case for the structure looks pretty watertight, and the Great Programmer (who is presenting the case that we should be using classes) should be looking nervous. But she doesn't. Perhaps this is because she knows something we don't.

Game Objects Should Be Classes Managed by Reference

The Great Programmer doesn't say a great deal at the start of her presentation. Instead, she just opens up a diagram that she has brought with her and shows it to you. Look at Figure 14-5.

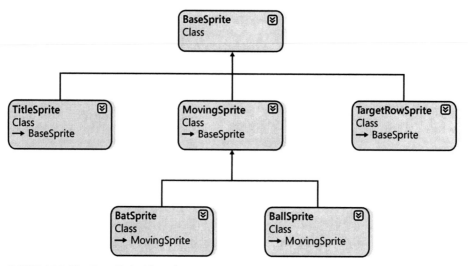

FIGURE 14-5 The *GameSprite* hierarchy.

It looks a bit like a family tree, with a BaseSprite at the top and others descended from this parent. At the bottom, you can see BatSprite and BallSprite, and there are some other sprite types in the middle of the tree. The Great Programmer explains that if you use classes, you can build a class hierarchy where you can create a child class that inherits the behaviors of a parent. The great thing about this, she says, is that you only have to write a behavior in the parent and then the child class can pick this up and just has to add any new behaviors that it needs. In other words, it is much easier to reuse code.

You find this interesting; you have not heard of object hierarchies before (this is not the first time that a case has been swayed by the sudden arrival of new evidence), and so you ask for more information. As an example, she produces Exhibit A, which is a version of the BreadAndCheeseGame that she has created using classes. She tells you that it is over 150 lines shorter and much simpler because she used the class hierarchy that she has shown you.

This is all very well, you reply, but it does not really answer the question as to why classes are managed by reference and not value. The reason, says the Great Programmer, is that using references actually makes a class hierarchy possible. For example, a BallSprite object must contain a bit of ball behavior (to check for collisions with the bread bat) and a bit of BaseSprite behavior (to draw itself on the screen). This means that the elements that make up a BallSprite are not necessarily held in one place in memory. Therefore, it is not possible to think of a single block of memory that holds the "value" of a BallSprite; bits of it might be stored in different parts. Fortunately, this is not a problem for the programmer because the environment in which your code runs takes care of this automatically.

When your program follows a reference to a BallSprite instance, the underlying system can work out the whereabouts of each part of the object. However, this makes it impossible to manage a BallSprite as a single value, and so classes must be managed by reference. But, she continues, the fact that you can reuse code means programs can be simpler and smaller. The previous version of the BreadAndCheeseGame contained five copies of the LoadTexture method. Her new version contains just one. Furthermore, she concludes, using classes makes adding new game elements really easy.

That sounds like a convincing argument, and so you decide that game objects should be classes and resolve to find out more about class hierarchies. So let's do that now.

Creating a Sprite Class Hierarchy

A class hierarchy is a great way that similar types of object can all share the same code. The Great Programmer has created one for our Bread and Cheese game to show how they work.

The *BaseSprite* Class

The starting point for the hierarchy is the class at the very base. (This is drawn at the top of the diagram.) The class that the Great Programmer has put at the base of the hierarchy is called BaseSprite. It does not seem to do very much:

```
public class BaseSprite
{
    protected Texture2D spriteTexture;
    protected Rectangle spriteRectangle;

    public void LoadTexture(Texture2D inSpriteTexture)
    {
        spriteTexture = inSpriteTexture;
    }
}
```

```
    public void SetRectangle(Rectangle inSpriteRectangle)
    {
        spriteRectangle = inSpriteRectangle;
    }
    public virtual void Draw(SpriteBatch spriteBatch)
    {
        spriteBatch.Draw(spriteTexture, spriteRectangle, Color.White);
    }

    public virtual void Update(BreadAndCheeseGame game)
    {
    }
}
```

The BaseSprite is the simplest type of sprite. It contains the bare minimum of sprite behaviors. It can be given a texture and a destination rectangle and be asked to draw itself. It also declares an update behavior, although in this version of the sprite, it doesn't do anything. We shall see how you can add an actual Update behavior later in this chapter. This BaseSprite class serves as the starting point for all the sprite classes. It brings together some fundamental data items (the texture and the drawing rectangle) that all sprites need, along with the essential methods (LoadTexture, SetRectangle, Draw, and Update). Every sprite class that we are going to create needs these facilities, and so it is put in the parent class, which every child class extends.

Using the *BaseSprite* to Store the Background

The BaseSprite class is perfect for the game's background. This is created, set to the size of the display, and then drawn at the start of each call of the game's Draw method. It is used in exactly the same way as the BackgroundSpriteStruct you saw earlier, so the game contains an instance of a BaseSprite to manage the background display.

Extending the *BaseSprite* to Produce a *TitleSprite*

The next most complicated sprite is the TitleSprite. This is exactly the same as the BaseSprite, except that it has an Update behavior that checks to see if the player has pressed the A button on the gamepad. If this button is pressed, the sprite must then start the game. Here's the code for that:

```
public class TitleSprite : BaseSprite
{
    public override void Update(BreadAndCheeseGame game)
    {
        if (game.GamePad1.Buttons.A == ButtonState.Pressed)
        {
            game.StartGame();
        }
    }
}
```

The interesting part about this sprite is the size of the code. There is only one method present, which gives the new Update behavior. The rest of the methods are inherited from the parent sprite. This means that a TitleSprite has LoadTexture, SetRectangle, and Draw behaviors, but it gets them from the BaseSprite class it extends. The compiler is told that the TitleSprite is extending the BaseSprite by the way that TitleSprite is declared, as shown in bold here:

```
public class TitleSprite : BaseSprite
```

The name of the class being created is followed by a colon and the name of the class being extended. The compiler now knows that the class is being based on another, and so inherits all the methods and data properties in the parent.

Overriding Methods from a Parent Class

The BaseSprite has an empty Update method. This is fine for our background, which does not need to do anything when it updates itself. However, the TitleSprite has to test the A button on the gamepad to see if the player wants to start a new game. What you want to do is provide a replacement Update method that works for the TitleSprite. It turns out that this is very easy to do. The empty method in the BaseSprite class has been marked as *virtual*, as shown here in bold*:*

```
/// Empty Update method in BaseSprite
public virtual void Update(BreadAndCheeseGame game)
{
}
```

A method that is virtual can be *overridden* by a method with the same name in a child class. When a program calls the Update method on a reference to a TitleSprite instance, this Update method is used instead of the one in BaseSprite. In other words, the TitleSprite class can contain a new version of the Update method that behaves in the way it needs:

```
public override void Update(BreadAndCheeseGame game)
{
    if (game.GamePad1.Buttons.A == ButtonState.Pressed)
    {
        game.StartGame();
    }
}
```

Note that the compiler is told that some overriding is taking place by the override key word.

Building a Class Hierarchy

The Great Programmer has grouped together the sprites in a very sensible way (as you might expect). She has created another child class called MovingSprite. These are sprites that need to move around the screen. They have extra properties and methods that allow them to be set up and their movement managed. There are two moving sprites in our game at the moment: the BatSprite and the BallSprite, both of which inherit all their movement information from the MovingSprite parent. The only method that differs between these classes is Update. In the BatSprite class, the Update method reads the gamepad and uses it to control the position of the bread bat. In the BallSprite class, the Update method bounces the cheese ball around the screen and checks for collisions between the ball and other game objects.

Using Protected Members from a Parent Class

One thing worthy of note here is the way that data is protected in class hierarchies. You know that members of an object can be marked public (everyone can use them) or private (nobody outside the object can use them). This protection also works between classes in hierarchies, in that if the parent class contains private members, they are not visible to code in the child classes. However, it is sometimes useful for the children of a class to be able to use things in the parent. In the case of the bread bat and cheese ball, these classes need access to the texture and the rectangle in the BaseSprite. The Great Programmer has solved this problem by using another feature of C#. Members of a class can be marked as *protected*, which means that they are visible to code in children of the class, but not to any code in classes outside the hierarchy. Note the following code:

```
public class BaseSprite
{
    protected Texture2D spriteTexture;
    protected Rectangle spriteRectangle;
    // Other BaseSprite content here
}
```

You can regard protected as a halfway house between private and public.

> **Sample Code: 05 Bread and Cheese Classes** The sample project in the 05 Bread and Cheese Classes directory in the resources for this chapter contains a version of the game that is implemented using classes. Because it has been designed and written by the Great Programmer, you can regard it as pretty much the last word on our simple game.

Adding a Deadly Pepper

The Bread and Cheese game is now reasonably playable, but it needs a few extra features. You ask your younger brother for advice, and he suggests a "deadly pepper" that constantly moves about the screen. Sometimes the pepper is green, at which point it is harmless, but at other times it is red. If the bread bat collides with the pepper when it is red, the player loses a life. Shooting the pepper with the cheese when it is red gains 50 points and turns the pepper green again. We already have an image of a pepper in our arsenal, and so this should be easy to add.

Creating a *DeadlySprite* Class

The first thing you need to decide is where in our class hierarchy the deadly pepper sprite should be located. The Great Programmer has arranged things so that there is a class called MovingSprite that provides all the elements required to make a sprite that moves across the screen. This includes working out the size of the sprite and how fast it should move. This seems to be a good place to start, and so you start by extending the MovingSprite class to make a new class called DeadlySprite. This needs to contain an extra data field that records whether or not the pepper is deadly, as follows:

```
private bool isDeadly;
```

If the value of isDeadly is true, the sprite is deadly; if it is false, the sprite is harmless.

Drawing the Deadly Pepper Sprite

Your younger brother wants the pepper to be red when it is deadly, and green when not. You need to provide an updated Draw behavior to do this. It turns out that this is really easy to do, and you can achieve it using only one pepper texture. The first thing you do is convert your image of the pepper to black and white. You can use any image-processing program to do this, including Paint.NET, which you can download from *http://www.getpaint.net/*.

Then you just have to provide a new version of the Draw method for the DeadlySprite class that uses a different color to draw the pepper, depending on whether it is deadly or not:

```
public override void Draw(SpriteBatch spriteBatch)
{
    if (isDeadly)
    {
        spriteBatch.Draw(spriteTexture, spriteRectangle, Color.Red);
    }
    else
    {
        spriteBatch.Draw(spriteTexture, spriteRectangle, Color.Green);
    }
}
```

This method overrides the Draw method in the MovingSprite class. This means that when Draw is called on a DeadlySprite instance, this code runs instead of the method in the parent class. It tests the value of isDeadly. If the sprite is deadly, it draws the texture using a red light. If the sprite is safe, it draws the texture using green. This works quite well, and you can use it if you want to display the same texture in a game using different colors. You can also use it to show things "heating up" by changing the draw color from white to pink.

Setting Up the Deadly Pepper Sprite

The next thing you need to do is provide the method that sets up the pepper at the beginning of the game. The MovingSprite class provides a method called StartGame to set up a moving sprite. It works out the size of the texture to use, and also calculates the speed of movement.

However, the version of StartGame in DeadlySprite must also set the isDeadly property to false, so that the pepper is green when the game starts. What you want to do is override the StartGame method in MovingSprite and replace it with one that does everything the parent method does, plus the action of setting isDeadly to false. This turns out to be really easy. The power of XNA Game Studio and the C# language is extremely helpful at this point. If you start to override a method, XNA Game Studio provides Intellisense to help you choose the method to override. When you type "public override" into the code inside the DeadlySprite class, XNA Game Studio shows you a menu of methods that can be overridden. Figure 14-6 shows how this works.

FIGURE 14-6 Intellisense helping override a method.

XNA Game Studio uses the comments that the Great Programmer put in the code to display information about the method as you step through them in the Intellisense list. You want to override the StartGame method, so you select that from the list and press Enter. At this point, XNA Game Studio makes an empty version of the method to get you started, as shown in Figure 14-7.

```
public class DeadlySprite : MovingSprite
{
    bool isDeadly;

    public override void StartGame(float widthFactor, float ticksToCrossScreen, float inMinDisplayX,
    {
        base.StartGame(widthFactor, ticksToCrossScreen, inMinDisplayX, inMaxDisplayX, inMinDisplayY,
    }
}
```

FIGURE 14-7 An empty *StartGame* method in the *DeadlyPepper* class.

This empty version contains a key word we haven't yet discussed. The base key word is used to call the method that has been overridden. If you think about it, this is exactly what you want. You don't want to have to replace the entire StartGame method; you just want to add something to set the isDeadly value. This is very easy to write:

```
public override void StartGame(float widthFactor, float ticksToCrossScreen,
    float inMinDisplayX, float inMaxDisplayX, float inMinDisplayY,
    float inMaxDisplayY, float initialX, float initialY)
{
    isDeadly = false;
    base.StartGame(widthFactor, ticksToCrossScreen,
        inMinDisplayX, inMaxDisplayX, inMinDisplayY,
        inMaxDisplayY, initialX, initialY);
}
```

The base key word is very useful when creating class hierarchies. It means that you can use the behavior of the parent method and then add something extra. You have actually seen base lots of times in the XNA programs that we have written already. The Draw and Update methods in the games that you have written so far are overrides of methods that exist in the parent class of the game you are creating. They always call the base behavior of their parent, and you have seen this call of base at the bottom of every Draw and Update method in the game class.

Updating the Deadly Pepper Sprite

The final thing you need to do is write the Update behavior for the DeadlySprite class. This is the largest method you need to make. It must move the sprite around the screen and also check for collisions with bat or ball. Finally, it needs to control when the sprite becomes deadly.

The movement code is easy to write—it is the same as that used for the ball:

```
x = x + xSpeed;
y = y + ySpeed;

spriteRectangle.X = (int)(x + 0.5f);
spriteRectangle.Y = (int)(y + 0.5f);

if (x + spriteRectangle.Width >= maxDisplayX)
{
    // sprite has hit the right side
    xSpeed = Math.Abs(xSpeed) * -1;
}

if (x <= minDisplayX)
{
    // sprite has hit the left side
    xSpeed = Math.Abs(xSpeed);
}
```

```
if (y + spriteRectangle.Height >= maxDisplayY)
{
    // sprite has hit the bottom
    ySpeed = Math.Abs(ySpeed) * -1;
}

if (y <= minDisplayY)
{
    // sprite has hit the top
    ySpeed = Math.Abs(ySpeed);
}
```

The only difference is that the player does not lose a life when the deadly sprite hits the bottom of the screen.

The collision code is also easy because you have seen this kind of code in the ball before. The only new bit is that the program must test for collisions only when the sprite is deadly. Here's the code:

```
if (isDeadly)
{
    if (game.BreadBat.CheckCollision(spriteRectangle))
    {
        // bat has hit the sprite.
        isDeadly = false;
        // lose a life
        game.LoseLife();
    }

    if (game.CheeseBall.CheckCollision(spriteRectangle))
    {
        // ball has hit the sprite
        isDeadly = false;
        // update the score
        game.UpdateScore(50);
    }
}
```

When the deadly pepper sprite collides with the cheese ball, the player is awarded 50 points, as this is a skill shot. When the pepper collides with the bread bat, the player loses a life, because this is not very skillful.

The final part of the Update method deals with the appearance of the deadly sprite. You talk it through with your younger brother and agree that the pepper should become deadly after the player has scored 200 points, and every 100 points after that. This means that the deadly pepper sprite needs to be able to obtain the score of the game. You look to see if the Great Programmer has thought of this and, sure enough, there is now a method in the BreadAndCheese class that returns the current score of the game:

```
public int GetScore()
{
    return score;
}
```

The deadly sprite needs to keep track of the next score to trigger its deadly behavior. To do this, it uses two variables:

```
int deadlyScoreStep= 100;

int deadlyTriggerScore = 200;
```

The code in Update gets the score and compares it with the trigger value:

```
if (game.GetScore() > deadlyTriggerScore)
{
    // Score has passed a threshold.
    // Turn deadly mode on and move the threshold.
    isDeadly = true;
    deadlyTriggerScore = deadlyTriggerScore + deadlyScoreStep;
}
```

When the score passes the trigger value, the sprite turned deadly and the trigger level is moved to the next step. It is up to the player whether to shoot the deadly pepper sprite or just avoid it when it is deadly. At the start of a game the deadlyTriggerScore value must be set back to 200. You can do this in the StartGame method.

> **Sample Code: 06 Bread and Cheese with Deadly Pepper** The sample project in the 06 Bread and Cheese with Deadly Pepper directory in the resources for this chapter contains a version of the game that adds a deadly pepper to the game. The game has now become quite challenging.

Conclusion

This has been another packed chapter. You have learned how to organize a solution properly using object-based design. You now know the meaning of coupling and cohesion in software engineering. You have finally solved the mystery of the difference between values and references and learned about classes for the first time. You have also discovered how a class can build on the behaviors of an existing class to create working systems from objects that cooperate together. And to cap it all, you have seen some code written by the Great Programmer.

Chapter Review Questions

What better way to follow a chapter than with a review? You know what to do.

1. High cohesion is bad for programs.

2. High coupling is bad for a system.

3. Data in an object should be made public to protect it.

4. Structures are managed by reference.

5. Using references makes a program run more slowly.

6. References make class hierarchies possible.

7. A class can only have one child class.

8. Methods must be marked `virtual` if they are to be overridden.

9. It is impossible for an overriding method in a child class to use the method that it has overridden.

10. Protected members of a class are also visible to code in child classes that extend that class.

11. The key word `this` refers to the class that a child class is overriding.

12. A child class must override all the methods in the parent class.

13. You can have only one reference to an object.

14. Objects without references referring to them are destroyed automatically by the garbage collector process.

Chapter 15
Creating Game Components

In this chapter, you will

- Find out what turns an object into a component.

- See how Microsoft XNA really uses components to make game creation easy.

- Experiment with artificial intelligence (AI) in a game.

- Turn "Bread and Cheese" into an arcade-quality game.

Introduction

You now know a lot about how programs are made. You have traveled all the way from performing simple calculations with your programs to creating complex game objects that show high cohesion (that is, they can look after themselves) and low coupling (that is, they interact in the simplest manner possible). In this chapter, you are going to find out how to take a high-level view of your programs and use this perspective to create software components that can be used in many different games. You also write your first code which displays AI and find out how to store large numbers of game objects in a program.

Objects and Abstraction

I take the view that as you develop as a software writer, you go through a process of "stepping back" from problems and thinking at higher and higher levels. The Great Programmer calls this *abstraction*. This is the progress that you have made so far:

- Representing values by named locations (variables).

- Creating actions that work on variables (statements and blocks).

- Putting actions into lumps of code to which we can give names. We can reuse these actions and also use them in the design process (methods).

- Creating things that contain member variables as properties and member methods as actions (objects).

- Making constructions that contain objects that are related in some way and want to share resources (class hierarchies).

As you think about a design in a more abstract way you will initially describe the actions that are needed in general terms. Rather than looking at specific behavior and low-level detail with statements like, "A sprite will draw itself using the spriteRect rectangle and the spriteTexture texture," you are thinking about things in more general terms and saying things like "A sprite will have to draw itself." This is because at the early stages of the design process, you are trying to focus on what things need to do rather than on the specific details of how they do them. Later on, you can come back and fill in precisely how the draw behavior works.

It is frequently the case that different components in your system that share a need for a draw behavior (for example, different kinds of game object) actually implement that draw behavior differently (some might draw a texture, whereas others might just draw a dot or a line), but from the point of view of the top-level design, it is best to think of them as just having the Draw behavior.

Creating an Abstract Class in C#

From a C# point of view, you can create abstract classes, which contain placeholders for methods that need to be present when actual instances of the class need to be created. Look at the following code:

```
public abstract class AbstractSprite
{
    public abstract void Draw (SpriteBatch spriteBatch);
}
```

This is a very simple abstract class called AbstractSprite that contains a single Draw method. You would not be able to create an instance of the AbstractSprite class. If you tried as follows, the compiler would reward you with an error:

```
AbstractSprite s;
s = new AbstractSprite();  // would cause a compilation error
```

The Draw method is not actually present in the class—it is an abstract placeholder. It is saying to the compiler, "A class that extends AbstractSprite must have a Draw method if you want to make an instance of it."

You could think of an abstract class as a really strict family business. To join the business, you have to be related to someone already in it and be able to do all the things that the business needs. Members of the AbstractSprite business must have a Draw method and be a child of a class in the hierarchy that has AbstractSprite at the base.

Extending an Abstract Class

The idea of an abstract class is that it provides a template of behaviors that are required in all the children of the class. We can create a child class called MySprite that satisfies these requirements. In fact, XNA Game Studio makes it very easy to do this. All you have to do is start typing the class declaration, then right-click the parent class name. This action brings up a menu from which you can select the Implement Abstract Class option, as shown in Figure 15-1.

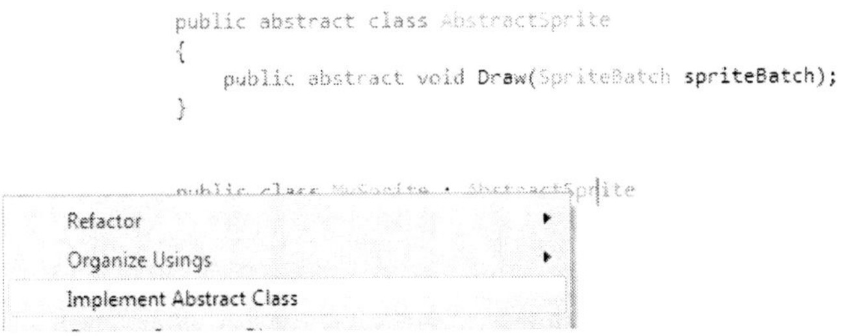

```
public abstract class AbstractSprite
{
    public abstract void Draw(SpriteBatch spriteBatch);
}
```

```
public class MySprite : AbstractSprite
```

Refactor	▶
Organize Usings	▶
Implement Abstract Class	

FIGURE 15-1 Implementing an abstract class in XNA Game Studio.

When you select the option, an empty child class that contains a placeholder Draw method is created automatically. If the parent class contained many abstract methods, the new class would have a placeholder for each. This is a lovely example of just how an intelligent editor that is aware of the design of the language you are using can make life much easier for the programmer. Figure 15-2 shows how XNA Game Studio fills in the child class started in Figure 15-1.

```
public abstract class AbstractSprite
{
    public abstract void Draw(SpriteBatch spriteBatch);
}

public class MySprite : AbstractSprite
{
    public override void Draw(SpriteBatch spriteBatch)
    {
        throw new NotImplementedException();
    }
}
```

FIGURE 15-2 XNA Game Studio filling in an abstract class.

The code for MySprite that XNA Game Studio has created allows a program to create an instance of the MySprite class. This is because the MySprite class contains an implementation of the abstract Draw method and therefore fulfills the entry requirements to join the AbstractSprite "club." Here's the code for this:

```
public class MySprite : AbstractSprite
{
    public override void Draw(SpriteBatch spriteBatch)
    {
        throw new NotImplementedException();
    }
}
```

The next thing that you would do is fill in the Draw method with the code that performs the draw behavior for this particular type of sprite. If you forget to do this, you can still create instances of the AbstractSprite class and call the Draw method, but the version of Draw shown here throws an exception and stops the program.

An exception is a way that a program can signal it is unhappy and bring this to the attention of an exception handler that might be able to sort things out. You have seen exceptions before in this book: in Chapter 4, "Displaying Images," in the section entitled "Loading XNA Textures," and in Chapter 8, "Creating a Timer," in the section entitled "Using Data in an Array." However, in these situations, things that you are using have thrown exceptions when something bad happens (such as trying to load a texture that isn't there, or trying to read elements beyond the bounds of an array). This time it is the other way around, in that the code you are writing is signaling that something has gone wrong—in this case, that the programmer has not filled in a placeholder produced by XNA Game Studio.

Designing with Abstract Classes

Abstract classes let you design a system by working out what a particular kind of object needs to do and then setting a specification or template to ensure that all the objects of that kind can do these things. You have already been working along these lines in this book. In Table 14-1 in Chapter 14, "Classes, Objects, and Games," you saw how we set out the requirements for a bat sprite. If you were using abstraction, you would find those behaviors that are common to all sprites (Draw, Update, BeginGame, and EndGame) and put them in an abstract parent class, so you could be sure that all classes in the sprite hierarchy had those minimum behaviors. The class could even have some data members and non-abstract methods that could be used by all the child classes.

> **Note** Of course, the fact that a class contains a Draw method does not actually mean that it can draw itself properly. A properly built system also has some tests that can be applied to objects to ensure that they really can do what is needed, just like you should have to pass some kind of interview to join the family business even if your dad owns the company. You have seen this test-driven approach in the section entitled "Playing with Images," in Chapter 10, "Using C# Methods to Solve Problems."

References to Abstract Parent Classes

You have seen that it is not possible to create an instance of an abstract class like AbstractSprite. This is because if the program ever needed to perform the Draw operation on such an object, it would not know what to do. However, you might find it surprising that you can create references of type AbstractSprite, and in fact, this is a very sensible thing to do. Here's code that does this:

```
AbstractSprite anySprite;

anySprite = new MySprite();

anySprite.Draw(spriteBatch);
```

This code creates a reference called anySprite of type AbstractSprite. It then sets this to a new MySprite instance and calls Draw on it. You might think that the compiler would take issue with this, but in fact, it is completely happy. A reference to a parent class can always refer to any of the child types. This is because a child is always able to do everything that a parent can. (Note that this is in direct contradiction to real life, in that none of my children seem to have inherited my dancing ability—and they are very relieved about this.)

The compiler knows that an instance of MySprite has a Draw method that can be called when required. This would be true for any child of the AbstractSprite class, although which actual code runs depends on precisely what class is on the end of the reference.

This turns out to be very useful. You might change the design of your game so that all the sprites on the display are managed using an array. You would want to hold a large number of sprites in such an array and not have to worry about precisely what kind of sprites they are. This can be achieved by making the array of type AbstractSprite:

```
AbstractSprite[] screenSprites = new AbstractSprite[100];
```

This would create an array that could hold references to 100 sprites, which could be any of the classes that are in the hierarchy that has AbstractSprite as its root. Actually, references like this also work with parent classes that are not abstract, so you could manage the game objects in BreadAndCheese using an array of BaseSprite objects as well.

> **The Great Programmer Speaks: Abstraction Is a Good Idea**   The Great Programmer is a big fan of abstraction. She says that "stepping back" from a problem and just concentrating on what the system needs to do is a great way to start. She reckons that too many software projects fail because the developers focused on the programming aspects of the problem rather than on what the customer wants. In fact, her first question to a customer is even more abstract than asking what he or she wants. She tends to ask, "What is the budget for your project?" so that she can decide in advance whether she even wants to do the job.

We will see an even better abstraction tool, the C# interface, a little later in this chapter.

Constructing Class Instances

The Great Programmer takes code writing very seriously. She is always concerned that objects in her programs contain valid data at all times. To her, this means that if an object has been created, it must contain values that mean it will not do something stupid if someone tries to use it. She had a look at the BreadAndCheeseGame code when she created her class hierarchy for Chapter 14 and she reckons that it has a serious flaw: it is possible to create sprites that would cause the game to crash if it ever tried to draw them.

> **The Great Programmer Speaks: Code Review Really Is a Good Idea** Letting other programmers see your programs (or "code review" as the professionals call it) is actually a really good idea. It might not be that good for your self-esteem as other people find problems with your solution that you hadn't thought of, but it does result in a better program. The Great Programmer has taken part in a lot of reviews (both as a reviewer and someone being reviewed) and she reckons that so long as you check your ego at the door, they work pretty well.

You take a look at the code and it turns out that she is right. The following statements create a BaseSprite reference called b and then try to draw it:

```
BaseSprite b = new BaseSprite();
b.Draw(spriteBatch);
```

These statements cause an exception to be thrown because the Draw method would try to use values of spriteRectangle and spriteTexture in the class that haven't been set up yet. What you want is a way of making sure that whenever a BaseSprite is created, it must be given a texture and rectangle. It turns out that this is very easy to do—you just need to add a *constructor* to the BaseSprite class. This is code that gets control when your object is being created, and can be used to set it up. Your constructor method, shown in bold in here, has the same name as the class and accepts two parameters:

```
public class BaseSprite
{
    protected Texture2D spriteTexture;
    protected Rectangle spriteRectangle;

    public void LoadTexture(Texture2D inSpriteTexture)
    {
        spriteTexture = inSpriteTexture;
    }

    public void SetRectangle(Rectangle inSpriteRectangle)
    {
        spriteRectangle = inSpriteRectangle;
    }

    public virtual void Draw(SpriteBatch spriteBatch)
    {
        spriteBatch.Draw(spriteTexture, spriteRectangle, Color.White);
    }

    public virtual void Update(BreadAndCheeseGame game)
    {
    }

    public BaseSprite(Texture2D inSpriteTexture, Rectangle inRectangle)
    {
        LoadTexture(inSpriteTexture);
        SetRectangle(inRectangle);
    }
}
```

This constructor for BaseSprite is given the texture to draw and the rectangle to be used to draw it. The constructor then calls the methods in the class to set these values. This means that now the only way that you can create a BaseSprite is by supplying a texture and a rectangle when you use the new key word to create a BaseSprite instance:

```
Texture2D background = Content.Load<Texture2D>("Images/Background");
Rectangle position = new Rectangle ( 0,0, 500,500 );
BaseSprite b = new BaseSprite(background, position);
```

Any BaseSprite instance referred to now always has a texture and a rectangle, which means that it can be drawn without problems. You have been using new in this way ever since your first program. Even this code uses new in the constructor call to set up the Rectangle being used to make the BaseSprite.

You can provide as many constructors as you like for a class, so that if there are different ways of providing the initial values, you can provide a constructor for each. You have already seen this in action, too: the Color type provides lots of different constructors so that you can make a new color value in many different ways.

Constructors in Structures

There is a subtle difference in the way that constructors are applied to value types. If you create a constructor for a value type, it must set a value for every data member of the structure:

```
struct demo
{
    int i;
    int j;
    int k;

    public demo(int newi,  int newj, int newk)
    {
        i = newi;
        j = newj;
        k = newk;
    }
}
```

The structure called demo (which is a value type) contains three data members. If you create a constructor for it, the compiler insists that the constructor must accept some parameters and must explicitly set all three members of the structure. This is not the same as for types managed by reference, where the compiler is much more relaxed about what has been initialized and automatically sets member data to default values (0 for numbers and null for references).

Constructors in Class Hierarchies

You haven't had to create constructors before because the compiler has provided an "empty" constructor (that is, one that accepts no parameters) automatically for each object you have created. However, once you add your own constructor, the compiler stops doing this. The designers of C# worked on the basis that if you provide a constructor you are indicating that you want complete control over how classes are created. This can lead to problems, as you now discover.

Armed with your knowledge of how constructors work, you now decide to sort out all the classes in the BreadAndSprite game. The constructor is very simple. It just sets the texture and rectangle values:

```
public BaseSprite(Texture2D inSpriteTexture, Rectangle inSpriteRectangle)
{
    spriteTexture = inSpriteTexture;
    spriteRectangle = inSpriteRectangle;
}
```

This does not go well. As soon as you add a proper constructor to the BaseSprite class to improve the program, it actually breaks everything. Figure 15-3 shows the errors that are produced by XNA Game Studio from this "improvement."

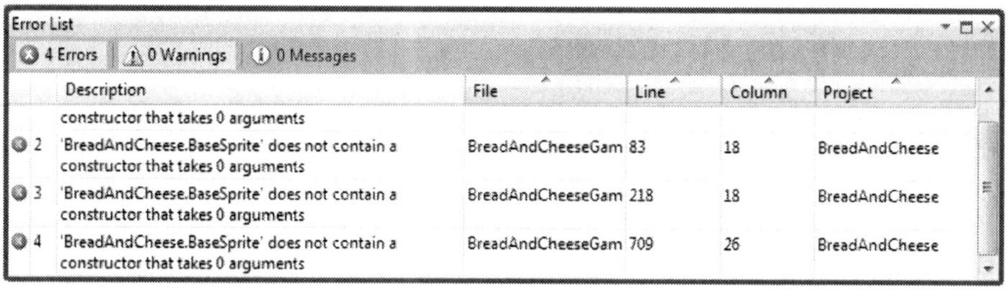

FIGURE 15-3 Compilation errors after adding a *BaseSprite* constructor.

The compiler is not very happy with the BaseSprite class. It seems to want back the empty constructor, the "constructor that takes 0 arguments." The compiler is trying to tell you that some parts of your program are trying to use the empty constructor to create a BaseSprite class. This no longer exists because you have provided your own constructor. You could start by fixing the Background sprite, which is a BaseSprite instance that draws the background. When it is created, the game must provide the texture and rectangle for this sprite:

```
Background = new BaseSprite(
    Content.Load<Texture2D>("Images/Background"),
    new Rectangle(0, 0, displayWidth, displayHeight));
```

The Background is now created in the LoadContent method because this is the point at which the texture is loaded. This gets rid of one of the errors, but there are still quite a few left.

Constructors in Child Classes

The next class that you could fix is the TitleSprite class, which is a child of the BaseSprite class. From what we know of class hierarchies, this means that when a TitleSprite instance is created, the system must create a BaseSprite first. If a parent class contains a constructor (as ours now does), this means that the child constructor must call the parent constructor to ensure that the parent class is set up properly before the child is constructed. The C# language provides a means of doing this very easily, as shown here in bold:

```
public class TitleSprite : BaseSprite
{
    // TitleSprite contents

    // TitleSprite constructor:
    public TitleSprite(Texture2D inSpriteTexture, Rectangle inRectangle)
        : base (inSpriteTexture, inRectangle)
    {
        // The constructor doesn't actually have to do anything
    }
}
```

The constructor for TitleSprite actually just needs to call the constructor for the base class. The preceding code shows how this is done. The parameters to the TitleSprite call are passed into a call of a method called base. We have seen this before when we called parent methods from overridden ones. In this context, it is doing something very similar, calling the constructor of the parent class (sometimes called the *base class*). The rather strange syntax, with the call actually appearing outside the body of the constructor method, is designed to make it clear that the constructor for the parent must run before the code in the child constructor runs.

To make the program compile all the children of the BaseSprite class must include a call of the base constructor like this. This calls for some changes to the code, but it is worth the effort as we shall see in a moment.

Sample Code: 01 Bread and Cheese with Constructors All the sample projects can be obtained from the Web resources for this text, which can be found at *http://oreilly.com/catalog/9780735651579*. The sample project in the 01 Bread and Cheese with Constructors directory in the resources for this chapter contains a version of the game that has proper constructors for all the classes. The MovingSprite constructor is more complicated than the others, as it has to use the scaling information to make the rectangle that bounds the texture.

The construction of objects in your system is something that you should plan carefully when you design your program.

Adding 100 Killer Tangerines

Your younger brother (who seems to have taken on the role of lead game designer) has come to you with an idea for 100 "killer tangerines" that appear on the screen once the player has scored 500 points. He is not sure what they would do, or how they would work, but he reckons that they would "scare the player to death," as he puts it. Because you are making up the game as you go along, you reckon that this might be a fun thing to do, and you can work out what to do with them once you have created them. The first thing you need is a picture of a tangerine to use for a sprite. Fortunately, the Great Programmer likes oranges, and so you are able to take a picture of one and convert it for use as a game texture. You decide to call this new type of sprite a `KillerSprite` for now; you can always change its name later if you need to.

Creating a *KillerSprite* Class

You use the `MovingSprite` as the basis of your `KillerSprite` sprite:

```
public class KillerSprite : MovingSprite
{
    public KillerSprite(
        Texture2D inSpriteTexture,
        float widthFactor, float ticksToCrossScreen,
        float inMinDisplayX, float inMaxDisplayX,
        float inMinDisplayY, float inMaxDisplayY)
        : base(inSpriteTexture, widthFactor, ticksToCrossScreen,
            inMinDisplayX, inMaxDisplayX,
            inMinDisplayY, inMaxDisplayY,
            0, 0) // set the initial position to 0,0 for now
    {
        // TODO: Calculate a random initial position for the Killer Sprite
    }

}
```

The big scary lump of code in the class is the call of the constructor of the `MovingSprite` class. This needs to be given all the information it needs to create the sprite rectangle and set up the movement of the sprite. At the moment, the constructor for `KillerSprite` doesn't actually do anything—it just passes all the values to the base constructor of its parent class.

The base constructor for the parent `MovingSprite` class must be given an initial position for the sprite. At the moment we don't know where to put the sprite, so all `KillerSprite` objects are initially placed at 0,0. The constructor code for the `KillerSprite` will calculate a random position of this sprite, so there is a TODO comment in the constructor to remind us to add this code later.

Your game could construct a `KillerSprite` instance like this:

```
KillerTangerine  = new KillerSprite(
    Content.Load<Texture2D>("Images/Tangerine"),
    0.03f,      // a tangerine takes 0.03 of the screen width
    1000,       // tangerine takes 200 ticks to cross the screen
    minDisplayX, maxDisplayX, minDisplayY, maxDisplayY);
```

Positioning the *KillerSprites* Using Random Numbers

Your younger brother wants the tangerine killer sprites to appear at random all over the screen. This means that you need a source of random numbers to position them. Computers are carefully designed to do exactly the same thing when given the same sequence of instructions. A computer that did not do this would be called a "broken" one. From a programming perspective, getting truly random behavior is difficult. Fortunately, the Microsoft .NET Framework provides a way of getting "pseudorandom" numbers very easily.

Pseudorandom Numbers

A source of pseudorandom numbers is not completely random, but it is random enough to be useful. It uses the previous random number to generate the next one and so produces a sequence of numbers that appear random.

The sequence starts with a particular "seed" value. The process always produces the same sequence from the same seed. This is why it's called "pseudorandom" rather than "completely random." Pseudorandom numbers are actually quite useful, in that they can produce complex but repeatable behavior. You are going to use this feature so that the killer sprites always appear in the same places on the screen. This would make it possible for a keen player to learn these locations and use this to improve their game play.

The .NET *Random* Class

The .NET Framework provides a class called Random which exposes a number of methods that can be used to obtain random numbers in a variety of ways. The first thing the program must do is create an instance of the Random class:

```
Random rand = new Random(1);  // create a random number generator seeded at 1
```

This statement creates a new Random instance and sets the variable rand to refer to it. The instance has been seeded with the value 1, so that it will always produce exactly the same sequence of values. The program can now call methods on this reference to get a hold of random numbers from it:

```
int diceSpots;
int winner;

diceSpots = rand.Next(1, 7);   // get a value between 1 and 6
winner = rand.Next(100);       // get a value between 0 and 99
```

The constructor for the KillerSprite must generate random numbers that will place the sprite somewhere within the boundary of the playfield. To do this it can use the maximum and minimum values for the screen size along with the width and height of the sprites that will be drawn:

```
initialX = rand.Next((int)minDisplayX,                       // min value
                 (int)(maxDisplayX - spriteRectangle.Width)); // max value
initialY = rand.Next((int)minDisplayY,                       // min value
                 (int)(maxDisplayY - spriteRectangle.Height)); // max value
```

The previous code sets the initial position for a KillerSprite so that it is random but within the screen boundary. Note that the Next method requires integer parameters, and so the values must be cast to int before being passed into it.

Creating a Static Random Generator for the *KillerSprite*

The KillerSprite class must have one random number generator which is shared among all instances of the class. If the program made a new random number generator each time it made a new KillerSprite instance this would not work. All the sprites would be placed in the same location because they would each contain a brand-new random number generator seeded with the value 1. They would then set their positions by using the same first two numbers produced by the identically seeded generator.

You can get around this problem by making the random number generator a *static* member of the class. When a class member is made static it is not held inside an instance, but is actually part of the class, and shared by all the instances.

```
static Random rand = new Random(1);
```

Whenever an instance of KillerSprite uses the rand member variable, it will use the single, static variable which is part of the class.

You first saw static class members in Chapter 11 in the section "Static Classes and Methods," where you saw how useful it can be to make methods static so that they can be called without needing to create an instance of a class. This is a situation where you want a particular data item to be shared among class members. The KillerSprite constructor uses the random number generator to position a sprite at a random position, as shown here in bold:

```
public class KillerSprite : MovingSprite
{
    static Random rand = new Random(1);

    public KillerSprite(
        Texture2D inSpriteTexture,
        float widthFactor, float ticksToCrossScreen,
        float inMinDisplayX, float inMaxDisplayX,
        float inMinDisplayY, float inMaxDisplayY)
        : base(inSpriteTexture, widthFactor, ticksToCrossScreen,
            inMinDisplayX, inMaxDisplayX,
            inMinDisplayY, inMaxDisplayY,
            0, 0)  // set the initial position to 0,0 for now
    {
        initialX = rand.Next((int)minDisplayX,
                        (int)(maxDisplayX - spriteRectangle.Width));
        initialY = rand.Next((int)minDisplayY,
                        (int)(maxDisplayY - spriteRectangle.Height));
    }
}
```

Getting a Random Sequence of Numbers

Your younger brother has been reading this section with interest. He is obviously planning some kind of card game program where he can know exactly what cards the other players are holding, because of the way that he can get a predictable sequence of values from the Random class. If you need to get truly random behavior you can create a Random instance without giving it an initial seed value:

```
Random rand = new Random();  // create a truly random number generator
```

If you do not provide a seed value the .NET Framework uses a seed that's obtained from the precise time that the program runs, so that the game program gets a different random sequence each time the game is played.

Using Lists of References

The next problem to solve is how to store all the KillerTangerine variables that you are going to create. Arrays are, at the moment, the only way we know to hold large numbers of things. We used them when we were decoding the scores in the section entitled "Finding Winners Using Arrays," in Chapter 8, "Creating a Timer." They let you create a storage area of a particular size and fill the elements in the store with data.

You could use arrays to hold all the game objects, but the C# libraries provide a much better mechanism for doing this. It is called a List. The List is a "collection" class, which is designed to hold lists of things. It is so useful that you feel like taking it home to meet your parents.

The List collection uses a C# feature called *generics,* where a program construction can be designed and made to work on items independent of their type. The great thing about a List is that you can create it and add items to it without worrying about it filling up. Some clever software behind the scenes (that you don't have to know about) reserves extra space when required. The List collection seems to have arrived just in time. For now, you need to create something that can manage a very large number of sprites.

Creating a *List* Collection

You declare a List collection as you would any other variable, as shown in bold here:

```
// The Game World
public BreadSprite Bread;
public CheeseSprite Cheese;
public DeadlyPepper Pepper;
public TomatoRowSprite Tomato;
public TitleSprite Title;
public BaseSprite Background;

public List<BaseSprite> GameSprites = new List<BaseSprite>();
```

This is the game world for our game. It includes all the original sprites, plus the list variable called GameSprites, which is going to hold all the sprites that are on the screen when the game is active. The type of the items you want to put in the list is given between the left-angle bracket (<) and the right-angle bracket (>) characters. In this case, you are creating a list of BaseSprite references, but you can create lists to hold any type. Note that because a reference to a parent class is able to refer to any of the child classes of that parent, we can add any of our sprite types to the list.

Adding Items to a List

The List class provides a method called Add, which can be used to add things to the List, as shown here in bold:

```
for (int i = 0; i < 100; i++)
{
    KillerSprite Tangerine;
    Tangerine = new KillerSprite(
        Content.Load<Texture2D>("Images/Tangerine"),
        0.03f,    // a tangerine takes 0.03 of the screen width
        1000,     // tangerine takes 200 ticks to cross the screen
        minDisplayX, maxDisplayX, minDisplayY, maxDisplayY);
    GameSprites.Add(Tangerine);
}
```

This code creates 100 tangerines and adds them to the GameSprites list. Note that if we wanted 1,000 of them (which would really scare the player), we just have to change the upper limit of the for loop and hope that the Xbox can keep up.

Accessing List Elements

Getting a hold of elements from a list turns out to be very easy. You can use subscripts just like an array, as follows:

```
for (int i = 0; i < 100; i++)
{
    GameSprites[i].Draw(spriteBatch);
}
```

This code would call the Draw method on all the tangerines in the list. If the program tries to access an element that is not present (perhaps the one with a subscript of 100), then the program fails with an exception, just as an array would. The List class provides a Count method, which can be used to find out how many items the list contains:

```
for (int i = 0; i < GameSprites.Count(); i++)
{
    GameSprites[i].Draw(spriteBatch);
}
```

This version of the loop would work correctly for any size of list. In this respect, the Count method is directly analogous to the Length property of an array.

Working Through List Elements Using *foreach*

Lists (and indeed arrays) can also be used with another form of C# loop construction called foreach. This provides a really neat way of performing an operation on a large number of items in a collection. It removes the need for you to create a control variable and worry about the size of the collection:

```
foreach (BaseSprite sprite in GameSprites)
{
    sprite.Draw(spriteBatch);
}
```

The foreach construction takes each item out of a collection and feeds it into the statements to be repeated. This code asks all the sprites in the game to perform their Draw operation. The elements of the List collection are fetched by the foreach loop in the same order that they were added. You can also use foreach to work through the elements of an array in the same way. Note however that other collection classes might not return the elements in the same order that you stored them; only lists and arrays are guaranteed to do this.

Setting Up the Game Sprites

It makes sense to add all the sprites into the game into the GameSprites list. This means that the Draw and Update methods can be made much simpler because they just have to use a foreach construction. The sprites would be added to GameSprites when they are created:

```
CheeseBall = new BallSprite(
    Content.Load<Texture2D>("Images/Cheese"),
    0.07f,   // a cheese takes 0.07 of the screen width
    200,     // cheese takes 200 ticks to cross the screen
    minDisplayX, maxDisplayX, minDisplayY, maxDisplayY,
    displayWidth / 4,    // a quarter across the screen
    displayHeight / 4); // a quarter down the screen

GameSprites.Add(CheeseBall);
```

Note that you now have two ways that to get to the BallSprite instance that represents the cheese in the game. The program can either follow the CheeseBall reference, or use the reference stored in the GameSprites list. You can now remove the use of the individual references in the Draw and Update methods so that they are now even simpler, as shown in the complete Draw method below:

```
protected override void Draw(GameTime gameTime)
{
    GraphicsDevice.Clear(Color.CornflowerBlue);

    spriteBatch.Begin();

    switch (state)
    {
        case GameState.titleScreen:
            Title.Draw(spriteBatch);
            drawHighScore();
            break;
        case GameState.playingGame:
            foreach (BaseSprite sprite in GameSprites)
            {
                sprite.Draw(spriteBatch);
            }
            drawScore();
            break;
    }

    spriteBatch.End();

    base.Draw(gameTime);
}
```

The only sprite that is not added to the list of GameSprites is the Title sprite, which is drawn when the title screen must be displayed.

Extra *List* Features

The List collection also provides Remove methods that let you remove elements from a list. When an element is removed, the list is "shuffled down" to so that there is no empty slot. This would be a very useful way of removing items from game that have been destroyed. If they are removed from the list, they are not drawn.

> **Sample Code: 02 Bread and Cheese with Tangerines** The sample project in the 02 Bread and Cheese with Tangerines directory in the resources for this chapter contains a version of the game that draws 100 tangerines when it starts.

Figure 15-4 shows how the tangerines are drawn. Note that because the code uses a random number generator seeded with the same number each time, the tangerines are placed in exactly the same position each time the program runs.

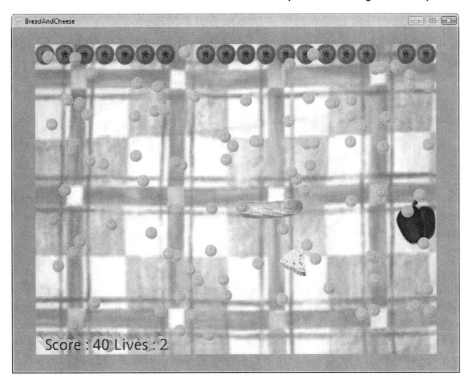

FIGURE 15-4 100 tangerines (count them if you like) in the Bread and Cheese game.

Adding Artificial Intelligence

At the moment, the tangerines just stay at their initial positions on the screen looking dangerous, which is rather boring. Perhaps they could chase the bread bat instead (your younger brother really likes this idea). The posh name for what you are doing now is artificial intelligence (AI). You want to make it look as though the tangerines are being controlled by an intelligent opponent who knows where you are and is heading that way.

Chasing the Bread Bat

To change the way the tangerines behave, you just have to override the Update method in the KillerSprite class. To chase the bread bat, a killer sprite first has to know where the bat is. At the moment, this information is hidden inside the Bat class, so we need to add some code to make this information visible. The best place to put this code is the MovingSprite class; then we can get the position of any of the moving sprites on the screen, including the Cheese and the DeadlyPepper.

Using Properties to Read the *Bread Bat* Position

We could provide a method called GetX to read the X position of a MovingSprite, but C#
provides something called a *property*, which makes this much easier. Look at this code:

```
public float XPos
{
    get
    {
        return x;
    }
}
```

When placed inside the MovingSprite class, the code provides a property that lets objects
read the value of x (which is the member of the sprite that holds the position). The new XPos
property can be used very easily:

```
float breadX = Bread.XPos;
```

This assigns the x location of the bread to the value of breadX. This looks a lot like direct
access to a member of a class, but what is actually happening is that the code inside the get
portion of the property is running and the value following the return is being sent back as
the result of the property. At the moment, there is no way that the position of the bread can
be changed (which is what we want in this case). However, this would not stop programmers
like your younger brother from trying, as in the following code:

```
Bread.XPos = 99;
```

Because there is no set behavior, this fails to compile. However, you can provide such
a behavior if you like by adding a set part to the property declaration, as shown here
in bold:

```
public float XPos
{
    get
    {
        return x;
    }

    set
    {
        x = value;
    }
}
```

The set behavior of a property uses the key word `value` as a placeholder for the value specified on the right side of the assignment operator. So if your younger brother's code to write to the property was performed, the value of x would be set to 99.

Properties are quite neat, and they can make code look simpler.

Creating the *KillerSprite*-Chasing AI

The code to make a killer sprite chase the bread bat is actually quite simple:

```
if (game.BreadBat.XPos > x)
{
    x += xSpeed;
}
else
{
    x -= xSpeed;
}
if (game.BreadBat.YPos > y)
{
    y += ySpeed;
}
else
{
    y -= ySpeed;
}
```

This is pure AI. These statements are doing exactly what you would do if you were steering a tangerine towards the bread. They work on the principle that if the bread was to the left of you, you'd move left. If the bread was below you, you'd move down, and so on. If this code is placed in the `Update` method, the tangerines try to head towards the bread. The speed of the tangerine has been set so that the tangerines move quite slowly, but it definitely feels like they are chasing you. If you really want to scare the player, you can speed the tangerines up. Figure 15-5 shows the situation in the game a few seconds after the tangerines have been made to appear. This is actually quite a scary point in the game, as the pepper is also deadly.

If you want to make tangerines that ran away from the bread bat (to make a kind of chasing game), you just have to reverse this behavior.

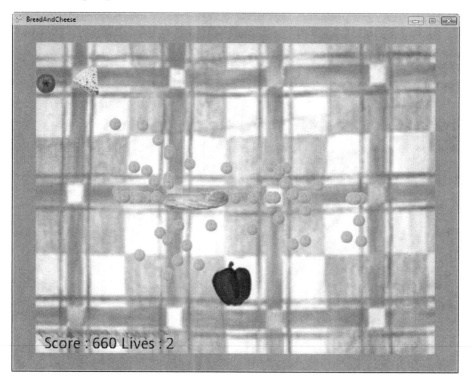

FIGURE 15-5 Starting the chase.

Hitting the Killer Sprite Tangerines

The only problem with the tangerines is that we can't really have them make the player lose a life when they touch the bread bat. This would be very unfair because the player would almost certainly die quickly. We get your younger brother to test this form of the game play and see how long he can survive and the answer is what we expected—not very long.

However, we can arrange things so that the player suffers in other ways. Every killer sprite that hits the player's bat could cost them 10 points, whereas every one they manage to get rid of by hitting it with the cheese could earn them 10 points. This makes the killer sprite a bit like the pepper in some respects. The final Update behavior for the KillerTangerine looks like this:

```
public override void Update(BreadAndCheeseGame game)
{

    if (game.GetScore() > killerTriggerScore)
    {
        // Score has passed a threshold.
        // Turn the killer sprite on and move the threshold.
        isDeadly = true;
        killerTriggerScore = killerTriggerScore + killerScoreStep;
    }
```

```
  if (isDeadly)
  {
      if (game.BreadBat.CheckCollision(spriteRectangle))
      {
          // bat has hit the Killer Sprite.
          isDeadly = false;
          // lose some score
          game.UpdateScore(-10);
      }

      if (game.CheeseBall.CheckCollision(spriteRectangle))
      {
          // ball has hit the Killer Sprite.
          isDeadly = false;
          // update the score
          game.UpdateScore(10);
      }

      if (game.BreadBat.XPos > x)
      {
          x += xSpeed;
      }
      else
      {
          x -= xSpeed;
      }
      if (game.BreadBat.YPos > y)
      {
          y += ySpeed;
      }
      else
      {
          y -= ySpeed;
      }
  }

  spriteRectangle.X = (int)(x + 0.5f);
  spriteRectangle.Y = (int)(y + 0.5f);

  base.Update(game);
}
```

Note that, unlike the pepper, the tangerines are drawn and moved only when they are deadly.

> **Sample Code: 03 Bread and Cheese with Killer Tangerines** The sample project in the
> 03 Bread and Cheese with Killer Tangerines directory in the resources for this chapter contains a
> version of the game that creates 100 killer tangerines when the score reaches 500. It also creates
> them every 400 points after that.

The interesting thing about this is that we have added only a few lines to the game to get the new character, and many of the lines we have added were copied from other methods. We could easily add other kinds of sprites and make them appear and disappear when we want them. It would also be quite easy to add things like "Extra Life" sprites if we wanted the game sprites that increase the number of lives available.

Adding Game Sounds

The BreadAndCheese game is now quite playable. It has a bit of variety and it can get quite hectic, with the player having to keep an eye on lots of things at the same time to stay alive and rack up a big score. However, there is one thing missing from it, and that is sounds. At the moment, playing the game is very much like watching the TV with the sound turned off.

Such is the value of sound to a game that even the very first computer games had sound output, even if it took the form of primitive beeps. You now need to think about how sounds can be added to the game. You have seen how easy it is to load and play sound effects; now you have to bind them into the game sprites so that when something happens to each sprite it plays an appropriate sound effect. But before we can add sounds, we have to decide how to do it and decide who makes the sounds in the game.

This is actually a profound question. Does the BreadAndCheeseGame class make the sound, or do the sprites do it themselves? After some thought, you probably come to the same conclusion that I did, which is that the sound of a sprite is a bit like the texture that is used to draw it; it is a property of the sprite. Furthermore, on the principle of high cohesion being good (that is, it is best if an object can look after itself and not rely on any other objects), it makes sense for the sprite to make the sound. Sprites that need to make sounds can be given the sound effects when they are constructed and play the appropriate ones as required. You can make the sounds any way you like. I created mine using a little electronic sound generator. Figure 15-6 shows the sounds after I had imported them. Note that the name of each sound file directly reflects its purpose.

FIGURE 15-6 All the sound effects in the Bread and Cheese game.

Each of them is loaded into the game as content, and the constructor of each sprite class is modified to accept the sound effect resources when the sprite is created:

```
CheeseBall = new BallSprite(
    Content.Load<Texture2D>("Images/Cheese"),
    0.07f,    // a cheese takes 0.07 of the screen width
    200,      // cheese takes 200 ticks to cross the screen
    minDisplayX, maxDisplayX, minDisplayY, maxDisplayY,
    displayWidth / 4,    // a quarter across the screen
    displayHeight / 4,   // a quarter down the screen
    Content.Load<SoundEffect>("Sounds/BreadHit"),
    Content.Load<SoundEffect>("Sounds/TomatoHit"),
    Content.Load<SoundEffect>("Sounds/EdgeHit"),
    Content.Load<SoundEffect>("Sounds/LoseLife"));
GameSprites.Add(Cheese);
```

This code creates a new CheeseBall and passes it all the information it needs, including the sound effects. The constructor of the class stores the sound effects so that they can be used to produce the sounds as required:

```
public BallSprite(Texture2D inSpriteTexture,
    float widthFactor, float ticksToCrossScreen,
    float inMinDisplayX, float inMaxDisplayX,
    float inMinDisplayY, float inMaxDisplayY,
    float inInitialX, float inInitialY,
    SoundEffect inBatHitSound,
    SoundEffect inTargetHitSound,
    SoundEffect inEdgeHitSound,
    SoundEffect inLoseLifeSound)
    : base(inSpriteTexture, widthFactor, ticksToCrossScreen,
        inMinDisplayX, inMaxDisplayX,
        inMinDisplayY, inMaxDisplayY,
    inInitialX, inInitialY)
{
    batHitSound = inBatHitSound;
    targetHitSound = inTargetHitSound;
    edgeHitSound = inEdgeHitSound;
    loseLifeSound = inLoseLifeSound;
}
```

This code actually looks rather horrible, and for that I apologize. The constructor for the cheese actually does very little work because most of the heavy lifting is done by its base constructor, which sets up the moving sprite. All the constructor does is copy the incoming sound effects into members inside the BallSprite class, so that they can be used in the Update method to make the appropriate sounds. I think it is fair to say that when you understand this lump of code, you properly understand constructors and class hierarchies.

Here is part of the `Update` method in the `BallSprite` class that plays a sound when the cheese ball hits the top of the screen:

```
if (y <= minDisplayY)
{
    // ball has hit the top of the screen.
    edgeHitSound.Play();
    ySpeed = Math.Abs(ySpeed);
}
```

> **Sample Code: 04 Bread and Cheese with Sound** The sample project in the 04 Bread and Cheese with Sound directory in the resources for this chapter contains a version of the game that has all the existing game play with sounds added. I have used the code from the music player that we created in Chapter 7, "Playing Sounds," to play background music and to make the sound for the deadly pepper repeats when it is on the screen. And you should make sure that you have the volume turned down a bit before the tangerines turn up.

> **Note** The game will run on a Windows Phone but because the Windows Phone has fewer sound channels than the Xbox or Windows PC it may fail when the bat or the ball collides with a large number of killer tangerines. This is because the game will try to play a sound for each collision, and these are all played on separate sound channels. To fix this problem you could make a Windows Phone version that does not play a new collision sound if the existing one is already active. I will leave this for you to sort out.

From Objects to Components

We now have a whole set of sprite components that are used in the `BreadAndCheeseGame`. These components use some methods in the game itself, so that they can tell the game when something important happens. As an example, the `Update` method in the `Ball` is given a reference to the `BreadAndCheeseGame` that it is part of so that it can tell the game when a life has been lost, as shown here in bold:

```
public override void Update(BreadAndCheeseGame game)
{
    ...

    if (y + spriteRectangle.Height >= maxDisplayY)
    {
        // cheese has hit the bottom. Lose a life.
        LoseLifeSound.Play();
        ySpeed = Math.Abs(ySpeed) * -1;
        game.LoseLife();
    }
    ...
}
```

The LoseLife method is part of the BreadAndCheeseGame class and is how game sprites tell the game that a life has been lost. You use a similar method when you score points. Sprites need to have this form of coupling so that the sprites can affect the game where required. However, this means that they are tightly linked with the BreadAndCheeseGame class and can be used only with it. This is actually a serious restriction. We would like to use the same set of sprites in an "Alien Wars" game that we are also working on, but because this is held in a class called AlienWarsGame, our sprites can't talk to it. We can't use abstract classes to solve this problem, because the game classes are children of the XNA Game class, whereas our sprites are all children of the BaseSprite class.

C# Interfaces

However, it turns out that we can use another C# feature to solve this problem and turn our sprites into genuine components. This feature is called an *interface*.

> **Note** One point I should make here is that we are *not* talking about the user interface to our game. The user interface is the way a person using a program would make it work for them. These are usually either text-based (that is, the user types in commands and gets responses) or graphical (that is, the user clicks "buttons" on a screen using the mouse). In programming terms, an interface just specifies how a software component could be used by another software component.

You can think of interfaces in terms of plugs and sockets. When you plug your computer into the wall socket, you are actually using an interface. The power company has created a standard that describes the shape of the outlet on the wall and the voltage and frequency of the power that comes out of it. This interface lets you plug in anything built to use that connection, whether it is a computer, a toaster, or an Xbox 360. You can create a software interface to specify the connection between your game and the sprite you would like to plug into it. You can design this interface by deciding what a sprite needs to be able to do with the game that it is part of:

- Update the lives
- Update the score
- Get the current score in the game
- Get the gamepad state
- Start the game
- End the game

Anything which provides these behaviors can act as a "host" for our sprites, in that it can do anything that they need.

Creating an Interface

I worked out the contents of the interface by looking at the existing classes and deciding which methods the sprites actually needed. These methods can be put into a C# interface as follows:

```
public interface ISpriteBasedGame
{
    void UpdateLives(int update);
    void UpdateScore(int update);
    int GetScore();
    GamePadState GetGamePad();
    void StartGame();
    void EndGame();
}
```

A C# interface looks a lot like an abstract class. It is a collection of method specifications. The idea is that rather than using a reference to a particular class, you can instead use a reference to a class that can implement that interface. In other words, rather than thinking of the host of a sprite as a BreadAndCheeseGame, we think of it as a class that implements the ISpriteBasedGame interface. The BreadAndCheeseGame class can indicate that it implements the interface, as shown in bold here:

```
/// <summary>
/// This is the main type for your game
/// </summary>
public class BreadAndCheeseGame : Microsoft.Xna.Framework.Game,
                              ISpriteBasedGame
{
    // All of the game class code goes here.
    // This must include implementations of UpdateLives,
    // UpdateScore, GetScore, GetGamePad, StartGame;
    // and EndGame
}
```

When you declare a class, you can state that it extends a parent (in this case, the Microsoft.XNA.Framework.Game class) and also give a list of any interfaces that it implements (in this case, the ISpriteBasedGame interface). A class can implement many interfaces, depending on the number of things you want to be able to ask it to do.

Note The name of the interfaces I have created is ISpriteBasedGame. There is a convention in C# that interfaces have names that start with I. This is so that a programmer can tell whether a given item is an interface or an object. You do not have to use this convention, but the Great Programmer has told me that she will hunt you down if you don't.

Implementing an Interface

When a class implements an interface, it is saying, "I can do these things." In other words, it contains public versions of all the methods described in the interface. You can regard an interface as a kind of resume if you like. My resume says that I can teach computer science. This means that you can stand me in front of a class and call my "StartTeaching" method, and I do something in response. You could replace me with any other teacher, or perhaps even a robot, or anything that also has "teach computer science" on its resume because you know that means it contains the required method.

> **Note** The interface doesn't say anything about what the methods actually do (any more than me having "computer science teacher" on my resume says how I will teach my class); it says only that the object contains them. If we want to prove that a component can provide the expected behaviors appropriately, we have to create tests for these methods.

References to Interfaces

From the programming point of view, this means that we can now refer to objects in terms of what they can do, as opposed to what they are. We can refer to an object of type BreadAndCheeseGame by using a reference of type BreadAndCheeseGame. But we can also refer to such an object by using a reference of type ISpriteBasedGame. A reference of type ISpriteBasedGame can refer to any object that implements the interface. The compiler is quite happy with this. It knows that if it needs to use any of the methods in the interface, they are there, and it doesn't need to care precisely what type of object the instance actually is. The Update method in the sprites is now passed a reference to the ISpriteBasedGame so that it can use the methods it provides. For example, here is the Update method in the TitleSprite class:

```
public override void Update(ISpriteBasedGame game)
{
    if (game.GetGamePad().Buttons.Start == ButtonState.Pressed)
    {
        game.StartGame();
    }
}
```

This Update method reads the gamepad of the game using the GetGamepad method and calls the StartGame method if it is time to start the game. It doesn't know exactly what it is being given to work with, but it does know that the object that the game parameter refers to contains the GetGamePad and StartGame methods because the game reference is only allowed to refer to objects that implement the interface.

Linking Bread, Cheese, and Tomatoes

Earlier versions of the Bread and Cheese game used the game class itself to link the Bat, Ball, and Target classes. In other words, when the ball wanted to find out if it had collided with the bat, it would access the BreadAndCheeseGame class to get a hold of the reference to the breadBat that is stored within the game.

You are trying to make the behavior of the bat, ball, and targets independent of the game they are part of, and to do this you need to couple the bat, ball, and targets together, and not have them use the game to find each other.

This means that the constructor of the ball must now be passed a reference to the bat and the targets it must interact with so that it can store these for use later. This is actually quite sensible design, in that it makes the coupling more direct; rather than coupling via a third party, the bat, ball, and targets are directly connected.

Designing with Interfaces

Interfaces provide a very neat solution to the problem of wanting to reuse our sprites in the AlienWarsGame game. If the AlienWarsGame class implements the ISpriteBasedGame interface, the sprites can be used with that game.

Our sprites can work with any class that implements the ISpriteBasedGame interface. You could also create an interface that works the other way. An ISprite interface would have all the methods required to control a sprite. This would make it possible to plug any kind of sprite into a game, not just ones that are children of the BaseSprite class.

> **The Great Programmer Speaks: Interfaces Are Very Useful** The Great Programmer uses interfaces a lot when she designs her programs. When she has decided what objects are needed to implement a solution, she next works out how they need to communicate with each other and creates interfaces based on these interactions. The result is that she can plug in new versions, or even plug in test versions, of objects very easily.

> **Sample Code: 05 Bread and Cheese with Interfaces** The sample project in the 05 Bread and Cheese with Interfaces directory in the resources for this chapter contains a version of the game that uses interfaces to connect the game sprites with the game of which they are a part.

Conclusion

This has been another very busy chapter. We have seen how abstract classes can be used as templates, to make sure that a child class provides implementations of the methods it needs to perform its work. We have also discovered how a class can take control during its construction and how this can be used to set the initial values of the class. We have used the List collection to store a large number of sprites in our game and we have written our first piece of AI code to control a tangerine. Finally, we have explored interfaces as a way of creating true component-based software.

Chapter Review Questions

And now for some chapter review questions for you to interface with.

1. An abstract class cannot contain any working code.

2. An abstract class is not allowed to contain a constructor.

3. You can make only one instance of an abstract class.

4. You can mark data in an abstract class as abstract.

5. A C# class can extend more than one parent class.

6. An abstract class can be used as the base of a class hierarchy.

7. A reference to an abstract class can refer to any instance of children of that class.

8. The constructor of a class is called when a new instance of the class is created.

9. If a class contains one constructor, this must be called to create an instance of that class.

10. In a class hierarchy, the data members of an instance of a child class must be initialized before the data members of the parent class are initialized.

11. The .NET system can be used to provide random numbers.

12. The List collection class must have its length set when it is created.

13. The foreach construction can be used to work through all the elements in a List.

14. Artificial Intelligence involves adding brain cells to a program.

15. An interface contains a list of methods.

16. A reference to an interface can refer to any object that implements the interface.

Chapter 16
Creating Multi-Player Networked Games

- See how Microsoft XNA games can be made to connect together.
- Look at the C# constructions that let network games exchange data.
- Create a multi-player game for Microsoft Windows PC or Xbox.

Introduction

You are well on the way to becoming a full-fledged programmer. You don't know every-thing yet, but you have enough programming and XNA knowledge to produce very playable (and marketable) games. One XNA feature that is worth exploring, though, is the way that XNA makes networked games possible.

In this chapter, we are going to find out a bit about how networks function and create a simple networked game for PC or Xbox.

 Note At the moment, it's not possible to use these XNA features on Windows Phone

Networks and Computers

It should come as no surprise to you that networks are used to link computers. Before we look at how XNA provides network connections, we need to learn a little bit about how networks work. This is not a detailed examination of the field, but it should give you enough background to understand what the XNA networking support does.

Starting with the Signal

The first computer networks used wires to send their data signals, although more modern networks can use radio or fiberoptic cables. Whatever the medium is, the fundamental principle is that you have hardware that can put data onto the medium in the form of bits and get it off again. A bit is either 0 or 1 (or you can think of a bit as either true or false) and can be signaled by the presence or absence of a voltage, a light from a light-emitting diode (LED), or a radio signal.

If you imagine signaling your friend in the house across the road by flashing your bedroom light on and off, you have an idea of the starting point of network communications. Figure 16-1 shows how such a bedroom-to-bedroom signaling system might work.

FIGURE 16-1 Sending messages from one bedroom to another using a light.

Once we have this raw ability to send a signal from one place to another, we can start to transfer useful data.

Building Up to Packets

Just flashing your light to your friend willy-nilly does not allow you to send much information. To communicate useful signals, you have to agree on a system. You could say, "If my light is off and I flash it twice, it means it is safe to come round because my sister is out. If I flash it once, it means don't come, and if I flash it three times, it means come and bring pizza with you." This is the basis of a thing called a protocol, which is an arrangement by parties on the construction and meaning of messages.

Addressing Messages

Your bedroom light communication system would be more complicated if you had two friends on your street with whom you needed to communicate. You would have to agree with them that you would send two sets of flashes. The first one would indicate who the message was for, and the second would be the message itself. Computer networks function in exactly the same way. Every station on a network must have a unique address. Messages sent to that address are picked up by the network hardware in that station.

Networks also have what is called a *broadcast* address. This allows a system to send a message which will be picked up by every system. This is the network equivalent of "Calling all cars…" In our communication network, this could be used to warn everyone that your sister has come home and brought her boyfriend, so your house is to be avoided at all costs.

Everyone can receive and act on a broadcast. In fact, if it wanted to, a station could listen to all the messages traveling down its part of the wire or WiFi channel. This illustrates a problem with networks. Just as both of your friends can see all the messages from your bedroom light, including ones not meant for them, there is nothing to stop someone from eavesdropping on your network traffic. When you connect to a secure Web site, your computer is encoding all the messages that it sends out so that someone listening other than the intended recipient would not be able to learn anything.

Routing

If you had a friend on the next block, she might not be able to see your bedroom light. But she might be able to see the light of your friend across the road. This means that you could ask your friend across the road to receive messages and then transmit them on for you. Your friend across the road would read the address of the message coming in, and if it was for your friend on the next block, she would transmit it again. Figure 16-2 shows how this works. Your friend uses the window on the left to talk to you and the window on the right to relay messages to your more distant friend.

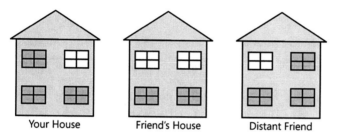

FIGURE 16-2 Using your friend to route messages to a friend farther away.

This is the basis of routing, and it is how the Internet works. Messages that you send from your home PC to distant machines are passed to the network hardware at your Internet service provider (ISP), which then passes them along to the next system in the path to the destination. Messages might have to be sent over several machines to reach their destination. The Internet constantly changes the routes that messages take. This makes the Internet very reliable and able to manage sudden surges in traffic and failures of systems in the network, but it can lead to situations where a message arrives before another which was sent first. Sometimes messages can get lost (although this is fairly rare), so you can't be sure that one has arrived until you receive an acknowledgement. One thing you should remember is that you do not really "connect" your system to the Internet. Whenever your system is connected, it actually becomes part of the Internet.

Anything that you send via the Internet will be transferred using one or more individual messages. Each message contains the address of the destination and each message is numbered, so that missing messages can be detected and messages can be put into the right order when they are received (if you want that). If you need to transfer a large file, this will be broken down into a number of messages.

Calls and Datagrams

The Internet provides two forms of connection: calls and datagrams. A datagram is a single message that is sent from one system to another. You don't know if a datagram has been received. This is like flashing your bedroom light to ask for pizza (message 3) and then just waiting for someone to turn up.

You could agree with your friend that she would flash her light once to indicate that she has received your message. Then perhaps you could send another message. When she was leaving to fetch the pizza, she could flash her light twice to indicate that she was "going off the air." This would be the basis of a call between the two of you.

When two systems are in a call, they have to perform extra work to manage the call itself. When one system sends a message that is part of a call, the network either tells that system that the message was successfully transferred (once the network have received an acknowledgement) or gives an error saying that it could not be delivered. Some Internet services use datagrams, and some use calls.

Datagrams are used for things like broadcasting video. In this situation, if a message is lost by the network, there is no point in asking for it again because by the time the replacement arrives, it will be too late to display it. So the display program must make up for the missing data and just keep going, hoping the viewer does not notice. Datagrams are used when you want to send data as fast as you can and it doesn't matter if some gets lost on the way. Game data is often sent like this because you want the objects in the game to update as smoothly as possible and there is no time to resend missing information. Datagrams are also used for streaming media, where moving video is being sent and the priority is to get the signal to you as fast as possible.

Calls are used when it is important that the entire message gets through. When your browser is loading a Web page, your computer and the Web server are connected by a call across the network. This makes sure that all parts of the Web page get through and that any pieces that don't arrive are retransmitted. The effort of setting up and managing the call and requesting retransmission when things fail to arrive means that data in calls is transferred more slowly and places heavier demands on the systems communicating by means of a call.

Networks and Protocols

A protocol is a set of rules that tells you how to behave in a certain situation. There is a protocol that tells you which knife and fork to use in a posh banquet, and another that tells you to kiss a maiden on her hand having just rescued her from a dragon. You already have one with your friend, where you have agreed on the meaning of the various messages that you send with your bedroom lights.

In networking terms, a protocol sets out the design of all the messages and how stations in a network should cooperate to move data around. There are essentially two levels at which this must take place. There must be a "local-level" protocol that lets local stations (ones on the same piece of physical media) exchange data, and there must be an "internetwork" protocol that allows messages to be sent from one local network to another.

You can regard a local-level network as the same as the internal mail that is used in many organizations, including my university at Hull. If I want to send a message to our chemistry department, I just put the address "Chemistry Department" on the envelope and drop it in the internal mail. There is a local protocol (called the internal mail system) that makes sure that the message gets there. However, if I want to send a message to the chemistry department at York University, I must put a longer address on the envelope. When the letter gets to the mailroom, the staff notice that the destination is not local, and they route it out to the postal system, which sends it to York. This is the "Internet Protocol" for letters.

The Internet is powered by a local protocol (Transport Control Protocol, or TCP) and an internetwork protocol (Internet Protocol, or IP). Put these together, and you have the familiar TCP/IP name that refers to the combination. You can also use the TCP/IP protocol to connect machines without linking them to the Internet. In effect, you can create an "Internet in your bedroom" from just a few machines. Windows PCs and Xbox consoles connected in this way can be used to play games using a connection called "System Link," which we'll discuss in the next section.

Xbox Live

Xbox Live uses the TCP/IP protocol to connect Xbox consoles and Windows PCs for networked game play. All Xbox games provide support for some form of network connection using Xbox Live. This can be as simple as the uploading of high scores and achievements to your gamertag. However, many games provide very advanced network play facilities, with Xbox Live connectivity allowing gamers to set up and play multi-player sessions.

Gamertags and Xbox Live

If you have used Xbox Live, you know about "gamertags." A gamertag is a name by which a player is known on the Xbox Live network. You have created an account on the Xbox Live network associated with a unique gamertag that other gamers can use to find you. Your gamertag is also linked to your game achievement records and other game-related information that is stored for you by the Xbox Live system. You can also create an avatar which lets other gamers see what you look like.

It is possible to create XNA programs that make use of the Xbox Live gamertags and world-wide servers and provide a multi-player experience just like that from any full-fledged game. However, to develop and test such a game requires multiple App Hub memberships and some fairly complex coding that is beyond the scope of this introductory text. However, you can still create multi-player games using the somewhat simpler System Link technology, which XNA also supports.

System Link and XNA

System Link is a game networking technology that allows Xbox 360 consoles and Windows PCs on the same physical network to engage in network game play. When I say "same physical network," I mean the network is connected to the same piece of wire or WiFi access point. The bad news is that this means for multi-player action, your friend has to bring her computer or console to your house and plug it into your network. The good news is that PC and console owners can play against each other.

System Link provides a set of methods that can be used to allow a program running on one system to send a message to another. What the message contains and how it is formatted are completely up to the game developer. You also get a means by which a network game can be set up between two or more players. A System Link game is "local," which means that it does not need to use the Xbox Live gamertag system to find players; instead, you can create local Gamer Profiles on machines.

> **Note** By "local network," I really do mean local. I have encountered problems creating System Link games using machines connected via WiFi adapters. It seems that XNA works best when communicating across real wire. Bearing in mind that during network play it is important that the systems have a reliable and speedy network connection, it is probably best to use wire anyway.

Bread and Cheese Pong

To find out how to create a network game, you are going to make a new game called "Bread and Cheese Pong." Your younger brother really likes the name. It will be a simple pong game, with each player controlling a bat and hitting the cheese towards the opponent. You can use a lot of the bread and cheese sprite code that you have already written in previous chapters. A good starting point would be a simple, two-player pong game, as shown in Figure 16-3.

This game finally answers the question, "Which is better, white bread or brown bread?" with bread bats being used to hit the cheese ball. The players are defending their back wall— if cheese hits the back wall, the player on the opposing side gains a point.

> **Sample Code: 01 Bread and Cheese Pong Game** All the sample projects can be obtained from the Web resources for this text, which can be found at *http://oreilly.com/ catalog/9780735651579*. The sample project in the 01 Bread and Cheese Pong Game directory in the resources for this chapter contains a two-player pong game that uses two gamepads to control the bread bats. This is the starting point for our game.

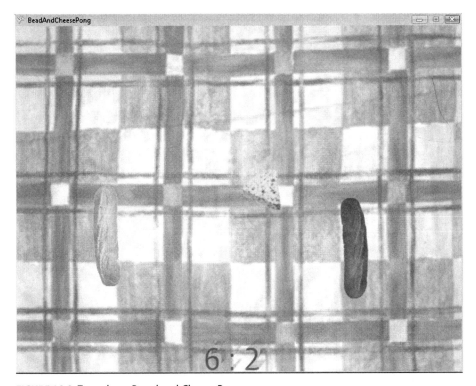

FIGURE 16-3 Two-player Bread and Cheese Pong game.

Managing Gamer Profiles in XNA

Before a game can start network play, the players must be signed in. On an Xbox 360, you perform this kind of task using the Guide part of the user interface, which you access by pressing the big silver X button in the middle of the gamepad. This facility is part of the Xbox and is always available. When running XNA programs on a Windows PC, you can access a similar facility by pressing the Home key on the PC keyboard. However, if you start one of the games we have already written and press the Home key, you find that nothing happens. This is because the Guide behavior is managed by the GamerServicesComponent, which is part of XNA and must be loaded into a game if the game wishes to use it. This is simple to do—you just have to add an extra line to the constructor of your game class.

```
public PongGame()
{
    graphics = new GraphicsDeviceManager(this);
    Content.RootDirectory = "Content";

    this.Components.Add(new GamerServicesComponent(this));
}
```

This creates a new GamerServicesComponent instance and connects it to your game. Now, when you run your game, you can press the Home key to call up the display. Figure 16-4 shows the initial sign-in screen.

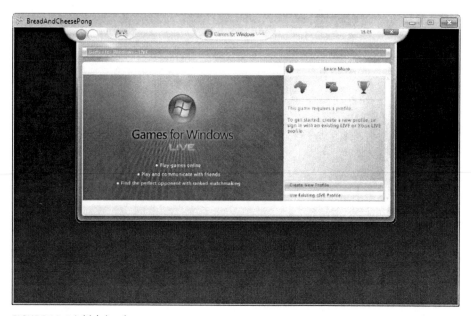

FIGURE 16-4 Initial sign-in screen.

Creating a Profile

The very first time you use the GameServicesComponent on your Windows PC, you do not have any gamer profiles on it. This means that it displays the screen shown in Figure 16-4, from which you can create a new profile. You can control the screen from an Xbox gamepad or from the keyboard. You should move the highlighted menu option to select Create New Profile, and then press the A button on the gamepad, the A key on the keyboard, or the Enter key to select this option. You can also use the Windows PC mouse to select options on any of these screens.

Once you have selected Create New Profile, the screen changes to a Create Gamer Profile screen. Do not click the Continue button on this screen. Instead, you should scroll down to find the Create A Local Profile link, as shown in Figure 16.5, and click the link instead. This will open a dialog box in which you can enter the name of the local profile, as shown in Figure 16.6. Type in a name, and select Submit.

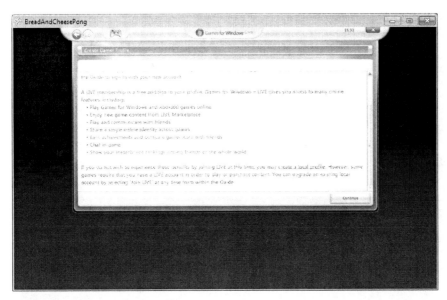

FIGURE 16-5 Creating a local profile.

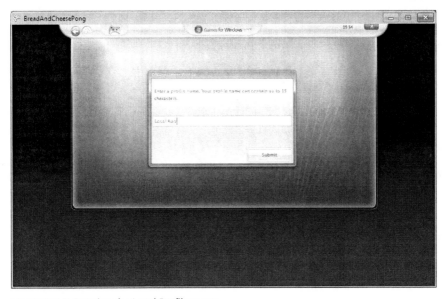

FIGURE 16-6 Entering the Local Profile name.

Once you enter your profile name and select Submit, you are taken to the Save Gamer Profile screen shown in Figure 16-7. You are allocated a random icon, but you can change this by selecting Customize Profile. The profile that you are about to create is local to the Windows PC you are using. Select Done to save your profile. At this point, the system has signed you in.

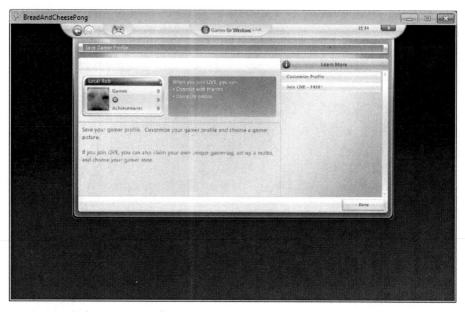

FIGURE 16-7 Saving a gamer profile.

You can close the guide by pressing the Home key again or the B button on the gamepad, or by clicking the X in the top right corner of the display.

Automatic Sign-In

The next time you start an XNA game that has GameServicesComponent active, it automatically signs in for you using the last active profile. It shows you that this has happened by momentarily displaying a message at the base of the screen, as shown in Figure 16-8.

The message also reminds you that you can sign out and change to a different profile, or even create a new profile, by pressing the Home key.

> **Sample Code: 02 UserDisplay**   The sample project in the 02 UserDisplay directory in the resources for this chapter is a brand-new, empty project that has the GameServicesComponent loaded. You can use it to create a new profile for yourself.

FIGURE 16-8 Notice of automatic sign-in.

Ensuring a Gamer Is Signed In for Network Play

It is impossible to start a network game until a gamer has signed in. This is because the gamertag is used to identify this player on the network, and if the player is not signed in, there is no tag. The Gamer class provides a property called SignedInGamers, which contains a collection of the gamers currently signed in at your game. On the Xbox 360, it is possible for more than one gamer to sign in to a single console (this is so they can use split-screen multi-player mode in networked games). On the Windows PC, there can never be more than one signed-in gamer at a machine.

The game must make sure that a gamer has signed in for network play. It can test to see if a gamer is signed in by checking the number of items in the SignedInGamers collection. If this is zero, no players are signed in. This means that the game must display the menu that lets a player sign in with his or her profile. The XNA menus are created using the Guide class, which can display a number of different menus. The one that you want is activated using the SignIn method on the Guide. The Guide also provides a property called IsVisible, which is set to true when the guide is active. You can use this to stop the guide being displayed on top of itself. Your program should only try to display a new guide menu if the IsVisible property is false:

```
protected override void Update(GameTime gameTime)
{
    // Allows the game to exit
    if (GamePad.GetState(PlayerIndex.One).Buttons.Back ==
            ButtonState.Pressed)
      this.Exit();
```

```
        if (Gamer.SignedInGamers.Count == 0)
        {
            if (Guide.IsVisible == false)
            {
                Guide.ShowSignIn(1, false);
            }
        }

        base.Update(gameTime);
    }
```

This version of Update displays the sign-in screen if there are no signed-in gamers. If a user closes the guide without signing in, this code displays the sign-in screen again. Note that the ShowSignin method for the Guide has two parameters. The first is the number of sign-in screens to display. For a Windows PC game, this must always be 1. The second is whether or not to restrict the sign-in to permit only online gamers to sign in. Online gamers have profiles linked to Xbox Live. For our game, we want to allow local gamer profiles as well, and so this parameter should be false.

Creating a Game Lobby

Playing a network game is just like any other. If you wake up one morning with a strong desire for some "Snakes and Ladders" action, you have to find your copy of the game and then get a hold of enough people to join you and start playing. This might involve standing somewhere shouting, "Who wants to play Snakes and Ladders?" until you have enough people who want to take part.

In computer gaming terms, this is sometimes called a "game lobby," where one system on the network proposes a game session and other players enter the game lobby and wait together until there are enough of them there to play the game. To create a network game, you are going to have to add code to set up a lobby and invite people to join your game. In the case of Bread and Cheese Pong, you need only one additional player, but the system we are going to build will handle more than two players.

Network Games and State

We have looked at game states before. The original Bread and Cheese game had a "Title Screen" state and a "Playing" state and would switch between them. In the case of a networked game, state is even more important. There are a number of possible states that the networked game might occupy. The best way to represent these is to use an enumerated type as follows:

```
public enum GameState
{
    titleScreen,
    NotSignedIn,
```

```
    SelectingRole,
    WaitingAsHost,
    WaitingAsPlayer,
    PlayingAsPlayer,
    PlayingAsHost
}

GameState state = GameState.titleScreen;
```

These are all the possible states that the game can occupy. For each state, there will be events that cause the game to move from that state into another. Figure 16-9 shows the states, the screens that they display, and the events that cause the states to change. The variable `state` holds the current state of the game.

The `Update` and `Draw` methods contain `switch` statements that control what the game does when in each state, something we used before when creating the original Bread and Cheese game. We can now look at how the states are used to start the game and play it.

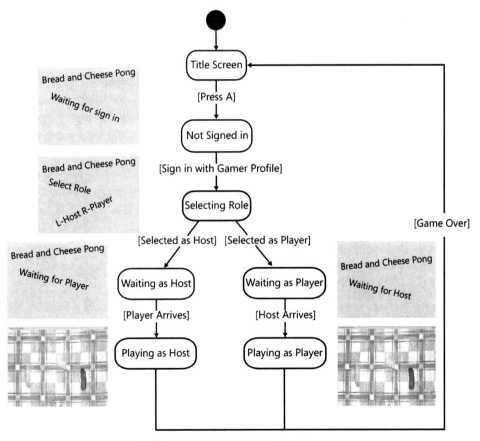

FIGURE 16-9 States in the Bread and Cheese Pong game.

Starting at the Title Screen

The titleScreen state is the state the game occupies at the start. A title screen is displayed and the player is invited to press A on the gamepad to continue. The game returns to this state when a game finishes. You have seen the code for this state before—it simply reads the gamepad of the player and checks whether the A button has been pressed. This is the part of the switch statement in Update that deals with the behavior of the game when in the titleScreen state:

```
case GameState.titleScreen:
    if (gamePad1.Buttons.A == ButtonState.Pressed)
    {
        state = GameState.NotSignedIn;
    }
    break;
```

When the player presses A, the game state is changed to the NotSignedIn state.

Signing In Players

The first thing the game must do is make sure that the player is signed in with a gamer profile. The code for the NotSignedIn state in the Update method must check whether a gamer is signed in and display the ShowSignIn page from the Guide if not.

```
case GameState.NotSignedIn:
    if (Gamer.SignedInGamers.Count == 0)
    {
        if (!Guide.IsVisible)
        {
            Guide.ShowSignIn(1, false);
        }
    }
    else
    {
        state = GameState.SelectingRole;
    }
break;
```

As XNA automatically signs in a player, the game normally moves straight through this state into the SelectingRole, where the player selects the role he or she is going to play.

Selecting the Role of Host

One player must be the host of the game, and the other will be the player. The host sets up the game lobby and waits for the player to join. The role to be taken is selected using the D-pad on the gamepad, which is tested when the game is in the SelectingRole state.

Note The lobby system works fine whether the player waits for the host or vice versa. However, you might have to wait a second or two after both systems have selected their roles as the systems find each other on the network.

Pressing the left button on the pad selects the Host role. The host must create a network session and wait for other players to join. The session is created using the `Create` method, which is told the type of the game, the maximum number of local gamers on a machine and the maximum number of players the game can support:

```
if (gamePad1.DPad.Left == ButtonState.Pressed)
{
    // Selected Host role
    // Create the session
    session = NetworkSession.Create(
        NetworkSessionType.SystemLink,
        1, // only 1 local gamer
        2  // no more than 2 players
        );

    session.GamerJoined +=
      new EventHandler<GamerJoinedEventArgs>(hostSession_GamerJoined);
    session.GamerLeft +=
      new EventHandler<GamerLeftEventArgs>(hostSession_GamerLeft);

    state = GameState.WaitingAsHost;
```

Once the session has been created, the game program must bind to events that tell it when more players arrive. At this point, we need to digress into events.

The Great Programmer Speaks: You Need to Know About Events The Great Programmer reckons that events are, quite literally, what make programs tick. They underpin the way that software responds to user actions on your Windows PC, including mouse movement, key presses, and even the system clock. A good understanding of how events are managed in a program is a very good thing to have, and the game sessions of XNA provide a good place to start exploring this subject.

Events let programs deal with things when they happen instead of the program having to hang around waiting. In the case of the Pong game, it might take several seconds for a player to join the host in a game. However, the XNA system wants to keep calling the `Draw` and `Update` methods until a player arrives. So instead of waiting for a response, the program tells the session what to do when a gamer arrives by connecting, or binding, a method to the events the program wants to know about.

To do this, the program needs a way of creating a reference to a method. You have seen references to objects before, but references to methods are different. They are called *delegates.* A delegate is an object that refers to a particular method in a class. You declare a delegate by telling the compiler the type returned by the delegate, and the type of the parameters to the delegate:

```
delegate int DoSimpleSum(int v1, int v2);
```

This creates a delegate type called DoSimpleSum. This particular delegate accepts two integer values and returns an integer result. It can be made to refer to any method that accepts two integers and returns an integer result, such as the two methods below:

```
int DoAdd(int v1, int v2)
{
    return v1 + v2;
}

int DoMultiply(int v1, int v2)
{
    return v1 * v2;
}
```

To create an instance of the delegate that refers to one of these methods we must declare a variable and create an instance of the delegate, as shown below.

```
DoSimpleSum mySum = new DoSimpleSum(DoAdd);
```

This code creates a delegate variable of type DoSimpleSum, which has the identifier mySum. This is then set to a new delegate instance that refers to the DoAdd method. This means that if I use the mySum delegate it will call the DoAdd method:

```
int result = mySum(3, 3);
```

The code above would put the value 6 into the result variable, because the delegate points to the DoAdd method.

A program can use the mySum delegate to tell another part of the program which method to call when a sum needs to be performed. Because mySum is an object like any other, I can pass it into a method as a parameter.

Delegates are *type-safe,* in that they are allowed to refer only to methods that match their declaration. For example, it would not be possible to create a delegate of type DoSimpleSum that referred to a method that only accepted a single parameter.

If I give a program a delegate value, it can use that to call the method that the delegate points to. The first event the game is interested in is when a gamer joins. You will create a method called hostSessionGamerJoined that will deal with this situation and then connect it to the event. The C# that connects to this event is shown here:

```
session.GamerJoined +=
    new EventHandler<GamerJoinedEventArgs>(hostSession_GamerJoined);
```

The event that we are interested in is the GamerJoined property of the session object. The event manages a list of people to contact when a gamer joins the session. The += operator is one we have seen before. It lets you add a value easily. For example, x += 3 adds 3 to the value x. In this case, the += is adding a new delegate value to the GamerJoined event in our session.

The delegate is set up to refer to an EventHandler method that accepts GamerJoinedEventArgs. The method being connected to the event is called hostSession_GamerJoined. This method must check to see if there are enough remote gamers connected, and if there are, it must start the game and change the state of the game to PlayingAsHost. It is actually quite a simple method. It checks to see if we have enough gamers available and then, if we have, it calls StartGame to set up all the game elements and changes the state to indicate that the game is now playing with this machine as the host, as shown here:

```
void hostSession_GamerJoined(object sender, GamerJoinedEventArgs e)
{
    if (session.RemoteGamers.Count == 1)
    {
        StartGame();
        state = GameState.PlayingAsHost;
    }
}
```

This version of hostSession_GamerJoined lets anyone join the game. It is, however, possible for the event handler method to get the gamertag of the player wishing to join and start playing only with certain people.

Events and delegates are used extensively throughout the Windows operating system to allow programs to bind to events such as button presses in the Windows graphical user interface. If the code looks a bit confusing, do not worry. The nice thing is that XNA Game Studio creates most of the code for you automatically.

Just remember that delegates provide a way that you can connect an event generator (something that wants to tell our program something) with a method (that needs to do something to respond to that event). The game also binds a method to the event for when a gamer leaves. If a gamer leaves, we want the game session to end and return to the title screen. The following method handles this event:

```
void hostSession_GamerLeft(object sender, GamerLeftEventArgs e)
{
    session.Dispose();
    EndGame();
}
```

Calling the Dispose method on a session causes it to shut down. This means that the player should be able to initiate a new game at this point. The EndGame method tells all the sprites in the game that it has ended and resets the game state to titleScreen so it is ready for the next game.

Displaying the Contents of the Lobby

While the game is acting as a host, waiting for players to join, it shows a list of players already in the game waiting to take part:

```
case GameState.WaitingAsHost:
    displayMessage = "";
    foreach (Gamer g in session.AllGamers)
    {
        displayMessage += g.Gamertag + "\n";
    }
    session.Update();
    break;
```

This part of a game is sometimes called the "lobby display." The foreach loop assembles a string called displayMessage containing the gamertags of all the gamers who are presently in the lobby waiting to play the game. For your game, this just shows the gamertag of the host of the game (because a host is always part of the session she is hosting), but if a game was waiting for several players, it would let the host see how many people had joined so far. The string displayMessage is drawn on the screen by the Draw method.

Note that there is also a call of an Update method on the session that is being managed. When a system is using the network, it must do this to keep the network active.

Selecting the Role of Player

The role of player is selected by pressing the right button on the D-Pad when the game is in the SelectingRole state. When in this state, the game looks for game sessions being presented by hosts and joins one if it finds it. This is much simpler than the host behavior. As shown here, the game just moves into the WaitingAsPlayer state, where all the work is actually performed.

```
if (gamePad1.DPad.Right == ButtonState.Pressed)
{
    // Selected Player role
    state = GameState.WaitingAsPlayer;
}
```

Waiting for a Host

If the game is in the WaitingAsPlayer state, it is waiting for a host. The game must repeatedly look for hosts who are presenting sessions that it might want to join. In a full-fledged lobby system, players would be able to choose which games they might like to join. Your game is much simpler, in that it simply finds the first available hosted game and joins it:

```
case GameState.WaitingAsPlayer:
    AvailableNetworkSessionCollection sessions =
        NetworkSession.Find(NetworkSessionType.SystemLink, 1, null);

    if (sessions.Count > 0)
    {
        AvailableNetworkSession mySession = sessions[0];
        session = NetworkSession.Join(mySession);
        session.GamerLeft +=
          new EventHandler<GamerLeftEventArgs>(playerSession_GamerLeft);
        StartGame();
        state = GameState.PlayingAsPlayer;
    }
    break;
```

The Find method is called on the NetworkSession class, which looks for games and returns a collection of the ones that it finds. It can be supplied with the properties of the game you want it to look for, in terms of the type of game, the number of local players, and other filtering options. The call shown previously looks for SystemLink games with no more than one local player. If it finds some games, it joins the one at the start of the collection (sessions[0]) and then adds the method playerSession_GamerLeft to the GamerLeft event so that the game is informed if the host leaves the game. It then starts the game and sets the game state to PlayingAsPlayer, so that the players can start their networked battle.

At this point, you now know how the lobby system works, and what happens to get the players this far in the network game. This would be a good time to go for a cup of coffee.

Playing the Game

The lobby mechanism has brought the two players to the point where one game is in the PlayingAsHost state and the other is in the PlayingAsPlayer state. Both games also have an active session instance that is providing the link between the two XNA programs. Now they can start playing the game.

Game Topology

You can arrange a network game in a number of ways. Some games are based on a configuration called "peer to peer," where no one player is in overall control and each player must exchange game status information with all the other players in the game. This works for small numbers of players, but for games with many systems, it can result in a lot of network traffic.

A better way to arrange network play is to have one system operate as a server and have all the others send their information to it. The server can then send out a message to everyone that contains the position of all the elements in the game. This results in much less network traffic. In terms of game arrangement, it is often the case that there must be one system in overall control of the game. The server for a game is usually, but not always, the system that proposed it in the first place.

In the case of our game, the system that is in the PlayingAsHost state works as a server and manages the game state, with the PlayingAsPlayer system working as a client. This means that if you wanted to add players (whole-grain bread, anyone?), then this would be easy to do.

Creating the Server Behavior

The host system performs all the game mechanics for player 1. These are very recognizable from previous games. The first part of the update is very familiar:

```
CheeseBall.Update(this);
Player1Bat.Update(this);
```

These two calls move the cheese ball and update the position of the bread bat for player 1. The ball update method also checks for collisions between the bats and the ball and performs the scoring.

Once the ball and the player 1 bat have been updated, the host must then send this information to the client system so that the game running on the other player's machine can use it to drive the display. You can think of the connection between the server and the client as two pipes which are plugged into your program. A system can push information into the "send" pipe and also check to see if anything has arrived from the "receive" pipe. The connection itself is not aware of the meaning of the data that is being transferred, and so we must make sure that it is clear to the receiver what they are getting.

XNA provides classes that take our data and convert it into a format suitable for transfer over the network connection. These classes are called PacketWriter and PacketReader. They do the same kind of thing for a network connection that SpriteBatch does for the graphics. They let a program assemble a bunch of items and then transfer them in one lump. We declare the reader and writer as part of the game world along with the network session that we are going to use:

```
// Game World

NetworkSession session = null;

PacketWriter writer = new PacketWriter();
PacketReader reader = new PacketReader();
```

The host system needs to tell the clients three things:

- The position of the cheese

- The position of the player 1 bat

- The message containing the score

The client can use this information to update the display. Note that the client is not handling any of the collisions between ball and bats or keeping track of the score. The code to use a packet writer to assemble this information is as follows:

```
writer.Write('H');

writer.Write(Cheese.XPos);
writer.Write(Cheese.YPos);

writer.Write(Player1.XPos);
writer.Write(Player1.YPos);

writer.Write(displayMessage);
```

The `Write` method provided by a writer can be given any number of simple values (number or string), and it assembles this into a message. The first thing that is sent is the character *H*, to indicate the message is from the host. A character is a single letter. The C# type `char` is provided for holding such single characters, and a `string` of text is made up of individual char values. You need to put this on the front of the message so the receiver can tell which message it is. The character is followed by the X and Y positions of the cheese, and then the positions of the Player1 bat, and finally the message presently being displayed.

Having assembled the message in the writer, it can now be sent to the game session for delivery for all the players in the game:

```
LocalNetworkGamer localHost = session.LocalGamers[0];
localHost.SendData(writer, SendDataOptions.ReliableInOrder);
```

The first statement gets a reference to `LocalNetworkGamer` from the session. The next statement uses the SendData method on this gamer to send the contents of the writer. The second parameter to the SendData method selects how the message is to be sent. There are a number of possible settings for this:

- ***Chat***   The message is part of a chat between systems. This option lets your game send chat messages in a properly formatted manner.

- ***InOrder***   Data is not guaranteed to be delivered, but messages are received in the same order they were sent.

- ***None***   There is no guarantee that the messages get to their destination or that they arrive in the order they were sent.

- ■ *Reliable* Messages are guaranteed to arrive, but they are not guaranteed to arrive in the same order they were sent.

- ■ *ReliableInOrder* Messages are guaranteed to arrive, and they will be in the same order they were sent.

The option that you select depends on the importance of data integrity and synchronization. You should remember that if you ask for a `Reliable` or `ReliableInOrder` transfer, this means that the transfer is slower and involves more effort to manage. In effect, the system must manage a virtual call to implement `ReliableInorder`. It must wait for late packets so that they can be given to your program in order, and it must also request retransmission of lost ones. On the other hand, selecting None means that data arrives more quickly, but some pieces of the data might be missing or out of order.

In our game, it does not really matter if messages are missing or out of order; all that happens in that case is that the ball or bats might seem to jump slightly. However, because the data is small and the systems are on the same network, I've selected the `ReliableInOrder` setting. You might like to experiment with other ones.

The next thing the host must do is read the position of the player 2 bat. This is managed by the client game, which uses a call of SendData to transfer the data to the host. To read data is actually very easy; it is done as follows:

```
while (localHost.IsDataAvailable)
{
    NetworkGamer sender;
    localHost.ReceiveData(reader, out sender);
    char messageType = reader.ReadChar();
    if (messageType == 'P')
    {
        Player2Bat.XPos = reader.ReadSingle();
        Player2Bat.YPos = reader.ReadSingle();
    }
}
```

The `localHost` provides a property called `IsDataAvailable`, which is `true` when data is available. This is used to control a loop construction that we haven't seen before. The `while` loop repeats a block of code while the condition controlling it is true. In this case, we want the game to read packets repeatedly until there are none left. The code inside the loop reads messages and processes them. The first statement in the loop uses the `ReceiveData` method. This is provided with a reference to a `PacketReader`, which it fills up with data, and also sets a reference to the `NetworkGamer` description of the system that sent the message. It does this by using an out parameter:

```
NetworkGamer sender;
localHost.ReceiveData(reader, out sender);
```

We have seen that normally parameters are passed into methods by value. In other words, the value of the parameter is copied and sent into the method. In this case, however, we want the `ReceiveData` method to actually change the value of sender to make it refer to the `NetworkGamer` object that describes the system from which the message came. The method has been declared as wanting to write to the value of the *parameter*, so when you use the method, we have put the `out` keyword in front of the variable name.

If a method wants full control of a parameter (that is, it wants to read and write), it can use the `ref` key word to modify the way the parameter behaves. Your game doesn't actually use this information, but you could use this in a multi-player game with lots of players to find out who sent the message. The host wants to see a message that starts with the character *P* because it knows that it comes from the player and contains the position of the player's bat. The following code reads the first character of the message, and if it is a *P*, it knows that it can read two single-precision, floating-point values to set the X and Y positions of the player 2 bat.

```
char messageType = reader.ReadChar();
if (messageType == 'P')
{
    Player2Bat.XPos = reader.ReadSingle();
    Player2Bat.YPos = reader.ReadSingle();
}
```

To make the game work, we have created a little protocol of our own. If a message starts with the character *H*, it contains four numbers (for the positions of the ball and the player 1 bat) and a string (the message for the display). If a message starts with the character *P*, it contains two numbers (for the position of player 2 bat). For a more complicated game, you could invent more messages, each with a different format.

Creating the Client Behavior

The client behavior looks very similar to the server:

```
Player2.Update(this);
writer.Write('P');
writer.Write(Player2.XPos);
writer.Write(Player2.YPos);

LocalNetworkGamer localPlayer = session.LocalGamers[0];
localPlayer.SendData(writer, SendDataOptions.ReliableInOrder);

while (localPlayer.IsDataAvailable)
{
    NetworkGamer sender;
    localPlayer.ReceiveData(reader, out sender);
    char messageType = reader.ReadChar();
    if (messageType == 'H')
    {
        Cheese.XPos = reader.ReadSingle();
        Cheese.YPos = reader.ReadSingle();
```

```
        Player1.XPos = reader.ReadSingle();
        Player1.YPos = reader.ReadSingle();
        displayMessage = reader.ReadString();
    }
}
session.Update();
```

First, the player 2 bat is updated, and then its position is sent to the host in a packet starting with the character *P*. Then the code looks for a message that starts with *H*, which it can use to set the position of the cheese, player 1 bat, and the message to be displayed. Note that the Update method on the network session is also called to keep the network active.

The Completed Game

The completed game works well, although it is not without its faults. The screen dimensions of the two systems being used must be the same because the present version passes the position of the items in terms of absolute screen coordinates. However, it would be comparatively easy to perform some scaling of these values.

Another slight problem is that because the host system performs all collision detection, it is the only system that makes sounds. However, it would be quite easy to extend the design of the messages sent from the host to include information to tell the client to play particular sound effects.

> **Sample Code: 03 Networked Pong Game** The sample project in the 03 Networked Pong Game directory in the resources for this chapter contains a fully working version of the game that provides networked gameplay for PC or Xbox 360

Conclusion

You have learned a lot in this chapter, starting with a quick introduction to the way that networks operate and then moving on to consider how Xbox Live uses the network to provide to multi-player games the profile of the gamers that use it.

You have seen how the Guide can be used on Windows PCs to allow XNA gamers to create their own gamer profiles and store them on their systems. You have also seen how a system can use a state machine to set up a lobby and wait for players to turn up and take part in a game. Finally, you have seen how to format data so that it can be passed from one system to another during game play and how to set up a server and client arrangement that can serve as the basis of any kind of networked game. All in all, not a bad place to end up.

Chapter Review Questions

And now we end with some review questions that should separate the networkers from the notworkers.

1. Networks are made using wet string.

2. Every station on a particular network must have a unique address.

3. Messages sent over a network to your system cannot be received by other systems.

4. You can use XNA network gaming without a gamer profile.

5. A router is connected to only one network.

6. You can create the Internet in your front room.

7. XNA cannot be used to create games that provide full Xbox Live network game play to gamers all round the world.

8. The XNA NetworkSession class drives the network gameplay in a multi-player XNA game.

9. Only two players can take part in a network game.

10. A state machine can be used to store the score gained in a network game.

11. One XNA system must create a session that others can join to play a networked game.

12. An event is a way of attracting the attention of a program.

13. A delegate is a type-safe reference to a method in an object.

14. XNA games can only transfer floating-point values between each other when playing network games.

15. In a server-client network game configuration, the clients send information to each other about the state of the game.

Part IV
Making Mobile Games for Windows Phone 7 with XNA

Chapter 17
Motion-Sensitive Games

- Discover how a device can be sensitive to orientation and movement.
- Find out how XNA programs can use the accelerometer hardware provided by the Windows Phone.
- Understand how easy it is to create a simple physics model in XNA.
- Create the "Cheese Lander" game for Windows Phone.
- Create a "Shaker" game for Windows Phone.

Introduction

In this chapter, we are going to develop some games for Microsoft Windows Phone 7 that use one of the special input features this platform provides—the accelerometer. We'll explore the physics behind the sensor in the device and how to make use of the sensor from software. Finally, we'll create some simple games that use the accelerometer in their gameplay.

The Accelerometer

The first mobile phones contained nothing more than, well, a phone. However, modern ones have much more hardware. A Windows Phone contains a powerful graphics processor, huge amounts of internal memory, and a range of sensors, one of which is the accelerometer. From a programmer's point of view, these sensors provide new ways that people can interact with their phones. In the case of the accelerometer, it means phone users can do things like select a new music track by shaking the phone or control objects in a game by tipping the phone in a particular direction.

What Does the Accelerometer Actually Do?

You might think that your game programs will just use the accelerometer to measure acceleration. While this is true, and it means you could use your Windows Phone to compare the performance of sports cars, it turns out that the accelerometer is actually much more useful than this. For the games we are going to write, we'll also be using the accelerometer to work out the orientation of the phone (that is, whether it is being held flat or tipped in any particular direction). To understand how this works, we are going to have to look at some physics.

Acceleration and Physics

It's difficult to talk about acceleration without mentioning physics. The good news is that we don't need to know a lot of physics to understand what is going on, and we can use physics in games to very good effect. We are only going to consider one physics equation for now, and here it is:

```
Force = Mass * Acceleration
```

This is Newton's Second Law of Motion. Sir Isaac Newton was a mathematician famous for having an apple fall on his head and for being one of the greatest scientific minds of our age. When he came up with the equation just shown, he was trying to set out mathematically what happens when we try to move things. As you already know, if you want to move something you have to push it. If you don't push something, it just stays where it is. This is the basis of Newton's First Law of Motion.

Having established that things stay in the same place unless you push them, Newton moved on to consider what happens to things when you do push them. He realized, and this is where the falling apple is supposed to fit in, that everything on the earth is subject to the force of gravity, which is constantly pulling us down toward the center of the planet. Whatever other forces are applied to objects on the surface of the earth, they will always have gravity pulling them down. This is why no matter how hard you kick a football into the air, it will always come back down to earth again. The only way to prevent the football coming back is to strap it to a rocket and send it into orbit around the earth.

"So," asks your younger brother, "having dropped apples on our head and shot footballs into space, how does this relate to the accelerometer in a Windows Phone?" Well, it means we can determine acceleration by measuring the forces acting on a weight. We can get the acceleration value if we know the amount of the weight we are using and the amount of the force being applied. All we have to do is rearrange the earlier equation a bit:

```
Force / Mass = Acceleration
```

All I've done here is divide the values on each side of the equals sign by the value of Mass. This equation passes my "Motor Racing Sanity Test." To get better acceleration for a car, you can either put in a bigger engine (increase the value of Force) or hack things off the car (reduce the value of Mass). If you feed values into the equation just shown, you'll find that either approach (increasing Force or decreasing Mass) makes the value of Acceleration larger. I always make up little "Sanity Tests" to prove my equations when I do physics so that I don't end up doing anything stupid.

Now that we have our physics sorted out, we need to build a sensor that can measure the forces acting on a weight. One way to measure a force is to look at the effect it has on things. Applying force to a spring will compress it if I push it or stretch it if I pull. The harder I push or pull, the greater the effect is on the spring. This means I can make a simple accelerometer by attaching a weight to a spring as shown in Figure 17-1.

FIGURE 17-1 Our first accelerometer.

If you do this experiment, you find that the weight hangs down from the spring, causing the spring to stretch. This is because the force of gravity is acting on the weight, pulling it down toward the earth. The heavier the weight is, the greater the force acting on the spring is and the longer the spring gets. This is the basis of a simple weighing machine—the spring balance. If we go to a place where there is no gravity (for example, into outer space), the spring would not be stretched because there is force acting on the weight and our spring balance would not work.

> **Note** This is a problem for astronauts in space stations, who have great difficulty weighing things. This is probably why they have to eat ready-made meals all the time—it would be impossible for them to follow a recipe that contained instructions like "Take two ounces of butter."

If we want to use an accelerometer to work out the orientation of the phone, we have to measure the direction of the force acting on it. We could do this by attaching three springs to the weight, one for each of the X, Y, and Z directions. By measuring the length of each spring, we can work out the force and, hence, the amount of acceleration in that direction. In the phone, the acceleration is not measured using a weight as such; instead, the readings are taken on the surface of a tiny semiconductor. However, the principles being used are exactly the same.

Making Sense of Accelerometer Readings

The accelerometer in the Windows Phone produces readings for acceleration along the X, Y, and Z axes. You can visualize the accelerometer as a weight on the end of a spring, attached to the back of the phone. Figure 17-2 shows us how this might look.

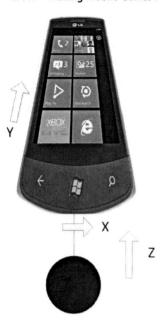

FIGURE 17-2 The accelerometer weight hanging off a Windows Phone.

If we hold the phone flat, as shown, the weight will hang straight down underneath the phone. If we were to measure the distance in the X, Y, and Z directions of the weight relative to the point where it is attached to the phone, we'd get 0, 0, –1, assuming that the spring is length 1. The value of Z is –1 because the position of the weight is now below the phone and the coordinate system being used has Z, the third dimension, increasing as we move up from the display.

If you tip up the near edge of the phone so that the far edge points toward your shoes, the weight swings away from you, increasing the value of Y that it has relative to the point where the string is attached. If you tip the near edge of the phone down so that you can see the screen properly, the weight moves the other way, and the value of Y becomes less than 0. If the phone is vertical (looking a bit like a tombstone), the weight is directly below and in line with the phone. In this situation, the value of Z will be 0 and the value of Y will be –1. Twisting the phone will make the weight move left or right and will cause the value of X to change.

These are the values we actually get from the accelerometer in the phone itself. So, at the moment, the accelerometer seems to be measuring orientation (that is, the way the phone is being held), not acceleration. We'll discuss acceleration later; for now, we'll use these values to make a game that can be controlled by the player tipping the phone.

Creating a "Cheese Lander" Tipping Game

The game we are going to create is a variant of the "lunar lander" games you might have played. These games have you guide a spacecraft down onto a landing pad. However, because we all like cheese, we'll create "Cheese Lander." This game, shown in Figure 17-3, involves landing a piece of cheese on a piece of bread.

FIGURE 17-3 Playing the "Cheese Lander" game.

The cheese starts off at the top of the screen, with the bread at the bottom. By tipping the phone, the player must guide the bread down onto the cheese. If the player doesn't land the cheese properly, she loses.

Game World Objects in "Cheese Lander"

Because we have only two game objects—the bread and the cheese—it seems like overkill to create a set of sprite objects. So we can just use textures and rectangles:

```
// Cheese
Texture2D cheeseTexture;
Rectangle cheeseRectangle;
int cheeseWidth;
float cheeseWidthFactor = 8;

float cheeseX;
float cheeseY;
```

This is all the information the game uses to manage the cheese sprite. It needs to hold the texture to draw on the screen (cheeseTexture), the rectangle that defines the draw position of the cheese (cheeseRectangle), and the width value. It uses the value of cheeseWidthFactor to set the size of the cheese on the screen. In the example just shown, the cheese is an eighth of the width of the screen.

The game uses two floating point variables—cheeseX and cheeseY—to determine the position of the cheese. We use the floating point type for this task because we'll need more precision than we can get from integers. The idea of this game is that the player must control the cheese by moving it at very low speed. This means the game needs to update the position of the cheese by amounts that are less than one. The Update method takes the floating point values and converts them into integers to position the cheese-drawing rectangle:

```
// Set the cheese Draw rectangle to cheeseX and cheeseY
cheeseRectangle.X = (int)(cheeseX + 0.5f);
cheeseRectangle.Y = (int)(cheeseY + 0.5f);
```

The Update behavior must also read the accelerometer in the Windows Phone and use it to update the position of the cheese. The good news is that it is easy to use the X and Y values supplied by the accelerometer. We can use them as direct replacements for the X and Y values provided by one of the thumbsticks on a gamepad. The bad news is that reading the accelerometer is not as simple as using the other input devices.

Getting Access to the Accelerometer Class from XNA

The accelerometer in a Windows Phone is managed by a class with the sensible name of Accelerometer. This is a software object that sits between our program and the hardware. We have seen this approach before—an object of type GamePadState hides how the hardware works and provides values that correspond to the physical settings of the gamepad. So to interact with the accelerometer hardware in the phone, we have to create an instance of the Accelerometer class.

The first thing we have to do is get the class itself. Up until now, everything we have used in our games has been directly available to our programs. Unfortunately, this is not the case with the Accelerometer class. The reason for this is that the part of the system in the Windows Phone that deals with the accelerometer is not provided in the standard XNA libraries. To use the Accelerometer class, we first have to add the program library that will provide access to that class. We have not done this before. Up until now, the only resources we have added to our games have been images and sounds.

Program resources are not managed by the Content Manager; they are handled directly by Microsoft Visual Studio. Each resource is a library file that contains the compiled code for a number of C# classes. A Visual Studio project contains a list of program resources that are being used by this project. You can take a look at this list by using the Solution Explorer view in Visual Studio 2010. Figure 17-4 shows the list of references created by Visual Studio 2010 when you open a new XNA game project.

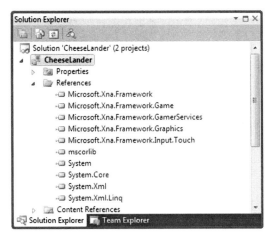

FIGURE 17-4 The references for a new XNA game.

These libraries contain code for the objects you have created in your games—for example, the Texture2D and Rectangle classes. Some of the elements in a game are from XNA libraries. Others are part of the standard .NET libraries. What we need to do is add the Microsoft.Devices.Sensors library to the list. This library contains the code for the Accelerometer object that we want to use in our game. The first step in adding the library is to open the Add Reference dialog. You can do this from the Project menu item as shown in Figure 17-5.

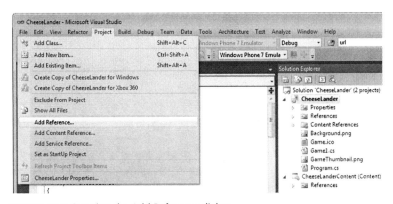

FIGURE 17-5 Opening the Add Reference dialog.

The Add Reference dialog shows the libraries that are available and lets you pick the ones you want to add to the project.

Note If you don't see any options to add a reference in the menu that appears when you click on Project, you must make sure that the project is selected in Solution Explorer as shown in Figure 17-5.

The library we need is the one shown in Figure 17-6. Click this library to select it, and then click OK to add the reference.

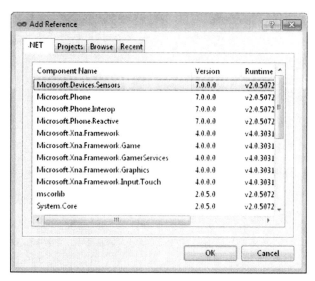

FIGURE 17-6 Adding the `Microsoft.Devices.Sensors` reference.

Our program can now use the `Accelerometer` class, but at the moment we have to use the full name of the class to find it in the `Microsoft.Devices.Sensors` namespace. To make it easier to use this class, we can add a `using` directive at the top of our program:

```
using Microsoft.Devices.Sensors;
```

We can now create an instance of the `Accelerometer` class in our game. The next thing we need to know is how to use it.

Using the Accelerometer in an XNA Game

In the past, we have obtained the status of objects in our game by just asking them for state information. When a game wants to know the state of the gamepad, it asks the GamePad class for an object that describes the state of that gamepad:

```
GamePadState pad1 = GamePad.GetState(PlayerIndex.One);
```

The game can then find out which buttons are pressed by reading members of the object pad1:

```
if (pad1.Buttons.A == ButtonState.Pressed)
{
    // Do things if button A is pressed
}
```

The `Accelerometer` doesn't work like this. It doesn't like being bothered by requests from users for values. Instead, our program must ask it to get in touch whenever it has a new reading available. This is just like going for an audition to appear in a Broadway show and being told, "Don't call us, we'll call you." In that situation, you will give the producer your phone number; in the case of the XNA accelerometer, we'll create a delegate that refers to the method we want to have called each time the accelerometer has a new reading available.

A delegate is a C# object that holds a reference to a method in an object. We have used references to objects for a while. A delegate doesn't just refer to an object, it refers to a method in that object. We must give the accelerometer a delegate so that it knows which method to run when a new reading is ready, just like we give the producer our phone number so that she can call us and tell us that we have the lead role in her musical.

We can get Visual Studio 2010 to do a lot of the hard work to create the delegate and the method that it connects to. The first thing we need to do is declare a variable in the game world that will hold the accelerometer we are using:

```
Accelerometer accel;
```

We can call the variable `accel`. The next thing we do is create an instance of the accelerometer when the game starts running. The best place to do this is in the `Initialize` method:

```
protected override void Initialize()
{
    accel = new Accelerometer();

    base.Initialize();
}
```

Now that we have our accelerometer variable we can connect a method to the `ReadingChanged` event that it provides. We can use Visual Studio IntelliSense to help with this. It will create the delegate that refers to the method and also the event hander itself. Start by finding the Initialize method and typing the two statements as shown in Figure 17-7.

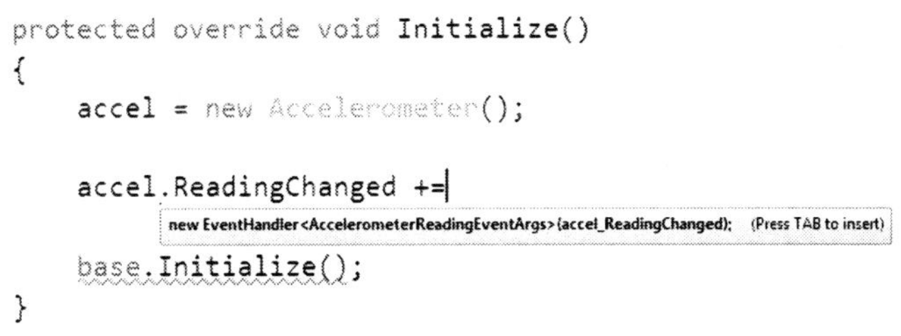

```
protected override void Initialize()
{
    accel = new Accelerometer();

    accel.ReadingChanged +=|
          new EventHandler<AccelerometerReadingEventArgs>(accel_ReadingChanged);    (Press TAB to insert)
    base.Initialize();
}
```

FIGURE 17-7 Adding an event handler delegate to the `ReadingChanged` event.

After you have typed "+=" as shown in Figure 17-7, IntelliSense in Visual Studio will offer to create the delegate for the event handler if you press the Tab key. When you press Tab, you are invited to press it again, as shown in Figure 17-8.

```
protected override void Initialize()
{
    accel = new Accelerometer();

    accel.ReadingChanged +=new EventHandler<AccelerometerReadingEventArgs>(accel_ReadingChanged);
    base.Initialize();      Press TAB to generate handler 'accel_ReadingChanged' in this class
}
```

FIGURE 17-8 Adding an event handler method to the ReadingChanged event.

If you press Tab a second time, the event handler is created automatically, although it just contains a statement that will throw an exception if the method is ever called. You should end up with code that looks like the following:

```
protected override void Initialize()
{
    accel = new Accelerometer();

    accel.ReadingChanged +=
      new EventHandler<AccelerometerReadingEventArgs>(accel_ReadingChanged);

    base.Initialize();
}

void accel_ReadingChanged(object sender, AccelerometerReadingEventArgs e)
{
    throw new NotImplementedException();
}
```

Note Sometimes IntelliSense can be a bit fickle and not turn up when it is supposed to. If you find that the menus do not appear as shown, make sure you have added the using statement as shown and that your source file is part of a project. Failing all that, you can of course type in the preceding code by hand.

The next thing to do is fill in the accel_ReadingChanged method with some code that will store the new accelerometer readings. When accel_ReadingChanged is called, it is given two parameters: a reference to the object sending the message (which will be the Accelerometer we created) and a reference to an AccelerometerReadingEventArgs object that contains the new reading values. The program must copy the values from the parameter into a variable in our game that will be used by the Update method to update the cheese position. The best XNA data type to use to store the accelerometer reading is Vector3. This contains X, Y, and Z components. It is the slightly larger brother of the Vector2 class we first saw in Chapter 5, "Writing Text," when we used one to position text on the screen. We need to create a vector to hold the accelerometer readings:

```
Vector3 accelReading;
```

Now we need to add code to the method to copy the readings over:

```
void accel_ReadingChanged(object sender, AccelerometerReadingEventArgs e)
{
    accelReading.X = (float)e.X;
    accelReading.Y = (float)e.Y;
    accelReading.Z = (float)e.Z;
}
```

These three statements take the X, Y, and Z properties out of the parameter e and copy them into the X, Y, and Z values of accelReading. Note that the code must cast the values read from the accelerometer to floating point ones—that is what the (float) part of each statement is for. This is because the type of the parameter that delivers the sensor values will allow it to produce ultra-accurate, double-precision results.

Starting the Accelerometer

The accelerometer must be turned on before it will start generating values. This is easy to do—the program just needs to call the Start method. I do this in the Initialize method:

```
protected override void Initialize()
{
    accel = new Accelerometer();
    accel.Start();

    // rest of initialize here
}
```

This starts the accelerometer, at which point it will begin to generate new values. If you want to stop the accelerometer for any reason, you can use the Stop method. It is unlikely you would want to do this, but your program might save a tiny amount of battery power if it enables the accelerometer only when it is actually required. My games start the accelerometer immediately after I have created it.

Using Accelerometer Values in a Game

Now that we have the accelerometer producing values, we can use them to control the movement of the cheese.

```
// Update the X and Y positions
cheeseX = cheeseX + (accelReading.X * acceleratorPower);
cheeseY = cheeseY - (accelReading.Y * acceleratorPower);
```

The two statements shown take the accelerometer readings that have been stored and use them to update the X and Y positions of the cheese. The variable acceleratorPower is a factor we use to control the effect of tipping the device. The larger this number is, the more sensitive the game is to movement. I have found that a value of 8 works well. Note that because the Y coordinate for texture drawing works in the opposite direction to the values from the accelerometer, we have to subtract the accelerometer reading from the Y position.

> **Sample Code: 01 Cheese Lander Game**   The sample project in the 01 Cheese Lander directory in the resources for this chapter contains a lander game where you must guide the cheese onto the bread by tipping the phone.

Improving Game Play by Adding Physics

You give your younger brother a copy of the Cheese Lander game, and he seems quite impressed. However, it is not long before he is back with a complaint. Apparently, the game is too easy. He and all his friends have been able to successfully land the cheese on the bread. He says, "What is the point of a game if you can't beat your friends at it?" We could make it a bit harder by making the bread target smaller or changing the value of acceleratorPower so that the cheese is harder to control. However, a better way to improve the game would be to add some more physics.

At the moment the tipping of the phone controls the speed, or *velocity*, of the cheese. Velocity is defined as the "rate of change of position" and is expressed in terms of distance traveled in a particular time. You can say that a car has a velocity of "60 miles per hour" or that the cheese has a velocity of "10 pixels per second." Each time Update runs, it adjusts the position of the cheese by a particular number of pixels. This update value is the velocity or speed of the cheese, in that it gives the distance that the cheese will travel during that clock tick. We can add cheese speed variables to our game as follows:

```
cheeseX = cheeseX + cheeseXSpeed;
cheeseY = cheeseY - cheeseYSpeed;
```

If these values are constant, the cheese will move at a constant speed around the screen. We have seen this code before. Whenever we have made an object move around the screen, we have done it by changing the position of the object each time Update is called. For our physics-controlled game, the initial speed values for our cheese will be 0 because the cheese is not moving at the start. Each time the game updates, the speed values will be changed according to the current acceleration. We can add acceleration by using two new variables:

```
cheeseXSpeed = cheeseXSpeed + cheeseXAcceleration;
cheeseYSpeed = cheeseYSpeed + cheeseYAcceleration;
```

Each time Update runs, the speed of the cheese is changed by the acceleration value. We apply acceleration in the direction the phone is tipping. We can work out the acceleration by using the accelerometer values (which seems very appropriate to me):

```
cheeseXAcceleration = accelReading.X * acceleratorPower;
cheeseYAcceleration = -accelReading.Y * acceleratorPower;
```

We again need to multiply the raw readings by a factor that makes the game work properly. This time a value that works well for `accceleratorPower` is 0.1. If we put all these together, we end up with speed calculations that look like this:

```
cheeseXAcceleration = accelReading.X * acceleratorPower;
cheeseYAcceleration = -accelReading.Y * acceleratorPower;

cheeseXSpeed = cheeseXSpeed + cheeseXAcceleration;
cheeseYSpeed = cheeseYSpeed + cheeseYAcceleration;

cheeseX = cheeseX + cheeseXSpeed;
cheeseY = cheeseY + cheeseYSpeed;

// Set the cheese Draw rectangle to cheeseX and cheeseY
cheeseRectangle.X = (int)(cheeseX + 0.5f);
cheeseRectangle.Y = (int)(cheeseY + 0.5f);
```

If we make the cheese bounce off the edges of the screen (as we have done in other games where we have a "ball" object), we have something that is very close to the behavior of a ball on a snooker table (assuming we were strong enough to pick the table up and tip it). This is exactly what we should have, because we are simulating the physics in such a situation to control the movement of the objects in our game.

The final change we can make is to force the player to make only soft landings on the bread. The previous version of the game just checked that the cheese had landed properly on the bread; it did not care how fast the cheese was going at the time. This is not very realistic. When landing her spaceship, a pilot will usually take a great deal of care to make sure that she doesn't hit the ground too hard. We can measure the softness of the landing by testing the values of the cheese velocity when the cheese reaches the bread. If they are above a certain speed, we can call that a crash landing:

```
if (cheeseRectangle.Intersects(breadRectangle))
{
    // May have won
    if (cheeseRectangle.Top < breadRectangle.Top &&
        cheeseRectangle.Left >= breadRectangle.Left &&
        cheeseRectangle.Right <= breadRectangle.Right &&
        Math.Abs(cheeseXSpeed) < cheeseMaxXLandSpeed &&
        Math.Abs(cheeseYSpeed) < cheeseMaxYLandSpeed)
    {
        // cheese is properly landed - player wins
        gameWon();
    }
    else
    {
        // cheese is badly landed - player loses
        gameLost();
    }
}
```

The lines in bold show the test that makes sure the X and Y speeds are below a particular threshold before the landing is considered a good one. I've found that a threshold of 0.4 seems to work well, providing gameplay that is not too easy but possible to achieve with care. I'm using the Math.Abs method in this code. This takes in a parameter and returns the absolute value of that parameter (that is, a value that is always positive). This is so I can handle collisions that occur when moving in any direction.

> **Sample Code: 02 Cheese Lander Game** The sample project in the 02 Cheese Lander directory in the resources for this chapter contains a lander game where you must guide the cheese onto the bread by tipping the phone. This version uses a physics model, and is therefore much harder to control.

Using Vectors to Express Movement

At the moment, we are using separate variables to express the movement and acceleration of our cheese in the X and Y directions. This works OK, but XNA can make life a lot easier for us if we use the vector classes it provides. We have seen vectors before—we used them to specify the position of text on the screen in Chapter 5. The Vector2 type can hold two values: an X and a Y. It also provides a whole set of operators we can use to manipulate vector values.

```
cheeseAcceleration.X = accelReading.X * acceleratorPower;
cheeseAcceleration.Y = -accelReading.Y * acceleratorPower;

cheeseSpeed = cheeseSpeed + cheeseAcceleration;

cheesePosition = cheesePosition + cheeseSpeed ;
```

We can still use the X and Y properties of the vector, but we can add two vectors together by using the + operator provided by Vector2. The * operator can be used in the same way.

You can also ask a vector to tell you how long it is by calling the Length method it provides. This is useful when testing the speed of our cheese. Rather than having to test the X and Y elements of the speed individually, we can just get the length of the speed vector. The longer the vector is, the faster the cheese is moving.

```
if (cheeseRectangle.Top < breadRectangle.Top &&
    cheeseRectangle.Left >= breadRectangle.Left &&
    cheeseRectangle.Right <= breadRectangle.Right &&
    cheeseSpeed.Length() < cheeseMaxLandSpeed )
{
    // cheese is properly landed - player wins
    gameWon();
}
else
{
    // cheese is badly landed - player loses
    gameLost();
}
```

Adding Friction

After we have given the cheese a velocity, it will have this value until we apply a new force to make it move in a different direction. At the moment, the cheese is in outer space with no friction to slow it down. However, you will often want to add friction to a situation. You could use the physics engine described to control the puck in a game of air hockey, but it would be very hard to play if the puck moved forever after it had been hit. Friction is a force that opposes movement, reducing the velocity of a moving object. We can simulate this effect in our game by multiplying the cheese velocity by a value that is less than one each time it is updated. This means that over time the velocity will reduce to 0.

```
float frictionFactor = 0.99f;
```

The smaller this value is, the faster the velocity will drop and the greater the friction effect will be. The Vector2 class lets you multiply a vector by a single value:

```
cheeseSpeed = cheeseSpeed * frictionFactor;
```

Adding friction to Cheese Lander makes it much easier to play because the cheese will slow down by itself rather than requiring the player to apply reverse thrust to stop it.

Controlling Sounds with Vectors

We can also use the length of a vector to make our game even more interesting. We can make an engine sound that is controlled by the length of the acceleration vector. The further the player tips the phone, the more power the engines are given and the faster the sound is played. The game can control a SoundEffectInstance during sound playback to get this effect:

```
float engineSoundThreshold = 0.07f;
float enginePitchFactor = 20.0f;

private void setEngineSound(float control)
{
    engineSoundInstance.Volume = Math.Min(control / engineSoundThreshold, 1);
    engineSoundInstance.Pitch = Math.Min(control * enginePitchFactor, 1);
}
```

This method is given the length of the accelerometer vector and uses this to control the volume and pitch of a playing sound. The Math.Min method is used to make sure that these values don't go beyond 1. The Math.Min method returns the minimum of the two values supplied as parameters. The two floating point variables control how rapidly the sound gets louder as you tip the phone and the change in pitch of the sound playback. The values you can see are ones I came up with during play testing. We can call the setEngineSound method from the Update method as follows:

```
setEngineSound(cheeseAcceleration.Length());
```

I have found that adding sound to the game actually makes it much easier to play. Players can hear how much "power" they are applying, and this makes the game easier to control.

> **Sample Code: 03 Cheese Lander with Sounds and Friction** The sample project in the 03 Cheese Lander with Sounds and Friction directory in the resources for this chapter contains a lander game where you must guide the cheese onto the bread by tipping the phone.

As an aside, I also discovered that by using sound like this I can use the Windows Phone as an *audible bubble level*. When the phone is flat, it makes no sound at all. If it is tipped, it makes a noise. You can use this to help you hang things on the wall. It actually works rather well.

Detecting Shaking

You can use the accelerometer to detect more than orientation. The length of the accelerometer vector will tell you the magnitude of the acceleration force acting on the phone. Normally this will be 1, which reflects the effect of gravity. However, if we start to move the phone around, this value will change. If we take the phone on a roller coaster, we would find that the acceleration becomes much larger when we are pressed down in our seats and much smaller when we are in a freefall moving downwards. The number also changes if the phone is shaken, which has the effect of rapidly changing the acceleration on the phone. You can use this as the basis of a very silly game:

```
protected override void Update(GameTime gameTime)

{

    float currentAccel = accelReading.Length();

    if (currentAccel > maxAccel)
    {
        maxAccel = currentAccel;
    }
}
```

This Update method keeps track of the largest acceleration length that it has seen. This value is then displayed by the Draw method. Players can compete to see who can get the largest value by taking turns shaking the phone.

> **Sample Code: 04 ShakeTester** The sample project in the 04 ShakeTester directory in the resources for this chapter contains the shake tester game. Please be very careful when playing this game. If you lose your grip on the phone, it could end badly (and expensively).

If you want to detect when the phone is being shaken, your program can just test for acceleration values above a certain threshold.

A Quick Digression About Threads and Synchronization

There is one other thing to consider that is not an enormous problem in these games but might cause you problems in future programs. This is the fact that our program now contains two things that are active at the same time. One of these is our game, which is drawing and updating as fast as it can. The other is the accelerometer, which is generating new readings. The fact that we have two processes running at the same time might lead to problems if they "fight" over the shared data in our game. The shared data is the variable that holds the acceleration values. If the Update method tries to read that variable at exactly the same time as the accelerometer event is writing to it, the Update method might read values that are invalid. It might get a fresh X value but old values of Y and Z.

To understand what is happening here, we can consider the behavior of a chef and a waiter in a restaurant. (Funny how lots of my examples involve food, isn't it?) The chef is busy in the kitchen putting food on dishes, and the waiter is busy taking dishes out to the customers. In this situation, you might have a problem that every now and then the waiter delivers a dish before all the food has been added. The chef might have added the burger and gone to get the fries, while in the meantime the waiter picks up the half-completed plate and delivers it to a diner.

We get this kind of problem because the two processes (chef and waiter) are *asynchronous*. Both are running without any awareness of the other. To solve this problem, the chef needs a way that she can grab the dish and stop the waiter from taking it until it is finished. The waiter would be forced to wait (which makes his job title all the more appropriate) until the dish is ready before he could take it out of the kitchen. This solution makes the two processes synchronized with each other.

The C# language provides a way of doing this. It is called a *lock*. A given process can grab a particular lock object and start doing things. While that process has the lock object, it is not possible for another process to grab that object. In our restaurant, the dish serves as the lock object. In the program, we create a lock object that can be claimed by either the event handler or the code in Update that uses the accelerometer value:

```csharp
object accelLock = new object();

void accel_ReadingChanged(object sender, AccelerometerReadingEventArgs e)
{
    lock (accelLock)
    {
        accelReading.X = (float)e.X;
        accelReading.Y = (float)e.Y;
        accelReading.Z = (float)e.Z;
    }
}
```

This is the final version of the event handler. The `lock` keyword is followed by a reference to the lock object (which is called `accelLock`). The block of code that follows the lock is obeyed with the event handler holding the lock. In the `Update` method, I have a similar piece of code:

```
lock (accelLock)
{
    cheeseAcceleration.X = accelReading.X * acceleratorPower;
    cheeseAcceleration.Y = -accelReading.Y * acceleratorPower;
}
```

The two statements that read the accelerometer are obeyed with the `Update` process owning the lock. When the block following the `lock` keyword is completed, the lock object is released for use by other processes. The lock object itself does not store data as such—it is there to provide a single item that is used by the processes to synchronize.

If a process tries to enter a block of code protected by a lock object and the object is already in use, that process will be paused until the lock is released. If a number of processes all want to use one lock object, the system will put them into a queue and let each have the lock as it becomes available. If the lock is never released, processes that are waiting for it will wait forever. This is very important. If the chef never lets go of the dish, the restaurant will be in trouble because nobody will get any food. All the time a process has a lock, it could be stopping other processes from running. The code in our program that uses locks is tiny and will complete very quickly, and that is how such code should be.

The Great Programmer Speaks: Locks and Processes Cause Pain The Great Programmer doesn't admit to having many coding nightmares, but she does worry about systems that use multiple processes and synchronization. The problem, she explains, is that systems that work this way can contain faults that appear only every now and then. These kinds of errors might appear when two users both press their Enter key at exactly the same instant and cause processes to start up and get stuck waiting for each other. Most of the time, the system will run correctly, until a perfect storm of events triggers the failure.

We have all experienced problems where our computer has gotten stuck and the only solution is to turn the machine off and back on again, at which point it works fine. These problems are often caused by faults like these.

The Great Programmer attacks this problem by having processes either produce data or consume it. That way, it is unlikely that two processes would get stuck waiting for each other.

Conclusion

In this chapter, you took a look at the principles behind the accelerometer sensor and how we can use these to make objects in our games behave in a realistic manner. You also found out how to obtain and use the Accelerometer class in your games and respond to the events that it generates. Finally, you saw how to create games that use the accelerometer as their starting point and behave in the same way as physical objects in the real world.

Chapter Review Questions

And now let's accelerate (sorry) into a set of review questions for this chapter.

1. Sir Isaac Newton discovered gravity.

2. The greater the force applied to an object, the greater its acceleration.

3. The accelerometer in a Windows Phone measures acceleration only in the X and Y directions.

4. The *Accelerometer* class is part of XNA.

5. The accelerometer produces new readings each time the XNA Update method is called.

6. A vector describes a direction and a distance.

7. When at rest on a desk, the accelerometer in a Windows Phone will return a vector with a length of 0.

8. Friction should cause the speed of objects in your game to increase over time.

9. The velocity, or speed, of an object is expressed as the distance traveled in a particular time.

10. Acceleration is expressed as the change of speed over a particular time period.

11. A lock causes all the processes in a system to stop until the lock is released.

Chapter 18
Exploring Touch Input

- Touch input management.

- Simple touch input: creating a panic button.

- Simple touch input: creating a set of "touch drums."

- Touch tracking.

- Touch event life cycle.

- Using touch to move game objects around.

- Creating a shuffleboard game.

Introduction

The Windows Phone device does not provide any gamepads you can access from an XNA program, but it is fitted with a touch screen you can use to get input from a player.

In this chapter, we'll develop some games for Windows Phone 7 that use the touch panel. We'll start with an upgrade to the drums we created in Chapter 7, "Playing Sounds," and then move on to how we can use touch to allow a player to move items around the screen.

The Windows Phone Touch Screen

All Windows Phones are fitted with *capacitive touch* screens for user input. These are a significant improvement on earlier mobile devices, which have *resistive* touch screens. The major difference between the two technologies is that the capacitive screens can detect and track multiple touch actions, whereas a resistive screen is able to detect only one contact point. This capacitive ability is used to good effect in the user interface, where screens can be "pinched" to zoom images out and "unpinched" to zoom in. XNA games can also make good use of this multitouch ability, and in this chapter we'll see how XNA provides access to touch input.

Getting Touch Input

Reading the touch panel in an XNA game program is easy. It uses the same input model as the gamepad and the keyboard. Our game can ask the TouchPanel object to give us status information. This works in the same way as the GamePad object we saw before. We make this request during the Update method. The information we get back from the panel is a collection of TouchLocation items. Each of these items describes a particular touch location on the panel. The Windows Phone specification says that a device must be able to track at least four individual touches, so our game could receive a collection of TouchLocation items. Each item gives the present location of the touch, along with some status information and a unique identifier value. We'll explore the more advanced features a bit later in the chapter.

Creating a Panic Button

The first thing we are going to create is a panic button. (See Figure 18-1.) This is a button that can be pressed during a boring meeting or at any other time you think is worthy of a bit of panic.

FIGURE 18-1 A panic button.

The button is simply a texture that is drawn on the phone screen in an appropriate position. The game world for this game consists simply of the texture, draw rectangle, and sound to be played:

```
Texture2D buttonTexture;
Rectangle buttonRectangle;
SoundEffect panicSound;
```

The texture and the sound are loaded by LoadContent when the game starts, and the panic sound will be triggered by touching the phone screen.

Reading Touch Events

The TouchPanel class provides the connection to the touch-input hardware on the phone. Methods in this class read the information from the touch panel and make it available to our program. The hardware on the phone can track up to four touch positions, so the GetState method for the TouchPanel class returns a collection of TouchLocation values:

```
TouchCollection touches = TouchPanel.GetState();
```

If the touches collection returned by the call of GetState contains any items, the screen is being touched in some way. This means we can create a simple panic button behavior as follows:

```
TouchCollection touches = TouchPanel.GetState();


if (touches.Count() > 0)
{
    // If we get here, the screen is being touched
    panicSound.Play();
}
```

This code plays the sound effect if the collection of touch locations returned by the GetState method has anything in it. So the sound effect is played if the screen is touched.

> **Sample Code: 01 Simple Panic Button**   The sample project in the 01 Simple PanicButton directory in the resources for this chapter contains a panic button program that works as shown here. If you touch the screen, you will hear a suitably panic-inducing sound.

Touch Location Types

The problem with our first version of the panic button is that touch location information is not just generated when the screen is touched. There is also touch location information that describes the status of existing locations. Any given touch location actually goes through a life cycle, as shown by the state machine in Figure 18-2.

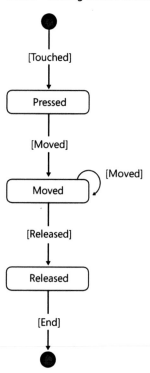

FIGURE 18-2 Touch location life cycle.

The first location is the position where the screen is first pressed. This is followed by a number of locations that describe the latest position the user has moved her finger to. Finally, when the user lifts her finger, we get the location where the touch was released. Our panic button should play the sound effect only when the user first presses on the screen; it should ignore all the moved and released locations. This is easy to do because a TouchLocation provides a State property that we can test:

```
TouchCollection touches = TouchPanel.GetState();

if (touches.Count() > 0)
{
    TouchLocation touch = touches[0];
    if (touch.State == TouchLocationState.Pressed)
    {
        panicSound.Play();
    }
}
```

The preceding code takes the first item out of the touch collection and plays the sound only if the location describes the position where the user has just pressed the panel. Note that we use a subscript (in this case, [0]) to get hold of the first TouchLocation in the collection.

> **Sample Code: 02 Touch Pressed PanicButton** The sample project in the 02 Touch Pressed PanicButton directory in the resources for this chapter contains a panic button program that plays the sound only the first time the button is pressed.

Using the Location of a Touch

At the moment, our panic button works, but it is not really a button. The sound is played irrespective of the location of the touch event. What we really want is a way that we can play the sound only if the button itself is pressed and make the program ignore touches on other parts of the screen. This turns out to be easy to do because the TouchPanel class does a lot of the hard work for us.

As the name implies, a TouchLocation value contains the position of the touch. The position information is given in the same coordinate system as the one we use to draw items on the screen. In other words, our program can take the position of a TouchLocation value and compare it with the rectangle being used to draw the panic button to see if that particular button has been touched. To make life even easier, a Rectangle value provides a method called Contains that returns true if the rectangle contains a particular point. The only complication is that the TouchLocation position information is given as a Vector2 value that contains floating point values for the X and Y coordinates but the Contains method accepts integers. The game must do some conversion to make this work:

```
if ( buttonRectangle.Contains( (int)touch.Position.X,
                               (int) touch.Position.Y) )
{
    panicSound.Play();
}
```

This test makes sure that the sound is produced only when the touch is inside the rectangle used to draw the button on the screen.

> **Sample Code: 03 Touch Location PanicButton** The sample project in the 03 Touch Location PanicButton directory in the resources for this chapter contains a panic button program that plays the sound only when the button is pressed.

This code is not completely perfect, however. The button shape being drawn covers a circular part of the display, but the touch detection is being performed on the entire drawing rectangle. This means that the sound will play in response to touch locations in the corners of the button region, not just on the button itself. Our program could do some math to determine if the touch was actually inside the button, or we could simply make the button a rectangle.

Creating a Touch Drumpad

Now we are going to make a phone-based version of the drumpad we created way back in Chapter 7. This will let us explore how to manage inputs from multiple touch sources. The drumpad game is simple. It allows the player to create a simple drum kit that plays sampled drum sounds. The first version we created used the buttons on the gamepad to trigger the sound playback. Now we are going to create a drumpad that is triggered by touch. This gives us a starting point for any game where we need to perform actions based on the player touching parts of the screen. (See Figure 18-3.)

FIGURE 18-3 A touch-controlled drum kit.

Creating a *soundPad* Class for Each Drum Sound

The program works by setting out particular areas of the screen for particular drums. As you can see in Figure 18-3, touching the Cymbal part of the screen will cause the cymbal sound to be played, and so on. For each drum sound, the game must store three items of information:

- The texture used to draw the image on the screen

- The rectangle that gives the draw position (which will also be used to determine when this sound has been activated)

- The sound effect to be played for this drum type

We can create a class that will hold these:

```
class soundPad
{
    public Texture2D padTexture;
    public SoundEffect padSound;
    public Rectangle padRectangle;
}
```

The class soundPad is declared inside our game because that is the only place we are going to use it. It brings together the three items that are needed for a sound effect. We have made the members of the class public because there are no great security issues to be considered here.

We can add a constructor to the class to make it easy to create new sound pads:

```
public soundPad(Texture2D inPadTexture, SoundEffect inPadSound,
                Rectangle inPadRectangle)
{
    padTexture = inPadTexture;
    padSound = inPadSound;
    padRectangle = inPadRectangle;
}
```

When the constructor is called, it is given the three items that will set up this soundPad. It stores each of these in the data members inside the class.

> **The Great Programmer Speaks: Using Classes from the Start Is a Good Idea**   The Great Programmer really likes this design approach. We don't really know exactly what the soundPad class needs to do, but we do know that it must bring together these three items and use them in some way. After we have the items, we can start to think about what the soundPad must do.

Storing *soundPad* Values in the Game

This version of the drum kit will have four drums, but we would like to be able to add more sounds if required. The best way to allow for this is to use a List that will hold references to all the soundPad instances our game is using. If we want to add more drum sounds or perhaps even a cowbell, we can just add a new soundPad instance to the list. We have seen lists before. They allow a program to store a collection of items without needing to reserve an area of memory of a particular size.

```
// List of touch pads
List<soundPad> pads = new List<soundPad>();
```

The list of soundpads will be set up by the LoadContent method when the game starts running. It will create soundPad values and add them to the list.

```
int halfWidth = displayWidth / 2;
int halfHeight = displayHeight /2 ;

pads.Add ( new soundPad(
        Content.Load<Texture2D>("Images/cymbal"),
        Content.Load<SoundEffect>("Sounds/cymbal"),
        new Rectangle(0, 0, halfWidth, halfHeight))
    );

pads.Add(new soundPad(
        Content.Load<Texture2D>("Images/top"),
        Content.Load<SoundEffect>("Sounds/top"),
        new Rectangle(halfWidth, 0, halfWidth, halfHeight))
    );
```

The preceding code shows how the first two soundPad instances are created and added to the list of pads. These are the cymbal and top drum sounds. Each of them is given a particular area of the screen where their texture will be displayed.

Note This code looks a bit scary, but actually it isn't. To understand what is going on, you need to break down the needs of the various methods that are being called. The Add method wants a soundPad that it can add to the list. The constructor in the soundPad needs a Texture2D, SoundEffect, and Rectangle. The first two of these are fetched by the Content Manager, and then the Rectangle is created to cover the part of the screen where that soundPad is to be displayed.

Drawing the Soundpads

If we are going to stay on the right side of the Great Programmer, we'll have to make sure our class design is as good as we can make it. When it comes to drawing a soundPad on the screen, the best place to put the code that does this is in the soundPad class itself. This means that the soundPad class will contain a Draw method. For this to work, the Draw method needs to be passed a spriteBatch to be used for the draw operations:

```
class soundPad

{

    // Other soundPad stuff

    public void Draw(SpriteBatch spriteBatch)
    {
        spriteBatch.Draw(padTexture, padRectangle, Color.White);
    }
}
```

Adding a Draw method to the soundPad is a good thing to do because it makes the class more *cohesive*. To get a soundPad drawn, the Draw method in the game just has to ask the soundPad to draw itself. The Draw method in the game will work through all the pads on the screen and ask each to draw itself:

```
protected override void Draw(GameTime gameTime)
{
    GraphicsDevice.Clear(Color.White);

    spriteBatch.Begin();

    foreach (soundPad s in pads)
    {
        s.Draw(spriteBatch);
    }

    spriteBatch.End();

    base.Draw(gameTime);
}
```

The game will also work through the list of soundpads during the Update method and ask each one to update itself.

Updating the Soundpads

The soundPad also needs an Update behavior that allows it to check to see whether the pad has been touched. We must detect multiple touches because the player might want to play two drums at the same time. The Update method in the soundPad class must work through all the touch locations and check to see whether any of them should trigger a drum sound:

```
public void Update ( TouchCollection touches )
{
    foreach (TouchLocation touch in touches)
    {
        if (touch.State == TouchLocationState.Pressed)
        {
            if (padRectangle.Contains((int)touch.Position.X,
                                      (int)touch.Position.Y))
            {
                padSound.Play();
            }
        }
    }
}
```

The Update method is supplied with the TouchLocation instances that are currently active. It looks for newly pressed touch locations that are in the draw rectangle for this soundPad, and it plays the sound if it finds one. The Update method in the game just calls each of the Update methods on all the soundPad values that were created when the game started:

```
protected override void Update(GameTime gameTime)
{
    TouchCollection touches = TouchPanel.GetState();

    foreach (soundPad s in pads)
    {
        s.Update(touches);
    }

    base.Update(gameTime);
}
```

Note I have created two Update methods. One lives inside the soundPad class and is given a collection of touches that it uses to decide whether to play the sound effect it contains. The other is the Update method that is part of our game. They have the same name, but they do that job in the context of the object they are part of. This is perfectly OK from a program design point, but it can be a bit confusing at the start.

Sample Code: 04 Touch DrumPad The sample project in the 04 Touch DrumPad directory in the resources for this chapter contains a four-pad drum program you can play by touching the required soundpad.

Making the Soundpads Flash

Your younger brother quite likes the drumpad program, although he wants you to replace some of the sounds with different ones. But he does have one observation: he can't tell when he has activated the sound. He says that in "proper" sound programs the button will flash to let you know it has been pressed. Because we want to write "proper" programs as much as we can, this sounds like something we should fix.

The start of a flash should be the point at which the sound effect is activated. The end of the flash should be a fraction of a second afterwards. The Update method inside the soundPad is called 30 times a second when the game is running. We can time a flash by using a counter that is set when we start playing a sound and reducing the counter each time Update is called:

```
int flashCount = 0;

public void Update(TouchCollection touches)
{
    foreach (TouchLocation touch in touches)
    {
        if (touch.State == TouchLocationState.Pressed)
```

```
        {
            if (padRectangle.Contains((int)touch.Position.X,
                                        (int)touch.Position.Y))
            {
                flashCount = 10;
                padSound.Play();
            }
        }
    }
    if (flashCount > 0)
    {
        flashCount = flashCount - 1;
    }
}
```

The soundPad now contains a flashCount member that holds an integer. The value of flashCount is usually 0. When a sound is played, flashCount is set to 10, and each time that Update is called this value is reduced by 1 until 0 is reached.

The Draw method in the soundPad can use flashCount to control the way that the pad is drawn:

```
static Color flashColor = new Color(255, 255, 255, 128);
static Color drawColor = Color.White;

public void Draw(SpriteBatch spriteBatch)
{
    if (flashCount > 0)
    {
        spriteBatch.Draw(padTexture, padRectangle, flashColor);
    }
    else
    {
        spriteBatch.Draw(padTexture, padRectangle, drawColor);
    }
}
```

This code uses drawing with a transparent color to make a button appear to light up. When flashCount is not zero (which means the button should light up), the draw operation uses a white color that is semi-transparent so that it shows the background through. Because the background is drawn as white, this has the effect of making the button appear to light up.

Sample Code: 05 Touch DrumPad with Flash The sample project in the 05 Touch DrumPad with Flash directory in the resources for this chapter contains a four-pad drum program with flashing buttons.

You can use this principle to make game elements animate themselves when they are used. You can even use different textures for buttons in the pressed and released states. The Great Programmer is very impressed because the changes to make an animated soundPad have not affected any other part of the game program, which just calls the Update and Draw methods on them.

Creating a Shuffleboard Game

The next game we are going to make is a shuffleboard type of game. In this game, players will take turns flicking a puck into a playfield that contains a set of regions, as shown in Figure 18-4. Each region of the board contains a particular score value. The player gets a score equivalent to the value of the region the puck comes to rest in. If the puck ends up in the red area at the back of the board, the player loses his entire score.

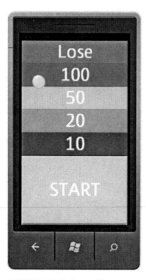

FIGURE 18-4 A shuffleboard game in progress. Someone has just earned 100 points.

We are going to focus how the player controls the puck. The game must detect when the player touches the puck and move it underneath the player's finger until the player releases it, at which point it must move across the playfield and come to rest on a score location. This code is worth taking a good look at because it provides a basis for any finger-controlled game objects you might want to create.

The *PuckSprite* Class

In the tradition of the Great Programmer, we are going to create a class that manages the puck on the screen. In the great tradition of me (and also the Great Programmer to some extent), I'm going to base some of the behavior of the puck on something I've built before—in this case, the cheese sprite in the "Cheese Lander" game we created in the previous chapter.

The cheese sprite contained methods that were called by the game to ask the cheese to update itself and draw itself. The PuckSprite class will work in the same way. However, it will be slightly more complicated because the behavior of the puck depends on what state it is in. At any given instant, the puck will be in one of three possible states:

- Being dragged by the player
- Moving across the screen
- Stopped at a particular position

We can show these states and what happens to cause the puck to move from one state to another by using a state diagram, as shown in Figure 18-5.

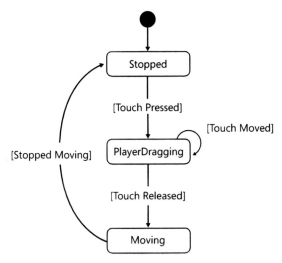

FIGURE 18-5 States of the puck.

At the start of the game, the puck will be stationary. The player will start dragging the puck by touching on it, and during the dragging action the puck will follow the player's finger. When the player releases her finger, the puck must move across the playfield until it comes to rest on a score value. This is actually a good way to design our objects. It makes it clear that, for example, touching the puck when it is moving should have no effect on the puck. It is only possible to start dragging the puck when it is stationary.

We can represent this by creating a new enumerated type that has a value for each of the states. We can then create a variable of this type and use it to control the behavior of the Update method:

```
public enum PuckState
{
    playerDragging,
    moving,
    stopped
}
```

```
PuckState state;
public void Update()
{
    switch (state)
    {
        case PuckState.stopped:
            updateWhenStopped();
            break;
        case PuckState.playerDragging:
            updateWhenDragging();
            break;
        case PuckState.moving:
            updateWhenMoving();
            break;
    }
}
```

The Update method just contains a switch construction that selects a different method, depending on the state of the puck. Now we can create each method in turn.

Updating a Stationary Puck

If it is not being controlled by the player, the puck must check to see whether there is a new TouchLocation with the Pressed state that is on that puck. If this happens, it means that the player is starting to drag the puck across the screen.

```
private void updateWhenStopped()
{
    foreach (TouchLocation touch in game.Touches)
    {
        if (touch.State == TouchLocationState.Pressed)
        {
            Vector2 vectorToPuck =
              Vector2.Subtract(PuckPosition, touch.Position);
            if (vectorToPuck.Length() < PuckRadius)
            {
                lastTouch = touch;
                PuckPosition = touch.Position;
                state = PuckState.playerDragging;
            }
        }
    }
}
```

The method works through each TouchLocation to find one that indicates the start of a Pressed event. If it finds one, it then does some vector arithmetic to find out whether the player has touched the puck. Figure 18-6 shows how this works.

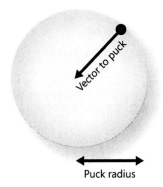

FIGURE 18-6 A Pressed event on the puck.

We can work out the distance between the puck and the TouchLocation by creating a vector that points from one to the other and then getting the length of that vector. We can do this by subtracting one vector from the other. After we have the vector between the puck and the touch event, we then test to see if the length of this vector is less than the radius of the puck. If it is, the touch event is inside the puck and we must give the player control of it. This is better than testing to see if the TouchLocation is inside the draw rectangle for the puck because it means that only touch events that are actually on the puck will be registered.

If a touch sequence is starting, we change the state of the puck to indicate that the player is controlling the puck. We also set the current puck position to the touch position, and we set the variable lastTouch to hold the most recent touch event. The program needs to know the value of previous touch events so that it can work out the direction the player is moving the puck as she drags it across the screen. This will be the direction the puck will move when the player releases it.

Dragging the Puck Across the Panel

If the player is dragging the puck, the touch panel will produce a sequence of TouchLocation events that describe the movements. We can use these to make it appear that the puck is following the finger. The program can tell which TouchLocation events refer to the puck because each set of events that refer to a particular location have the same Id value. By looking for events with the same Id as the last event, we can track the progress of this TouchLocation as the user drags the puck over the screen:

```
private void updateWhenDragging()
{
    foreach (TouchLocation touch in game.Touches)
    {
        if (touch.Id == lastTouch.Id)
        {
```

```
            if (touch.State == TouchLocationState.Moved)
            {
                Vector2 vectorToPuck = PuckPosition - touch.Position;
            }

            lastTouch = touch;
            PuckPosition = touch.Position;

            if (touch.State == TouchLocationState.Released)
            {
                state = PuckState.moving;
            }
        }
    }
}
```

The preceding code looks through the touch locations to find the TouchLocation value with the same Id as the previous one. The value indicates that either the location has moved or the player has released her finger. If the location is a movement event, the game can work out the velocity of the puck by subtracting the vector describing the previous position from the current position. Remember that velocity is the rate that the position of something is changing and this calculation will give us the change in position since the last time Update was called.

This code must also update the position of the puck and record the current location as the last one. The final task is to check to see whether this location is where the puck was released by the user. If this is the case, the state value must be set to moving so that the puck will now move according to the velocity it has been given by the player. We don't know how many movement events we are going to get because the player can drag the puck around for as long as she wants.

Puck Movement Across the Board

When the puck is not being driven by the player, it will just move across the board according to the velocity it had when the player let go of it. The behavior of the puck when it's not being touched is much like that of the cheese in the "Cheese Lander" game in the previous chapter. The puck will bounce off the sides of the board and slow down because we have simulated the effect of friction.

```
private void updateWhenMoving()
{
    PuckPosition += PuckVelocity;

    if (PuckRectangle.Right > game.DisplayWidth)
    {
        PuckVelocity.X = -(float)Math.Abs(PuckVelocity.X);
    }
```

```
    if (PuckRectangle.Left < 0)
    {
        PuckVelocity.X = (float)Math.Abs(PuckVelocity.X);
    }

    if (PuckRectangle.Bottom > game.DisplayHeight)
    {
        PuckVelocity.Y = -(float)Math.Abs(PuckVelocity.Y);
    }

    if (PuckRectangle.Top < 0)
    {
        PuckVelocity.Y = (float)Math.Abs(PuckVelocity.Y);
    }

    PuckVelocity = PuckVelocity * Friction;
    if (PuckVelocity.Length() < 0.05f)
    {
        PuckVelocity.X = 0;
        PuckVelocity.Y = 0;
        game.PuckStopped();
        state = PuckState.stopped;
    }
}
```

Most of the behavior of the puck in this part of the game came from the cheese in the "Cheese Lander" game. We even could have added tipping to this so that a player could add "aftertouch" to their puck movement and try to guide the puck by tipping the phone.

After the game has updated the movement of the puck, it checks to see whether it has stopped. The puck is slowed down by multiplying its velocity by a friction value that is less than 1. Each time the puck is updated, the velocity value gets smaller, but because of the way that math works on computers it will take a long time for the speed to reach 0. We solve this problem by using a limit value (in this case, 0.05). When the length of the velocity vector drops below this value, we say that the puck has stopped. The puck then does two things. It calls a method in the game it is part of to say that the puck has now stopped moving. This allows the game to work out where the puck has ended up and give the player a score for that turn. It also sets the state of the puck back to stopped so that the player can drag the puck around again.

> **Sample Code: 06 Emulator ShuffleBoard** The sample project in the 06 Emulator ShuffleBoard directory in the resources for this chapter contains a working shuffleboard solution. Drag the puck toward the playfield and release it, and it will move and then come to rest over a score area. At the end of a turn, the player can tap the start area to move the puck back to start again. The players take turns and attempt to build the highest score they can.

Emulators and Real Devices

The version of the game just described works very well when you use the Windows Phone emulator on the PC. You can use the mouse to click on the puck and drag it around. When you release the puck, it will continue to move in the direction you dragged it, creating a very nice effect.

Unfortunately, you might not get this behavior on the real device. When I used the program, I found that when I released the puck it stopped moving. I did some tests and discovered that the touch panel quite often produces a number of readings for the same location. If the program works out the velocity of the puck by subtracting the previous touch position from the current touch position, it will produce a speed of zero in this situation. The problem occurred because the touch panel on the phone I was using was not able to produce readings at the same rate that Update was being called. As a result, the same readings were being used for several updates. We can fix the problem by ignoring any velocity values that are zero:

```
if (touch.State == TouchLocationState.Moved)
{
    Vector2 newVelocity;
    newVelocity = touch.Position - lastTouch.Position;
    if (newVelocity.Length() == 0)
    {
        sameValueCount = sameValueCount + 1;
    }
    else
    {
        PuckVelocity = newVelocity / sameValueCount;
        sameValueCount = 1;
    }
}
```

This code calculates a new velocity value and uses the value only if it is not zero. It keeps a count of the identical values it has seen so that it can divide the final velocity to produce a value that only reflects movement for a single call of Update. We have to do this; otherwise, the puck might fly away from the finger at different rates depending on the performance of the touch panel at that instant.

> **The Great Programmer Speaks: You Must Always Test Your Programs on Real Hardware** The preceding code solves a hardware problem, which is that on some Windows Phone devices the touch screen might not produce a new reading for every update. We notice the issue only if we use real hardware because on the Windows PC emulator the touch screen input is simulated by the mouse, which is able to produce results very quickly. The Great Programmer says that you must test your programs on real devices as soon as you can, and be prepared to add extra code to deal with things that work differently on proper hardware.

> **Sample Code: 07 Device ShuffleBoard** The sample project in the 07 Device ShuffleBoard directory in the resources for this chapter contains a shuffleboard solution for the device.

Conclusion

In this chapter, we explored the touch panel, seeing how we can use it to produce single events so that we can create button-like objects on the screen. We also saw how we can track touch locations as they are moved around the screen. You are now in a position to create just about any touch-powered behavior that you like. You might also find it useful to take a look at the gesture support provided by the touch panel. This panel provides touch and dragging support, along with gestures that let you "pinch" items to scale them.

Chapter Review Questions

This is the point where we touch upon (sorry) some review questions for this chapter.

1. Touch input works only on the Windows Phone device.

2. You can detect only when a particular part of the screen is touched.

3. The position of a touch location is given using the same coordinates that XNA uses to draw things on the screen.

4. The touch panel generates touch events when it is touched.

5. The touch panel can track only one touch event at a time.

6. Each touch location is given a unique ID by the touch panel.

7. The emulator always behaves exactly as a Windows Phone would.

8. Objects can contain state information that controls how they behave.

Chapter 19
Mobile Game Development

- Mobile game development on Windows Phone.

- Creating multiplatform games.

- Storing high scores: using persistent storage

- The Windows Phone application life cycle: making a game that can survive a phone call.

- Getting your game out there: an introduction to Windows Phone Marketplace.

Introduction

As far as I am concerned, there is only one kind of programming that is cooler than writing games for your console. And that is writing games for your phone. It is one thing to drag everyone home to your house and fire up your Microsoft Xbox 360 and show them what you have made; it is quite another to be able to just get your phone out and show how clever you are.

In this chapter, we'll focus on the Microsoft Windows Phone as a platform for writing games. We'll take a look at some of the problems you have to solve when you write a game for this device and how you can make a game that works well in the environment of a mobile phone.

The Windows Phone

The Windows Phone is one of the most powerful mobile devices you can get. It has the kind of computing power that a few years ago would have filled a room and been used to keep entire companies in business. However, we need to remember when you write games for it that it is a portable, battery-powered device. We also need to remember that the device being used to play our games is also a telephone and might need to be used to respond to an incoming phone call at any time. This adds a few challenges to Windows Phone development that will require us to flex our programming muscles a bit.

The Windows Phone Marketplace

Many of the items discussed here are not just good programming practice. If you want to submit your games to the Windows Phone Marketplace and maybe make some money from selling them, you have to make you games work in the way I describe in this chapter.

Maximizing the Phone Battery Life in XNA Games

You probably noticed how the fans in your computer or console run faster when you move from the menu of a game into the game itself. This is because the hardware uses more power when it starts to do a lot of work. More work means more heat, so the cooling system needs to push this heat out of the back of the computer. If you were in the basement watching your electricity meter, you would notice that it speeds up a bit during gameplay as your console starts to use more power. Exactly the same thing happens in a phone. The more programs you run on the phone, and the more you ask them to do, the more power the phone will need. Unfortunately, your phone can't take more power from the grid. All the power for a phone has to come from a limited-capacity battery.

Because of this reality, the update rate of an XNA game on the Windows Phone platform has been reduced to 30 updates a second, from the 60 updates on the Xbox 360 or Windows PC. This is actually not a problem. One reason we have faster updates in our games is to reduce the flicker that you see on large screens. Windows Phone screens are small compared to TVs, so a slower update does not affect gameplay.

Setting the Update Rate of a Game

The rate at which a game updates is controlled by a property of the game class called TargetElapsedTime. This is a value of type TimeSpan. A TimeSpan variable does exactly what it says in the name—it contains a value that describes a particular length of time. A TimeSpan variable can hold a value that represents a very long time (days or even years), or it can hold a very short time interval (a thirtieth of a second). There are a number of ways to construct a TimeSpan value. XNA uses a constructor that is supplied with a particular number of ticks. A single Tick is equal to 100 nanoseconds or .0000001 seconds:

```
public Game1()
{
    graphics = new GraphicsDeviceManager(this);
    Content.RootDirectory = "Content";

    // Frame rate is 30 fps by default for Windows Phone.
    TargetElapsedTime = TimeSpan.FromTicks(333333);
}
```

This is the constructor for a Windows Phone game that is created when you start a new Windows Phone game project. This constructor sets the value of TargetElapsedTime to a timestamp that is a thirtieth of a second long. (A thirtieth of a second is 333333 ticks.)

If you want your game to run at any other speed, you can change the value of TargetElapsed time as required. Note that, as the name of this property implies, this is a target speed. If your Draw or Update method takes longer than a thirtieth of a second to run, your game will run slowly. So you need to be careful and test the program on the device to make sure you are not trying to do too much.

> **Note** Changing the update rate of a game is not a decision you should take lightly, and you might not want to go there at all. Although you can, in theory, make your XNA games appear to run faster by changing the update rate, this might not make them look or play any better. Making a game update more quickly definitely reduces the battery life of the phone when you're playing that game.

Your program can read the `TargetElapsed` property as well as write to it. This is especially useful if you want to use the same game code for both an Xbox and a Windows Phone version of a game. By automatically adjusting to the update speed, a game can provide the same player experience irrespective of what platform it is running on.

Dealing with Changes in Phone Orientation

One advantage of a phone is that it can be used in different orientations. There is little chance that you would be allowed to tip your TV on its side just because that is the best orientation to play a particular game. However, on a phone a game can work in either landscape or portrait mode with no problems. The "ShuffleBoard" game we created earlier works very well in portrait orientation, with the phone held upright. However, the "Bread vs. Cheese" tennis game is best suited to a landscape view, with the phone held on its side.

Selecting Orientations in an XNA Game

It is easy to make a game work in a specific orientation. You can tell XNA which orientations your game can support by setting a property of the graphics device in a game:

```
graphics.SupportedOrientations =
    DisplayOrientation.Default |
    DisplayOrientation.LandscapeLeft |
    DisplayOrientation.LandscapeRight |
    DisplayOrientation.Portrait;
```

In the preceding case, we created a game that can be used with the phone held in any orientation. If the player changes how she is holding her phone, the XNA system will redraw the screen to match that orientation. If you want to use fewer orientations, you just leave out the resolutions you don't want.

The `graphics` value refers to the graphics device being used by the game. This is the software component that manages the drawing operations. We can tell it which orientations to make available by setting the value of the `SupportedOrientations` property. We do this by creating a value that combines all the selections we support in the game.

The C# arithmetic OR operator (expressed by a vertical bar) combines the settings values to make a single number that identifies which ones we want to use. The arithmetic OR operation makes a single result that combines the values that it is given. This is a new operation. It works in a similar way to the *logical* OR we have seen before. We use the logical OR to combine two logical conditions (for example, if it is raining OR the forecast says it will rain, I must take my umbrella). The arithmetic OR combines values in similar way, but rather than create a result that is true or false, it produces a numeric result that combines the bit patterns of the values it is given.

Getting Messages When the Orientation Changes

If the orientation of the phone changes, the width and height of the display available to a game will change. You can connect a method to the OrientationChanged event so that your game can be told when this happens:

```
public PanicButtonGame()
{
    graphics = new GraphicsDeviceManager(this);
    Content.RootDirectory = "Content";

    graphics.SupportedOrientations =
        DisplayOrientation.Default |
        DisplayOrientation.LandscapeLeft |
        DisplayOrientation.LandscapeRight |
        DisplayOrientation.Portrait;

    Window.OrientationChanged +=
        new EventHandler<EventArgs>(Window_OrientationChanged);

    // Frame rate is 30 fps by default for Windows Phone.
    TargetElapsedTime = TimeSpan.FromTicks(333333);
}

void Window_OrientationChanged(object sender, EventArgs e)
{
    positionButton();
}
```

This is the constructor for a new version of the "Panic Button" game. This version will display the panic button correctly irrespective of the arrangement of the phone. The constructor connects the method Window_OrientationChanged to the OrientationChanged event so that it can call the positionButton method to calculate a new position rectangle for the button when the phone orientation changes. (See Figure 19-1.)

FIGURE 19-1 A panic button in multiple orientations.

> **Sample Code: 01 Multiple Orientation PanicButton** The sample project in the 01 Multiple
> Orientation PanicButton directory in the resources for this chapter contains a panic button
> program that automatically adjusts the screen when the phone orientation is changed.

Using a Specific Display Size for Windows Phone Games

We have seen before that Xbox and Windows PC systems can be configured to use displays
of different sizes. Some screens are 800 pixels wide and 600 high, and others can be 1280
pixels wide and 768 high. One of the things a well-designed game must do is make sure that
it will work correctly on any display. However, Windows Phone lets you turn this on its head,
in that it is possible for a Windows Phone game to insist on a specific display resolution:

```
graphics.PreferredBackBufferWidth = 240;
graphics.PreferredBackBufferHeight = 400;
```

This tells the graphics hardware to use a low-resolution display that is 240 pixels wide and
400 high. You make this request in the constructor of the game.

If a game requests a screen size that is not the same shape as the screen, the hardware will
draw borders around your screen as required. This is similar to what happens when you
watch a wide-screen movie on an old TV. The movie is shown with black borders. It is best to
have the dimensions requested match the orientation you want to use. In other words, if you
want a game to use only portrait mode, the sizes you ask for should have a height greater
than the width.

Forcing a particular resolution on a game makes the game easier to write, because you don't
have to worry about how the game looks on different-sized devices. The other good reason

for forcing a specific screen size is to improve the graphics performance of a game. The more dots there are on the screen, the more work the hardware has to do when drawing. Remember that when you double the resolution of the screen—for example, when moving from 240x400 pixels to 480x800 pixels—the amount of memory required for the screen is quadrupled. This means that in the higher resolution game the graphics chip has to move four times as much memory around to draw on the screen. By using a lower resolution, you can improve the smoothness of the graphics at little cost to the gameplay experience. If the screen is physically quite small and the game graphics are moving quickly, it is unlikely that the player will notice the difference, anyway.

Hiding the Windows Phone Status Bar

The Windows Phone reserves the top row of the screen for information such as signal strength, the battery gauge, and notifications about things such as Bluetooth and WiFi status. The status bar will appear on the phone whenever you touch the top area to activate it. Figure 19-2 shows what the status bar looks like.

FIGURE 19-2 The status bar when using the emulator.

When an XNA game starts, the bar is hidden; however, touching the screen toward the top might cause this bar to appear. The bar also steals screen space from your game. To get the space back and stop the status from ever appearing during your game, you can tell the graphics device to always use the full screen:

```
graphics.IsFullScreen = true;
```

You can put this statement in the constructor for your game (the same place you select the orientation and screen size above), and it will prevent your player from being distracted by the sudden appearance of signal strength messages during crucial parts of the gameplay.

Stopping the Screen Timeout from Turning Off Your Game

There is nothing quite as frustrating as having a game stop just as you are doing well at it. A pinball machine of my acquaintance has an annoying habit of actually blowing a fuse every time I approach the high score. This is not likely to happen on a Windows Phone, but one thing that can happen is that the phone can activate *screen timeout*. The Windows Phone operating system monitors user activity, and if nothing is detected for a while it will stop the currently running program and shut down as much of the hardware as it can to conserve battery power. Activity on the touch screen will keep the phone "awake," but if your game is controlled only by the accelerometer the screen timeout might be inclined to turn up uninvited. The user of the phone can solve this by adjusting his phone settings so that the screen never times out, but your game program can also turn off the screen timeout:

```
Guide.IsScreenSaverEnabled = false;
```

The setting is part of the `Guide` options. Your game can turn the timeout on again by setting this value to `true`.

> **Note** If you turn off the screen timeout, your game will keep going until the phone battery runs out. This is good for someone who is really enjoying the game, but it's bad if the player forgets to stop your program and just puts the phone back into his pocket. A better solution to this problem might be to change your game so that the player does something on the touch panel every now and then. This would stop the screen timeout from activating and make sure that your game is never the cause of a dead phone.

Creating a Phone State Machine

Have you ever seen one of those films where the hero has to battle through loads of obstacles to get the girl/save the world/kill all the zombies? Whatever the hero does, he is faced with more problems and more messages of doom. This is a bit like the life of an XNA game on a Windows Phone. Games that run on a Windows PC or Xbox have an easy life. They just run until the player gets bored and turns them off. A Windows Phone game has to contend with suddenly being ejected from memory because the phone user wants to take a photograph or being interrupted by an incoming phone call. It also has to behave properly when the user presses the Windows Phone Back button to move through menus in the game.

In a movie, the hero often has special powers that help him deal with all the bad things that come his way. Our special power is going to be a state machine that ensures that whatever happens the game will be able to do the right thing. We are going to create a framework based around a state machine that will control the way our game is used and how it responds to the various events that can occur when the game is being played. We can then use this framework in every other XNA game we write for Windows Phone. We have used state machines before; they crop up in games at various levels.

Games and States

When you start a game, you usually begin at the menu for the game. This is where you select your character, set the difficulty level, and so on. Quite often, the game menu covers several screens. For example, a racing game will let you select the track you want to race on and the car you wish to drive. At some point, you make a selection that starts the game running. During gameplay, you can press a pause button to pause the game. When you are in the pause state, you have the option to either resume the game from where you left off or return to the game menu. Figure 19-3 shows how this might work.

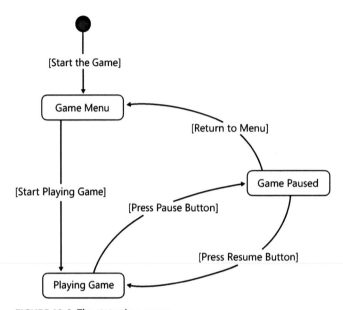

FIGURE 19-3 The states in a game.

Each of the states is shown, along with the events that cause the state to change. Game designers use diagrams like these when they are creating games. This type of diagram makes it clear how the system should work. For example, from the information in Figure 19-3 you should be able answer the question, "Is it possible to pause the game when you are in the Game Menu state?"

If you take a close look, you should be able to work out that this is not possible, because there is no direct path to the Game Paused state from the Game Menu state. You have to play the game first and then press the pause button.

Note If you look at the state diagram in Figure 19-3, you might be wondering how a player can leave the game. At the moment, it looks like a game can start but never end. If the game was running on a Windows PC or Xbox, we would need to add an Exit event in the Main menu or Game Paused states to allow players to finish their games. However, as we shall see later, when a game is running on the Windows Phone it is possible for a game to be stopped at any time (for example, when the user wants to respond to a text message that has just arrived), so we will have to deal with this separately.

Creating a Simple Game State Machine

We have created game state machines before. The best way to do this is to create an enumerated type that contains a value for each of the states we want to store:

```
enum GameState
{
    GameMenu,
    PlayingGame,
    GamePaused
}

GameState state;
```

The variable `state` is of type `GameState` and can hold any one of the following three values: `GameState.GameMenu`, `GameState.PlayingGame`, or `GameState.GamePaused`. In the Update method, we use a `switch` construction to select a different behavior for each state:

```
protected override void Update(GameTime gameTime)
{
    switch (state)
    {
        case GameState.GameMenu:
            updateGameMenu();
            break;

        case GameState.PlayingGame:
            updatePlayingGame();
            break;

        case GameState.GamePaused:
            updateGamePaused();
            break;
    }

    base.Update(gameTime);
}
```

We put the behavior for each game state into a separate method. This is a very good idea, because it means we can use this framework for any game we create in the future. The Draw method has exactly the same arrangement:

```
protected override void Draw(GameTime gameTime)
{
    GraphicsDevice.Clear(Color.Black);

    spriteBatch.Begin();

    switch (state)
    {
        case GameState.GameMenu:
            drawGameMenu();
            break;
```

```
            case GameState.PlayingGame:
                drawPlayingGame();
                break;

            case GameState.GamePaused:
                drawGamePaused();
                break;
        }

        spriteBatch.End();

        base.Draw(gameTime);
    }
```

We are using a consistent arrangement for the names of the methods so that it is easy for another programmer to take a look at what we have made and work out the methods that are called from the name of the states. The Great Programmer is very impressed with this, and reckons that we are turning into proper developers. Which is nice.

Creating More Complex State Machines

Your younger brother is getting into programming now and has taken to looking at our listings and making comments. We are worried that he might see himself as some kind of Great Programmer. He has just looked at our Draw method and has asked the question, "Where is the Game Over screen?"

This is a good question that is rather hard to answer, because at the moment there isn't one. The Game Over display is the one that shows the player the score she reached when the game ended and perhaps lets her enter her name if the score is the new highest. At the moment, we don't have this in our game design. When the game is over, the player is sent straight back to the game menu. Your younger brother doesn't like this very much. He reckons that part of the fun of playing games is beating your previous score. So we need to modify our design to provide this new screen.

There are two ways we can approach this design problem. We can add a new state to the game itself, which we could call GameState.GameOver. The game would enter this state when the player uses up her last life. We would make methods called updateGameOver and drawGameOver and select these from the Draw and Update methods.

The second way to solve the problem is to add a new state type and use this to control the state of the game when it is in the PlayingGame state:

```
enum GamePlayingStates {
    gameInProgress,
    showingGameOver
}
```

```
GamePlayingStates gamePlayingState;

void updatePlayingGame()
{
    switch (gamePlayingState)
    {
        case GamePlayingStates.gameInProgress:
          updateGameInProgress();
          break;

        case GamePlayingStates.showingGameOver:
          updateGameOver();
          break;

    }
}
```

The updatePlayingGame method is called when the game is being played. The behavior of this method is controlled by a variable of type GamePlayingStates. This contains a switch that controls what happens when the game is being played. When the player has lost all her lives, the game is still in the "game playing" state—it is just that this state will now behave differently.

We can see that either way can be made to work. The first method has the advantages that it is easy to understand and would require only small changes to the program. The second method is better, says your younger brother, because it means the game can be extended even further so that it can have Boss Fight states and lots of other things too. Because we can't agree which technique to use, we ask the Great Programmer to tell us which is best.

It turns out that she doesn't really care that much. She reckons that in many situations there are lots of designs that could be made to work. After you have eliminated all the stupid ones (and she doesn't think that either of the ideas is particularly stupid), it is best not to get too worked up about the ones you have left. It is certainly not worth fighting over it with your brother.

> **The Great Programmer Speaks: Don't Worry Too Much About the Best Approach** The Great Programmer reckons that the nicest thing a customer can say about your program is, "Hey, it works!" Users don't care about program design in the same way that you don't really care about the properties of hydraulic fluid when you press the brake pedal in your car. You just want the car to stop.
>
> After you have a design that will work and doesn't look stupid, don't worry too much beyond that. You can make arguments that a given approach is better because it is easier to extend, but if that extension might never take place you might have wasted effort adding that flexibility. When the Great Programmer is making code, the most important considerations for her are "How easy is this to understand?" and "How easy is this to test?" along with "How much will I get paid?" and "When do we get coffee?".

With that in mind, you decide to just add a new state to the game itself. You might like to have a go at updating the state diagram yourself before looking at Figure 19-4.

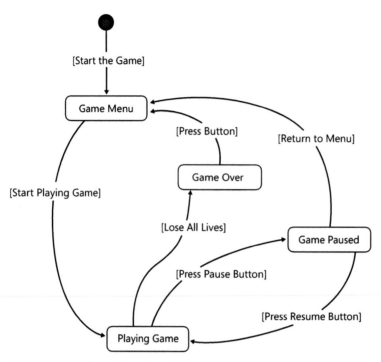

FIGURE 19-4 Adding a Game Over state.

Designing state machines is something you will need to get used to. Any game that has different types of gameplay and things like Boss levels will be managed as a state machine.

Handing Incoming Phone Calls

Now that we have our states properly designed, we are nicely positioned to deal with events that will affect a game. The first one we are going to deal with is an incoming call arriving on the phone being used to play the game. The game will keep running, but the phone call information will be displayed on top of the game screen. This means the player might be upset when he comes back from his call to find he has lost all his lives and a chance for the high score. What the game needs to do is go into pause mode when a phone call arrives. When the call ends, the player can then resume the game from where he left off.

We tell the Great Programmer our cunning plan. She seems fairly impressed, but she has a question: "What happens when the phone rings when the player is at the game menu?" This turns out to be a very good question.

The game must not go into pause mode in this situation because there is no game to pause. The reaction to an event depends on the state the game is in when the event takes place. Humans do this all the time. If the phone rings when you are in the shower, you are very likely to ignore it and let the answering machine (or your mom) take the call for you. However, if you were seated on the couch watching TV, you would just answer the call directly.

As programmers, we have to be very careful to ensure a program always does something sensible with an event. One of the most common causes of programs crashing or getting stuck is events occurring in a sequence or at a time that the software designer didn't expect. The way to solve this is in our games is to use the state of the game to determine what the event hander actually does:

```
private void handleIncomingCall()
{
    if (state == GameState.PlayingGame)
    {
        pauseGame();
    }
}
```

The handleIncomingCall method in the preceding code is the one that the game will call when a phone call arrives. It will pause a game only if it is playing. The method pauseGame sets the state of the game to paused:

```
private void pauseGame()
{
    state = GameState.GamePaused;
}
```

Now that we have a way for our game to deal with incoming calls, the final thing we need to do is get the handleIncomingCall method to run when the phone receives a call.

Note We seem to have worked out what to do when a phone call arrives before we know how to detect the phone call. This is not actually a bad thing. Quite often in a development, you will be working on many things at the same time, or you will be part of a team. In these situations, you will work on different components that will be fitted together to make the complete system. At the start of the project, a plan will be drawn up showing how these all fit together and the project will have an "integration phase" where the components are assembled to create the finished whole.

Now that we know what to do when a phone call arrives, we next have to detect the phone call itself.

Detecting Phone Calls

In Chapter 17, we saw how the accelerometer device in the Windows Phone uses events. A game gets acceleration readings by connecting a method to the event that is produced by the accelerometer when it has new values available. The process of responding to the start and end of phone calls is the same. The Windows Phone operating system provides events that methods in our game can be connected to. When the event occurs, the methods are called:

```
this.Activated += new EventHandler<EventArgs>(Game_Activated);
```

```
this.Deactivated += new EventHandler<EventArgs>(Game_Deactivated);
```

The two preceding statements connect event handler methods to the Activated and Deactivated events that are produced by XNA.

The Activated event is produced when a game starts running and also when a phone call ends. The Deactivated event is produced when a phone call starts. The two handler methods we have identified in the preceding statements are called Game_Activated and Game_Deactivated, respectively.

```
void Game_Deactivated(object sender, EventArgs e)
{
    handleIncomingCall();
}

void Game_Activated(object sender, EventArgs e)
{
    resumeGame();
}
```

The method that is called when the game is deactivated just calls the handleIncomingCall method. When the call is finished, the Game_Activated method calls the resumeGame method to restart the game if it is paused. If the game is a fast-moving one, the player might prefer to resume it manually rather than be pitched straight back into a space battle immediately after the phone call has finished, so we might remove the call of resumeGame for this kind of game.

With these methods in place, our game will now work correctly when a phone call arrives. When the player returns to the game, she will be pleased to find that she can just resume it from where she left off. The sequence goes like this:

1. The player opens the game.

2. The game begins running in the Main Menu state.

3. The player selects the game options and starts playing the game.

4. A phone call arrives.

5. The `Deactivated` event is fired by XNA, which causes the `Game_Deactivated` method to be called.

6. The `Game_Deactivated` method runs and calls the `handleIncomingCall` method in our game.

7. The `handleIncomingCall` method checks the state of the game. If the game is in the `GameState.PlayingGame` state, the `pauseGame` method is called and the game pauses.

8. The player answers the phone call.

9. The `Game_Activated` method runs and calls the `resumeGame` method to resume the game.

If this seems complicated, that's because it is. Unfortunately, it is often the case that to get a good user experience we need to write fairly complex code. You need to bear this in mind when deciding how much effort a particular project will involve. Often, solving the problem itself is actually only a small part of the work you need to perform. You will also need to spend a lot of time making your solution usable.

The `Activated` and `Deactivated` events are not just used for phone applications. They are also generated in XNA games that run on the Xbox or Windows PC. When a game player activates the `Guide` or minimizes a window on a PC desktop, these events are used to tell the game that the user is no longer interacting with it.

A Game as a Windows Phone Application

We can now make our game handle incoming phone calls. The next thing to deal with is the player ending the game program because she wants to do something else. Mobile phone users often play games to fill in the time while doing things like waiting for a bus to arrive. When the bus turns up, the player will expect to be able to stop her game and resume it later. When we make a game program, we have to ensure that it is a well-behaved Windows Phone application that can be stopped and started like this at any time. To do this, we have to make the game work with the buttons that are pressed on the phone.

The Windows Phone Back and Start Buttons

The Back and Start buttons are an important part of the Windows Phone user interface. They are physical buttons on the Windows Phone device that the user can press at any time when the phone is being used. All Windows Phones have these buttons, and the way they work has been carefully designed to help you use the phone. Their design is based on the way that you work. For example, you might be sitting at home watching a video. Then you get asked to help wash the dishes. So you pause the video, go into the kitchen, and start doing the dishes. Then you get asked to take out the garbage. So you put down your dishcloth, take out the trash, wash your hands, and then go back to washing dishes. When the dishes are finished, you then go back to your video (taking a well-earned drink with you).

Windows Phone works the same way. You can start doing new things at any time by pressing the Start button. You can then use the Back button to return to the previous program. You can open a document with Microsoft Office Word and then remember you need to send a text. You press the Start button, open up the SMS message application, and start writing. When the message has been sent, you press Back to return to your word processing. When you are using Word to write a document, the Back button is used to exit from menus you enter within the program. When you are at the "top" level of Word and you press the Back button, you are given the option to save your work before leaving the word processor.

I've taken over 250 words to explain something that turns out to be simple to use. The idea of pressing the Start button to do something new and the Back button to return to what you were doing is intuitive and works well. But, of course, our games have to work with these buttons correctly. This means five things:

1. If the player presses the Back button at the top level of our game menu system, the game must exit.

2. If the player presses the Back button when navigating any menus in our game, the navigation must return to the previous level. In other words, if the player enters a Car Selection submenu in a racing game, he can press Back to get out of that menu and return to the main menu.

3. If the player presses the Back button when playing the game, this must cause the game to enter pause mode.

4. If the player presses the Back button when in pause mode, the game should resume playing.

5. If the player presses the Start button at any time, the game will be ended.

Note that these are not rules you can ignore. If you want to sell your games in Windows Phone Marketplace, they have to behave in this way.

Detecting the Back button is easy. You can regard a Windows Phone as an Xbox gamepad with only one button: the Back button. This gamepad is always assigned to player 1. An XNA game on Windows Phone can test if Back has been pressed by getting the state of the gamepad and testing for that button:

```
if (GamePad.GetState(PlayerIndex.One).Buttons.Back ==
                               ButtonState.Pressed)
{
    // if we get here, the back button has been pressed
}
```

To add handling for the Back button, we just have to add tests for it at the appropriate points in the game:

```
private void updateGameMenu()
{
    if (GamePad.GetState(PlayerIndex.One).Buttons.Back ==
                                ButtonState.Pressed)
    {
        exitGame();
    }

    // Rest of update method here

}
```

This is the method that is called to update the game when it is in the GameMenu state. If the player presses the Back button, the exitGame method is called. This will exit the game.

The method that updates the game when it is playing also contains a test for the Back button. If the button is detected in this state, the game is paused:

```
private void updatePlayingGame()
{
    if (GamePad.GetState(PlayerIndex.One).Buttons.Back ==
                                ButtonState.Pressed)
    {
        pauseGame();

    }

    // Rest of game play update here

}
```

The Back button should also be used to exit from the game paused state to make it easier for a player to get back into a game he has paused. If we do this correctly, the user of the phone will find this easy to understand. The Back button will always take the user out of menus within the game and then, at the very top level, it can be used to exit the game itself. When the user needs to pause a game, he can always do this with the Back button, and a further press of Back will resume the game.

Note When we have used gamepad buttons in the past, we have had to detect the edge of the button press (that is, when the button state changes from up to down), rather than just the position of the button. If you think about it, we should have a problem if we use the Back button both as a way of entering game pause mode and a way of exiting pause. If the Back button is held down, we would expect the game to flip between play and pause mode, because it would if the Back button was on a gamepad. However, the Windows Phone environment does the edge detection for us, which means that our game paused method can just check for the Back button being pressed and everything will work out fine.

Starting New Programs with the Start Button

At the start of this section, I mentioned that you can think of your game as the hero in a film who is battling all manner of foes. In such films, there is always a big scene at the end where the hero must face his greatest challenge. We have just reached this stage now. We have to deal with the Start button. For the user of the phone, the Start button is very useful. It is the button that the user presses when she wants to do something new. When the Start button is pressed, the phone does the following:

1. Stops the current program from running.

2. Makes a note of which program was in use so that it can be restarted later if required.

3. Displays the start menu so that the user can select another program.

The Start button can be pressed at any time. This means that our game programs can be stopped at any time. To make things even more difficult for us, the Back button makes it really easy for a user to return to the game, and that user will expect the game to be in exactly the same state that it was when she left it. This means the game will have to store information on the phone so that it can remember where it was and return to this state later when she resumes playing. When our game is being removed from memory, it will get an event to tell it this is happening. We can connect to this event in exactly the same way that we connect methods to the Activated and Deactivated events we saw earlier:

```
this.Exiting += new EventHandler<EventArgs>(Game_Exiting);
```

We put this in the constructor for the game class along with the other statements we used to connect handlers to events. The actual event method calls a method to save the game state:

```
void ShuffleBoardGame_Exiting(object sender, EventArgs e)
{
    saveGame();
}
```

When our game is being stopped, the saveGame method is called to save the status of the game. We also need a loadGame method to fetch this saved status. This can be called from the LoadContent method when the game starts.

Note It is important that the saving process doesn't take much time. If our save routine takes too long, the Windows Phone operating system will step in and forcibly eject our program from memory. This might be very bad, because it might mean our saved file was half finished. The saving that we are going to do will write only a few items to memory and will complete quickly.

Using Isolated Storage to Store Game State

Now to get control when the game state needs to be saved, we have to write the code that actually saves our game state. Fortunately, for us it is easy for a game to store information on a Windows Phone. It is called *isolated* because each game is only able to use an area of storage that is set aside for that particular game. One game is not able to access stored information for any other game on the system.

On the Windows PC and Xbox systems, this isolation is extended to individual gamer tags. This is sensible, because it means that someone playing as Fred Blogs would not be able to modify the saved games of Rob Miles. If an XNA game on Windows PC or Xbox wants to use isolated storage, it must first ensure that the gamer is signed in. We have seen how to do this in Chapter 16, where we signed in a user with the Guide system so that the user could take part in networked gameplay. On a Windows Phone, there is no need for a gamer to sign in because the owner of the phone is assumed to be signed in at all times.

Storing Files in Isolated Storage

Data on computers is organized into files. Each file contains information of a certain kind— for example, a C# program, a photograph, or a music track. A given file has a name that we use to locate it. Files can be organized into folders. We know that when Microsoft Visual Studio 2010 creates a new game project, it creates a number of files and folders for us automatically, and we are used to browsing through files on our computer to locate them. What we are going to do now is find out how a game program can create and read a file that we are going to use to hold the status of a game. The file will be created when a game stops and then used to restore the status of the game when the game resumes. To find out how information is stored, we must first understand the way that programs connect to data storage. Figure 19-5 shows how it all works.

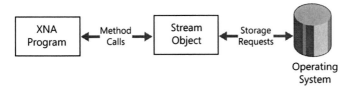

FIGURE 19-5 Files and streams.

A Stream object sits between a program and the operating system that is providing the storage. We have seen how software objects can provide connections to hardware. The GamePad class allows a game to interact with a physical device by calling methods exposed by software that drives it. A stream works in the same way. It means that XNA games can use the storage of an underlying device, whether it is a hard disk, memory key, or internal phone memory.

Our game will create a stream instance that is connected to the file we will use to store the status of the game. If a program needs to connect to lots of files at the same time, it can create multiple streams. The isolated storage facility also provides methods that can be called to create folders inside the isolated storage area. If your game needs to store lots of different kinds of game data and user settings, you can design a file storage system as appropriate.

Connecting Streams Together

Once they had the idea of stream objects that accept method calls and pass them on to other objects, the designers of the C# input/output system decided to use this to add even more flexibility to their input/output classes. They were working on the basis that there are lots of different types of items we might want to save to a stream (for example, text, images, and sounds) and there are lots of different kinds of things we might want to connect to (for example, network ports, files, and isolated storage). We are going to store our game status information as text in a file, so we need to use a text stream to do this. We can connect a text stream to the raw stream provided by the isolated storage on the device, producing an arrangement like that shown in Figure 19-6.

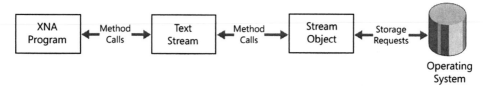

FIGURE 19-6 Connecting streams together.

The program sends messages to the text stream, which in turn sends messages to the isolated storage stream. This is actually how the XNA Content Management system works, in that the content pipeline (which looks similar to the sequence shown in Figure 19-6) provides interchangeable "filters" that connect to the system that fetches the raw data from the game storage.

Saving the State of a Game

We are going to save the state of the ShuffleBoard game we developed earlier. Figure 19-7 shows a game in progress.

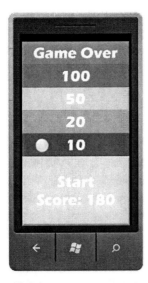

FIGURE 19-7 A ShuffleBoard game in progress.

The player flicks the puck onto the board and gets the score on the tile that the puck stops on. If the player flicks the puck onto the Game Over tile, the game is over. The aim of the game is to build up the largest possible score. For the game to be resumed at any time, it must store the following information:

- The position of the puck on the screen

- The score achieved so far

- The high score for the game

- The current state of the game

The saveGame method must write all these items into a file in the isolated storage area. It will create a stream that is connected to a file in the isolated storage. It must then write this information out into the file and then close it. How the data is actually stored is not a concern; our program just uses the methods provided by the stream. Before a program can use the isolated storage and stream input/output classes, it needs to specify the namespaces that contain them:

```
using System.IO;
using System.IO.IsolatedStorage;
```

Now the game program can ask the isolated storage classes to create streams that can be used to store game status data:

```
private string filename = "GameStatus.txt";

private void saveGame()
{
```

```
using (IsolatedStorageFile isf =
            IsolatedStorageFile.GetUserStoreForApplication())
{
    using (IsolatedStorageFileStream rawStream =
                isf.CreateFile(filename))
    {
        StreamWriter writer = new StreamWriter(rawStream);
        int stateInt = (int) state; // convert state into an integer
        writer.WriteLine(stateInt); // save the state
        writer.WriteLine(puck.PuckPosition.X);
        writer.WriteLine(puck.PuckPosition.Y); // save the puck
        writer.WriteLine(GameScore);  // save the score
        writer.WriteLine(HighScore);  // save the high score
        writer.Close();
    }
}
}
```

The saveGame method in the preceding code uses the isolated storage to create a file called
GameStatus.txt, which contains the state of the game. Each of the items is written out in
turn. The state of the game, which is actually a value of type GameState, is converted into
an integer for saving. The method creates a stream called rawStream, which is then used
to create a StreamWriter called writer. This class provides a method called WriteLine,
which is called to write a line of text into the file the stream is connected to. The WriteLine
method is given the value to be written out.

After all the lines have been written to the stream, the connection to the file is removed
by using the Close method. Programs *must* close files when they have finished with
them; otherwise, other programs will not be allowed to access them. If you could see
inside the memory of your Windows Phone, you would see something like this in the file
GameStatus.txt:

```
1
26
415
180
500
```

The first value is the game state. The values of an enumerated type are actually numbered
from 0, so a value of 1 means PlayingGame. The next two values are 26 and 415, which represent the X and Y positions of the puck, respectively. This means that the puck is toward the
left edge about halfway down the screen. The final two values are the current score, which is
180, and the highest score so far, which is an impressive 500. When the game restarts, it must
load these values back.

Loading a Saved Game

The game status must be loaded when the game restarts. However, it is not quite as simple as just loading the file and setting up the game. The problem is that the very first time the game is run there will be no saved file to load from. The load method must therefore check to see whether the file exists. If it doesn't, it must start the game in the GameMenu state:

```
private void loadGame()
{
    using (IsolatedStorageFile isf =
        IsolatedStorageFile.GetUserStoreForApplication())
    {
        if (isf.FileExists(filename))
        {
            try
            {
                using (IsolatedStorageFileStream rawStream =
                    isf.OpenFile(filename, System.IO.FileMode.Open))
                {
                    StreamReader reader = new StreamReader(rawStream);
                    int stateInt = int.Parse(reader.ReadLine());
                    state = (GameState)stateInt; // convert into a state
                    puck.PuckPosition.X = float.Parse(reader.ReadLine());
                    puck.PuckPosition.Y = float.Parse(reader.ReadLine());
                    GameScore = int.Parse(reader.ReadLine());
                    HighScore = int.Parse(reader.ReadLine());
                    reader.Close();
                }
            }
            catch
            {
                // Select the main menu if the load fails
                selectGameMenu();
            }

            // Remove the file so that it isn't used next time
            isf.DeleteFile(filename);
        }
        else
        {
            // Select the main menu if there is no file to load from
            selectGameMenu();
        }
    }
}
```

This method checks to see whether the file exists before trying to open it. If the file is not found, the method just selects the game menu state. If the file is found, a StreamReader called reader is created that is connected to this file. The program calls the ReadLine method on this reader to read each line of the file in turn. When a program reads a line of a file, it is actually read from the file as a string of text. This text needs to be converted into a number for use in our program:

```
GameScore = int.Parse(reader.ReadLine());
```

This is the statement that reads the current game score. It uses a method called Parse, which is provided by the int type. The job of Parse is to take a string and read the integer value it describes. If the string contains "180", the Parse method returns the integer value 180. If the string contains "Hello Mom", the Parse method will fail because this is not a proper number. When Parse fails, it does this by throwing an *exception*. An exception is a way that a method can say, "I just can't go on any more." The throw keyword in C# lets a method throw in the towel, to coin a phrase. It causes the method to return instantly and send a message that something terrible has gone wrong.

Exceptions in Number Reading

Exceptions are reserved for situations where something really bad has happened, like expecting to see some digits and getting a message for your mom instead. We can make our programs deal with exceptions by enclosing code that might throw an exception in a try – catch construction as shown earlier. If everything in the try block of the method works correctly, the code in the catch part is ignored. However, if one of the methods throws an exception, the code in the try block jumps to the code in the catch part and obeys that.

So the job of the code in the catch part of the method is to try and recover from the error that has occurred. In the case of our game, there is not much the method can do. It is not really able to work out what has gone wrong; the best it can do is put the game into a "known good" state, which in this case means setting the game to the MainMenu state.

It is unlikely that these methods will throw exceptions very often, if at all. However, it is still important that the game handles them. If a file becomes damaged because of battery failure during the write process, we must make sure that our game does not get stuck the next time it is played. After an exception has been caught, the program will continue to run at the statement after the catch block. If an exception is not caught (that is, code that is not in a try – catch construction throws an exception), no more statements will be obeyed.

Erasing Saved Files

The final thing the load method does is erase the save file after it has been read in. This is to make sure that the same saved game file is not used more than once. If you think about the life cycle of the game, you can see that the next time the game is stopped a new save file will be created at that point. The isolated filestore system provides a range of commands that can be used to test whether files exist and also create and manage folders of files.

Creating a Well-Behaved Game

We now have save and load behaviors we can use to make it appear to the player of our game that it has never stopped. However players find their way back to the game, it will seem as if they are picking up from where they left off. These events are also fired when the user locks the phone or starts using the camera during gameplay. These actions will also cause our program to be removed from memory, with the events we have already seen being fired.

> **Sample Code: 02 Well-Behaved ShuffleBoard game** The sample project in the 02 ShuffleBoard Game directory in the resources for this chapter contains a shuffleboard game that works correctly on Windows Phone. You can stop the game and return to it, and it will always return to where it left off. You can use this game as the basis of any Windows Phone games you create that you want to work correctly.

A game doesn't have to wait until it is being removed from memory to save information in the isolated storage. If you want to save high scores and the position reached in a game during the game itself, this is a good idea. You should remember that bad things can happen to mobile phones—they can be dropped or the battery can fall out. If this happens in the middle of an exciting bout of gameplay, your user will be very unhappy if he loses all his progress. It is therefore sensible to store progress through the game at regular intervals.

Getting Your Games into the Marketplace

The great thing about writing games for the Windows Phone is the ease with which you can sell your games when you have made them. After you have developed your game, tested it on a real device, and then added all the handling for the Start and Back buttons as described earlier in the chapter, you can think about putting the game into the Windows Phone Marketplace. Maybe you will become rich.

The Windows Phone Marketplace

The Windows Phone Marketplace is part of the App Hub community for application and game developers, which also includes XNA Indie Games. If you are a member of the App Hub, you can create XNA games and submit them to the Indie Games part of Xbox Live. The games that are submitted are *peer reviewed*, which means that other App Hub members will download and rate your games. The Xbox Live Indie games scene is a vibrant and creative one that runs alongside the mainstream Xbox Live. Indie games might have rough edges in gameplay and behavior that make them frustrating and confusing to play. But, then again, they might provide completely novel gameplay you can't get anywhere else. People who dip into the Indie games scene know they are running programs that are community developed and will make allowances for this.

App Hub members can also submit applications and games to the Windows Phone Marketplace. A program that you submit to the Windows Phone Marketplace will be available to all Windows Phone users. It will sit alongside offerings from the big games studios and can be downloaded by any phone user, including folks in your family or even your mom. You can charge money for your games, and buyers will expect them to behave in the same way as other programs they have bought and used. This means that programs destined for the Windows Phone Marketplace are subject to a much more rigorous approval process before they are allowed to be put on sale. Some of the tests are automatic; others are performed by specialists who check your game to make sure it meets the required standards. If it is judged to be lacking in any way, you will be given a list of the things you need to fix and you can then resubmit it. As a developer, you have access to a "dashboard" on the developer Web site that shows you the status of any registrations you have.

Registering for the App Hub

Registration is managed from the App Hub site, which you can find at *http://create.msdn.com*. To register, you need a Windows Live account. If you register for the Windows Marketplace, you can submit an unlimited number of "paid for" games and up to five free games every year you remain registered. The cost of registration is $99 a year. The registration process is quite complex because it includes the validation of your identity. Games that you create and submit are signed with a special software key that is unique to you. The key is created for Microsoft by a key generation authority and ensures you can always be identified as the author of your games. It is impossible for anybody else to create games and pass them off as yours. The registration process also includes validation of your bank details and tax status so that the money your games earn can be passed back to you. If you are a student, there is a good chance you can get developer registration for free under the Microsoft DreamSpark initiative. You can find out more at *https://www.dreamspark.com*.

Using a Windows Phone Device

A developer can register up to three Windows Phone devices, which can then be used to run programs they have created. The Windows Phone Developer tools include a program you use to perform this registration. Student developers who have registered using their DreamSpark account can register a single device. The actual communication between the Windows Phone and Visual Studio is performed by the Zune software, which is also used to load media content onto the Windows Phone.

Creating Games for Sale

If you want to write games and sell them, you do this in exactly the same way as we have already seen. However, there are some things that are worth remembering:

- Make sure your game can survive the dreaded Start and Back buttons. This is tested during the game submission process, and any game that fails to return correctly after being stopped and started will not be accepted.

- You can increase the size of your market by allowing your game to be played by people from all over the world. This means it should be easy to change the language of the game. You make this easier by ensuring that your help information and all the displays on the screen are drawn as text on the screen and that all your messages are stored in one place. You can then ask a friend with language skills to translate them for you.

- Follow the submissions guidelines. When you register as a developer, you gain access to your own little part of the Windows Marketplace. This contains lots of useful documents, including the "Windows Phone 7 Application Certification Requirements." This gives you lots of useful detail about how to prepare your game for submission.

If you follow the guidelines in this book, you are nicely positioned to turn your ideas into a money-making reality. I wish you the best of luck in your endeavors.

Conclusion

In this chapter, we explored the Windows Phone device and took a look at the special challenges that face developers who are writing programs for a small, battery-powered device. We also learned about the way a game can be sent messages as the environment it is running changes, and we found out how to make use of the isolated storage feature of XNA to allow a game to retain its state when it is not running. Finally, we took a look at Windows Marketplace and what we need to do to make a program we can sell.

Chapter Review Questions

This is the point where you get some questions. And you are not allowed to use your Windows Phone to phone a friend.

1. The Windows Phone device has unlimited power.

2. The faster a computer runs, the hotter it gets.

3. XNA games on Windows Phone update at half the speed of those on the Windows PC or Xbox.

4. The update rate of an XNA game is fixed by the platform it runs on.

5. The Windows Phone can play games only in landscape mode.

6. XNA games can be told when the orientation of the Windows Phone changes.

7. A state machine can have only up to five states.

8. A given program can contain only one state machine.

9. When in a particular state, a program must be able to respond to any event.

10. When the Windows Phone receives a call, your game program is terminated.

11. When a game receives an "Activated" message, it should always come out of pause mode.

12. When the Back button is pressed, an XNA game should always terminate.

13. When the Start button is pressed, an XNA game will always be terminated.

14. An XNA game has no way of knowing when it has been terminated.

15. The isolated storage area is shared among all games on the device.

16. A stream connects a program to a file.

17. Files are closed automatically when they are no longer needed.

18. When an exception is thrown, your program is always stopped.

Appendix A
Answers to the Chapter Review Questions

Chapter 1

1. False. If you enjoy solving problems and working with people, that will make you a great programmer.

2. False. You can write XNA game programs and run them on your PC if you don't have an Xbox.

3. False. XNA is a framework for writing games. It is written in a programming language and is used by programs, but it is not a programming language.

4. Indeed it is.

5. False. The C# compiler produces a file containing a sequence of machine instructions that the computer can follow when the program runs. Once you have the instructions, you don't need the compiler anymore.

6. False. C# is a programming language; XNA is the framework.

7. Indeed you do. But you don't need to be a member to write games for the PC.

8. No. You have to be a Windows Phone developer and have registered your phone as a developer device before you can send programs to it, but this is completely separate from App Hub.

9. No. This program is used to manage the connections between your PC and XNA devices that you want to use.

10. False. The compiler converts your source code into lower-level instructions for the computer to follow. But once the compiler has done this, you can just run the program that the compiler has produced.

11. Nope. The screen is initially blue.

12. Actually, you can do this, and it works very well (especially for games on a PC that require a joystick).

13. No you don't. The version of XNA you use to write Windows Phone games is just the same; you just need to select the appropriate device to run the program.

14. True. This folder will also contain all your assets such as images and sounds that your game will use. Visual Studio will put all these together into an item that is then trans- ferred into the required target device when the game runs.

Chapter 2

1. False. A program is a sequence of statements. A variable is the way that we represent values that we want our program to work on.

2. False. We can call the file what we like; when coding in C#, it must have the language extension (the bit after the dot) of .cs. XNA Game Studio puts our game program into a file called Game1.cs by default, which is a good start.

3. True. We need to think of a name that represents the value that the identifier is going to hold or the action the method is going to do for us.

4. True. A method contains a sequence of statements. It also has an identifier as a name. Our program can "call" the method by name, and when the method is called, it performs the statements in the method. We don't have to write every method ourselves; instead, we can call methods provided by other programmers.

5. False. The Draw method is not in charge of updating the game. Instead, it is supposed to perform the drawing. The method that performs the update is called, not surprisingly, Update.

6. False. A block of statements is a number of statements that have been enclosed in curly brackets. C# can treat an entire block as a whole.

7. False. A comment is put into the program by the programmer as a kind of "note to self." The compiler completely ignores any comments.

8. False. A byte can hold only a number in the range 0 to 255. When creating a color, each of the primary colors (red, green, and blue) has a byte value that represents the intensity of that primary color. So a Color must be held as at least 3 bytes.

9. True. The C# compiler always ensures that we don't combine variables in an incorrect way. Trying to place a Color into a byte would not work because it would not fit. Therefore, the compiler refuses to compile a program that does this.

10. False. A local variable is held inside a block. It is not visible to statements outside the block; each time the block is entered, a new version of the variable is made.

11. False. We create the identifiers. If we need to keep track of the highest score in the game, we might want to create the identifier HighScore, which can be used to identify the variable where we store the high score.

12. True. This is exactly what a variable does. We create a variable every time we need to store something in our program. Each variable has a different identifier and has a particular type.

13. False. The Boolean type has just two possible values, but they are true and false, not 0 and 1.

14. False. The word that starts a conditional statement is if.

15. False. You don't need to add an `else` part to an `if` condition unless your program needs it.

16. True. A recipe tells you how to combine and process ingredients to cook something. An algorithm gives a sequence of actions that you can perform to achieve something.

17. False. A single equals character (=) is used to assign a value to a variable.

18. True. The methods provide the class with things it can do (behaviors) and a place to hold information (data).

19. False. `PlayGame` sounds like a good identifier for a method (an action of some kind), but it is not a good name for a class. Classes have names like `Sprite`, `Session`, `Game`, `Invoice`, and `Car`. A class represents a whole thing that you want to create and interact with, not just a single action.

20. True. `Explode` is a word that implies that an action is being performed; perhaps we are going to make one of our game objects perform an explosion behavior. Method names should be "doing" words, like verbs.

21. False. A byte holds 8 bits organized in one lump. Each of the bits can be either true or false, which means that a byte can actually occupy 256 different states.

22. False. ++ works on a single numeric operand and makes the value in the thing it works on one bigger. We use it to increase the intensity of the color values in our program. It has a complementary -- operator.

23. False, for two reasons. One is that the compiler does not have control when your program runs. It just prepares the program for execution, so there is no way that it can react to things that happen when the program runs. The second reason is that when some numbers overflow (for example, if we try to overfill the byte type), the processor typically doesn't notice. We have to make sure that the values in our programs always stay within the range of the variables that we create to hold them.

24. True. In programs, we often need to represent things that can be either true or false. These allow us to decide whether we do something (true) or not (false).

Chapter 3

1. False. A method does something. A desk is just a holder for values. It is more sensible to regard a method as a person in the office who can do something when the method is called.

2. False. The compiler converts your C# source code into machine language instructions for the computer, Zune, or Xbox, but it is not around when your program is running. The class instances are created when the program runs.

3. False. You need to add the `else` part only if you want to perform some other statement or block of statements if the condition is not true.

4. False. The parameter feeds information into a method.

5. False. It is performed only if the condition controlling the `if` statement is false when the program runs.

6. False (aren't we having a lot of false answers this time?). The gamepad is represented by a special Microsoft XNA structure that holds all the gamepad settings. The structure is called `GamePadState`.

7. False. This method gives your program a `GamePadState` structure. You can use the `GamePadState` structure to find out what the button state is.

8. True (at last). This is exactly what a block is.

9. True. The logical expression (`true || false`) works out to true, as do (`true || true`) and (`false || true`). In fact, the only condition involving explicit values and a single logical *OR* operator that works out false is (`false || false`).

10. False. I feel terrible about this one. The condition is fine, but it does not test the value of `greenIntensity`.

11. False. We may have to do this ourselves when the game is stopped.

Chapter 4

1. False. The compiler is the program that converts C# source code into machine instructions for the computer. Images are held by the XNA Content Manager, which ensures that they are incorporated into your program once it has been compiled successfully.

2. True. A texture is a special type of data that can hold images. The examples in Chapter 4 use the Texture2D data type to hold an image because the examples are for textures that are to be displayed as flat.

3. False. This method brings the images into the program. It gets the item of content and loads it into the target texture, but it does not display the image.

4. This might be true, but it is not relevant to Microsoft XNA graphics. A sprite is a texture and a position. It represents something in the game you want to draw at a particular position. In your programs, you've used a `Texture2D variable` to hold the image to be drawn and a `Rectangle` to express where the image is to be put on the screen.

5. True. The clue is in the name. You can use `SpriteBatch` to perform a number of drawing operations, and then, when the Draw method is called the SpriteBatch actually does the drawing, it can organize all the draw operations in the most resource-efficient way.

6. True—but with reservations. The `Initialize` method is simply a placeholder where you can put C# code that runs when the game is being initialized. If you need to get control at this point in the game process, you can add code to this method. Otherwise, you can leave it empty.

7. True. It also has a `Height` field for the height and `X` and `Y` fields that describe where on the screen it is to be positioned.

8. False. An XNA game can store many image resources. Each of them is given a name and can be loaded by the Content Manager when required.

9. False. I'd say that an inch is a better measure of screen size. A 20-inch monitor could have different numbers of pixels depending on the quality of the images it can show. A monitor with 1,024 pixels across displays a more detailed picture than one with only 800. The number of pixels really gives you an idea of the resolution of the images, not the actual size as displayed.

10. True. Unlike graph paper, which has the origin on the bottom left, the XNA display area has the origin at the top left corner.

11. False. Although you could use a Portable Network Graphics (PNG) picture in this way, you might find that a large image (such as you would use for a background) stored in this file format would be quite a large file. If you do not need transparency (and background images do not) then I would suggest that you use a Joint Photographic Experts Group (JPEG) image for that. A JPEG image can be much smaller than an equivalent PNG picture.

12. False. The XNA system provides an easy way to find out this information. The `GraphicsDevice.Viewport.Width` and `GraphicsDevice.Viewport.Height` values will do this a treat.

Chapter 5

1. False. The font information is concerned with the shape of the characters. You decide the color of the text only when you use the font to draw the text on your output device.

2. False. You can incorporate as many fonts as you like in a Microsoft XNA game. You just need to remember that each additional font uses up space in the memory and make the game program larger.

3. False. The Content Manager is told which fonts are required. It then reads the font information and makes each requested font part of your game in a way that makes it possible for you to use the font.

4. True. This is exactly what a resource is. The resource itself is fetched only when the program is being created.

5. False. Nice thought, though. XML stands for Extensible Markup Language. XML is widely used in computing to allow two different programs to share information. An XML file contains the names of settings (for example, `<size>`) and the values that these should have (for example, 100).

6. True. A vector is given as coordinates that identify a point, such as (200, 300). You get the direction and distance of movement by considering how you would travel from the origin (0, 0) to that point. In the case of (200, 300), you would be moving across and down the screen if you were drawing in 2-D.

7. False. The first program you write should display "Hello World."

8. False. Although the Xbox can be programmed to update the clock by using a network connection, the hardware itself holds a clock, backed up by a battery, that keeps track of time for the Xbox device.

9. False. Both the PC and the Xbox have special software to "localize" them to a particular area. One aspect of localization is how the date and the time are displayed, so the same program code might display the date and time differently on machines in different countries.

10. True. That is exactly what it does. Inside the structure itself are fields that hold the day, month, year, hour, minute, and second that the particular value of DateTime represents.

11. False. For example, the DateTime structure provides a property called Now. This delivers a DateTime instance that is set to the current time. Properties are used by objects as a way for the outside world to interact with the data that they hold.

12. True. That is what ToString is for. Exactly what you get when you call ToString depends on what the object holds and what the programmer who created the type of object has decided that ToString should return. In the case of a DateTime object, the ToString method returns the date in a text format.

13. False. A programmer can make it run forever, either intentionally or by mistake. However, how long the for loop runs depends on your requirements. In Chapter 5, you've used it to draw items a particular number of times.

14. False. The first time around the loop, the value of layer is 0; the second time, it is 1; the third time, it is 2; and the fourth time, it is 3. At the end of the fourth time around the loop, the value of layer is increased to 4, and then the condition is checked before the next time around the loop. Because the value of layer is no longer less than 4, the condition is not true, and the loop ends after four times around.

15. False (nasty ones, these). The value left in layer when the loop has stopped is the value that caused the condition to fail. The value 10 would not cause the condition to fail, as layer would be equal to 10. The value of layer that causes the loop to end would be 11 because that is not less than or equal to 10.

16. True. The test is always performed before the code controlled by the for loop is obeyed. The first time the test is performed, the value of layer is 4. Because 4 is not less than 0, the test fails, and the loop never runs.

17. True—sort of. Because you're making the value of layer 1 bigger each time and it starts at 4, the condition (layer > 0) is always true, so you would expect the loop to repeat forever. But this is not quite the case, given what you know about variable types. If layer were a byte, you know that the range of a byte is from 0 to 255. This means that once the value of layer reached 255, it would wrap around to 0, and the loop would stop. Note that this kind of mistake would result in the program acting strangely and would be hard to uncover.

18. True. They can. This is where the idea of a color as a paint can or colored light breaks down. You'd be happy drawing red text on the screen by using the red color. However, you can also use red text through which the background can be seen by using a red color value with a transparency value. Furthermore, because you know that you can draw images in a particular color, this means that you can draw transparent images by drawing them with a transparent color.

Chapter 6

1. False. Any of the buttons on a gamepad can be used to detect edges.

2. True. The program can notice that a signal has changed only if it has before and after values that it can compare. If these two values are the same, there has been no change, but if they are different, it means that the signal has changed.

3. False. The whole point of an edge-triggered input is that you detect when the button changes state. They are used for flicking switches, changing gears in a car, or for your button-press-counting game. The only way that you can detect an edge is to compare the state now with the state it had last time you looked.

4. False. The clue is in the name. The compilation process, where your program is converted into executable statements, is where conditional compilation takes place. By the time the program runs, the statements have either been included in the program or ignored.

5. False. The preprocessor, as the name implies, looks at the C# code going into the compiler. If it's given commands to ignore sections of the program, these are not passed into the compiler for conversion into machine instructions in the finished program.

Chapter 7

1. True. The Content Manager provides a version of the Load method that loads and converts audio files for use in a game.

2. True. You can also use .wma and .wav files.

3. False. The files are copied automatically for you by the Content Manager.

4. False. Each hardware platform supports a different number of simultaneous sound samples, but it is always more than one.

5. False. The Play method is used to play an existing effect. The effect should have been loaded when the game started running.

6. False. The Play method actually returns a reference to a SoundEffectInstance that describes the particular instance of the sound being played. You can call methods on this to control the sound playback.

7. False. There is no such thing as a null object. A null reference is defined as explicitly referring nowhere. It is used to denote the fact that the reference does not refer to anything at all.

Chapter 8

1. False. The code creates a variable called scores that can refer to arrays of integers, but it does not create the array itself. The program must actually construct the array to use it: int[] scores = new int [4]; would do this. To make the array bigger, change the 4 to a different value. You can even use a variable to set the size of an array, so that a program can allocate the correct amount of storage for its needs automatically.

2. This is both true and false. You can create an array of any type, so you can have arrays of integers, arrays of strings, and pretty much arrays of anything you like. However, once an array has been created, it has a particular type and keeps that type forever; for example, an array of integers can hold only integer values.

3. True. When you create an array, you make an instance of an array object. You can tell this because making the array (that is, the step where you set up how many elements the array has in it) uses the key word new. The identifier you give the array is a reference that refers to the array object.

4. False. In some languages (Microsoft Visual Basic, for example), this is true. However, in C# the convention is that the first element in the array is zero. If you think of a subscript as giving the distance down the array you need to travel to get to the element, then it is reasonable to have a subscript value of zero. It is unfortunate that different languages handle this differently, but there's nothing you can do about it.

5. False—to the extreme. The system running your programs cares a great deal about this. If you try to get a hold of an array element that is not there, your program stops.

Chapter 9

1. False. Exactly how many keys can be pressed at once depends on the keyboard hardware, but multiple keys can be registered.

2. False. The Keys type holds information that describes a particular key on the keyboard. For every key on the keyboard (including the Shift, Ctrl, and Alt keys), there is a corresponding Keys value that matches that key.

3. False. The Keys type has values just for physical keys on the keyboard. The only way that you can determine whether an uppercase letter has been typed is by checking the state of the Shift keys when the key press is detected.

4. True. Each value of a variable of type Keys describes one physical key on the keyboard. There are as many Keys values as there are keys on the keyboard. An enumerated type allows programmers to create their own types that have just the values that are required by their application.

5. False. A reference provides a way that a program can find and use an object. However, you should not regard a reference as letting your programs find out where in memory something is stored. The way that C# works, you're not allowed to know where the objects in your program are actually located. In this respect, a "telephone number" analogy works best, in that a telephone number provides a way you can contact someone but does not tell you where he or she physically is. You can think of a variable that refers to an object in memory as holding the "telephone number" of that object.

6. False. It's very common in C# programs for a particular object to have multiple references referring to it. This is the best way that a large resource (for example, a particular texture or sound) can be shared in a program.

7. False. In C#, garbage collection takes place while a program is active. The garbage collection process runs alongside your program to make sure that the maximum amount of memory is available at all times.

8. False. You've used the break key word in two situations: when you wanted to exit from a for loop and when you wanted to exit from a case in a switch statement. It does not stop the program; instead, it says, "I've done all I want here, and I want to escape from this construct."

9. False. The idea of a program turning the computer off is interesting but is not what the switch statement is used for. It's used to select an option from a number of different possible ones, depending on the value of a control.

10. True. Note that this does not cause the contents of the string itself to change; instead, you should regard methods like ToUpper and ToLower as different views of the string, much as you can get a DateTime instance to give you a string that contains only the time information.

11. False. You can add strings together, but the effect is to put one string on the end of the other, which is called *string concatenation*. C# uses the same operator, +, for adding numbers and for concatenating strings but the meaning of the action changes depending on what it is applied to. A + between two integers would add them together. A + between two strings causes them to be strung together to make a longer string.

Chapter 10

1. False. The `Rectangle` tells the draw process the position and size of the drawing area, but it does not do the drawing itself.

2. False. Although the Microsoft XNA programmers have made methods for you to use, there's nothing to stop you from creating methods of your own.

3. True. A method is a member of a class. It's how you can ask an instance of a class to do something for you.

4. True. The statements are performed when the method is called. Used like this, a method lets you use a given sequence of statements from any part of your program simply by calling the method.

5. False. A method that specifies a return type of `void` does not return a result to the caller.

6. False. A method can contain many `return` statements. If the method returns a result, each `return` statement must be followed by a result that's an expression of the correct type.

7. False. You've seen methods that don't accept any parameters.

8. False. The C# compiler is very picky about method calls. If the call doesn't exactly match the header definition (the signature) of the method, the compiler produces an error.

9. False. When you work with test-driven development, you do the testing as you write the program. Often you write the tests before you write the code.

10. False. One of the many wonderful things about XNA Game Studio is the way that you can set a breakpoint in your code even if it's running on an Xbox. When you run the program in debugging mode, the next time the program reaches the breakpoint, it stops.

11. False. The `int` type holds a value that doesn't have a fractional part. This means that when you move a floating-point value (which does have a fractional part) into an integer variable, the fractional part of the data is lost. This is called *narrowing*. The C# compiler won't let a programmer unintentionally lose or damage data in this way, so it refuses to allow such a transfer unless the programmer explicitly takes responsibility for the effect of the action by adding a cast.

12. True. The double precision type can hold all integer values, so data is not lost when the move takes place. This is called *widening*.

13. True. It tells the compiler that although the actual data is in one type, for the purposes of the program, it needs to be converted into an alternative type. This is the programmer's way of "taking responsibility" for the consequences of the action. When you move a floating-point value into an integer location, you're destroying data because the fractional part of the floating-point value is lost. The cast is the way that you tell the compiler that you know what you're doing, and the compiler then allows the conversion to take place.

14. False. Although casting does perform conversion between similar types (programmers can cast between integers, bytes, doubles, floating points, and the like), it cannot convert any type to any other type automatically. Only conversions that have been predefined are allowed.

Chapter 11

1. False. You can use any image that you like in your games (subject to copyright laws, of course). The images must be in file formats that can be imported into the games, but you can create the images yourself.

2. False. The solution contains the project. A solution brings together a number of projects that are used to create a single application. When you create a new project, XNA Game Studio creates a solution that contains it.

3. False. The Program.cs file is created for you when the project is created by XNA Game Studio.

4. True. The Program.cs source code starts the game running in that it creates an instance of your game class, but it doesn't contain the game program itself.

5. True. The compiler is told to search namespaces by using directives at the start of the program source file. When the compiler comes across the name of a resource it hasn't seen before, it looks in the namespaces to find the resource.

6. False. But this is really unfair. The method that starts the program is called Main (with an uppercase "M"). In C# this is important because the case of letters in identifiers is significant.

7. False. The term *static* means that the static item is always there. It doesn't need to be created by your programs because static items are created automatically when the program is loaded.

8. True. When program execution exits the block of code after the using statement, it means that the item created at the top of the using statement can now be removed and that any resources it uses can be reclaimed.

9. False. When a floating-point value is converted into an integer, the fractional part is simply removed.

Chapter 12

1. False. Cows are held in fields, but structures are not. A field is a member of a structure that holds data.

2. True. Whenever you have a number of related items, you should think about creating a structure to hold them.

3. False. Structures are managed by value. You can tell this because you don't have to use the new key word to make a new structure variable. By default, the value in the structure is copied when passed into a method call.

4. False. Public is used to explicitly make members visible to code outside a class or structure. To restrict access to a member you would use the private modifier.

5. False. An absolute value is always positive or zero.

6. True. When a value type is passed as a parameter a copy is made of the contents of the variable. This is the value passed into the method. When a reference is passed as a parameter a copy of the reference is passed into the method. If you want the method to change the content of a value or change a reference to refer to a different object you must use the ref modifier to ask the compiler to generate a reference.

7. False. Oh, yes you can. XNA Game Studio lets you add breakpoints or pause a running program even when it's running in an Xbox or Zune.

8. True. If you make a method static, it means that it's always around and not part of any object. This means that you can use Abs without needing to make an instance of the Math class.

9. False. Nothing in C# forces you to keep the name of a method once you've written some code. It was once difficult to change the name of a method because you needed to make sure that you changed all the places in which it was used. Fortunately, XNA Game Studio makes it much easier to do this, so you should consider doing this (it is called *refactoring*) whenever you notice that the things a method does no longer fit its name.

Chapter 13

1. False. A programmer can add a return key word anywhere in a method. In fact, a method can have as many return statements as you like, although the Great Programmer won't approve of this because it can make programs harder to understand if you have too many ways that a method can return.

2. False. The type of the variables is not usually changed, although the name used to identify a variable might be changed if you decide on a better name to use.

3. False. The Refactor menu in Microsoft Visual Studio can be used to change the name of a method in your program. The only proviso is that you can't change the name of methods that are part of the system; for example, it's not possible to change the name of the Update method, as this is based on a method that's part of Microsoft XNA.

4. False. A code region is a way of grouping together a number of items in your program source file. A single source code file can hold a large number of regions.

5. False. A code region just lumps together parts of your program. Certain Intellisense information is retrieved from specially formatted comments that programmers can place inside the code as they write it.

6. False. A state machine can have as many states as the application requires. The Great Programmer uses an enumerated (enum) type to keep track of the states that a state machine can occupy. The state machine that we created for the game had two states: when the game was being played and when the title screen was being displayed. It would be easy to add a third state in which the high-score table is displayed.

Chapter 14

1. False. If an object has high cohesion, it means that it can go about its business with no need to use resources from other objects. This is good because it means that changes to the rest of the system do not affect the object.

2. True. The amount of coupling in a system reflects on how much objects rely on each other. Coupling is a form of dependency in that if A is coupled to B, you have to test A if you make any changes to B. Large amounts of coupling make it difficult to modify or repair systems because of the number of internal components that need to be checked if one is changed.

3. False. Public data can be read and written by code running outside the object, making it possible for unmanaged changes to be made to the data. The data in an object should be made private. The object should contain methods that provide managed access to the data so that objects can be created which always hold data that is in a valid state.

4. False. Structures are managed by value. When you work with a structure variable, you are actually using the value it contains. This means that during assignment, the data from the structure is copied from one variable to another.

5. True. When using the data pointed to by a reference, the program must follow the reference to get to the data itself. This introduces an extra stage into the use of a variable which adds a delay. However, modern processors run so quickly that this is virtually never a problem within a program. Furthermore, the delay can be compensated for by time saved moving data around memory.

6. True. A class hierarchy is a means of code reuse. A child class is created based on an existing one (the parent). This means that the new class contains its own data elements as well as those of the parent. The data from the parent and child portions of the variable may not necessarily be held in a single place in memory and so cannot be regarded as a single value. When you use references, the run-time system can find the requested data when a reference is followed.

7. False. A class can be extended by many other classes as required. There is no upper limit on the number of child classes that a parent can have.

8. True. Overriding is the process by which a child class replaces an existing method in the parent class with one that meets the needs of the child. However, it is possible to override a method in a parent only if the parent method has been marked as virtual.

9. False. The key word base allows the overriding method to use the method in the parent that it has replaced. This is very useful if you want to add to existing behaviors in the parent method.

10. True. The protected key word is provided so that child classes can be given access to data members in the parent.

11. False. The key word this means "a reference to the currently executing instance." If an object needs to supply a reference to itself for any code outside the class to use, it uses the key word this. We used it so that the BreadAndCheeseGame class could provide a reference to the currently executing game. The cheese needs this so that it can get hold of the bread in that game, and check for collisions.

12. False. The child class does not have to override any of the methods in the parent. It could just add new methods and leave all the old ones untouched.

13. False. A single object can have many references to it.

14. True. The garbage collector continuously searches for such objects and reclaims the memory they occupy.

Chapter 15

1. False. Although an abstract class can be used as a template for child classes and states which methods the child classes must contain, there is nothing to keep a programmer from putting full methods and member data inside an abstract class. In fact, this can be a very sensible design if a method or data must be used in all the child classes.

2. False. If there are data members of the abstract class that always need to be set up, there is no reason why the class shouldn't contain a constructor method to set these properties.

3. False. You can't make any instances of an abstract class. This is because it is intended to serve as a template for child classes.

4. False. Only the methods can be abstract. An abstract method is a way of signaling that there is a need for a particular behavior; it has nothing to do with member data.

5. False. In C#, a class is allowed to have only one parent class. If you are used to other languages like C++, this will be surprising because C++ lets a class have multiple parents. However, the designers of C# left this ability out, perhaps because it can make classes too confusing.

6. True. That is the best way to use abstract classes. A user of an instance of any child in the class can be sure that it provides implementations of all the abstract methods in the abstract class at the base of the hierarchy.

7. True. This is a good way to allow a program to manage collections of objects that must perform a particular function but do it in their own way.

8. True. If the programmer has provided a constructor for a class, the constructor must be called to create an instance. This is how a programmer can ensure that all instances of a class start out with valid data.

9. True. Once a class has a constructor, it must be called an instance of that class.

10. False. The child is always set up after the parent.

11. True. The Random class provides a "pseudorandom" sequence of values based on a starting value called the seed. If this starting value is based on something effectively random (such as the number of milliseconds since midnight), then from a programmer's point of view, the sequence can be sufficiently random. Note, however, that using a particular seed value allows the same sequence of random numbers to be generated repeatedly.

12. False. The great thing about the List is that you do not have to set the length of the list. It automatically expands to hold all the values that are added to it. In this respect, it is much more useful than an array.

13. True. That is exactly what foreach was created for. It removes the need to worry about managing a counter value to keep track of the particular length of the collection being used.

14. False. It just means making a piece of program that is intended to mimic the effect of intelligence in a particular situation.

15. True. If a class implements an interface, it must contain public implementations of all the methods in the interface.

16. True. This means that objects can be regarded in terms of what they can do rather than what they actually are. In this respect, interfaces are a very powerful way to let programmers create software components that behave according to a set of requirements given in the interface.

Chapter 16

1. False. A network can be made using radio, fiberoptic, or wires, but probably not wet string. The actual medium of the connection is not really the most important thing these days, though; it is the protocol that runs on top that makes it useful.

2. True. If the stations are actually wired together, all the machines on that particular wire (or radio channel) must have a unique address so that messages can be sent to them. If a particular physical network is connected via a route to another network (using an Internet Protocol, or IP) then they must also have an address that is unique in the world. The IP address of your computer must be the only one of its kind so that only you get the messages sent to you.

3. False. This depends on the precise type of network, but very often, the same physical media is used to carry traffic between lots of machines. This means that anyone with the right equipment could eavesdrop on conversations between any machine. The way this problem is solved today is to have software that scrambles (or encrypts) important information before it is sent so that eavesdroppers don't hear anything of use to them.

4. False. The profile provides the gamertag information that allows you to be identified on the network. If you do not have a profile, you cannot perform network gaming. Profiles can be held locally on your Windows PC, however, and they are easy to create.

5. False. The idea of a router is to send information from one network to another. This means that it must be connected to at least a couple of networks. Stations on the network send their messages to the router if they determine that the destination machine is not on their physical network, and the message must be routed to a distant network.

6. True. Well, perhaps not the complete Internet, but you can create a network using the Transport Control Protocol/Internet Protocol (TCP/IP) standard, which is used by the Internet. You could use such a network for System Link games. If you connected your little network to a router, it could then become part of the worldwide Internet.

7. False. If you wish, you can create highly advanced network game play with servers, lobbies, and vast numbers of players. However, to deploy and test such games, you need to have two memberships in the XNA App Hub. On the other hand, System Link network game play can be achieved between Windows PCs with no need to join the XNA Creators Club. You can also create network game play between Windows PCs and Xbox consoles.

8. True. This class is used to set up and manage the connection between machines taking part in a network game. It also provides lobby support so that systems can propose games that others can join.

9. False. When a game is proposed, the proposer can specify how many players the game is for. This takes the form of an upper limit.

10. False. A state machine is not really used to store scores. Instead, it is used to manage the state of the game itself, for example whether it is waiting for more players, it is being played, or it is at the title screen.

11. True. The system is notified when players join the game.

12. True—mostly. Rather than having a program waiting for something to happen, an event lets a program say, "When this happens, call this method."

13. True—exactly. It is like writing your phone number down on a piece of paper, giving it to a garage mechanic, and saying, "Call me when my car is ready to be picked up." A delegate is a lump of data that identifies a particular method. I give this to an event generator (perhaps the thing that fires when someone joins a game I'm proposing) so that the event can be bound to the method that needs to act on it.

14. False. The PacketWriter class can accept many different C# types and assemble them for transfer to another system. The PacketReader class can then extract these items.

15. False. This would result in a lot of unwanted network traffic. In a game that uses a server, the clients would communicate only with the server, not with each other.

Chapter 17

1. False. Any caveman that dropped a rock on his foot knew all about gravity way before Sir Isaac. What Isaac Newton did was put gravity into the right context when considering how things move and respond to forces acting on them.

2. True. This makes sense. The harder you kick a football, the faster it moves and the further it goes. The larger the engine in your car is, the more quickly you can speed up.

3. False. It also measures acceleration in the Z direction.

4. False. It is actually part of the Microsoft.Devices.Sensors library and your game must add this to the references it uses when it runs.

5. False. We don't actually know when the accelerometer produces new readings. All we know is that we can use a delegate to connect a method to that event that will run and capture new readings when they are available.

6. True. The values of X, Y (and Z if this is a Vector3D) express distance values along their respective axes. By joining the origin to the point that the vector coordinates describe, we can get a direction of travel and also a distance value. The distance value can also be called the length of the vector.

7. False. The accelerometer is calibrated so that when the phone is at rest it will return a vector with a length of 1, reflecting an acceleration of 1 G. The only time this statement would be true is when the desk is on a space station that was either in outer space or in a freefall.

8. False. Friction acts to slow everything down. This means that over time the speed of objects should decrease.

9. True. You can understand this by thinking about speeds such as "60 miles per hour."

10. True. When we say that a car is capable of an acceleration of "Zero to 60 in eight seconds," we are expressing how fast the speed is changing. The greater the force that is applied to an object, the greater the acceleration will be.

11. False. The lock does not stop a process, it provides a way that one process can obtain exclusive access to a resource. The process that has obtained the lock object is able to run, but any others that attempt to acquire the lock will be paused.

Chapter 18

1. False. The emulator that runs on the PC provides support for the touch screen, although with only one touch point if you use the mouse. If you have a Windows 7 system that supports multitouch input (for example, a monitor with a multitouch screen), you can use the screen as a multitouch input device for your Windows Phone 7 programs running on the emulator.

2. False. You can detect three touch events: the start of the event (pressed), movement during the event (moved), and when the touch is released (released).

3. True. This makes it easy to position items based on touch input.

4. False. In this respect, it is very different from the accelerometer we saw in the last chapter. The touch panel is used in the same way as other XNA peripherals, including the gamepad. We ask it for a list of the currently active touch locations, and we then use this in our program. We do not have to connect methods to events produced by the touch panel.

5. False. The actual number of touch events that can be tracked depends on the hardware in the phone, but a device will be able to track at least 4 points.

6. True. By this, I mean that a given set of locations that refer to a particular sequence of actions starting at a particular point (such as pressed, moved, and released) will have the same ID. This makes it easy for a game to track a particular movement action, based on the ID of the touch locations that are received.

7. False. It would be lovely if this was the case, but unfortunately it is not. The emulator does a fantastic job of appearing the same as a real device, but in the end you will have to try the program on a real device to make sure that the user experience is a good one.

8. True. That is how our puck works in the shuffleboard game. The puck can be in one of three states: stationary, dragged, or moving. Also, how it behaves is quite different in each of these states.

Chapter 19

1. False. If only. The phone is constrained by the amount of energy that can be stored in the batteries it uses. Although these batteries do provide an impressive amount of power, they are finite. This means that programs designed for the platform must take into account that they are working in a constrained environment.

2. True. You can see this on your console or laptop. When you start doing something that makes the processor work hard, the fans come on to cool everything down. This heat is a by-product of all the switching that is taking place on the processor chip when it is working hard. And, of course, if the computer is getting hot, this means it is consuming more power.

3. True. Windows Phone games are updated and drawn 30 times a second, as opposed to the 60 times a second used by the other platforms. This is because small, low-power, display systems on the phone are not able to update as quickly as larger displays. Also, on a smaller display it is much less likely that a player will notice any flicker.

4. False. You can set the update rate to any value you like. On a Windows Phone, there is no point in increasing the update rate beyond the initial settings because this will just increase the drain on the battery without providing much of an improved experience for the user. You can experiment with different settings on the other platforms if you wish, but generally I prefer to just stick with the original setting.

5. False. You can play games in any orientation you like (even held diagonally if you like). However, the XNA system will support any of three orientations: portrait and two land-scapes, with controls to the left or right. Your game actually tells XNA what orientations it is happy to support.

6. True. Your game can register to receive events when the Windows Phone system detects a change in orientation.

7. False. You determine how many states you want the machine to have based on the job the machine is doing. The simplest state machine has only two states (perhaps active and inactive), but a game might have many different states (attract mode, main menu, game active, paused, and game over).

8. False. We saw that a game can have a master state machine that holds the state of the game itself (Main Menu, Playing, or Paused). Then when in the Playing state a game can be in a variety of modes, depending on the game. For example, the game could have a "Boss" mode when the player is fighting the end of level "boss." A game will have lots of state machines inside it. And remember that individual game objects—for example, an alien game sprite—can have states as well.

9. False. A program has to respond only to events that are relevant to a particular state. However, keep in mind that it is not possible for events to "upset" a program and make it do the wrong thing if they occur.

10. False. The game receives a messages saying that it has been deactivated, but the game itself will continue to run. However, it will not have the foreground of the display, so the player will not be able to interact with it. When a game is deactivated in this way, it should go into pause mode.

11. False. This might be sensible. If the game is not fast and furious, the player might prefer it if the game just restarted. However, if the game contains fast-moving objects, the player might prefer to have time to get ready for the game and release pause mode themselves.

12. False. The Back button is how a phone user can move back out of one application and return to the previous one, but it is also used when navigating menus within an application. This means the Back button should cause your program to exit only if the player is at the topmost menu in your game. If the player presses the Back button when playing the game, it should enter pause mode.

13. True. When this button is pressed, it indicates that the user wants to go do something else. This means the currently running application will be stopped.

14. False. The game can connect methods to the Closing event so that it can save its state to isolated storage when this happens.

15. False. Each game has a storage area that is separated from any other area. This is what "isolated" means in this context.

16. True. The stream represents a connection to a particular file. A program can interact with the file by calling methods that are provided by the stream.

17. False. Your program must close each file when it finishes using it. If a program is writing to a file, it will be the only one allowed to connect to that file. The file is available for use by other programs only when the file is closed.

18. False. If the exception is thrown in a statement within a try - catch block, the catch code is executed and the program continues running. A program ends only if an exception is thrown on a statement that is not within a try-catch construction.

Index

Numbers and Symbols

About the Author

Rob Miles

I wrote my first computer game on the original Commodore PET in Microsoft Basic, having learned to program some time before that at school, where I began by writing my first programs on cards using a hand punch, posting them off to a distant mainframe, and getting a message back (two weeks later) that I'd omitted a semicolon. A good many years have gone by since then. I'm still omitting semicolons, but the turnaround has improved quite a bit.

I've been at the University of Hull in the United Kingdom for over 25 years now, moving from the Computer Center to Electronic Engineering to Computer Science where I teach programming (in C#, of course) and software engineering, amongst other subjects. In my time, I've also had a hand in quite a few industrial projects, and it is a matter of great personal pride to be the man who wrote the software that puts the date stamps on Budweiser beer cans, among many other products. I've also been known to turn out bad verse, the highlight of this being a whole page of poetry for the *Independent* newspaper in Britain. I'm a Microsoft Most Valuable Professional (MVP) for Mobile Development, and I've been a judge and Competition Captain for the Imagine Cup Software Design Challenge for a few years.

I live happily in East Yorkshire with number-one wife Mary (she calls me "husband zero") and a pinball machine. My kids, David and Jenny, return every now and then so that we can play happy families properly. You can find out more about my interesting times at *http://www.robmiles.com*.

What do you think of this book?

We want to hear from you!

To participate in a brief online survey, please visit:

microsoft.com/learning/booksurvey

Tell us how well this book meets your needs—what works effectively, and what we can do better. Your feedback will help us continually improve our books and learning resources for you.

Thank you in advance for your input!

Microsoft®
Press

Stay in touch!

To subscribe to the *Microsoft Press*® *Book Connection Newsletter*—for news on upcoming books, events, and special offers—please visit:

microsoft.com/learning/books/newsletter

Find the Right Resource for You

DEVELOPER STEP BY STEP	DEVELOPER REFERENCE	FOCUSED TOPICS	BEST PRACTICES

DEVELOPER STEP BY STEP

- Hands-on tutorial covering fundamental techniques and features
- Downloadable practice exercises and eBook
- Prepares and informs new-to-topic programmers

**Microsoft®
Visual C#® 2010
Step by Step**
John Sharp
978-0-7356-2670-6

**Microsoft
Visual Basic® 2010
Step by Step**
Michael Halvorson
978-0-7356-2669-0

**Microsoft ASP.NET 4
Step by Step**
George Shepherd
978-0-7356-2701-7

DEVELOPER REFERENCE

- Expert coverage of core topics
- Extensive, pragmatic coding examples
- Builds professional-level proficiency with a Microsoft technology

**Programming
Microsoft ASP.NET 4**
Dino Esposito
978-0-7356-4338-3

**Microsoft
Visual Studio® Tips**
Sara Ford
978-0-7356-2640-9

**Programming Windows®
Identity Foundation**
Vittorio Bertocci
978-0-7356-2718-5

FOCUSED TOPICS

- Deep coverage of advanced techniques and capabilities
- Extensive, adaptable coding examples
- Promotes full mastery of a Microsoft technology

**Microsoft ASP.NET and
AJAX: Architecting
Web Applications**
Dino Esposito
978-0-7356-2621-8

**CLR via C#,
Third Edition**
Jeffrey Richter
978-0-7356-2704-8

**Windows Internals,
Fifth Edition**
Mark E. Russinovich
and David A. Solomon
with Alex Ionescu
978-0-7356-2530-3

BEST PRACTICES

- Proven software-engineering practices from industry-leading professionals
- Delves beyond academia and theory
- Pragmatic approaches to real-world challenges

**Code Complete,
Second Edition**
Steve McConnell
978-0-7356-1967-8

**Agile Portfolio
Management**
Jochen Krebs
978-0-7356-2567-9

**How We Test Software
at Microsoft**
Alan Page, Ken Johnston, Bj Rollison
978-0-7356-2425-2

Microsoft Press

CPSIA information can be obtained at www.ICGtesting.com
Printed in the USA
BVOW081621080113

310073BV00009B/71/P

9 780735 651579